The Trekker's Guide
to the Himalaya
and Karakoram

by Hugh Swift

with additional material by
Rodney Jackson, Charles Gay, Helena Norberg-Hodge,
Milan M. Melvin, and John H. Mock

Sierra Club Books   San Francisco

The Sierra Club, founded in 1892 by John Muir, has devoted itself to the study and protection of the earth's scenic and ecological resources—mountains, wetlands, woodlands, wild shores and rivers, deserts and plains. The publishing program of the Sierra Club offers books to the public as a non-profit educational service in the hope that they may enlarge the public's understanding of the Club's basic concerns. The point of view expressed in each book, however, does not necessarily represent that of the Club. The Sierra Club has some fifty chapters coast to coast, in Canada, Hawaii, and Alaska. For information about how you may participate in its programs to preserve wilderness and the quality of life, please address inquiries to Sierra Club, 530 Bush Street, San Francisco, CA 94108.

Library of Congress Cataloging in Publication Data

Swift, Hugh.
    The trekker's guide to the Himalaya and Karakoram.

    Bibliography: p. 296
    Includes index.
    1. Hiking—Himalaya Mountains—Guide-books.
2. Hiking—Karakoram Range—Guide-books.
3. Himalaya Mountains—Description and travel—
Guide-books. 4. Karakoram Range—Description and
travel—Guide-books. I. Title.
GV199.44.H55S94   915.4'0452   82-738
ISBN 0-87156-295-2 (pbk.)   AACR2

Photographs not otherwise credited are by the author.

Cover design by Howard Jacobson

Book design by Drake Jordan

Maps by Tom Dolan

Composition by Dharma Press

Printed in the United States of America

10 9 8 7 6 5 4 3 2

Contents

Acknowledgments

This book has come about with the active help of many individuals and four governments. My parents first took me into the hills, instilling in me a love of mountainous country. Peter Yaple initially suggested that I write a book of treks. After seeing my first chapters, Andrew Fluegelman and Eric Harper sent helpful letters of advice.

I am particularly grateful to Ronnie Smith and Richard R. Cleverly who aided me with encouragement and editorial advice. Thanks also to Edwin Bernbaum, Stephen Bezruchka, Reverend and Mrs. S. R. Burgoyne, Charles Gay, Peter Gradjansky, Peter Hackett, and Pam Shandrick, who read and who advised on various parts of the book.

Arlene Blum, K. Garnay, and Chris Wriggins provided valuable information and showed me photographs of areas I have not visited. Mimi K. Calhoun contributed material about women's concerns in trekking.

Rodney Jackson, who at the present time is extensively studying snow leopards, wrote the informative natural history chapter. Charles Gay, Helene Norberg-Hodge, Milan M. Melvin, and John H. Mock contributed glossaries, and John Mock collaborated with me on three glossaries. Tom Dolan drew the fine maps, and Benjamin Ailes made the excellent photo conversions. Carey Charlesworth and my editor, Diana Landau, worked particularly hard to smooth and reorder the text. Susan Ristow's production coordination and Drake Jordan's design work helped to create the physical book.

I sincerely acknowledge the governments of Pakistan and India and the royal governments of Nepal and Bhutan for allowing me to visit the mountain regions of their countries.

Finally, I warmly thank those friends in Asia who helped me in many ways and patiently answered my endless questions. These include Ghulam Mohammed Beg, Ghulam Rasul Drasi, Padam Singh, and Pasang Khambache; the numerous people in many mountain areas who provided kind hospitality; and, finally, the people from the hills who have worked and walked with me, typified by the estimable Karma Chumbey and other companions including Mohammed Jon, Zerbali, Ramazan, Karma, Bir Bahadur Lama, Chandra Gurung, and Tenzing Gyaltso.

Acknowledgment is made for permission to reprint material from the following sources:

Afghanistan by W. K. Fraser-Tytler, 3rd ed., revised by M. C. Gillett. Oxford: Oxford University Press. Copyright © 1967 by Oxford University Press.

The Confessions of Aleister Crowley: An Autobiography by Aleister Crowley. London and Boston: Routledge & Kegan Paul Ltd. Copyright © 1969, 1979 by John Symonds and Kenneth Grant.

Preface

The Himalayan ranges are part of a supreme mountain system containing some of the most spectacular scenery to be found on earth. The Great Himalayan Range and the ice-bound Karakoram are among the world's youngest mountains. Peaks from Chitral to Assam are still growing from the geologic collision of the Indian land mass with the Eurasian continent. Together they separate as effectively as an ocean the oldest living cultures, those of India and China, yet ancient trade routes and pilgrimage sites abound in deep valleys beneath the snowy summits.

All along these ranges, thousands of trails interconnect through magnificent alpine terrain and valleys inhabited by many races and clans. Even today, however, few people have heard of a trekking route unless it leads to Mt. Everest, Annapurna, Amarnath Cave, or the Baltoro Glacier. In fact, with remarkably few exceptions, the entire Himalayan system from Chitral to Bhutan offers excellent trekking opportunities.

This book presents an overview of most regions within the Himalayan ranges other than Tibet, Bhutan, and the Indian state of Arunachal Pradesh. Three introductory chapters present, first, a brief history of foot travel in the Himalaya from the era of the Silk Route through the present. Today there are several different ways to trek, and these are described and compared. Other sections offer information about how to prepare for trekking, what to take, and what to expect while walking along the ancient trail system far beyond the roads. Details on how to reach cities and towns that are major starting points for treks are also supplied in the introductory chapters.

The bulk of this guide is composed of ten chapters that provide an overall description of the hill regions between the Afghanistan-Pakistan border and the Indian state of Sikkim, as well as specific routes and suggestions for other trekking possibilities in each region. The first three descriptive chapters cover areas in Pakistan: Chitral, the Gilgit River valleys, and Baltistan. The next four chapters take you through the mountainous areas of India: Kashmir, Ladakh, Himachal Pradesh, and Garhwal. The remaining chapters cover western, central, and eastern Nepal, with brief sections on Sikkim and Bhutan. (Up to the time of writing, entry into these last two regions has been restricted, and trekking possibilities are limited.)

The chapter on natural history by Rodney Jackson will introduce you to the flora and fauna of the Himalaya, and one or more of the book's seven glossaries will help you to begin speaking with the locals.

No book that encompasses a 1,200-mile span of some of the most rugged terrain on earth can pretend to be inclusive. Each chapter contains sufficient detail about routes and locales within its region to keep a trekker occupied for years, but my coverage by no means exhausts the possibilities. Trekking in the Himalaya is far more than walking through beautiful landscapes, however, and my hope is to guide you as well to the rich cultural and human experience that this part of the world offers. So a substantial portion of the text describes religious, cultural, and historic sites, and provides glimpses of some of the many clans that inhabit the Himalaya.

Further, my approach herein is to give you enough information to plan a route and get started, but not so much as to remove all sense of discovery in traveling it. Rather than precise itineraries, approximate times in days or weeks are given for principal walking routes. The joy of discovering details is left to you. Keep in mind that the maps located among the descriptive chapters are intended only for general orientation. If at all possible, obtain a detailed map of your planned route before you leave (see Appendix A for a full discussion of maps).

Although this guide discusses most mountainous regions south of the Afghan and Tibetan (Chinese) borders, the governments of Pakistan, India, and Nepal have restricted entry to certain areas, principally those near their northern or common borders. These regions are closed to entry for political reasons and out of concern that a foreigner might willfully or inadvertently cross into the adjoining country. Such areas tend to be found near disputed borders or in places where access to the adjoining country is unimpaired. I have attempted to note in the text which areas are restricted at the time of writing, but this is subject to change. By the time this book is available, some may be opened and others closed to entry. I have described numerous areas that cannot presently be entered, in the hope that they will become derestricted in the future. During September 1981, three groups of Indian pilgrims were permitted to depart by foot for sacred Mt. Kailas in Tibet for the first time in twenty years. Let's hope this is a harbinger of increased trekking possibilities to come.

Before you commit the time and money for traveling to Asia, consider your decision carefully. Trekking involves hard physical exertion. Most treks take several weeks at least, and whether you go by yourself or with one of the best trekking outfitters, there are bound to be times that will test your capacity for humor, your adaptability, and, very importantly, your ability and desire to walk in mountainous regions. This is not to say that you must be a super-athlete to consider Himalayan trekking. The region offers a great diversity of terrain, from easy walking to mountaineering on snow and ice. The information in this book should help you to observe the principal rule: know where you are going and what it will require of you.

Your experience in the Himalaya will be enriched immeasurably by learning even a modicum of the local language. Imagine how much a traveler in your country would be handicapped if he or she spoke none of your language. Use the appropriate glossary and add words to your vocabulary list as you walk. Even if you speak just a few words that are out of order and mispronounced, people will listen and respond to your efforts.

Most of the information about routes in the ten descriptive chapters comes from firsthand sources. However, paths can be relocated, bridges can wash out, and trail information can become outdated from one year to the next. Inaccuracies are bound to occur in a book such as this. If you believe that important information has been omitted (a 3,000-ft. climb that goes unmentioned, for instance), or if you find misleading information while trekking, please record your observations and write to me in care of the publisher so that subsequent editions can be updated.

Hugh Swift
Berkeley, California
September, 1981

Coming around a ridge, with the Annapurna massif in the background.

1
Foot Travel
in the Himalaya

*The art of Himalayan travel—and indeed of all adventure—
is the art of being bold enough to enjoy life* now.
W. H. Murray, 1951

Traditional Travelers

Until the mid-18th century, the Himalaya's countless isolated valleys within scores of autonomous princely states were virtually unknown to the western world. But long before Europeans ever set foot there—in fact for hundreds of years back into prehistory—the Himalaya provided homes and trade routes for many people. The inhabitants, who live at higher elevations year-round than their counterparts in the Andes or Caucasus, have maintained circuitous trails where no person could otherwise pass through the vast, convoluted ranges along the Himalaya's 1,800-mi. length.

The Himalayan trails are an extraordinary mountain network. These tracks vary greatly, from wide, professionally made, stone-paved routes to treacherous talus paths and narrow, exposed ledges. Many extremely remote areas of the Himalaya are visited by shepherds, hunters, or wood gatherers who have no reason to document what they easily remember. Winter migrations continue; entire northern hill communities moving south thread the paths to escape the grip of winter and to visit traditional camps, taking in the sights of such bazaar towns as Darjeeling, Kathmandu, Dharmsala, or Chitral. Aside from these migrants, and local householders who use the routes for access to field, pasture, and market, until quite recently only three types of traveler have used Himalayan trails.

Merchants and traders, the first group, have been important voyagers along the major trans-Himalayan trade routes for hundreds of years. Along the branches of the Silk Route in Chitral and Ladakh and the scores of winding paths leading north to Tibet through India and Nepal they traveled, carrying on the trade in *pashmina* (shawl wool), salt, tea, textiles, grains, spices, and more. The tattered, indomitable caravans of Bactrian camels no longer enter the bazaars of Chitral, Gilgit, and Leh, but hundreds of traders still carry goods through the mountains by various methods. Cow-yak crossbreeds in Baltistan and sheep and goat caravans in the Indian and Nepalese Himalaya carry goods in homespun woolen bundles, one to a side. And human beings have always been beasts of burden in these ranges; once, four of us (two *sahibs* and two Tibetan porters) accompanied a merchant and village chief from Torpa village in Humla, Nepal, as he and his three hired porters (one a woman) carried his merchandise on their backs from Jumla to his store in far northwestern Nepal, a 10-day walk. During the heyday of trade on the Silk Route, crossing from the north—the Turkestani or Tibetan highlands—to the southern slopes of the great mountains was an immense undertaking.

Since the days of small local kingdoms, emissaries of the prevailing rulers have visited remote areas. Government employees still travel the Himalayan trails in the line of duty, though civil servants often wear no uniform, hat, or identifying badge of their profession. In Nepal, anyone carrying only a portable radio and wearing stylish sunglasses is probably a V.I.P. In 1974, Chris Wriggins, my trekking companion, and I were descending from Jang Pass in central Nepal when we met a man with modish, wraparound dark glasses and a cloth-covered radio who asked several questions about our route. Later we were told that he was walking to his new position as police chief of Dolpo District. We also encountered soldiers, mailmen, tax collectors, and government workers on leave from their jobs in the city to see family at home.

The third traditional Himalayan traveler has been the pilgrim. From Baba Ghundi Ziarat in Hunza at the top of the subcontinent to Tashigang Monastery in eastern Bhutan, pilgrimage sites and the routes to them trace the mythological past of the Himalaya to its origins. The pilgrimages by foot that attract the greatest numbers take place in India: the Amarnath Yatra, the winter festivals of Ladakh, and a gathering of Tibetan refugees for an appearance by the Dalai Lama attract thousands, but religious-cum-trade festivals occur in every hill area.

The 3,500-year-old Vedas, Hinduism's oldest poetry and spiritual teachings, recommend that the last third of a person's life be devoted to seeking the Ultimate in a state of voluntary poverty. The varieties of "renouncing individuals" (*sannyasi*) are many, but most ascetics are called *sadhus*. A sadhu, whether he is independent or belongs to an order, will travel from shrine to shrine most of the year, rarely staying in one place longer than three days. Many older sadhus are well educated and have left professions. More than once I have had pleasant conversations in English with trident-carrying, ochre-daubed sadhus on the trail. During the summer months, those walking into the Indian and Nepalese Himalaya are joined for the Amarnath and Kedarnath yatras and for the yatras to the sources of the Ganges by thousands of householders eager to assure themselves religious merit and a better place on the karmic wheel in the next incarnation. Tibetans are inveterate travelers by nature, and they like to combine trading, visiting, and seeing holy places. The Tibetan word for pilgrimage is *gnas-skor*, which means "going around places." The Moslems of the Himalayan region make their pilgrimages to Mecca. At home, Moslems consider travelers to be guests and traditionally offer them warm hospitality.

The Himalaya Is Explored and Mapped

At its largest, Alexander the Great's empire extended east to Chitral and the Indus Valley. The Kalash in southern Chitral and some families in the Hunza Valley claim to be kin of dissatisfied legionnaires who did not follow "Sikander" home to Greece. After Alexander's forces departed south down the Indus River, nearly a thousand years passed before Chinese pilgrim-scholars began to filter across snowy Karakoram passes seeking the seminal texts of their Buddhist teachings. The best known of these Chinese was the indefatigable seventh-century pilgrim Hsuan Tsang. He arrived in the region called Gandhara, centered in the Peshawar Valley, and traveled for 14 years in

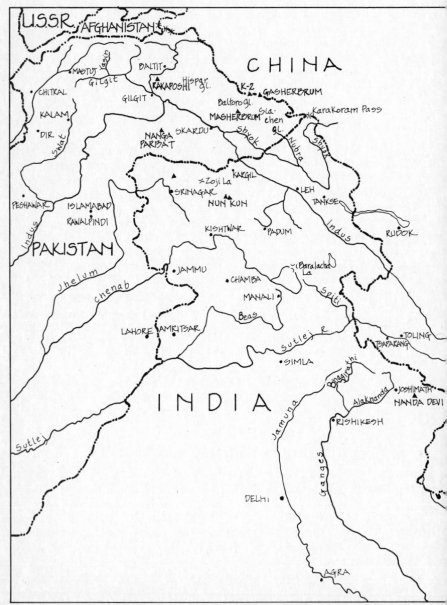

The Himalaya from Chitral to Western Bhutan

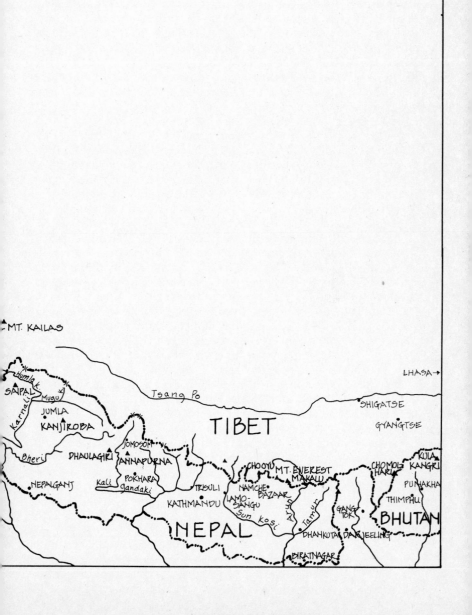

what is now Afghanistan, Pakistan, and northern India before returning to China by the Pamir caravan route.

At the beginning of the 14th century, Marco Polo made his voyage of discovery from Italy to China and back. He told Orient and Occident of the riches that each could offer the other, nearly single-handedly opening the era of the great Silk Route. The trans-Himalayan branches of this trail stretched from Chitral on the west to the Leh-Rudok route east from Ladakh. For many years the finest silk, tea, textiles, jewels, and other valuables were carried along it between Europe and Turkestan, then the gateway to China.

With trade came cultural diffusion. Catholic missionaries began to move eastward, and some descendants from their tradition still remain in the Himalaya. The first Christians into the mountains were two Portuguese Jesuits who established a church in the 17th century at the west-Tibetan city of Tsaparang. The Jesuit Society also set up a missionary outpost in Lhasa, which passed to the Capuchins and operated until that order was expelled by the Chinese emperor in 1740.

Aside from these few incursions, trails within the Himalaya remained the exclusive domain of Asian traders, civil servants, and pilgrims until the mid-19th century. The xenophobia of every Himalayan potentate successfully kept most *Angrezi* (foreigners, or English people) away from the formidable ranges. Those who entered the foothills were immediately suspected of trying to learn a region's geography, of arranging lucrative trade contacts, or of endeavoring to influence local political sentiment. The grapevine among people on the trail passed along word of the movement of any Angrezi, the information traveling as rapidly as the swiftest person. It was the rare Westerner who could disguise himself so skillfully or move so covertly as to avoid detection.

Eventually, however, the expanding British presence in the Ganges and Punjab plains to the south brought pressures too great to be contained. By 1800 the British needed imperatively to know more about the Abode of Snow (*Hima-alaya*) than the meager accounts previous travelers had brought back.

In 1803 Nepal's first British Resident had a preliminary survey done; until then, the extreme height of the Himalayan Range had not been known. And even then, European scientists refused to believe the British survey work, maintaining that the Andes were the world's highest mountains. The unassailable trigonometrical survey, begun in south India, was supervised by George Everest as it moved northward and undertook the Herculean effort to map the Himalaya and Karakoram. Not until 1845 was Dhaulagiri (26,810 ft.) officially recognized as taller than the Andes' Chimborazo (20,703 ft.), and not until 1852 did Mt. Everest (29,028 ft., named for Sir George) gain its rightful place in the record books.

In 1812 the British explorer and trader William Moorcroft and a friend named Hearsey disguised themselves as sadhus, crossing the Niti Pass in Garhwal on the Badrinath route to Lake Manasarowar and Mt. Kailas, the holy of holies for Hindus and Buddhists. They went to find the goats that produce shawl wool, and when they returned they brought a herd of the long-haired goats to spur interest in the lucrative pashmina trade. During this trip, Moorcroft made the first accurate sketches of the sources and drainages of the Indus, Sutlej, and Ganges rivers. Eight years after that clandestine journey, Moorcroft journeyed northwest from the Sutlej River—then the limits of British control—with 300 men and 16 pack animals carrying textiles for barter. He did not return for three long years. Herbert Tichy noted in the 1950s that Moorcroft's name could still be seen scratched on the cave wall of the great Buddha at Bamian in central Afghanistan.

The Gurkha War of 1814–16 resulted in Nepal's western boundary shifting east, from the Sutlej River to the Mahakali, by order of the British-dictated treaty terms; this opened the Ganges River headwaters to outside scrutiny for the first time. In the 1830s G. T. Vigne, another independent British adventurer, was the first Westerner to explore the Karakoram kingdom of Baltistan, conducting four journeys to that vertical, glaciated world. Most of its high peaks and major watersheds were known by the mid-1800s, but the arduous, valley-by-valley work of surveyors with plane-tables was done thereafter.

Despite these discoveries, large areas of the subcontinent's map were still marked UNEXPLORED in enticingly bold print: Nepal, Tibet, Sikkim, and Bhutan. To chart those sovereign, forbidden lands, the Indian Survey in 1865 trained carefully selected people from the hills, who traveled disguised as merchants, monks, pilgrims, or *fakirs*. These men came to be known as the pundits, and their stories remain some of the most remarkable in the annals of Himalayan exploration. Their mission was to map specific areas within those forbidden kingdoms, and they were able to fulfill it by allaying suspicion in a variety of imaginative ways: a Muslim mullah carried a special compass, said to point to Mecca; a Buddhist monk carried a *mala* (prayer beads) with 100 beads for counting paces instead of the 108 traditional in Buddhism; a merchant liked to camp alone at the base of the hills; and one pundit hid in a coconut his mercury for measuring altitude. They used code numbers and names, some of which became famous—the Mullah, A-K, the Pundit, and Hari Ram, who first fixed the latitude and longitude of Lhasa. Later, in 1873, Hari Ram also visited Mustang, the last outsider on record to have done so until H. W. Tilman passed through in 1950. Two of the pundits were away without contact for four years in the uncharted vastness of Tibet, Mongolia, and western China. The accuracy of the work they brought back astounded their university-trained British colleagues and the explorers of later years.

The Survey of India Quarter Inch Series sheets from the period 1914–24 that cover Nepal, Tibet, Sikkim, and Bhutan are drawn from information supplied by the pundits. Interestingly enough, the maps for these areas in the AMS U502 series (see Appendix A) are taken from that early Survey of India Series. So now we not only trace routes that were explored by the pundits, we use maps made from their drawings and measurements.

The explorer George Hayward, an Englishman who favored

traveling alone in Afghan dress (often that of a Pathan merchant), explored the upper Yarkand River drainage in 1868–69. Then he visited the previously unknown cities of Kashgar and Yarkand before succumbing violently—"in the wilds of Central Asia," as he had predicted. It fell to the renowned explorer Francis Younghusband to cross the Mustagh Pass of the northern Karakoram in 1886, the only known traverse from Turkestan south into Baltistan. The height and extent of the entire Himalayan mountain system was essentially known by 1900, but as recently as 1937 Eric Shipton (known along with H. W. Tilman for the lightweight equipage of his mountaineering explorations) could exult while in the Karakoram:

> To the east and west stretched an unexplored section, eighty miles long, of the greatest range in the world. We had food enough for three and a half months, and a party equipped and fully competent to meet the opportunity.... Carrying three weeks food which, with our equipment, was as much as we could manage without relaying, we set off up the Shaksgam. . . . We started by climbing a 20,000-foot peak to discover the lie of the land. . . . The next ten days were spent exploring the glaciers flowing north and west from K_2, the second highest peak in the world.

The exploration by land of the Himalaya still has not been exhaustively completed, although some sites only recently reached by Westerners are now much frequented. The Khumbu Glacier, destination of hundreds of today's trekkers yearly, had never been seen by outsiders until Dr. Charles Houston and H. W. Tilman reached the southern base of Everest in 1950.

A Short History of Himalayan Trekking

No, not shooting; not rocks-collecting, not flowers keeping; not heads measuring, not mountains measuring; not pictures taking. This my Sahib and my Mem-Sahib traveling where their felt are liked, camping always high place to look the country.

Rasul Galwan, 1923

Until quite recently high mountains put fear into the hearts of European and Easterner alike. Inhabitants of the Alps believed that dragons lived by glaciers (which is not surprising, for glaciers can emit frightening noises) and also assumed that survival overnight on a glacier was totally impossible. Only toward the end of the 18th century did mountain peaks, high-country lakes, and meadows begin to be aesthetically pleasing to Westerners. On the full moon of August in 1786, the Frenchmen Gabriel Paccard and Jacques Balmat became the first of thousands to climb 15,782-ft. Mont Blanc, the highest peak in the Alps. Carrying only iron poles as aids, they went up and back 8,200 ft. each way in one day, for they still believed it impossible to sleep on the mountain. The second ascent of Mont Blanc involved 18 porters carrying assorted wines, brandies, and scientific instruments, proving, as we see in the Himalaya today, that there are many ways to go into the mountains.

Beginning in the early 19th century, the British established summer "hill stations" on the Indian subcontinent at Simla, Mussoorie, Darjeeling, and elsewhere on high ridge tops well situated for viewing the eternal snows. Trekking and hunting enthusiasts on holiday set out from those well-furbished bases, and they wrote home about the glories of the Himalaya. W. W. Graham, an Englishman, was in 1883 the first person known to have traveled to the Himalaya from England "more for sport and adventure than for the advancement of scientific knowledge." In those days, when travel was far more involved than it is now, Graham certainly would have read the popular *Art of Travel* by Francis Galton, the period's required reading prior to an Asian trip. It was subtitled *Shifts and Contrivances Available in Wild Countries*, and it featured instructions on rope descents, making black powder, and defending a camp against marauders.

From the outset of travel into the Himalaya, a trek or a climb could be in either of two styles. Some people preferred to walk with a small group that ate the local diet and replenished most food supplies along the way, eschewing large numbers of porters. Others traveled as befitted a proper sahib, with porters, servants, cooks, guides, and, if not all the comforts of home, enough to take the edge off. Each method of travel has had its enthusiastic participants, and trekking styles today have evolved directly from the parties that went into the Himalaya a hundred years ago.

A perfect example of the grand, well-provisioned approach to Himalayan trekking was carried off first-class by Robert and Katherine Barrett in 1923-24. Well read in both Tibetan lore and Galton, this maverick American couple left Kashmir and trekked for a year in Ladakh and Baltistan, calling themselves Gypsy Davy and Lady Ba. En route, they reached the Baltoro Glacier, made a winter camp above Leh, and stayed by the Pangong Lake, before returning to British India. Their book, *The Himalayan Letters of Gypsy Davy and Lady Ba*, is a little-known classic, with an unexcelled map that shows every night's camp and depicts the glaciers as firewater-breathing dragons.

Toward the beginning, Lady Ba writes to a friend, "It is our pilgrimage to Mecca, this Himalayan journey. We go about in a sort of rapture. It may be years before we get back." Davy, in his fifties, went about in "neatly patched Shetlands" and liked to meditate on high view points. The Barretts lived Tibetan style in handsome embroidered tents. They hired Rasul Galwan from Leh, the best *sirdar* (caravan foreman) of the day, and gave him carte blanche to outfit the caravan. Davy and Rasul had traveled together 20 years earlier, and it was Rasul's knowledge that bestowed their pilgrimage with an extra dimension. "Up to now," Lady Ba wrote, "the mountains have been earth to us, beautiful, austere, impersonal. To Rasul they are places, backgrounds for stories of people."

The opulent style of Gypsy Davy and Lady Ba's journey "to the high quiet places" cannot be duplicated today, but it is quite possible to go with a sizable crew, eat western food, and maintain many amenities. However, many Himalayan travelers today, given economics and recent innovations in lightweight gear, are taking an unencumbered approach to trekking, and this style too had its enthusiasts in the days when few valleys had yet been breached by outsiders.

The first mountain explorer to advocate traveling lightly was Dr. Tom Longstaff, a British explorer and climber who made discoveries and ascents in the Gilgit valleys, Baltistan, Garhwal, and the Everest area at the beginning of this century. Another exponent of the unencumbered approach was the legendary British mountaineer Eric Shipton, who in 1934 amazed even Longstaff by telling him that he (Shipton) and Bill (H. W.) Tilman planned to travel to India by cargo ship, hire two Sherpas, and travel in the Himalaya five months for a total of £ 300. Not only were Shipton and Tilman £ 14 under budget for that trip, they were the first Westerners to reach the meadows of the Nanda Devi Sanctuary, and they explored the three major sources of the sacred Ganges River. Shipton later wrote in his autobiography, "Bill and I used to boast that we could organise a Himalayan expedition in half an hour on the back of an envelope."

In 1949, several years before Nepal opened its doors to tourism, Bill Tilman, Maj. James O. M. Roberts, and two scientists were allowed into the upper Marsyangdi and Kali Gandaki valleys to look about and climb a few peaks. Like Tilman, Roberts knew the mountains, but the major lived higher off the land on his trip than had Tilman and Shipton with their wheat flour, *tsampa* (roasted barley flour), butter, and tea. (Even the hardy Sherpas, while emphasizing that Shipton and Tilman were always fair, complained of the spartan diet they shared with these two Angrezi.) Major Roberts was fluent in Nepali, having commanded a Gurkha Rifles regiment, and had gone many times into the hills on recruiting missions. From time to time he did some climbing, once as leader of the only expedition ever sanctioned to attempt Machhapuchhare (the "fishtail"), stopping a respectful distance below the summit of the sacred peak.

When Jimmy Roberts retired, by then a colonel, he opened the first trekking agency, called Mountain Travel, Nepal. Roberts's idea was that, in order to trek comfortably in the exquisite and remote Nepal Himalaya, people would be willing to pay for porters, supplies, and Sherpas with know-how. It was a prescient choice, as events have shown.

When Nepal began issuing trekking permits, a world traveler named Jan Peiper became an early recipient. Later in Calcutta when I met Jan, he told me about the incredible experience of trekking there in 1967 and described a particularly fine *bhatti*, or village inn, at a town called Tatopani where hot springs were close at hand. At that time neither Jan nor I could have imagined the number of trekkers who would soon pass through Tatopani and stay at that inn with the tangerine trees. The path including Tatopani has since been hyperbolically called "the ultimate trek" in a *Washington Post* headline.

Trekking Today: Four Options

Times have changed since Francis Galton's book appeared in the mid-1800s. Then, you would have been foolish indeed to travel in the Himalaya without being capable of repelling a raid by the locals. As time passed, however, the people who live in and govern the Himalaya have undergone successive changes of mind about the Angrezi. Economics have undoubtedly been a factor in most areas; it is said that prominent Ladakhis pressured the central government to allow tourists into Leh because of all the rupees being made in Nepal from sightseers and trekkers. At any rate, with a few exceptions determined by political considerations, you can roam throughout the Himalaya today.

And you have a number of options as to trekking style as well. You can trek alone (recommended for very few) or with one or more friends; with a porter; with a sirdar and crew; or with a group arranged by an agency. The descriptions below of these four styles will help you decide which is closest to your inclination and means.

Note that while styles of trekking differ in convenience and load, the one doing the walking is always you. The first few days of a Himalayan trek can be daunting even though you know rationally that thousands of people (some of them quite out of shape) have preceded you, and that for countless thousands of mountain dwellers in the Himalaya, walking mountain trails is an everyday fact of life. A good way to break in, and also to help determine which style of trekking best suits you, is to take some short trail walks. There are one-day routes near or directly reachable from every important mountain bazaar, for example, Chitral, Gilgit, Skardu, Srinagar, Joshimath, Pokhara, and Kathmandu. (These day hikes are described in the appropriate chapters, 4–13.) You can practice your trekking act—and shove aside mountains of inhibitions—by carrying a small pack to or beyond the day-hike view point, then setting up camp and staying for the night. Two quick considerations if you do this: do not sleep in any religious temple or shrine (unless invited), and be certain that you are well above town and away from a road. As at home, the laws and denizens of the city are different from country ways and people.

Another way to warm up for a longer trek, or to help decide which style of trekking fits you, is to walk solo or with a porter for a couple of days to get the feel of things. Walking uphill from such towns as Pokhara, Pahlgam, Ayun, or Chalt, select an accessible roadhead and simply hike right into the mountains for two days or four. The danger is that in several hours or days you will indeed have a feel of things, yet lack the gear or permission to continue. Returning to "Go" is frustrating, as I learned the first time, when I had to return to Kathmandu from Pokhara to get a trekking permit.

Here, then, are the four styles of trekking.

Alone or with Friends

Yes, to dance beneath the diamond sky with one hand waving free. . . .

Bob Dylan, 1965

When we hike in the Sierra, Rockies, Appalachians, or the Alps, we plan for our food needs, take shelter, and head for the trail. This kind of trekking can be done in the Himalaya too, but several ifs and caveats are attached to going completely alone. The first-time trekker who will set off alone is rare, although many have done it. My decision to go trekking for the first time was arrived at one day in 1971 during a delightful two-hour walk west of Pokhara. In the course of that walk I easily came to the realization that, yes, the trail just kept going along and all I had to do was follow it. Serendipitously, I met some Peace Corps volunteers who were about to leave also, and we agreed to trek together. I am an explorative type, but I know that for the first two to three days of that trek I was very glad to be with the PCVs, learning the ropes and more vocabulary. Still, after five days I went off on my own, and I have since walked solo or with one friend in areas from Chitral to Khumbu.

Unfortunately, women are not safe camping alone in the Himalaya and in many areas are not safe hiking alone. If you are a woman, you had best go with a friend or a very reliable porter who is recommended by a reputable agency.

Trekking alone can be wonderful, but to do it you must be prepared to put more than walking along the trail into your day. If you plan to camp out and cook your own food, then you must have the stamina to do it. In some areas you may also stay in inns or homes; in them, you will need to know words learned from the appropriate glossary in this book. Also, you must have the energy to use the vocabulary after a day on the trail.

Walking alone or with just one or more friends over Himalayan periods of time (typically 10 days out at the absolute minimum) takes a knack that comes as you proceed. If you are intrepid enough to trek alone, you probably have good trail sense, and unquestionably should have a good map. A 100-word vocabulary and a friendly disposition are two of the best assets for any Angrezi walker, but they are particularly helpful to the solo trekker; just as families have traditionally given the traveler shelter and a meal, the traveler has traditionally reciprocated with local gossip, the word-of-mouth newspaper. Since you are not fluent and don't know the issues and personalities of the valley, you can talk with people about other subjects, such as their livestock, the children, or a neighboring valley, or you can ask and comment about the trail in the vicinity. Practicing your food words with the cook may lead to eating a better meal. You will be surprised how many subjects can be handled with so few words and how quickly you will learn new words if you jot them down and actively use the language.

A solo trek can be the most rewarding walk possible. It can bring you almost mystically close to both the people and land in a way impossible when traveling with a group. Carrying all your gear is the most tiring way to walk in the mountains, but you can be compensated by the freedom.

With a Porter

There came a time when I realized that he was teaching me more than I was teaching him.

Edward W. Cronin, Jr., 1979

For a great many people, trekking with one porter, who carries gear and (lacking inns on your route) cooks—or trekking with friends and several porters—is the best way to walk in the Himalaya. Going with a local person will introduce you to much that might otherwise pass by unnoticed, and you are spared the labor of lugging all your belongings and food, besides. If you show an interest in crops, forest plants, birds, people along the trail, or anything else, your porter will be able to pass on much lore, because he knows the country, probably better than you know your own home area. You will learn the old truth that you may be the sahib, but he is the teacher.

Soon after you begin walking with a porter, a lingua franca will develop, whether pidgin English, a pidgin version of the local language, or both. Speaking even minimal Hindi/Urdu or Nepali will set you apart from other trekkers. If your porter wants to work for trekkers in the future, he may use as much English as he can with you.

I had been on three treks without using a porter, but then one spring I found myself, along with friend Chris Wriggins, in dusty, windy Jumla, the wild west of Nepal. We would need porters for the long, rugged trip we planned. When we first saw the two thin, grinning Tibetan *Drok Pa* (nomads) who were to carry and cook for us, we thought they might not be sturdy enough to carry a good load. That erroneous notion was erased quickly. The first night away from Jumla, I wondered, too, whether our preparations had been adequate. But we ate a fine dinner, and during the eight weeks we were on the trail together we needed only to replenish basic food items. By the time we reached Pokhara, the four of us had walked halfway across Nepal together. And when we reached the road, we subjected one 40-year-old Tibetan nomad to his first bus ride.

Longstaff, Shipton, Tilman, and Murray walked the mountain trails with a similarly minimal approach to trekking. Because they trekked for months at a time, and departed from trailheads that were farther from the ranges than the trailheads used today, they needed more than one porter to a sahib. But everyone carried a load. If you are willing to carry a good load yourself, you and a friend can have a rewarding trek far into the Himalaya with one or at most two porters.

Do not assume that you can get a first-class porter on snap notice. If you must count every day of your time in the Himalaya, you should weigh the merits of trekking with a sirdar and crew or with a group arranged by an agency. The important subject of whom to hire as porter and how is discussed at length in Chapter 3.

With a Sirdar and Crew

It was clear that we must field a light party and live on the country, after the manner set by the pioneer of Himalayan climbing, Dr. Longstaff—a manner that subsequently lapsed but which had again been demonstrated by Shipton and Tilman in the nineteen-thirties. This meant that we must buy our food from small villages in the upper valleys. . . .

W. H. Murray, 1951

If you want to walk a chosen route through the mountains for a limited time with several friends, and if expense is not a prime concern, then hiring a sirdar (foreman), cook, and porters is the way to trek. By making arrangements with an agency at home or in Asia, or by hiring a sirdar after you arrive (which can be tricky), you can go on a private trek with all or most of the comforts enjoyed by commercial trekking groups. An agency, whether government or private, can do anything for you from arranging permits (if necessary) to completely outfitting a crew for your private group.

At least six months before your first trip to the Himalaya, you should write to several recognized trekking agencies. Consult advertisements in such magazines as *Outside* and *Adventure Travel* about agencies currently operating. Let them know where and for how long your group would like to walk, discuss the terms, and you can have an appropriate agency completely outfit your trek before you get there. Then you will not waste time in-country, and, although working with such an agency is more expensive, you can be reasonably sure that your group will have an experienced sirdar, adequate supplies, and a dependable crew. The job of the sirdar is to purchase all the food and to hire the cook and porters: the sirdar is in charge. Making these arrangements takes more time in Asia than does a similar production in the United States or Europe; if you do not plan in advance, allow several days at the absolute minimum for the sirdar to put together a crew and buy food.

If you organize your group on-site in Pakistan or India, the nearest office of the Tourism Development Corporation can help you. Or, in Kathmandu, go to Ason Tole (*ason* means "intersection"), along the main street of the old bazaar. On side streets just off Ason Tole, ask at the numerous smoke-enshrouded teashops and small restaurants; these gritty establishments are informal gathering places for sirdars, cooks, and assistants. And if you tell your hotel staff that you are looking for a trekking crew, you may not have to search long. Word of mouth is unbelievably quick in Asia, and much business that would be conducted in the West with the Yellow Pages or union hall is done in the East person to person, often through invisible nepotistic channels unknown to the outsider.

If you sign with an agency, you will pay a fixed price for everything and that will be it. But if you deal directly with the sirdar, you will make a verbal arrangement, called a *bandobast* in Hindi/Urdu, and you must agree on everything then. Any points left vague or open to interpretation may get hauled out later for renegotiation. Refer to the section on hiring a porter in Chapter 3 for details, if you hire someone yourself. In Asia, verbal agreement is as sacred as the handshake that once concluded business transactions in America, but take care: Many people like to call themselves sirdars nowadays. You must always ask for a person's *chits*—literally pieces of paper with information—his letters of reference from former employers. Read the letters carefully and form an intuitive sense of the man. Note particularly whether he has been along the specific route you want, and whether he is recommended by someone you know or know of. Be certain, too, that the chits are his and not on loan from a friend.

One consequence of trekking with your own English-speaking sirdar or with an arranged group is that the "us–them" fiction is more easily fallen into. "Us–them" signifies that we are *here* and they who live here are *there*, unapproachable. The language barrier is the principal invisible fence; without it the "us–them" split withers away. Time and again I have been freely offered warm acquaintance and assistance by local people whom at first glance I might have ignored. Rather than depend on your group's sirdar as the only source of your information, seek out your own encounters, paint your own canvas.

With a Group Arranged by an Agency

*1855–Thomas Cook organized the first international tour, an
excursion to the Paris Exposition.*
*1874–Thomas Cook offered the first world tour, by horse-drawn
coach, steamship, and train.*

Many people have enough money for special vacations but lack the time to make arrangements. For these people, there are agencies that offer treks along a remarkable variety of routes in the Himalaya, from Chitral to Bhutan. For more than 15 years, these outfitters have been sending people on walking excursions, and the best do an excellent job. Mountain Travel was the first and is the biggest. Organized trekking groups from Japan, Germany, France, Australia, and the United States fan out in many seasons, often with itineraries of obscure sites, and with increasingly sophisticated specialities. Before long some enterprising company will offer a cross-cultural tour to observe the making of first-class rakshi (Nepalese grain liquor) from rice, then corn, and finally from barley as the participants progress up a valley. Many agencies will gladly send colorful, informative catalogues—but please be warned: these catalogues are known to elicit drastic depletions of savings.

Whether a trekking group is on a brief walk in the midlands of Nepal or trying a little-known pass to Zanskar from the Kishtwar area, the sirdar must have a capable crew working under him. Experienced personnel can do everything from cooking to fixing ropes along dicey, exposed stretches. The cook on an organized trek bears much of the morale burden, and the best cooks rise daily to the occasion with meals that astound many trekkers.

A feature to keep in mind about the group treks is that the participants agree to a set schedule. They all know before leaving where they will be on any day of the trek, and no one can follow an individual impulse to set off on an overnight side trip, to rest for a day, or to climb a tempting minor peak. The group must stay together, even if someone ails. This style of trekking is probably not for the maverick, then. But for many people it's the ideal way to go; thousands have enjoyed trekking in groups, and many sign to go again.

Thoughts on Time

Meanwhile our lives have become geared, as it were, to the speed at which we move, so that of the few who have the will to cross mountains, even fewer have the time.

David L. Snellgrove, 1961

When we walk into the Himalaya and away from the web of roads and electricity, we are reaching for a unique experience, not a predictable vacation. In thinking about a trek, consider from the outset the time needed to do it. Thirty days from departure to return should be an absolute minimum. If you buy a 14-to-120-day excursion plane ticket and your stay in Asia approaches four months, you can have two or more good walks along Himalayan paths.

Most of us move at a pace entirely different from the Himalayan farmer's or merchant's, and it takes some time to accomplish the shifting of gears. Gradually, the terrain imposes a tempo. The long trekking day gives a vector view, as, for instance, one evening you look back across a gorge and see the morning's campsite less than 3 mi. away. The days of foot pace allow you to absorb awesome mountain scenery. The immediacy of such an experience imparts a perspective on home life that cannot be gained from long weekends at the state park.

2
Advance Planning

As often as possible, do what the others are not doing: go off-season instead of on, go in bad weather instead of good, walk when others ride, laugh when others cry. . . .

Ed Buryn, 1971

In every journey, there are as many objectives missed as there are objectives gained.

Arnold Toynbee, 1960

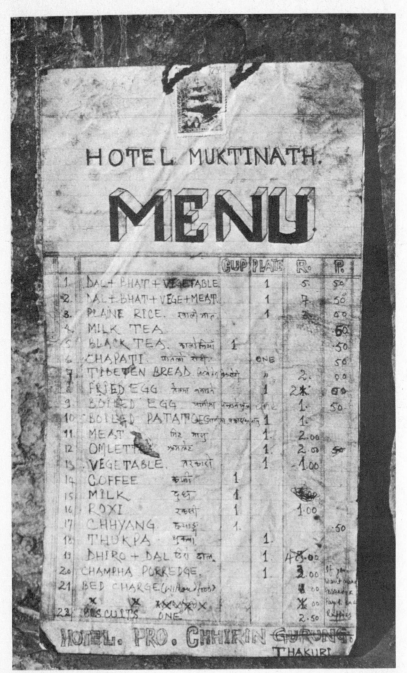

Menu from a village inn north of Annapurna.

Many of us tempt ourselves for years with the possibility of going to the Himalaya. Scenes from books come to mind, and we try to put ourselves into them. We imagine trekking north of the world's highest massifs into land indistinguishable from Tibet, or of walking up a glaciated pass between two medieval valley kingdoms. When the decision is finally made, it is as if you had been walking up a rolling hill and imperceptibly crossed its ridge line, finding yourself going down the far side. You *are* going. This chapter takes you from that decision to the airplane ride that will whisk you to Asia.

Eric Shipton could organize his excursions to the Himalaya "in half an hour on the back of an envelope," but you will require considerably more time and at least two full-size sheets of paper for making lists of inoculations to have, visas to obtain, and more. My second overland trip to Nepal was completely organized on 2½ weeks notice, from inspiration to departure. This can be done and we proved it, but if you take such a hasty approach, you'll likely be exhausted by the time you reach Asia. A Himalayan trek requires planning, and there are several projects to start at once.

General Preparation

Physical Conditioning

If you plan to trek in addition to sightseeing, you should initiate or continue a good conditioning program. Vigorous exercise that strengthens the cardiovascular system, lungs, and legs is the best way to prepare yourself for Himalayan walking. Hiking, running, swimming, bicycling, and cross-country skiing will help toughen you for walking in country so vertical that you may trek steadily uphill for days at a time. Exercise continuously for 60 to 90 minutes every other day, or every day, if you have the time, and certainly work up to that much exercise before leaving. This will not fully condition you for 6 to 10 hours of walking day in and day out, but it will strengthen your system to the point that your body can accept the rigors of trekking. Backpacking in your favorite hilly location is the best approximation of what you will do in the Himalaya and will help remind you of your physical capabilities. One of the many joys of a Himalayan trek is that you get far beyond the achy-muscles-and-groggy-evenings stage of hiking by the end of the first week. To get in shape if you have done no physical preparation, however, will take far longer than a week on the trail. Many people who set off on a whim don't get far without wishing fervently that they were in shape, and spur-of-the-moment trekkers are sometimes forced to turn back by physical ailments.

Background Reading

This book gives you an overview of the Himalaya from Chitral to Bhutan, but you will want to do more background reading. After finishing this book, you may have a greater interest in two or three areas

and want to seek out additional reading about them. One likely source
is the *National Geographic*; the stories are colorful, and most libraries
have the magazine's back issues. The annotated bibliography at the
back of this book will lead you a long way toward gathering all the
information you will need or can absorb.

Of the introductions to walking Asian mountain trails and glaciers,
Eric Newby's *A Short Walk in the Hindu Kush* remains one of the best.
Newby, his friend, and their crew of three Afghans trekked in Nuristan,
Afghanistan in 1956. With minimal paraphernalia, they walked in the
Panjshir and Ramgul valleys, then tried to reach the top of 19,880-ft.
Mir Samir, reading how-to-climb books on the ascent. After failing
in three attempts, they had an eventful look at rarely seen Ramgul in
Nuristan before returning by the standard route to Kabul. Newby
experienced and humorously detailed the range of predicaments and
pitfalls facing the neophyte trekker. A more scholarly but nonetheless
fascinating book is *Himalayan Pilgrimage*. In it, David Snellgrove
portrays his study trek to Dolpo and north-central Nepal's other
Buddhist areas during a five-month period in 1956. He gives tribute to
his guide and friend Pasang, without whose assistance "the whole
venture would scarcely have been possible." Snellgrove describes his
book as "a kind of scholar's travelbook." It is also an excellent evoca-
tion of village people and life in truly remote Himalayan places. Many
other volumes also tell about walking Himalayan trails from the contemporary outsider's perspective. Among them, Stephen Bezruchka's
A Guide to Trekking in Nepal is the best-detailed hour-by-hour trail
guide yet published for a particular Himalayan area, in this case the
central and eastern Nepalese Himalaya.

Aside from reading for background, make copies of this book's
glossary or glossaries for the areas you will visit. Post the word lists
by your dining area or near your bed, and you will begin absorbing vocabulary.

Maps

As you narrow down the areas you are interested in and plan the
trek, you must purchase maps that give the best possible bird's-eye
view. When you are trekking, a map can mean all the difference sometimes and most of the difference all the time in knowing where you
are. For some areas, specialty maps are available, particularly the
Erwin Schneider Research Scheme Nepal Himalaya maps. The best
overall series is the US Army Map Service (AMS) U502 Series, which
covers all non-Tibetan areas of the Himalaya east of 72°E in Chitral at
4 mi. to the inch (1:250,000). For some areas the U502 sheets are
nit-perfect; and on most sheets a "reliability diagram" shows the degree
of the map's accuracy. A Himalayan map list (with addresses of map
sellers) is contained in Appendix A, "Map Information." (All map-
purchase facts are in Appendix A to avoid scattering them about.) Do
read that appendix and acquire the U502 maps, at least, for the areas
you will trek in.

If maps are as foreign to you as Hindi, you can familiarize yourself with them in several ways. Try to stop thinking that "reading" maps is as difficult as trying to read a foreign language. When you fly in a plane and look straight down, what you see is like a map. Think of a map as an "Oh yes, now I see it" kind of picture. You can become accustomed to route following by tracing on a map the paths described in a narrative account as you read it. Once in the Himalaya, you can read towns off the map and talk with locals about them, even if you haven't figured out the exact relationship of one place to another. Become familiar with any area you will walk in. Use a map to figure out alternate routes, and try them if the usual trails are crowded or restricted. If at first the map appears to be a jumble of lines, you can become accustomed to the area represented by returning to the map and getting to know it in relation to what you see. Some people like to mark their maps with colored felt-tip pens, using one shade for the main rivers and another for the ridge lines. Such lines following valley bottoms and ridges can help you visualize the country shown on two-color maps. Don't hesitate to make notes right on a map or its border if your reading of the land disagrees with what the map shows.

Documents and Immunizations

If you have never been out of the country, or if your passport is expired or due to expire, you will need a new passport. In any case, you will need to get visas and immunizations. These are generally minor details, but they must be attended to and not put off—unforeseeable complications will be plentiful enough at the last minute without procrastination on these few chores.

Most post offices in the United States can give you forms for a passport. You will need two identical recent photos and your old passport, or, for a first application, you will need a certified copy of your birth certificate and a driver's license in addition to the photos and a fee. You should also get a dozen photos for visas and trekking permits. These do not need to be of the quality of the passport photos, but do get a full dozen visa photos; running out is a mistake to be avoided.

For Pakistan, a visa will be necessary if you plan to stay more than a month. With a visa, you will be allowed 30 days' stay in-country at any point of entry. If you wish to extend your visit beyond a month, you can request an additional two months' time at the Foreigner's Registration Office in any city's superintendent-of-police compound, where you will be given a registration certificate. You must have previously obtained a visa to qualify for an extension, however.

Americans need visas in order to enter or transit India. The Indian visa should be a triple-entry tourist visa valid for a three-month total stay. The visa is extendable for three more months once you are in-country; extensions are granted at district police stations. An Indian tourist visa must be used within six months of issuance.

Americans also need visas to enter or transit Nepal. The Nepalese tourist visa is good for a one-month stay within three months from the date of issue. In Nepal, you can have a visa extended for a total stay of three months by paying the fee required. Alternatively, you can get a one-week visa for Nepal upon arrival by air, and arrange extensions once in-country.

Travel in Bhutan is restricted. The Bhutan Travel Service, listed below, will provide information on groups going to that country. The tour agency you go with will arrange the actual visa.

The information on visas included here applies to the citizens of most countries. Passport holders from Commonwealth countries, however, have virtually no limits on length of stay in India.

To get visas, you must first request an application form from each embassy. After filling out a visa application, mail it back with payment, photos, a self-addressed and stamped envelope (SASE), and your passport. To be absolutely safe when mailing your passport, send the letter express or registered and include postage on the SASE sufficient for your stamped passport to be returned likewise by registered mail. Allow as much as two to three weeks for each visa to be processed. In the United States, contact the officials for Pakistan, India, Nepal, and Bhutan by writing to the following addresses:

Embassy of Pakistan, 2315 Massachusetts Ave. N.W., Washington, DC 20008

Consulate General of Pakistan, 12 East 65th St., New York, NY 10021

Embassy of India, 2107 Massachusetts Ave. N.W., Washington, DC 20008

Consulate General of India, 3 East 64th St., New York, NY 10021

Indian Consulate, 215 Market St., San Fancisco, CA 94105

Royal Nepalese Embassy, 2131 Leroy Pl. N.W., Washington, DC 20008

Royal Nepalese Consulate General, 711 Third Ave., Rm. 1806, New York, NY 10017

Bhutan Travel Service, 120 East 56th St., New York, NY 10022

Note: Trekking permits are covered in Chapter 3, as they are usually obtained in-country, but it should be mentioned here that trekking permits for Pakistan have to be applied for well in advance, according to new regulations.

As to immunizations, you should contact the nearest office of the United States Public Health Service (USPHS) for current information. At the time this is written, a cholera inoculation is the only shot required for entry into Pakistan, India, or Nepal. Your tour agency will let you know about any requirements for Bhutan. The initial cholera injection must be followed by a second shot in one week for you to become properly immune; the immunization then remains valid for only six months. As with all other immunizations, your cholera shots must be recorded in a yellow booklet called the International Certificate of Vaccination, which is available from many physicians or the

USPHS. Carry it with your passport when traveling between countries. Have your cholera shots officially validated by the proper authority in the yellow booklet.

There are several other shots you should consider having, including gamma globulin; oral polio vaccine; and immunization for yellow fever, typhoid, and diphtheria/tetanus. Gamma globulin is highly recommended as partial protection against most forms of infectious hepatitis. Get your gamma globulin shot as close as possible to the time you leave, for its protection begins to fade after three to four months. The oral polio inoculation, because it is a live vaccine, has to be taken separately from any other injections that contain live vaccine. Inoculation for yellow fever is now required only if you will be traveling in Africa or South America; you may find some border crossings, however, where this inoculation is asked for regardless. The yellow fever immunization, like that for cholera, must be properly certified in your yellow booklet.

If you will be traveling at low altitudes, you should take malaria pills (chloroquine). The standard dosage is 500 mg per week, beginning two weeks before you go and continuing at least six weeks after you return.

What to Take: The Trekker's Compleat List

You will be the final judge of what to take when you go trekking; to help you, I have compiled the following rather exhaustive list. It is divided into six categories so that you can visualize what you will be adding to your pack if you wish to trek on your own carrying camping and cooking gear, or if you go into the high snows off the trail. Not everything is applicable to everyone's use; the equipment in category 5, for instance, is only for those intending to walk up high peaks or glaciers.

Here are the six categories, then the Compleat List, item by item:
1. Clothing and Personal Gear
2. Camping Equipment
3. Cooking Equipment
4. Miscellaneous
5. Equipage for the High Snows and Glacier Walking
6. Optional Accessories

Clothing and Personal Gear

If you are going to be walking in the Himalaya for any length of time, the chances are quite good that you will need the clothing listed here. You may have to give a porter essentials acquired locally. As you choose which to pack, keep in mind that you will be hand-washing the most-used items in cold stream water.

Underwear. Take three pairs.

Bras. For women, a couple. Bras are recommended for modesty in traditional societies.

Tampons. Or sponges or pads for women. These may be difficult to locate in the local bazaar.

Swimsuit. For women, so you can wash in streams without scandalizing the inhabitants. For men, when washing in streams, shorts or cut-offs will do.

Socks. Take plenty. Liner socks of silk, nylon, or cotton are becoming popular nowadays. You must have, at minimum, two complete changes of socks plus an extra pair in case you need another layer. Few sensations are worse than the feel of wet or dirty socks when trekking.

Nonwrinkling walking skirts (mid-calf length). I recommend that women wear a skirt in places where the likelihood of pants offending the locals is greatest; that is, in places that have had minimal exposure to Westerners. Even in Nepal, it can be a thoughtful practice to wear a skirt while in villages, keeping shorts in your day pack to change into once on the trail for the day. The baggy, locally made pants described below are a good compromise for women between modesty and freedom of movement.

Tights. For women, one pair for warmth.

T-shirts. Take two or three.

Lightweight shirts. You should have one or two loose-fitting wash-and-wear shirts.

Medium-weight to heavyweight shirt. Two button-down pockets on your upper-altitude shirt will come in handy.

Walking shorts. One or more pairs. Shorts should not be worn by anyone in Muslim areas, however.

Trekking pants. For men and women a pair of pants in addition to those you wear on the plane. Many of us feel as if we were walking with an old friend when we wear jeans, but they make very poor trekking duds. Loose pants are a must if you want freedom of the hills. Baggy pants are universally worn in the Himalaya and, even if you are not used to them, will prove most comfortable after an hour or two on a hilly trail. In the West, the nearest we have to Himalayan-style pants are knickers. These give room for the knee to bend unconstricted, but many are tight in the crotch and pelvis unless you make or buy yours large on purpose.

Better than knickers is the Nepali *suruwal* or the Muslim *shalwar*, those wonderfully baggy pajama pants with a drawstring at the waist. When you arrive in an Asian city, consider having a local tailor measure you for a pair to take on your trek. After measuring you, the tailor will know how much cloth is necessary; you can then purchase the material (dark colors hide stains), and the pants can be sewn within hours. I direct the tailor to make the ankle openings just wide enough to fit around my trekking boots. For me, walking in shalwar is the only way to go except on tricky, exposed places off the trail, where the voluminous material can snag. These pants breathe when the temperature is hot, yet seem not to lose heat during cold weather. And their primary asset is that they permit unrestricted leg movement in any direction without rubbing.

Thermal underwear pants. (The shirt is optional.) In winter and in high camps, if you wear long johns with pants and the rest of your body is kept warm, the chill you are exposed to will have to become intensely cold before you become uncomfortable. For most treks, even with several high camps, these two garments will be enough cover on your legs. (If you carry rain chaps, you will have a third layer.)

Rain chaps. Coated nylon rain chaps are great for peace of mind. If they are tied at one end, you can carry flour in them.

Down or fiberfill jacket. You will want to have a good, stuffable down jacket on most treks to ensure comfort. I have gone without one in western Nepal's cool spring, wearing a cheap wool sweater from Kathmandu and a sleeping sheet thrown over my shoulders, but a down jacket would have been much better. Don't take an expedition parka, however, unless you are going up a high peak or have extremely slow metabolism. A jacket with only 10 ounces of goose down has kept me warm up to 20,000 feet. When you trek with a porter, he can use your down jacket to sleep under, with his blanket beneath him. A synthetic-fill jacket will be better if you trek in the monsoon, but remember that fiberfill jackets take up significantly more room.

Trekking boots. The medium- to lightweight trekking boots of your preference are the best to walk in. If you buy used boots, *they must be in good condition.* If you buy new boots, *they must be broken in.* I have had to learn these lessons from that master mentor, experience. My first three treks were done on three pairs of Bata jungle sneakers. Each pair cost a couple of dollars and lasted from two to four weeks, and for each pair my feet required at least five days to begin accustoming themselves to the meagre protection. When I carried a stout pack, my feet were always more tired than they would have been in boots. Once I bought a pair of used boots from a reputable Kathmandu used-trekking-goods store. The heavy boots lasted until halfway through the trek. One sole came off just beyond the highest snow pass, and, by the time I got east to Pokhara, the holes in my Chinese-made back-up sneakers were as big as 50-cent pieces. When I finally had the sense to get new boots, I did not wear them in, having imagined beforehand that my feet could "take it." My feet did not "take it" very well and neither will yours: never take new boots to the Himalaya without being certain that they and your feet are well acquainted.

Here is another misstep to avoid: don't get your shoes resoled anywhere unless you are quite sure the repairman knows his business. I took a pair of shoes and new Vibram replacement soles to a repairman in Rawalpindi who assured me that he could replace the soles like new. Soon after, by the third day up the uninhabited Rishi gorge in Garhwal, the right sole was detached from the ball of my foot to the heel, forcing me to tie on the flopping sole with twine for two weeks.

Insoles. Your feet may become more fatigued than you expect, and a soft cushion beneath them can give some relief. Insoles can also help keep a foot from rubbing when a boot stretches from extensive use. You can cut your own innersoles from the end of a foam pad.

Moleskin. This padding is used to cushion broken skin. Some people prefer Elastoplast to moleskin, and even cellophane tape can partially protect rubbed skin from further harm. Some sort of padding is a real essential.

Running shoes or tennis shoes. Running shoes are useful when you are not carrying much, must ford a fast-moving stream, or have blisters. The light shoes are great for switching off with your regular footgear, but beware of taking them as your only shoes. If you twist an ankle, you can walk only very slowly in running shoes. When you wear them on the trail, walk carefully until you get the feel of them. Waffle soles in particular are tricky; they tend to grab and can throw you off balance. If you hire a porter for a trek with a snow pass or glacier walking, he can wear your running shoes for those sections, unless, like one man I hired, he already has mountaineering boots with full-length steel shanks!

Gloves or mittens. For chilly mornings and high passes, you'll be glad to have hand protection.

Umbrella. That's right, a bumbershoot. Many cognoscenti of the Himalaya would never be without one. It is your best aid against the tropical or alpine sun: with an umbrella, you always have shade. Also, in the rain an umbrella is superior to a poncho (which tends to soak you in perspiration), and it provides a quick line of defense against charging Tibetan mastiffs. When you take back-lit photos, an umbrella is excellent for shading the camera lens. The best possible type is available in India's bazaars or in Kathmandu along the main bazaar street. It is called a *chhatri*, has a bamboo stem and black cloth, and is the same used by sadhu, funky trekker, and Sir Edmund Hillary alike. (Due to the lack of bamboo in Pakistan, the bamboo chhatri is not made there.)

Hat. A warm stocking cap or down hood is the best instant regulator of body temperature. Because more than 40 percent of the body's heat exits from the head, a thick cap will help keep heat in. If you don't plan to use an umbrella in the sun, take a wide-brimmed hat. You *must* have something with you to keep the sun off your head.

Money belt or pouch. A thin, sweat-proof money belt that holds passport, yellow health booklet, traveler's checks, and currency is most convenient for such valuables. It is the trekker's equivalent of the amulets that Buddhists, Hindus, and Muslims often wear around their necks. Before you get trekking, your money belt should be fastened around you, but on the trail it can be buried in your pack. Your passport (or trekking permit, in Nepal) will be needed along the route at checkposts, so don't become separated from it. At night you can put your money belt in your sleeping bag if you question the quarters.

Handkerchiefs. Hankies are great; take one to two large ones for swabbing sweat, carrying walnuts, and playing peek-a-boo with shy kids.

Poncho and groundcloth. Sometimes extra baggage, sometimes necessary protection, a poncho may serve as your groundcloth, rain gear, or extra padding. Be sure that yours has a hood, grommets in the corners, and snaps along the sides.

Sleeping bag. What makes a proper sleeping bag is up to you. Don't be awed by Himalayan heights and over-equip yourself for trekking. I have used a bag containing 26 ounces of goose down and one that had 42 ounces of goose down. The latter was always too warm below 6,000 ft. but fine in colder weather, particularly those winter nights at near-17,000-ft. elevations. Carry your sleeping bag inside your pack, if possible: "Not good to tempt fate, Sahib."

Sleeping sack. Last in this category, I list a personal favorite. Fold a thin bed sheet or like-size piece of cloth lengthwise and sew it closed across the bottom and along both sides to about 10 inches of the top. The sleeping sack that results goes into your bag at night to protect it from greasy nighttime sweat. To wash a sleeping sack several times is a lot easier than to wash a sleeping bag once. The sheet can also serve as a towel or padding for your pack's waistband.

Camping Equipment

The clothing and gear on the previous list are needed by most trekkers in the Himalaya. You will not need to carry your own shelter as well if you trek with a group, decide to sleep only in houses or inns, or decide to chance the rain. Most trekkers, though, need at least these two additional items in order to camp.

Tent. A sturdy, rainproof tent can make all the difference ... but you know that. Having a tent means you can camp anywhere with a flat spot and reachable water.

Foam pad. A half-inch or, preferably, five-eighths-inch-thick closed-cell foam pad under the proper sleeping bag will keep you cozy on a glacier. Use a pad everywhere you sleep to keep out the chill and damp.

Cooking Equipment

In order to trek fully self-contained, a few cooking implements (in addition to food, which is discussed in the next chapter) are necessary. These items can be bought locally, but will be heavier than the back-packer models you can bring with you.

Stove. Using a reliable kerosene stove that you can clean anywhere is preferable to using wood for fuel (unless you are in a remote, heavily forested area like western Nepal). Kerosene is available in Himalayan bazaars; it burns with a hotter flame than gasoline (petrol) and, unlike gas, will never explode. As the wood-fuel crisis spreads and standards of living rise in the mountains, kerosene-burning stoves are coming into general use. This helps to assure that you can buy fuel in the darnedest places if you ask people for it. Local makes of stove are heavier and bulkier than western models. Also, Asian stoves are less fuel efficient and less well built. Note that white gas, used in many popular models of American camp stoves, is not available in Asia.

Fuel container. Your fuel must not leak away, so think again before waiting until you reach the trailhead bazaar to buy your fuel container. Carry enough fuel, and in a sturdy container or containers.

Nesting cook pots. A minimum of two cook pots, or billies, are needed. Bring some, or purchase a pair in the local bazaar. The Asian variety is heavier but can be a bonus to your porter when the trek is over.

Stuff bags. To carry bulk rice, flour, sugar, and other foods, you need nylon or cotton-cloth bags with drawstrings at the top. In the United States they are called stuff bags; in Asia they have other names, and tailors can make them quickly.

Freeze-dried food. If your style of trekking includes freeze-dried food, bring packets from home. The supply in Asia is spotty at best, even in Kathmandu.

Miscellaneous

This is a long list, but look it over carefully. Many articles are lightweight and might be needed on the trail; others can be overlooked. Large and important items are listed toward the beginning. Some are unnecessary (such as cutlery) if you go on a group trek.

Backpack. As with a tent and a sleeping bag, you will have to choose for yourself what you want in a pack. A single-compartment, top-loading pack is the best for me. A broken zipper on an "easy access" pack is quite a nuisance, and that situation can be averted by using a zipperless, top-loading model. Try to avoid using a pack that has no sweat-evaporating back panel or webbing, or you will find that both back and pack become drenched with sweat in lower-elevation trekking. If you plan to go by yourself or go long distances with a porter, take a large-volume pack. Mine holds more than 5,800 cubic inches and it has been quite full several times. If you go with an organized group, you will need only a duffle bag for your porter to carry.

Stuff bags. You will need various sizes and colors to put things in. Stuff bags are described in the cooking-equipment list above.

Iodine tablets. These are absolutely necessary for purifying water. Don't leave without them. Small bottles of 50 tablets are available from mail-order outdoor-supply businesses. *Do not get halazone tablets.* Halazone does not protect against the amoebic cyst that causes amoebic dysentery, a debilitating, sometimes fatal disease. If you drink an iodine solution soon after the 10 to 20 minutes needed for the iodine to decontaminate the water, the taste of the water is remarkably unaffected. Treated water that has been standing overnight will have a much stronger taste.

Medicine kit. A small but complete medicine kit should accompany you. Note Appendix B, "Staying Healthy."

Maps. Take the best maps you can. Check Appendix A, "Map Information."

Notebook. Carrying a small spiral or bound notebook is almost a necessity for the traveler. Before leaving home you can make notes in it, include addresses and any information needed, and tape duplicated glossary pages to it. After arrival in Asia, you owe to your future memories a record of events and places, even if it is cursory. Use your notebook, or you will forget the color and small touches of an experience, despite its vividness at the time.

Day pack or shoulder bag. A day pack or locally made shoulder bag (called a *jhola*) is good for day hikes, but for some would be extra baggage. I carry a *jhola* when trekking to hold my camera, notebook, and maps. On a day walk above a town or high camp, the *jhola* contains food and water.

Toilet kit. The smallest kit may include toothbrush and paste, mirror, comb, soap (one bar will do for body and clothes), washcloth, and dental floss. The floss is important to have, for it is unavailable in South Asia, and a sliver of meat or husk in your teeth can be painful.

Toilet paper. Take it, buy it in the bazaar, or use the *Time* international edition for the wild juxtaposition of timeless mountains and ephemeral news stories. Burn the used paper.

Watch. A reliable watch is perfect for knowing when to arise for an early start or for getting an idea how much light is left on cloudy days. Some clever souls keep a few extra inexpensive watches in their packs. They barter their "only" watches and later replace them with others to be used again as trading material.

Enamel cup. Purchase a large enamel cup in a hardware store or in any Asian bazaar. Use it for tea bought at bazaar stalls, since the glass offered may not be clean. It will also hold coffee, milk, or yoghurt, and you can use it on the trail to count out quantities of dry food or milk products. A cup that holds at least 20 ounces is preferable; some entire meals of soup or *tsampa* will be eaten from it. (I object to the Sierra-cup style for two reasons: it doesn't hold enough liquid by far, and its metal rim is too hot on the lips.)

Spoon. A large soup spoon will enable you to eat nearly anything, if you are reticent to sup with your fingers, local style.

Can opener. Weighing about two grams, the "G.I." or "P-38" can opener is the best for the trail.

Pocket knife. One wide blade should be enough.

Scissors. I find scissors handy, though you might not need them.

Flashlight. An absolute must: for those obligatory nocturnal trips, for the time you find yourself benighted on the precipice trail, and for every other imaginable and unimaginable occurrence in the dark in village or wilderness. Take extra batteries and bulb.

Water bottle. Another sine qua non, your water container should hold one to two quarts or liters. Don't compromise on durability.

Sewing kit. Needles, light and dark nylon thread, numerous safety pins, and a few feet of two-inch-wide ripstop repair tape compose a good, minimal sewing kit. You may wish to carry extra clevis pins or eyebolts (for repairing your pack) in the sewing kit.

Boot protector. Take Sno Seal, mink oil, or your favorite boot grease. You will be surprised how much punishment your boots will suffer on a long trek, compared with a shorter outing at home.

Lip balm. Your lips will quickly chap when trekking, unless you ordinarily live out-of-doors. Without question, take some form of lip grease on any trek.

Suntan lotion. Many people need suntan lotion, although others do fine using only an umbrella or hat. If you burn easily, take lotion with a high sun-protection factor.

Cord. Twenty to 40 ft. of thin nylon cord has a multitude of uses. And few gifts please a person from the high Himalaya more than a nice length of nylon cord.

Photographs. They are great ice-breakers. Everyone likes to see "fotos" of your family, buildings where you live, and such places as stores or roads with cars. In the roadless hills, pictures of automobiles can set off wonderful discussions. Of the photographs I took on my last trip, the favorite showed my sister milking a goat—a very large-uddered goat, the sight of which often provoked exclamations of envy and awe.

Sunglasses. These are useful for low and medium elevations; for the highest elevations, you need more protection.

Spare glasses. If you use prescription glasses, take a spare set in a hard case.

Insect repellent. Insect bites are usually a minor problem unless you trek in the middle of the monsoon. Take strong insect repellent if you are especially sensitive to bites.

Bug powder. Even if you don't cross the threshold of a single dwelling in the Himalaya you can still acquire those tiny things that itch and bite in the night, merely by camping somewhere that has recently been frequented by livestock. I have found that for the rare times lice or bedbugs have materialized, lethal powder (available in Asia) has been necessary for dusting clothes and sleeping bag.

Odds and ends. You will always need a candle, large and small rubber bands, plastic bags, cellophane or masking tape, and extra pens.

Equipage for the High Snows or Glacier Walking

With a few things more, you can head for the high snows and get closer to the summits, or walk for days on a Karakoram glacier.

Mountaineering or glacier goggles. With nothing about but sun and snow at the teens of thousands of feet, your eyes will fail painfully unless protected from the immense amount of direct and reflected light. Be sure to use goggles with high-altitude lenses. Carry good dark glasses or goggles for your porter if you are going with one, for he, like you, will become sightless without eye protection.

Glacier cream. Get high-altitude (greasy) glacier cream to protect your face from strong radiation and reflection.

Extra mittens. Protect your fingers from the possibility of freezing in the heights with at least two pairs of good hand protection.

Cold weather headgear. Carry a balaclava or down hood that will keep your head warm in penetrating winds.

Gaiters. Walking through any deep snow will be a rugged experience unless you can cover the opening between your pants and boots—gaiters accomplish this best. A good stopgap method to keep out snow is to use rubber bands or cord around your cuffs.

Crampons. Take crampons only if you are quite certain you will be going well above the highest trails onto steep snow slopes. Many people, including me, have naively carried crampons about for weeks in Nepal, returning to Kathmandu with them unused. High passes on almost any intervalley route will not require crampons, because other walkers will have blazed the way.

Ice axe. An ice axe provides a bit of dash, but it weighs a pound or two and is not needed for trekking unless you plan to walk in snow or on glaciers.

Climbing equipment. If you are a technical climber, take your gear to the most challenging mountain range you'll ever find. Masses of used climbing gear are available for rent or purchase in Kathmandu—caveat emptor.

Rope. Rope is essential if you are walking on the upper part of a glacier where the moraine gives way to snow. Glaciers in the Karakoram above 16,000 feet are often covered with powder snow. To walk high on such a glacier, all members of your party must be roped together and have ice axes for self-arrest.

Optional Accessories

You will want to take along some of the following to record or illumine the world that you step into.

A good book. Most people have time for a good novel when trekking. A paperback with trading potential is best, in case you finish it and want to swap with someone en route. Some people prefer guides to the flora or fauna. (See the Bibliography.) After toting T. E. Lawrence unread on two successive Himalayan journeys, I have decided I won't ever get much reading done, unlike, according to H. W. Tilman, the traditional mountaineer: "His occupational disease is bedsores, and a box of books his most cherished load."

Camera and film. For tips about camera equipment and use, see the next section, on photography. Some people going to the Himalaya say, "I'm not going to take a camera, because with one, I wouldn't really see things there." Such a philosophy loses out in the long run, however, as memories fade and nothing is left.

Cassette recorder. Using one of the new mini-recorders, you can make friends with people by playing back dialogues, and you can also record singing or instrumental music that you hear. Tapes from afar will lend great immediacy to a slide show.

Binoculars. Some people prefer a lightweight monocular. Either way, field glasses are required if you want to observe animals or birds.

Compass. For most people, a compass is so much unused weight. Because the Himalayan landscape is so vertical, landmarks are usually visible and you will rarely have any doubt of your approximate location. As to using a compass for naming those white peaks on the horizon, I defer again to H. W. Tilman, who wrote, "The identification of very distant peaks is a harmless and fascinating amusement so long as the results are not taken seriously."

Frisbee. Not appropriate for impressing stuffy village elders with your seriousness of purpose, a frisbee can nevertheless be a good ice-breaker.

Afterword to the Compleat List

From T-shirts to frisbees, this is a fairly exhaustive list, and you couldn't carry everything on it plus food and walk very far. If you will be traveling on your own, then, even if you pare down your list to the minimum, you may want a porter to haul some of your gear and cook your food. Trekking with a lighter pack will enable you to enjoy, not merely endure, the entire trek and allow you to better assimilate and record the experience.

Photography

In the Himalaya, the extremes of distance and climate make extra preparation necessary. Some of the following hints may be helpful. The nearest qualified camera-repair shop will be far away when you are trekking, so take a well-built camera. Think twice before relying on a camera that utilizes an easily breakable electronic mechanism unless the camera can also be operated manually. To protect the lens, use an ultraviolet filter. Use a polarizing filter to reduce haze, make colors richer, and dramatize clouds and sky, but remember to take the polarizer off when not shooting in direct sunlight. Carry a camel's hair brush and lens paper to clean your equipment, and if your camera requires a battery, carry an extra one. Some people use a lightweight aluminum camera clamp as a tripod.

Be certain to carry enough fresh film to last the entire trip; you can't count on finding what you want overseas, and discounts are usually available if you buy more than 20 rolls at once. Film with processing charges included can be purchased reasonably from large New York photo-supply houses. High-speed film is useful for inside shots and night pictures. You can usually sell any extra rolls to another traveler or a camera store on the subcontinent for at least your purchase price. Unfortunately, film sold in camera stores there is often out of date or tampered with. One friend of mine bought new-looking rolls at a reputable shop and eventually found that he had purchased rewound film, already exposed. Don't let your film or loaded camera pass through the metal-scanning machines at airports, no matter what any signs say about no damage to film. If the scanning machine is adjusted incorrectly, it can harm your film. Save all color processing for your return. And don't mail home exposed rolls; take the advice of someone who lost five irreplaceable rolls from Nepal. Film that is mailed may be exposed by inspectors looking for contraband, stolen by someone who will sell the film as unused, or thrown away by someone who wants the uncancelled stamps on the mailer.

To preserve your equipment, minimize sudden temperature changes. For example, don't move a camera directly from your sleeping bag into subfreezing outside air. Avoid extremes in temperature if at all possible. Change film in a shaded area, of course, and be very careful that grit does not enter the camera when you replace film or lenses.

Some locals do not want to have their pictures taken; others will ask for payment. The decision whether to pay is yours, but consider the effects of payment on both the subjects and future hikers. Last, elab-

Woman grinding lentils in West Nepal. She has worked as a porter for foreigners (photo by Kevin Bubriski).

orate camera gear is less important to the quality of a photo than care in composition. Look before you shoot—but not too long, or your image may vanish.

Reaching the Subcontinent and Estimating Expenses

In 1973 I flew from New York City to London and traveled overland as far as Kathmandu for a total of $260 in transportation expenses. During those heady days in the early 1970s, the 14-to-120-day round-trip excursion fare from New York to New Delhi was $400. Since then the fare has more than tripled.

Recent turmoil in Iran and Afghanistan has made the exciting overland route impossible, and nowadays the lone travel option for most people is a flight to Rawalpindi, New Delhi, or Kathmandu. The 14-to-120-day excursion fare, a standby ticket, or an around-the-world flight with a long stopover may be your least-expensive choice. Alternatively, it is still possible to fly with a small charter airline or airlines. You can find out about these various kinds of flights by calling travel agencies anywhere that use the code words budget, student, or charter in their advertising. Confirm, confirm, and reconfirm air tickets for in-country travel anywhere in South Asia, particularly Nepal. If you don't absolutely ensure that you have a seat, your name may be mysteriously dropped from the manifest.

If you are without reservations for a hotel in your city of arrival, do not be concerned. Rawalpindi, New Delhi, and Kathmandu each have an adequate number of hotel rooms, from dollar-a-day specials to five-star accommodations. Preconfirmed, computer-made reservations are not necessary, not if you are a trekking type. The arrival area of each international airport has a booth with personnel whose duty is to assist you with arranging lodging in the nearby city. Taxi drivers are always glad to take you to a hotel. No matter where you are and what you may be told at first, remember that in Asia the outcome of a situation is never known until that situation is completely resolved. Information as first stated will be amended, and there is a vacant hotel room.

Inflation fools anyone who tries to estimate expenses far in advance precisely. An approximate rule of thumb is that your costs on the Indian subcontinent will be slightly less than your normal monthly living expenses. Depending on your standards of cuisine and accommodations and the trekking style you prefer, your costs in Asia can vary widely, just as at home. If you are trekking with a prearranged, organized group, most of your in-country expenses will be taken care of, and the only extra money you will need will be for any souvenirs, meals, and extras that you buy.

Take enough money with you. Having funds sent is difficult, subject to delay, and may produce only local currency. If money must be sent, do it through American Express. Carrying both cash dollars and traveler's checks will enable you to convert your funds into local currency.

Receiving Mail

Postal service, having been established by the British in Pakistan and India, is an institution there and in Nepal. In many a Himalayan village unreached by vehicle road, you will see the round red PTT box attached to a tree or post in the square, to be emptied by the mail carrier passing on foot.

Advise your correspondents to underline or capitalize your family name when they address your mail, to ensure that the letters held for you are filed correctly, and be sure to give them the names of the district and state where you'll be, if you know them, as well as the city and country. Remember that to receive a package through the post may be costly: customs duties may well be 100 percent or more of the contents' value. If an item must be sent, consider air freight. Never send cash through international mail, and remember that, although bulky letters are often slow to reach their destination, aerogrammes travel quickly. The vagaries of international mail are many; be ready for delays. Here are the best addresses for receiving mail, country by country.

The poste restante (general delivery) system is not over-used in Pakistan, as it is elsewhere, so you can use it in any city or large town: Trekker's Name, Poste Restante, City, District, State, Pakistan. If you use American Express (AMEXCO) traveler's checks, in Rawalpindi you can collect your mail c/o American Express, Haider Road. AMEXCO does not have an office in Lahore. Mail can be sent c/o your embassy in Islamabad or c/o the American Consulate in Peshawar if your passport is American.

A useful address in north India is c/o American Express, Wenger House, Connaught Place, New Delhi. There you can expect a colorful, international queue and efficient, professional handling of your mail. Note that in New Delhi, AMEXCO is open for clients' mail only 4 hours a day. If you are not a client for AMEXCO traveler's checks, mail can be sent to you in New Delhi c/o your embassy, but the diplomatic enclave is some distance from the center of the city, whereas AMEXCO is in the midst of it. If you will be in Ladakh, Kulu, or elsewhere in the mountains, your mail will be held in large towns if it is addressed to you there c/o poste restante.

In Nepal, everything is centralized and you should probably get your mail in Kathmandu. AMEXCO is a reliable place to have your mail held there, too, if you carry the traveler's checks. You may also direct mail to be held by your embassy; Kathmandu is not large enough to keep you from reaching any embassy by cab or bicycle, or perhaps by foot from your hotel. The address to be avoided in Kathmandu is general post office, or the GPO. The GPO keeps hundreds upon hundreds of letters in about 20 small canvas bags labeled with the letters of the alphabet. The bags are ransacked daily by travelers, each with complete access to the entire pile of mail in any given sack. Some people have told me they always get their mail that way, but I give Poste Restante, Kathmandu a wide detour.

When to Go: Weather in the Himalaya

Climate in the Himalaya is primarily dependent upon two factors: elevation and time of year. Because of the great vertical distances involved in most treks, you will have to be prepared to encounter temperatures ranging from oven-like warmth to below-freezing cold. Heat drops 3.5° F. for every 1,000-ft. elevation gain. Be prepared for cold weather after the sun goes down whenever you are above 10,000 feet. On glacier treks in the Karakoram, the thermometer can rise by 100° F. from sun-up to noon. The Karakoram is, however, the extreme. People on their first Himalayan walk usually bring enough warm clothing, but some fail to include thin wash-and-wear shirts and loose pants or skirts, and then swelter at low altitudes.

Fall is definitely the best time to trek in most areas. The monsoon usually relents by the beginning or middle of October, and temperatures fall until mid-December. Most years, winter snows begin to close the high passes in December. From December to February, the weather is cold and clear except for the occasional winter storms. March, April, and May are usually good months for trekking, although the heat can be fierce below 5,000 ft., and deep, wet snow remains on the high passes. Also in springtime, a thick haze that rises from the dry Ganges plain (where ground fires are intentionally set) often obscures the view in Nepal and the central Himalaya.

The subcontinent's life-giving monsoon comes from the southeast: it normally arrives in Sikkim about June 5, reaches western Nepal 10 days later, and appears in Kashmir by the beginning of July. The monsoon causes muddy trails, obscures the view, and brings out leeches, but it also gives rise to a profusion of greenery. Monsoon rain is not continual, but should be expected for a few hours daily through September. The mountainous areas in Pakistan and Ladakh are not subject to the monsoon, but drenching storms, sometimes lasting for days, can occur there during the summer. No matter what the region or season, vicious localized thunderstorms can occur anywhere in the mountains, particularly during spring and summer. Go prepared!

3

Into the Himalaya

*photographs studied before leaving
prepared me for such majesty. Truly
does have to be seen to be believed,
ust be continually yearned for when
as incurable a fever of the spirit as*

Dervla Murphy, 1967

*y first day's march in the Himalayas,
thrilled me. I kept squeezing my fists
mphatically to myself and to the uni-
es! Oh yes! This really is splendid!
How splendid! How splendid!"*

Francis Younghusband, 1924

Gateway Cities to the Himalaya

Now we plunge into Asia. This section gives you enough information to pass through or to get started seeing the cities of Rawalpindi, Peshawar, New Delhi, Varanasi, Kathmandu, and Pokhara. From these six, plus a few others noted along the way, you can reach most major hill towns adjacent to Himalayan trailheads. Areas of town to stay in are noted for each place, as are local sights and directions for reaching the mountains.

A stupa at Leh, Ladakh.

Pakistan

Rawalpindi, like the three other cities in India and Pakistan, is divided into an old city and a new city of cantonment (often called a *cantt*). The new city was developed when the British began to settle there during the last century and built a completely new town with colonial buildings and a Western-style street grid next to the existing city with its bazaars and *galis* (the winding lanes mostly too narrow to admit vehicles). So present-day travelers can choose between hotels in the old or new cities.

In Rawalpindi Cantt, several hotels are situated on Hospital Road south of the railroad, and other, newer hotels are nearby on the Mall. The Rawalpindi Tourist Information Office (TIC) is also on the Mall. After establishing your quarters, head for the TIC to get the latest information on trekking areas up-country. The old city has many hotels in Raja Bazaar and some on College Road. Don't fail to try the delicious, rich yoghurt (*dahi*) in milk shops scattered about the old city. If a shop is out of yoghurt, then you have probably found one of the better places; be sure to return later.

If you have a half day or more at your disposal, a pleasant walking excursion would be to the cave tomb of the area's most important saint, Bari Imam. You may rent a taxi, but most people take the van that leaves from a small *serai* (an open area surrounded by walls) on Liaquat Road, halfway between College Road and Raja Bazaar. You will go north or Islamabad to the roadhead at the edge of the Margala Hills. From there, walk past the shrines of other saints, fakirs, and *malangs* (religious mendicants) on a path that leads in 3 mi. to the whitewashed cave shrine visible on the rock face. Ecstatic singing with musical accompaniment called *quawwali* is performed at the roadhead shrine area, called Nirpur Shahan, particularly during the yearly Urs (death anniversary) of Bari Imam, celebrated about May 4–10.

From Rawalpindi, roads connect with Peshawar, Swat, Gilgit, and with India via Lahore. You can reach Peshawar in 3 hours or Lahore in 4½ hours by taking the 11-passenger mini-buses. Gilgit, to the north, is a long but spectacular 15-to-20-hour bus ride away, through the Indus Valley gorge on the Karakoram Highway. You can reach either Gilgit or Skardu by plane, passing 26,600-ft. Nanga Parbat on one of the most scenic flights imaginable.

A Note on Islamabad: Pakistan's newly built capital city. Islamabad, is located 8 mi. north of Rawalpindi. Most visitors miss Islamabad unless they need trekking permits or visas. To reach most of the embassies (including India's) in Islamabad from Rawalpindi, take the route 2 mini-bus from Rawalpindi Cantt. The Indian Embassy is open 9:00 to 12:00 A.M., Sunday through Thursday at 482 F Sector G64, Islamabad. With the new trekking regulations, you may have to visit Islamabad to get a trekking permit.

A note on Lahore and the Indian Border: A daily train leaves the Mughal-style Lahore Railroad Station for the border and continues to Amritsar, where yoy can book one of two evening trains for New Delhi. In addition to the train, a land route is open between Lahore and

Amritsar 7 hours each day. The border post on the Pakistan side is called Wagha; in India the checkpoint is named Attari Road. Buses are located across from the Lahore Railroad Station, or you can rent a taxi to reach the border. If you go by road and are carrying much luggage, note that you must walk 200 yards or more between the Indian and Pakistani checkposts. When you are carrying a lot of gear, the train is easier.

Peshawar is one of the most fascinating cities in this part of the world, along with Varanasi and Kathmandu. The Peshawar we glimpse today is an amalgam of Buddhist, Mughal, Sikh, British, Pathan, and modern influences. When the mountain snows were deep across the Himalaya one recent year, I wintered in Peshawar's Qissa Khawani Bazaar for five weeks and was always kept busy. The bustling copper, jewelry, cloth, and money bazaars, the crowded restaurants serving *keema, karai*, chicken *tandoori*, and other specialties, and Peshawar's gregarious, colorful people—Pathan, Punjabi, Chitrali—all combined to assure me that the personality of its storied past is not entirely dimmed. In early 1977 an ancient tradition passed, when, due to a fractious election campaign, the open carrying of rifles, pistols, and ammunition belts in public was disallowed. The practice has not been permitted since in Peshawar itself. But a few miles west, in the tribal areas, only Pathan tribal law is obeyed, and many men carry rifles.

Several good, old-style hotels stand near Kabuli Gate at the end of Qissa Khawani Bazaar, the old Street of the Storytellers. Most hotels in the cantonment are within several long blocks of each other, west of the venerable Dean's Hotel and the Tourist Information Center. The fame of Peshawari food, including spicy meat dishes, light *roti* wheat-cakes, and rich milk products is justly renowned. Ask your hotel manager to recommend a restaurant and he will gladly suggest several nearby establishments.

Peshawar's old bazaars and tranquil parks are its prime attractions, although its museum contains some excellent pieces of Bactrian art and finer wooden funeral figures from the Kalash valleys in Chitral than are left now in the valleys themselves. If you have the better part of a day, you might take a local bus from Peshawar's Shuba intersection to Landi Kotal Bazaar in the Khyber Pass, an hour's ride west and only 5 road miles from the Afghan border. Landi Kotal is the only place where people come up and proudly volunteer, "This free country, Mistar. No police here. What you want, I can get." If what you want is *charas,* opium, or locally made guns, copies of Sten guns, English rifles, Mausers, Berettas, Kashnolinkovs, or merely an eyeful of such contraband with a later peek into Afghanistan from the upper story of a teahouse, then you have found it. Landi Kotal is the most remarkable bazaar town I have yet encountered in Asia. Don't fail to note that there is a customs inspection on the city's outskirts as your bus returns to Peshawar.

When the border with Afghanistan is open, daily buses leave Peshawar for Kabul, passing through Landi Kotal and the Khyber Pass.

Buses and planes leave daily for Chitral and Swat; see the section in the next chapter called "The Way to Chitral" for details. Mini-buses leave Peshawar regularly for Rawalpindi.

India

New Delhi International Airport is often the Western traveler's humid introduction to South Asia, and, due to the vagaries of flight scheduling, most passengers arrive in New Delhi between 1:00 and 3:30 A.M. A passenger bus called E.A.T.S. (Ex-servicemen's Airlink Transport Services) operates between the airport and Connaught Place (except in the middle of the night, when you are likely to arrive), or you can share a cab for the 10-mi. ride. Connaught Place is the center of New Delhi, and thereabouts you will find hotels of every type. I favor the modest guest rooms in private homes, several of which are located just west of Jan Path near the Indian Oil Building. These pleasant homes feature unrestricted access to your private room, yet the acting manager—who may be any member of the family—is always ready to give tips, answer questions or discuss politics, as Delhi *walas* like to do. (In Hindi, "wala" describes a maker, doer, or be-er of anything.) If you prefer to stay in old Delhi, then the Pahar Ganj area, within easy walking distance of Connaught Place, is the place to find a hotel. Be forewarned, though, that the street scene of pedlars, rickshaws, taxis, and ambling cows can often be frenetic. Old and New Delhi each offer many good restaurants. Ask at your hotel or guesthouse for recommended places near you.

The Mughal-built Red Fort and nearby Chandi Chowk Bazaar are two of the old city's attractions; and dotting New Delhi are numerous landscaped tombs and gardens. Jantar Mantar, a series of pink observatory structures, features a tall, stairway-topped lookout with a good view of the locale. If you find yourself withering in Delhi's summer heat, visit the nearby air-conditioned U.S. Information Service (USIS) Library.

To help you find your way around town, ask for a city map at the main Tourist Office, 88 Jan Path, not far from Connaught Place. If you are flying anywhere, particularly to Kathmandu in the fall, be certain to confirm, confirm, and reconfirm your reservations. You may hear that no seats remain for a flight; in that case, you might be happily surprised if you nevertheless show up at the airport 90 minutes before flight time with cash or an open-dated ticket in hand and establish with the people behind the counter your interest in a seat.

New Delhi has good bus connections with many hill towns from the Inter State Bus Terminus (ISBT) on Qudsia Marg just north of Kashmiri Gate in the old city. From the ISBT you can get direct buses to Simla, Mussoorie, and Hardwar, with connections for Dharmsala, the Kulu Valley, and all the yatra roadhead towns in the upper Ganges watershed.

India's extensive railway system is readily available to foreigners, who may request seating and sleeping reservations from the quota of them set aside for tourists. To obtain a reservation, first go to Baroda House on Kasturba Gandhi Marg in New Delhi and get a chit, then take it to the appropriate city railway station for seat and sleeper tickets. Overnight sleeper trains run to Amritsar for Lahore, Jammu for Srinagar, and east to Varanasi, Patna, or to a connecting point for the Nepal border's closest station, Raxaul. Try to get a two-tiered sleeper, which is softer than a three-tiered bunk. You can take a morning train to the incomparable Taj Mahal in Agra (even stay overnight to see it in all its moods) and still have a confirmed reservation from the nearby rail junction of Tundla. This reservation system works. When you approach the railway car numbered on your ticket through the throng on the platform, it is always comforting to find the mimeographed reservation list and see your misspelled name with your assigned berth number alongside.

As you settle into your seat on the Indian train, just as when you take a seat on a Nepalese bus or a passenger van in Pakistan, you will be part of a typical Asian activity. Those you meet may nod kindly (perhaps in the side-to-side fashion that is so difficult for Westerners to comprehend as meaning *ahcha*, yes or ok), act slightly reserved, or engage you, the Angrezi, in conversation. Often people will mirror your demeanor. For all of us, whether meeting Asia for the first time or returning for the fifth, here are two reflections:

Everyone finds his own India.

Arthur, a British traveler, 1967

A shrewd observer, who will make numerous mistakes in describing details, will understand the general tendency of the sum total of Indian life more accurately than one who has lived so long in the country that he has ceased to see it except as a moving mass of detail.

Dwight MacDonald

The holy city of *Varanasi* was called Benares by the Muslims, and its original Vedic name is Kashi. Varanasi has a past that extends back thousands of years into the mists of prehistory. Situated 200 mi. south of Nepal's Himalaya, Varanasi is a lodestone for Hindu pilgrim travelers and is often sought out by Angrezi travelers visiting the Himalaya. The bathing and cremation steps and platforms collectively called *ghats* along the Ganges riverbank near the heart of town are considered to occupy some of the most sacred ground in all of India. *Melas*, religious festivals attracting thousands of devotees, occur with frequency in Varanasi. Walk along the ghats and galis at dawn or in the evening. You will behold a kaleidoscope of pilgrims, votive statues daubed with vermillion and flowers, houses large and small, animals, temples, and crooked walkways, while pungent smells—acrid, spicy, and sweet—mingle with the sounds of voices in conversation or prayer, bells, and green parrots squawking in the trees above.

Varanasi's pulsing central district is located at Godolia. If you wish, you can find lodging close by, or stop at the hotels in the cantonment some distance from the river, where the pace is quieter but bland. The Varanasi Tourist Office is at 15B the Mall, Cantt. This city is *sui generis*, and you will be discovering how unique it is continually as you wander along or near the several miles of ghats.

Varanasi is on the main railway line between Delhi and Calcutta. If you want to go to Varanasi and your ticket says Mughal Serai, you will have to take either a short connecting train across the Ganges or a taxi to reach Varanasi itself. The Kashi-Vishwanath Express is the fastest direct train between New Delhi and Varanasi. Flights from Varanasi to Kathmandu are less expensive than from Delhi or Calcutta. Note that the cheapest airfares from India to Kathmandu are for the daily flights from Patna, 150 mi. east of Varanasi, on the Delhi-Calcutta rail line. The alternative to flying between Patna and Kathmandu is a day on trains from Patna to Muzaffarpur to Sagauli to Raxaul, and a long and tiring but very beautiful day's bus ride from the Nepalese border town of Birganj to Kathmandu.

Nepal

Fortunately, excellent guides to *Kathmandu* are available. Otherwise I would be tempted to write at length about the still-enchanting Kathmandu Valley and its numerous diversions. *Kathmandu and the Kingdom of Nepal*, by Prakash Raj (Lonely Planet Publications), is my favorite guidebook to the city, but Robert Rieffel's *Nepal Namaste* (Sahayogi Prakashan, Kathmandu) is also very complete. The areas of Kathmandu named Besantpur and Thamel each contain numerous lodges (with fewer amenities than hotels have) where trekkers of all ages often stay. When I explored Kathmandu in 1967, the inexpensive restaurants numbered precisely four and as many lodges had a traveler clientele, whereas now scores of eateries and hostelries are oriented to the budget traveler.

While you wait for a trekking permit to be issued, the sights of Kathmandu's Elizabethan-style wood and brick old city await your discovery. Put on those walking boots and roam about the narrow, helter-skelter lanes: you may well be reminded of Shakespeare's London, as scraps land at your feet for the onrushing pig, yet you are jolted back to Nepal by the sight of a large pagoda temple with Buddhist and Hindu images, adjacent to red peppers drying in the sunlight.

The stroll to Swayambhu Temple is an obligatory one: go west from the temple-studded Durbar Square past the golden Maru Ganesh Shrine. Across from the Ganesh Temple is a small statue of Ganesh's "vehicle," Muso the Mouse God. Continue between the Ganesh and Muso images down through Maruhity on the narrow brick walkway, past the *stupas* (tall votive shrines) and Vishnu Temple to the foot-bridge across the Vishnumati River, on by the brick houses and rug factories to the foot of the steep Swayambhu Hill. Several minutes' steep walk ahead at the top of the staircase is the ancient Swayambhu Stupa, a monastery, and a Buddhist school. Long ago this temple complex was built around the sacred gas flame that burns at the peak of the conical 300-ft.-tall hill. Swayambhu is also called the Monkey Temple, owing to the legions of rhesus monkeys that make their homes in the trees thereabouts and successfully beg from worshippers.

A protector deity in the village gomba, Braga, Nepal.

You can try out a pleasant unimproved path by following the Jamacho Hill trail up from Balaju Water Gardens, north of Swayambhu. At the top, some 1,800 ft. above Balaju, you will find several whitewashed stupas and an excellent panorama of the Kathmandu Valley. Take some biscuits and water for this warm and unshaded half-day walk.

Like spokes, roads lead from Kathmandu's outskirts across the valley, and you can enjoy delightful bicycle rides to the Chaucerian villages along the way: Patan, Kirtipur, Bodnath (with its large stupa and extensive Tibetan refugee colony), Sandkhu, Chapagoan, and the botanical gardens at Godavari. Another road for biking—wide and little used—is the anachronistic Ring Road that circumambulates Kathmandu, offering valley perspectives. On clear days, the road's southern reaches have wide vistas of the snowy Himalaya.

If you lack any conceivable item of trekking or mountaineering paraphernalia, you will surely be able to rent or purchase it at one of the many stores in Kathmandu that deal in used gear.

With permit in hand and gear assembled, you are ready to leave Kathmandu for the trailhead. Transportation will involve a bus, chartered Jeep or other four-wheel-drive vehicle, or a plane. Of the three types, plane travel can prove the most fickle. If your trek depends on a plane to get you to or from the trailhead, don't expect anything to go awry, but do make plans knowing that acts of weather and lack of spare parts sometimes delay or cancel flights. If you are flying to a busy airport such as Pokhara's or Biratnagar's, you can be fairly sure that, if weather does cancel your flight, extra flights will be put on when the weather clears—and you can always take a land route to your destination. However, if you are going to a STOL (short take off and landing) field such as at Jumla, Silghari-Doti, or Tumlingtar, delays of weeks between flights can occur, and you should have bail-out plans in mind—walking farther south, for example. Such busy STOL fields such as those at Jomosom and Lukla may receive extra flights when needed, but if your "service," or scheduled flight, to, say, Jumla is cancelled, you must scramble for a seat; those people holding tickets for the next flight still have priority for that flight. If your plane leaves Kathmandu but cannot land at its destination, remember that you can get a full ticket refund.

Most of Nepal's well-known trekking routes can be reached by bus, or, if you are several people, vehicle rentals are possible. Also, by morning or midday bus you can be deposited at Pokhara, Dumre, Trisuli, Panchkhal, or Lamosangu. Longer rides will take you to the flat southern Terai roadheads farther west or east. Most bus tickets can be booked from offices near the GPO.

Pokhara is the last and most atypical of these six gateway cities to the Himalaya. The town itself consists largely of a one- or two-building-deep bazaar that extends more than 2 mi. along the western edge of Nepal's second largest valley, not 20 mi. from peaks that rise 4 mi. above the 2,500-ft. valley floor. The gems to the north are the white *himals* (snow peaks) of Dhaulagiri, the Annapurna summits, Lamjung, and Manaslu. But Machhapuchhare, the Fishtail Peak, is the symmetrical giant we look to first in the morning or evening, when its high, rose-hued triangle glows.

The mountains dominate this tranquil valley, but its lakes draw the weary or wistful. Modest lodges are numerous near Pewa Tal, the largest lake, a couple of miles southwest of the airfield. By Pokhara Airport there are large hotels, and more lodges at several places along the bazaar. You can rent a bicycle and ride to Begnas and Rupas lakes, or to an overlook on the narrow Seti River gorge.

Pokhara is best for most people as a rest haven upon return from the mountains, a quiet place for only nudging toward the hubbub of the outside world again; a place to reminisce, eat continually, finish the journal, and commune once more with the mountains.

Last, here are two notes on the gateway cities particularly for travelers who will go there for the first time. From April to late August, every one of these cities except Kathmandu (at 4,440 ft.) will be very hot during the daytime. Pace yourself in this summer heat, and try to get business taken care of early or late in the day. And there is a hotel room. Remember this from Chapter 2. If the first place is full, you can be certain that nearby you will find a room. These six cities all have adequate hotel or lodge space, no matter how large the festival or busy the season.

Trekking Regulations

The two primary considerations about walking in the subcontinent's mountains are historic and political. Traditionally, the many Himalayan kingdoms from Chitral to Bhutan were reluctant to admit outsiders—at least anyone who was not a government official, trader, or pilgrim, and certainly not foreigners. Today's policies have evolved from this position, as well as from the political reality of China's extreme sensitivity to having foreigners approach the Tibetan frontier. The countries to the south of the Himalayan and Karakoram ranges know that roads and communications are better within Tibet than on their own northern frontiers, owing to the flat Tibetan plain called the Changtang. All three subcontinent governments have forbidden foot travel near their northern borders except where the high passes require technical gear as the only means of access northward.

Each of the Himalayan countries has distinct regulations concerning trekking. The information provided for each country covers, first, how to obtain the necessary permits, and second, which areas are restricted in each nation as of mid-1981. (Bhutan is treated separately in Chapter 13.)

Pakistan

In April 1982, Pakistan's Tourism Division announced many new areas to be "Open Zones" where "Foreigners are allowed to trek without permit and guide, etc." From the Nazbar Pass west of Yasin to the Bilafond Glacier in easternmost Baltistan, newly permitted trekking routes (most of which are described or noted in Chapters 4, 5 and 6) have been added in Chitral, Nagir, upper Hunza, around Nanga Parbat and especially in Baltistan. A detailed list of treks in the Open Zones can be obtained by writing the Deputy Chief, Tourism Division, College Road, Sector F-7/2, Islamabad. For information about arranging treks and mountaineering expeditions, write Mr. Sayeed Anwar Khan, Pakistan Tourism Development Corporation (PTDC), the Mall, Rawalpindi. Sayeed, Pakistan's foremost trekking expert, has been nearly everywhere and can be of great assistance. Once you arrive up-country, you may need to register. Once, when I was registering in Chitral, the civilian-clothed policeman assigned to tourists and visiting VIPs looked up as he was noting my particulars in his ledger and waxed philosophical: "Where do we come from, where are we now, and where will we go? That is the question."

Pakistan has a 10-mi. Closed Zone along the Afghan border in Chitral (with the exception of the Kalash valleys); where Pakistan's land adjoins the Wakhan Corridor, a Closed Zone extends 30 miles. The area near the cease-fire line with India is closed for approximately 10 mi., as is the Chinese frontier.

India

India requires no permits for trekkers in its mountainous areas. As long as your visa is valid, you may walk as long as you like, with the following important proviso: No foreigners may cross north of what is called the Inner Line. Although the exact location of this line parallel to the northern border is subject to alteration, it is rarely set closer to the border than 15 air miles. In mid-1974, Inner Line restrictions were greatly modified, allowing trekkers to reach many hitherto closed areas, including large parts of Garhwal and Ladakh. If you have specific questions about current regulations, you should contact the Indian Tourist Office closest to you, or write the embassy in Washington. (See Chapter 2.)

The exception to the above guidelines is Sikkim, where permits are required for tourists and trekkers. Permits for going into Sikkim are issued by the Ministry of Home Affairs in New Delhi and may require at least three months to process. (See the section on Sikkim in Chapter 13 for more details.) When you apply for your Indian visa, inquire whether a permit is necessary for Darjeeling, which is near the politically sensitive area; if so, request to have the permit stamped in your passport with your visa.

Nepal

Every visitor to Nepal who wishes to travel off the roads outside the Kathmandu or Pokhara valleys (or in the Chitwan Game Preserve in the southern Terai) must get a trekking permit, issued only by the Ministry of Home Affairs at the Immigration Office in Maiti Devi, east of Ram Shah in Kathmandu. One working day only is usually required to process applications for trekking permits. (Most permit requests also include visa extension applications.) As soon as you have determined your intended walking route, make your application for the permit. List on the application form the farthest points you may reach; you might be turned back later if you have not gotten an appropriate permit. Also, when you apply, be absolutely certain to figure in time to take side trips and to rest while trekking. Kathmandu and Pokhara are the only places where you can extend your visa-trekking permits—don't be embarrassed with expired visas or permits. You can usually extend your visa up to three months. Difficulty may be encountered in staying longer than 90 days at one time in Nepal.

Trekking permits note on their reverse side that the bearer must remain 25 mi. off the northern border, although this caveat does not include places such as Mt. Everest base camp and the Langtang Valley, where steep mountain barriers make border crossings unfeasible. Aside from the prohibited northern zone, three areas in Nepal are (at this writing) restricted to trekking: Dolpo District, upper Mustang District, and the northeastern corner of the country near Mt. Kangchenjunga. Also, such other areas as Humla and Mugu are often restricted.

Finally, here are several points to keep in mind for all countries:

1. Keep your passport and any permits with you at all times.

2. Respect the restricted areas in each country and know where their limits are reached.

3. Give yourself as much distance to trek and time to get somewhere as are allowed on any permits and your visa. Westerners, thinking in rush-rush terms, consistently underestimate the time they will need and the distance they will want to travel in the mountains. But after getting the trail underfoot, they often change their minds and want more time, for more distance.

Using Local Equipment

At the start of one of my Nepal treks, worse came to worst for my cousin Ellen Swift: the airline lost her pack as she arrived in Kathmandu. All four of us scurried around and fortunately managed to replace her entire outfit from socks to pack in a day. Like organizing an overland trip to Nepal on 2½ weeks' notice, you can outfit yourself in Asia, but it's best not to be faced with having to try.

Many items locally made and available in hill bazaars are appropriate for backpacking. The following list covers gear that you can expect to find in every roadhead bazaar. Better-quality products are often available in larger cities. Used Western gear also is sold, or can be rented in Kathmandu on a wide scale, and in such other places as Skardu and Namche Bazaar, but they are the exceptions.

Kerosene. Because this is the fuel you can expect to buy most readily back in the hills, have a stove that uses kerosene and keep yourelf supplied.

Cigarettes, loose tea, and matches. These lightweight items are appreciated as thank-you gifts. If you have qualms about giving tobacco, take good-quality tea or matches.

Small-denomination currency. Obtain 1-, 5-, and 10-rupee notes in equal numbers, with an extra packet of ones thrown in. With these, you can bargain to the rupee and never need change. You can get bills in packets from a bank or neighborhood shopkeeper.

Doka. If you are trekking in Nepal, you can purchase a *doka*, a conical woven bamboo basket, for your porter. If no doka is available, buy a burlap sack from a merchant for the porter's load.

Rope. Rope, called *rassi* throughout the Himalaya, will hold together the porter's load. Purchase enough to give plenty to your porter.

Fuel and water containers. Sometimes excellent water-tight containers are available in the bazaars. Don't count on finding one, however.

The articles below have already been described in the Trekker's Compleat List in Chapter 2; they are noted here as well because they can be purchased locally:

Stove. Kerosene stoves are available, but they are not as sturdy as Western-built models.

Enamel cup. The twenty-ounce size is an all-purpose cup and bowl. Use this cup to drink tea purchased at stalls; the glass provided may not be clean.

Cook pots. Nesting pots are sold by weight; you will need at least two.

Umbrella. A bamboo chhatri is essential.

Pants. The baggy pants made locally are the best to trek in.

Food for Trekking

Our own experience coincides with that of Shipton and Tilman, who proved how economically one can live in the Himalayas. . . . Our diet [consisted] mainly of rice, barley, wheat, and millet . . . we enjoyed the most excellent health throughout, on an almost strictly vegetarian diet. . . .

Arnold Heim and August Gansser, 1938

Dietary Alternatives

A good, balanced diet with adequate calories is essential for enjoyable trekking. Depending on your weight, activity level, and individual metabolism, you will need between 3,000 and 4,500 calories to sustain you each day of vigorous trekking, and these calories should come from a mixture of proteins, carbohydrates, and fats. One pound of pure protein or carbohydrates will provide 1,800 calories, and one pound of fat will give 4,500 calories. Carbohydrates (such as crackers, rice, and sugar) provide energy quickly; the energy from proteins and fats becomes available later but over a longer period of time.

A local person eats about 2 pounds of grains each day, which provides about 3,200 calories that are primarily from carbohydrates. The grains are supplemented with *dal* (lentils), milk (if available), and salt. Vegetables, dairy products, legumes, eggs, and sugar are also consumed, if they are obtainable. On this seemingly meagre diet, porters can carry enormous loads through difficult terrain day after day, and many trekkers have enjoyed good health and fitness following the local example. If you rely primarily on local grains, your total dry weight of food per person-day will be about 2½ pounds.

You may want more variety than the local diet provides, however. You could take along fresh and dried vegetables, canned goods, and spices from local markets. From home, bring canned food and packaged sauces; such luxuries as chocolate bars, cocoa powder, drink mixes, dried fruits and nuts; or other high-calorie, low-weight favorites. But keep in mind that with such additions you may easily end up carrying 3 pounds of food per person-day. If what you bring from home is freeze-dried foods, your total food weight can be lower than 2 pounds per person-day. Bringing freeze-dried rations probably won't be worthwhile, however, unless so much of your trekking route will be through uninhabited country that supplies aren't otherwise available. Another way to extend your menu is to occasionally buy chicken or meat in the hills.

These supplements are not essential, however. The local diet (with vitamin pills added if fruits and vegetables are not obtainable) is perfectly adequate for nourishment. Indeed, this diet is in line with the theory of protein complementarity popularized by Frances Moore Lappé, who explained in her book *Diet for a Small Planet* how you can get your complete protein requirements without the need for meat protein by using four basic food groups in three basic combinations. Said Lappé:

> The combination of grains plus beans, peas, or lentils evolved spontaneously, becoming the center of the diet in many different parts of the world—rice and beans in the Caribbean, corn and beans in Mexico, lentils and rice in India, and rice and soy in China.... Only recently has modern science truly understood what must have been known intuitively by the human race for thousands of years.

The four basic food groups from *Diet for a Small Planet* are:
1. Grains—such as rice, wheat, barley, corn, millet, pasta
2. Legumes—such as lentils, beans, peas, peanuts
3. Milk products—such as cheese, yoghurt, butter, *lassi* (similar to buttermilk), milk
4. Seeds—such as sesame, sunflower

The three basic combinations are:
1. Grains and legumes
2. Grains and milk products
3. Seeds and legumes

We Westerners are often surprised that we can trek for weeks eating only the locally available foods and emerge fit and amply nourished. My friend Chris Wriggins and I lived and trekked for 10 weeks in western Nepal eating foods entirely from the first three groups (with the addition of eggs when possible) and finished lean but strong: the last full day on the trail I walked 24 mi., ascending and descending a total of 15,000 feet. A high-bulk diet like the locals' in ample quantities is very sustaining.

Locally Available Foods

The items in the following lists are not the only foods you will find or can expect to eat while trekking; remember also that not all items will be found everywhere. Some areas are food deficient, and in those places you will have to offer a good price to make the sale of rations to you worthwhile. (In such a situation you can buy small amounts of food from several families.) When attempting to buy food in the hills, check the appropriate glossary for the proper local words.

If you are going into a very remote area, be certain to carry enough food; the extent of your foot travel will often depend on the amount of food you can carry and obtain in the hills, and often people have had to turn around for lack of it.

The most difficult time of year to get food in the hills is early spring before the harvest. Late fall is the best time to purchase food. Remember to ask about fruits in season, especially apricots in the Hindu Kush and Karakoram, or papayas, mangoes, bananas, and tangerines in Nepal and the central Himalaya. When buying canned food, examine the tin for signs of expansion, which may indicate spoiled food.

Food Available at Large Bazaars

Whole milk powder. Next to grains, I take more milk powder than anything else into the mountains. Milk is excellent food, whether taken in tea, with tsampa, or straight. The best way to mix the powder (which tends to cake) is to mix it with a few ounces of cool water in someone's cup. In Pakistan, imported whole milk powder is widely sold in Peshawar and Rawalpindi. In India, the best brand to use is Amul. (Avoid the ersatz preparations with glucose.) In Kathmandu you can purchase quality imported milk powder from the main dairy office in Lainchaur, off Kanti Path.

Peanut butter. Most local brands of peanut butter contain low-quality oils, but nevertheless the spread makes a good topping for wheatcakes and is an excellent source of protein.

Jam. Most local jams are good. Take plastic containers to repackage jam and any other food that comes in jars.

Tinned butter. If you think you will be unable to purchase butter along the way, buy it in cans. Butter or *ghee* (clarified butter) is an important source of calories in the trekking diet.

Dry soup mixes. Brought from home or purchased locally, dry soup packets come in handy; they add flavor to soups made on the trail and are a quick topping for grain dishes.

Dried fruit. This is excellent food. I walked for several weeks in upper Chitral on a diet of salt tea, wheatcakes, and dried apricots and mulberries. Pakistan produces its own dried fruit, whereas India and Nepal import most of theirs from Afghanistan.

Noodles. Pasta may be available in large bazaars; if so, you can carry along several meals of it. Remember to take enough; everyone's appetites will be gargantuan on the trail.

Salt. Moderate use of salt is a necessity when trekking because of the large amount used up in extensive exercise and the limited amount of sodium occurring naturally in the diet. If only rock salt is available, ask the shopkeeper to grind it for you. Pulverizing salt can be difficult to accomplish en route.

Sugar. Sugar is absorbed rapidly into the blood, providing quick energy when needed; it is usually taken with tea, and it helps some foods such as tsampa taste better.

Spices. There are two types of spices, hot (like chilies) and sweet. Get four or more of the powdered hot spices to flavor the basic dal and rice; you will find cumin, cayenne, turmeric, and other components of curry powder. Sweet spices, such as cardamom, ginger, cinnamon, and cloves, can be used in tea or curries. Also, check whether your porter wants the astoundingly hot green and red peppers that some locals favor. If so, for a rupee or two you can season food to his particular liking.

Coffee. You can usually purchase tinned instant coffee from India or East Africa in the larger cities.

Tea. Get lots of good-quality tea; don't buy lesser-grade "dust tea." Pakistan imports good tea from Sri Lanka; India has name brands sold loose or packaged; Nepal's best tea comes from Ilam.

Biscuits. "Biskoots" (an Anglo-Hindi, Anglo-Nepali word) are fine for snacks and can sustain you if necessary when you miss a meal, but are uniformly disappointing when damp. Squeeze the package; if the biscuits don't snap when they break, they are wet. In Pakistan and India, you can purchase locally made, English-licensed brand-name biscuits in most bazaars. The Nebico brand in Nepal is first class.

Candy. A good picker-upper for those day-long uphill tramps. Get individually wrapped sweets.

Food Usually Available in the Hills

Grains. Grains in one form or another will form the bulk of your diet on the trail. Wheat flour and roasted barley (most often ground into a flour called *tsampa* or *sattu*) and rice are the best-liked grains, but several others are to be had, and they are available in a number of forms. For example, pounded rice, called *churra*, is excellent with tea as a breakfast cereal or snack food. Plan on half a pound of grain (one cup) per hiker per meal. Your porter will eat half again that much grain.

To determine the total amount of grain needed, multiply one pound by the number of person-days (1½ lbs. per person-day for each porter).

The accompanying table shows at a glance how the different grains can be prepared and served ("X" signifies yes).

Dal. Lentils are called *dal* nearly everywhere in South Asia. With rice, this forms an important part of the diet, so take two or three varieties. Well-stocked bazaars sell many kinds of dal, and you can also buy it in low areas where people grow it. If you will constantly be at high elevations, get a quick-cooking type of lentil (orange-colored masur dal cooks quickest), or plan to use flour only.

Peanuts. A legume like dal, peanuts combine with grains to form a complete protein, and they are a great snack. Ask for peanuts and you may find them raw or roasted. In Nepal, also try roasted soybeans (*baatmas*) as trail food.

Milk products. These include milk, buttermilk, lassi, yoghurt, cheese, butter, and ghee. Milk products can be purchased seasonally in bazaars near the hills, but you can also ask along the trail and people will tell you where you can buy dairy foods. Remember that, eaten with grain, they produce the full protein complement. If you reach the

Common Ways to Prepare and Serve Grain

	Whole grain, to boil	Flour, for fried graincakes	Roasted flour for tsampa/sattu	Other form
Rice	X			Pounded, whole grain
Wheat		X	X	
Barley*		X	X	Roasted, whole grain
Millet	X	X		
Corn		X	X	Roasted, whole grain
Buckwheat		X		
Oats (tinned)	X			
How to serve	Rice and millet with butter, dal, yoghurt or cheese; oats as breakfast cereal	With butter, yoghurt, lassi, peanut butter, fruit, or jam	Eaten in tea or milk with sugar, butter, cheese, yoghurt, or jam	Out of hand

*There are both lowland and upland varieties of barley. The upland type is best for tsampa.

upland summer pastures, you can trade for, buy, or, depending on the circumstances, be freely given delicious, fresh milk products. Buttermilk is usually available only in the upper pastures, but the rich, sour milk called lassi may be found in bazaars or homes anywhere cows or water buffaloes are kept. Another delicious local food is the fresh white cheese that is produced in summer only.

Himalayan butter is nearly always of excellent quality, although it often comes protected in skins that shed hair. Travelers who have complained of being served rancid butter in salt tea probably were given some that had not been kept cool. Butter comes fresh from the summer pastures and has always been a cash crop, so you will have to pay well for it. *Ghee*, often misunderstood by Westerners to be inferior to butter, is actually a refined, pure product made by clarifying butter. Ghee is divine: rich and delicious.

Caution: Raw milk may contain harmful bacteria. Before drinking milk, ask if it has been cooked, making it safer.

Eggs. Virtually the most complete protein you can eat comes from eggs. Those you can buy along the trail are from chickens that run around, scratch in the earth, and eat all manner of food. Consequently these eggs, although smallish, have a deep-orange yolk and a rich, full flavor that is rare in the West. For their weight, eggs are some of the best food you can carry, but when buying them do ascertain the going rate. For years, this has been two eggs for a rupee in most areas, but the price has been going up so you may have to pay more. When porters carry egg-farm eggs into heavily trekked areas, egg prices are inflated and egg quality suffers drastically.

Vegetables. Most vegetables are available only in season, and many simply are not grown extensively in the Himalaya. Potatoes, called *alu*, are the principal exception: they are the staple in Khumbu near Mt. Everest and are being introduced in other areas. Squash, pumpkins, and root vegetables will keep into the winter and can be purchased by request, when you can locate them.

Honey. Sometimes you can buy the delicious Himalayan honey. Finding honey unexpectedly can lift spirits like sighting an ibex or coming across an unmarked spring.

Meals on the Trail

If you have even half of the foods listed above, you can eat well while trekking. You may carry additional food from home, but you will learn, if you or your cook is capable, that a grain-based diet is adequate to propel you to the snow-clad peaks. Trail food, though not in endless variety, is usually fresh and can be cooked temptingly with butter and spices. When your palate becomes accustomed to the locally grown food, prepared foods like glucose biscuits (with preservatives) taste suspiciously artificial.

During most trekking days you will have two large meals and one or two additional pauses for tea. Here is a typical outline of meals on the trail. After arising, you will have milk tea (or coffee) while striking the tent and preparing to leave. You might supplement this with biscuits, porridge, wheatcakes, rice, or food left over from dinner. After walking a good portion of the distance you will cover that day, everyone stops for 90 minutes to 2 hours while a meal is cooked. This break for the morning meal usually occurs after the sun's heat has been felt and before the afternoon breezes begin, but the time for it will vary with the terrain, preferences of the personnel, time of leaving, and other factors. You can catch up on your journal, wash, explore, or snooze while the dal and rice are cooking. A fried egg or some yoghurt goes well with rice, if either is available. Later in the afternoon, tea is made while camp is set up, and dinner comes later. The evening meal may be graincakes fried in butter or oil and washed down with potato soup. (Save a piece of graincake to eat with tea the next morning.)

Trekking at high elevations (above 10,000 ft.) requires a few meal changes, for dal never completely cooks and even rice is difficult to soften, higher up. In the uplands, most meals are of soups, graincakes, potatoes, or tsampa.

H. W. Tilman can have the final word on food: "If one professes and practices living on the country, one must take the rough with the smooth, rancid yak fat and frogs along with buckwheat cakes and raksi."

Hiring a Porter

Most trekkers who go into the Himalaya on their own need to hire a person who will carry some of the weight to be packed in. The subject of trekking with a porter was introduced in Chapter 1 in the context of choosing your preferred trekking option; this section provides specifics on the who, where, and how of porter hiring and gives you an idea of what it is like to trek with a porter.

Who Will Work as a Porter?

When a Wyoming rancher needs some extra money (and a diversion after haying season), he or she hires out as a guide, taking hunters into the Rocky Mountains and supplying horses and food, as well as whiskey and stories about ranch life. The rancher gets into some high country, doesn't work as hard as usual (without letting on about that to anyone), and makes a nice pile of untaxed income from the hunters, those "city fellers who sit behind desks all year."

A man or woman in the Himalaya or Karakoram who occasionally works for Angrezi trekkers or mountaineers is in much the same position as the North American counterpart. Nearly everyone who has portered and cooked for me has been a farmer or rancher, and probably a third have never worked for a foreigner before. Most likely your porter will be a local farmer, but, more specifically, let's note some types of people who might be available:

The first person you meet may be an English-speaker who has

worked as a sirdar before. He may not usually carry weight, himself, and may be expensive merely because of his language ability and experience with Angrezi. Despite his usual role, he may have time and be willing to carry for a paid trip into the hills, even at less than expedition salary. Otherwise, he may be the person who can locate the right porter for you.

A younger person who needs the wage for land or stock can be a good porter, but determine carefully that you are hiring someone who knows the countryside, not a pidgin-English-speaking cowboy type who has no experience in the hills and who may quickly falter.

The older woodsman or *shikari* (hunter) will be an excellent porter if you can find him and he wants to go. Often older porters are the hardest working, most reliable companions: wise to the old ways, knowledgeable about the land, and delighted to point out trail lore.

Whom Should You Hire?

Some Himalayan travelers have considered their private porter or expedition sirdar to be a living Buddha, an omniscient titan who can interpret all of nature's wordless hints, signs, and scents. These travelers, through choice or chance, have hired the right person. Others feel differently: "Porters are mostly local men of uncertain occupation and unsteadfast habit, notorious for giving trouble." The author of that statement trekked with a companion so "desperate to get under way" that virtually the first nine people who agreed to carry were hired.

Often the people who happen to be in the bazaar when you first arrive indeed are not the ablest or sturdiest. The best strategy may be to wait overnight for word to get around and for people to come in from the fields before hiring anyone. This usually saves more time in the long run than does barely slowing down to consider whom you are hiring, in your haste to leave the roadhead bazaar. You or your group can move faster and more comfortably with a good porter than with someone coaxed into going.

If you want to hire a sirdar as well as porters, you must ask to see any letters or chits held by someone claiming to be a sirdar, as noted in Chapter 1. The sirdar you hire as leader then will hire his own crew of porters.

Where and How to Hire

If your group is small, you may wait until you reach the trailhead bazaar before engaging a porter to go with you. If you are several people and you need a crew, then hire a competent sirdar before leaving the large hill bazaar where you get supplies, or get recommendations there for sirdars living near the trailhead. If you are in a tropical climate, you may be able to hire only people who will go up to about 5,000 ft. in elevation, where you will have to change porters. In this case, don't be as choosy in whom you hire initially as you would if you were trying to find someone to walk on a longer haul with two snow passes.

When you reach the place where you will first be hiring someone, you can expect one of two or three situations. Let's consider the three most likely scenarios:

First, there may be no one immediately about who is interested in working. Don't be in the least concerned. This is Asia and the telephone works by word of mouth. Tell whomever you think can help that you need a porter: the Jeep or bus driver on the way, the hotel manager and staff at the hotel, a friendly shopkeeper or two, or the local official whose duty it is to advise tourists. If possible, spread the word several days before you need to hire. Think about this process as you would about finding a hotel room: like the inevitable room, a good porter will certainly appear.

In a second likely scenario you may find an accomplished sirdar with a good command of English. If you need him and a crew, you're set. Otherwise, you can ask for his assistance. Drink tea with him, explain the differences between your trek and a well-financed mountaineering expedition (even though they are obvious, with your lack of equipment, sahibs, and turmoil), and request that he help you find a person to porter. Given overnight at most, he should be able to refer a friend or two to you.

A third possibility is that a group of people may be waiting at the bus stop or bazaar when you arrive. They will be looking for work and will know that you, as an Angrezi, may want to hire someone. Under these circumstances your best ploy is to feign disinterest in the whole affair. Claim to be doing something other than trekking and head for the teahouse, keeping any likely prospects in view or nodding to them. Take tea and rest, allowing the scene to quiet down. When my trekking partner Pancho Huddle and I arrived at Trisuli Bazaar with loaded packs, bedlam ensued; we made for the back of the Ranjit Hotel's restaurant and asked the waiter if he would whisper to the person who had impressed both of us. Bir Bahadur Lama proved to be an excellent porter.

Coming to Terms

When you are discussing portering with someone, you need to decide more than just how many rupees per day he will be paid. Work up to the subject of wages by discussing and agreeing on other points first, as discussed in this section. State your position or offer, then say "Teek hi?" If he agrees, he'll answer "Teek!" and that will be settled. Keep in mind that wages differ from person to person, as at home. One man will go for 20 rupees per day when another won't budge for less than thirty. Salaries will depend on the amount of work to be done, the person's need for money, the exorbitant wage scales introduced by large mountaineering expeditions in the Karakoram and parts of Nepal, and many other factors aside from experience and ability, for every agriculturalist can cook local foods and carry. The following list covers the principle terms upon which you will need to agree:

General itinerary. Some people will be able to go with you for weeks, while others will walk only as far up as the next climatic zone. Some men will want only a couple of days of work (in which case you would have to change porters again soon), while others don't want to be bothered unless they are going to earn at least a couple hundred rupees. You will want to agree on roughly how many days the person will work for you, in order to avoid misunderstandings later on.

Cooking. In a small group, things go best when everyone eats the same rations (although I recommend avoiding the porter's red peppers). Your porter is thoroughly familiar with cooking the food you'll be eating: let him do it. If he is Hindu, make certain that he has no caste restrictions against taking his food from the same pot you do.

Cigarettes. If you have no strong scruples against the use of tobacco, you might offer a few cigarettes a day to sweeten the pot. This can make a real difference to some people who would not otherwise be able to afford the luxury. I sometimes thought that Karma Chumbey (twice my porter in west Nepal) went along for the cigarettes above everything else. He was such a tobacco fiend that I had to carry the cigarettes and dole them out daily or he would have quickly used them up.

Wages (including food). Try to learn the local wage scale; then be willing to tamper with it, but don't bargain wildly, as if you were buying an antique. The person you want to hire is not a top-wage, high-altitude porter, but neither is he an ordinary load hauler, whose work is over the moment you reach camp. Your porter will be cooking for your group, and he will be unable to choose his own working hours as he could on his own. In the past, I have paid from 15 rupees per day in western Nepal (1974) to 35 rupees per day in Baltistan (1977), that is, from $1.20 to $3.50, but inflation will surely raise those amounts. Nowadays, you must expect to pay in excess of two to three dollars a day plus food for a good porter. If the person you are hiring has worked for expeditions and wants a high rate, explain with a twinkle in your eye that yours is a "first class, *naya* position expedition," a good, new-style expedition, in which everyone eats the same and (fingers crossed) carries the same. Offer a higher rate for days on snow. In addition to furnishing the porter's food, it is also proper to pay a half day's wages for every day the hiree must walk back in order to reach the point where you began (unless the return involves going by road, in which case you pay his bus fare). He will make the return trek much more quickly unloaded, but this payment is proper convention.

Clothing. Particularly if you are to be on snow or a glacier, you must provide for your porter companion's warmth at all times: shoes, socks, coat, goggles, and a hat are the minimum requirements. If he does not have these five items, see that he borrows the remainder or uses your spares—this should be arranged before leaving for the high country. He should have at least a blanket and coat of his own, but you can also contribute any extra tent space and your parka at night in cold conditions.

Bakshish. The universal Asian term for a gratuity means, in this case, a bonus. If your prospect is going to be working more than just a few days with you, then hint that some of the locally purchased equipment will go his way when you are done with the trek. If, by walk's end, you have gone several weeks together and gotten along well, there will be no question of giving him gear, extra food, or maybe even your jeans (now that's talking, Sahib!), along with a cash bonus.

Your relationship with your porter may optimally become one of companions on the trail. Using what David Snellgrove has called "a combination of quiet resolution and ingenuous friendliness," you can keep a warm spark within your group and foster good relations with those you meet.

Remember that while you are the sahib, he knows the country. Sometimes this lesson takes a while to learn. On my first west Nepal trek, Chris Wriggins and I thought we could make route-finding decisions, but only one day out of Jumla and one long detour convinced us we had better learn our place and include everyone in such decisions. When I have shown interest, porters have pointed out all manner of flora, fauna, mineral deposits, tracks, and trails, and have told me stories about themselves, their families, and the country we were traversing. These insights can be among the most rewarding aspects of a trek.

Notes on Acculturation

The following miscellany of observations about the culture you will be entering are offered in the hope of getting you off to a good start and smoothing your way. From the moment you meet the betel-stained Customs wala asking you to open your luggage at the airport, you will be forming impressions of who and what you see. Whether observing or taking part in a situation, try to reserve some judgment and set aside preconceptions as much as you can. Try not to fume or be frustrated by inexplicable behavior or situations that cause delay. You are part of the dance and can't always change its tempo.

As stressed earlier, to learn as much as you comfortably can of the lingua franca is very important, whether it be Hindi/Urdu or Nepali. Your time on the subcontinent, as in any foreign country, will be completely different if you learn even a hundred words. Again, don't neglect to study the appropriate glossary or glossaries in this book before leaving for Asia. On arrival, begin trying words with the Customs wala as he eyes your chattels. Don't be concerned with mispronunciation; you'll still be appreciated, and, in the process, the invisible barrier demarcating you from him and creating the us–them dichotomy will be lowered somewhat. You can always find English-speaking students, merchants, hotel employees, and others in the cities who will be most willing to help you with needed words or pronunciation. Misunderstandings can be ironed out surprisingly often with the right word or phrase. Often travelers and locals "misunderstand" each other not through non-agreement but literally from non-communication. Just a few words can establish connections with waiters, hotel managers, students, cab and bus drivers, shopkeepers, and others who want to make themselves understood, but can't, lacking the English.

The word *sahib*, pronounced "sahb," means sir. It is not reserved for you as foreigner, and it can connote varying degrees of respect in various situations. The manner in which the word is spoken implies the amount of esteem intended. "Barasahib" is used sparingly and may mean anything from boss to governor.

Chai, or tea, the beneficent, deserves a brief paean here. From Istanbul to Tokyo, most people drink black, green, or jasmine tea daily. To the world's billions of tea drinkers, the sipping of a cup is a refreshing break from the business at hand. Chai calms but revivifies; it cools a person in the summer and warms the body in winter, an ever-near balm. Important for the traveler, tea is quite safe to drink, whereas the fresh water it is brewed from may not be potable. Wherever you become involved, you may be asked to "take tea." Always pause to drink tea with officials if they offer it, but don't feel obligated with everyone or you might never finish drinking pots of tea in the bazaar. On the trail in the middle of a long day's afternoon, call an unplanned halt to the walking for a half hour by some inviting stream and brew tea. With every sip, you will appreciate the soothing, restorative value of chai, the traveler's magic catalyst.

Bargaining, like tea drinking, is a venerated Asian custom, but it is a tradition that most neophytes need some time to feel easy with. Bargaining is agreeing on a price or rate of exchange, and this process is usually played out with different mental attitudes on the part of local and visitor. The Angrezi often considers bargaining akin to a duel between adversaries, whereas the shopkeeper or porter prospect thinks of bargaining as a social exercise, not unfriendly at all, and at its conclusion, over and done. There is a matching of wits but never a winner or loser, and when the price or rate is decided, that is it: no paperwork, no bad feelings. You may prefer to begin practicing the bargaining process with small things; most ordinary items are fixed-price merchandise, however. For larger purchases, learn the ballpark price first. Think of bargaining as a good way to practice language—you can toss out words and see if they are understood. A polite, firm tone tinged with humor contributes to a good bargaining stance.

When you ask anyone for information, never imply the answer in the question. To suggest in the question the answer you expect is human nature, but so is agreement by the unsure or timid just to be done with it. ("Yes, that's the bus stop.") In rural or urban Asia, anyone is likely to go along with you if you answer your question as you pose it. Don't say,

Are there two buses today to Gilgit?

Is the next bus at eight o'clock?

Does this path reach Sinja?

The questions would be better phrased:

Are there buses to Gilgit?

When is the next bus?

Where does this trail go?

If the person understands your question and doesn't know your preference, you may hear "patta nahi," "I've no information"; or "nahi malung," "not known"; or you will get a more substantive answer.

Finally, a look ahead to the next section, with its preview of the trail underfoot. Some of us fantasize about trekking and prepare for it so long that by the time we actually begin we are set askew for a couple of days, experiencing mild fatigue from the outset of walking, minor aches, and a haziness. This is a dose of culture shock akin to that some people feel when they alight from a plane in a new country, almost expecting the clouds to be altered, the tarmac to be unrecognizable. Probably the few trekkers who do have these temporary symptoms undergo them not so much because there is a letdown, a leaving go of expectations, but because they experience either an overload of beauty or a repulsion at the different standard of living they see. Take things easy for the first few days and let yourself become accustomed to your new surroundings.

Notes for the Trail

This book does not attempt to mention every trail junction, bridge, village, and pass in the 1,300-air-mile distance from Dorah Pass in eastern Chitral to Thimphu, the capital of Bhutan. The hope is that the book instead gives an approach to trekking that makes such an exhaustively detailed guidebook unnecessary.

The book's chapters are organized from west to east. Within each chapter, the sections on trekking are mostly arranged either from west to east or progressively outward from the principal local bazaar town, if there is one.

Treks follow different kinds of courses, and often you will have a choice of possible routes in a given area. You may walk up one valley, climb over a pass, and return down another valley. You might come back to your starting point by the trail you took or by a different path. Or you may return to another roadhead entirely.

All the routes mentioned are along established paths (excepting glacier hikes), although, as you walk, you may become misled by divergent tracks that lead to other villages or grazing pastures than the ones you are attempting to reach. Most trails will be in good repair, but there can always be surprises, especially during or after the monsoon. The degrees of difficulty from one trail to another will be a factor of the elevation you can gain or lose on any day as you proceed. I have tried to indicate either the elevations at valley bottoms and passes or the approximate total elevation gains to reach most passes. If you are walking

through particularly high terrain, your pace will, of course, be somewhat slower than otherwise.

Many variables are involved in walking, say, from one valley to
another 12 mi. away over a 16,000-ft. pass. Heavily laden porters or
neophyte trekkers might take three days, while others would require
but a single day to traverse the same distance. Rather than setting
day-to-day itineraries, I have usually limited myself to suggesting that a
route may take four to six days, for example, or two to three weeks. If
you want to plan a trek to the day, read an agency's catalogue and note
the number of trekking days allowed for a walk that appeals to you. If
the route is easily passable, expect that you will take as long as the
organized group does to cover the same distance.

Trails themselves may be used differently from season to season: in
the winter during low water, valley routes are often used, whereas
higher paths may have to be taken during other times of the year.
Always ask directions if you have any doubt at all of the way. Locals ask
each other directions when unfamiliar with a trail. In fact, Asians have
asked me the way, especially on pilgrimage routes where they are far
from home and obviously uncertain. If you want hour-by-hour accounts, you will find detailed trail descriptions of central and eastern
Nepal in Stephen Bezruchka's *A Guide to Trekking in Nepal*. However,
such detailed guides do not yet exist for other parts of the Himalaya.

Buddhist prayer stone bearing the familiar chant:
"Om mani padme hum."

The horizontal distance traveled each day on a trek will not be great unless you are in a relatively flat river valley. The day's distance will not reflect the day's labor if you have just spent 10 long hours descending 6,000 ft. into a gorge and partially climbing the other side. To take an extreme example, I have hiked less than a single horizontal mile in a hard day on a faint trail, walking into the Nanda Devi Sanctuary. On the other hand, in Chitral's Yarkhun Valley I walked 29 mi. even with a leisurely start and a lunch break. Average daily distance covered tends to range from 6 to 12 miles. If you eat well, your average will increase after the first week, as your body adjusts physically.

In the first week of a trek particularly, don't set overly ambitious distance goals. Have an easy attitude toward trekking, and don't make it into an endurance contest. Experienced long-distance runners and hikers know that those who go the farthest and remain the strongest pace themselves at the outset. Later on, when your muscles and lungs are stronger, you can push yourself for a day or more. Then, when you ask yourself, "Shall I try for that next ridge?", you can push on for it and know that your aches, parched throat, and empty stomach will not rest as markedly in your memory as the far view you saw by gaining the ridge top.

An average trekking day's length likewise varies from group to group and person to person, but is often some variant of the local schedule. If you are cooking your own food, you can call the shots as you wish, but if you are eating in inns or homes, the two-meal schedule will apply. Rarely in the Himalaya do two days ever unfold exactly alike, but in general the day's journey is geared to the sun: because the cool hours in the morning are preferred for walking, you will often rise with the sun's earliest light and cover much of the day's distance before the morning meal is cooked; after the first meal, afternoon breezes or clouds may have arisen to cool the air. After camp is made in mid to late afternoon and you have had a chance to rest, the evening meal is eaten. Time of year is important to both the length of trail that can be covered and the meal routine. In midsummer, prepare to go to bed before dark so you can walk in the dawn hours before the heat builds.

The physical act of walking through the Himalaya (with or without a pack) may require adaptation because of the scale of things, the order of magnitude involved. In these, the world's highest ranges, river-to-ridge elevation differences can be two or more vertical miles and several climatic zones, not to mention numerous levels of settlements and fields. You will find yourself walking uphill for days at times, and when you have descended halfway down the other side you will feel that going down is as hard on the legs as climbing is on the lungs. Pace yourself when walking, take rests, carry water, and don't forget what you have learned from backpacking at home. A trick to going downhill is to use the bent-knee style of walking. It takes a bit of doing until your upper leg muscles strengthen, but when you can walk down trails in a bent-leg posture you will cushion your upper body, keep your weight directly over your feet, and save your stamina. Westerners who tromp heavily down a canyon and later complain of aching knees, or, worse, who must remain immobile with swollen knee joints suffer from the malady known as "sahib's knee." Only the foreign sahibs are foolish enough to put so much pounding pressure on their legs and knees.

Be as alert as you are able to your surroundings, especially if no one in your group has been on the trail before. Fill water bottles before you leave a stream's vicinity (especially in upper altitudes) and before climbing passes. And avoid becoming benighted on a narrow trail far from the nearest conceivable camping spot; in any case, do not tackle a pass late in the day without carrying water, fuel, and the know-how to make a high camp. Give your porter some voice in any decision to stop or go. In the Himalaya, your surroundings have many aspects to be aware of, and you will learn more of them as you walk.

As you walk into villages in the Himalaya, remember that you are the best act in town. Imagine for a moment that in the town where you live or in a nearby national forest a Balti shepherd or a Tibetan Drok Pa were to pass you. If you dwelt in Kathmandu or New Delhi, you would expect to see lots of tourists in certain parts of town, just as you would if you lived in Manhattan or San Francisco. In the sticks, however, unless you are trekking one of Nepal's most frequented routes, a foreigner is an oddity. You can almost gauge the degree to which foreigners are seen in a village by the response to you, especially by the initial reactions of children. Young children in any remote area who are playing outside will run in fear at the sight of a strange foreigner approaching. Their older brothers and sisters will walk away, to reappear in a window or on the roof. On a trail well-traveled by outsiders, however, kids' reactions will vary right on up to nonchalance. I have learned nonetheless that if I camp near a village or stay in someone's home, there may be overly inquisitive people at the campsite (until dinner time, when the crowd vanishes) or young, crying babies in the house. No matter what my mood when I reach a village, I try not to let myself forget that I am there entirely of my own accord.

Assume goodwill on the part of others. Travelers are often on their guard in new situations, but never does the Golden Rule and its corollaries apply better: expect the kind of treatment from villagers that you would accord a foreign visitor at home (albeit a well-to-do visitor). Better yet, try to imagine how the locals might see you. In cities most people are honest, but in the provinces even fewer people are used to shucking outsiders. A herdsman in Hunza tried to charge my brother Ken and me too much for cheese, but Ken with his good Urdu and some of the shepherds with their sense of right and wrong talked the man down. Agreed: there will be a fast talker about from time to time. But you will almost always be correct if you do assume that people's intentions are honorable. It's called trust, and it works.

Anywhere you walk south of the Himalayan crest, you will be in country that has a human history going back thousands of years, cultures that trace their ethical and spiritual beliefs to events so ancient they blend into pre-history, and have been mythologized. These traditional cultures have elaborate social, and, in some areas, caste systems, all of which will be largely invisible to you. As a visitor you are seeing only a slice of time, and much that will meet your eyes, your mind cannot interpret. If you should meet a Peace Corps volunteer, anthropologist, or any local who is competent in English, ask him or her just who is who in town, and you may be surprised: "Oh, he's the mayor and the richest man in town" (an older man in well-used work clothes); "this chap just came back from school and has nothing to do" (a well-dressed man who speaks a little English); "she moved here from down-valley to marry" (a woman with a light complexion). To figure out the cast of characters—and how they might be apprehending you— you either have to be told or must be an acute observer with some linguistic ability. As you become aware of the local customs, respect them, and note the courtesies that you see practiced by people about you.

Trekking rarely offers opportunities to acquire things. Take pictures, by all means try to keep a journal going, press some flowers, tape music and conversations, but collect your mementos in the bazaars or such larger cities as Peshawar, Delhi, or Kathmandu. There, the souvenir cum collectable industry is alive and well, but not many reliably old relics are left in the mountains anymore. Also, don't give trinkets away indiscriminately. Some trekking groups have hired porters to carry candy and balloons (of all things) for children, creating images of the Westerner that are difficult to dispel.

Trekking as Metaphor

Our principal metaphor is the trail of life. It includes all activity: our observations and experiences, our encounters with friends and strangers, our fantasies and recollections. For many thousands of people, walking trails in the Himalaya is an experience all the more powerful because its metaphorical teachings are couched neither in words nor within a system of organized thought. The occurrences of the day, and the days taken together, as they pass, acquire a connectedness and dimension that is missing in urban Western society.

This palpable "realness" about life on the trail is called, in the Tibetan tradition, "direct perception." Pilgrimage has long been recommended as a means of salvation not only for the merit that accrues in reaching a holy shrine or sacred phenomenon but because of the character and inner strength induced by such travel.

After some days of adjusting to the walking routine, you will begin to pay little or no attention to your hesitant thoughts and will become better acquainted with the milieu of the endlessly changing land that you pass through. You may feel that each day is more intensely etched during these periods of time when the ordinary course of your life is altered. Your initiation may occur when you cross your first high pass: the tough, sweaty, lung-pounding climb with its passing uncertainties and teasing false passes is offset by the growing panorama below, the giddiness of the height, and your exultation at reaching the top.

As you stand there between the past and the future, the present can be luminous. However high you do choose to go, travel at your own proper speed.

High above the passes are rarely touched places where nature is magnified and visual metaphors abound. Ama Dablam (the mother with two outspread, robed arms) and Machhapuchhare (the Fishtail with its double-peaked summit) are two mountains that have visibly metaphoric qualities. Glaciers appear dragon- or river-like depending on perspective, and individual glacial features translate immediately into mushrooms, incisors, eyes, and vast amphitheaters. While trekking, we all read meanings into nearby landforms and the human interactions that occur within their aura; no one can fail to be touched in some way by becoming, for a time, part of the Himalayan tapestry.

4
Chitral

[The Hindu Kush is] a wild, desolate, little-known country, a country of great peaks and deep valleys, of precipitous gorges and rushing grey-green rivers; a barren beautiful country of intense sunlight, clear sparkling air and wonderful colouring as the shadows lengthen and the peaks and rocks above turn gold and pink and mauve in the light of the setting sun.

W. K. Fraser-Tytler, 1950

On the Edge of the Subcontinent

Chitral forms the northwestern roof of the Indian subcontinent. The rugged Hindu Kush Range comprises Chitral's northern and westerly borders while the imposing Hindu Raj Mountains isolate it from

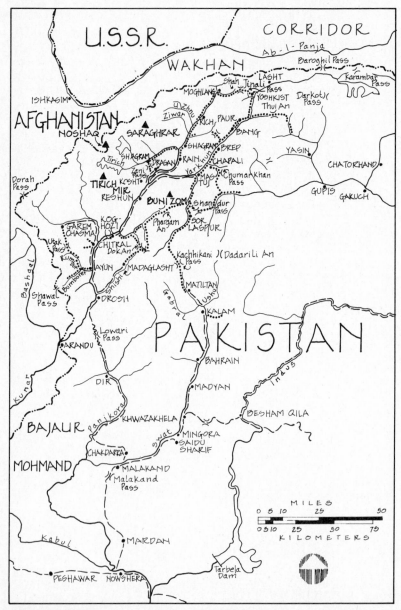

Chitral and Swat

the south. Within Chitral, the Adamzada, the old ruling clan, proudly traces its lineage to the 14th-century Tartar emperor Tamerlane; Adamzada governors called *mehtars* dominated the state for 350 years until about 1960, when Chitral's statehood ended. Now Chitral is directly governed by Pakistan. Surrounded by warlike tribesmen in the Afghan territories and the unruly Pathan state of Dir to the south, its 3½ centuries of autonomy represent a hard-fought accomplishment. Through Chitral's central valley, an arm of the great Silk Route led to the Boroghil Pass in the Hindu Kush. This provided a low-elevation passage to the ancient Turkestani bazaars of Kashgar and Yarkand, but marauding bandits forced most caravans to abandon this route for the punishing five-pass eastern trail through the Karakoram Range in Ladakh. Recently, a few travelers and trekkers have begun to discover Chitral, this intriguing, mountain-encircled land along the easternmost ramparts of the Hindu Kush.

Late 19th-century photographs show that members of the mehtar's court wore the long, bulky Afghan turban and pointed sandals. Today, a handsome woolen, Tudor-style hat is worn throughout Chitral. The occupation of the often blue-eyed, sandy-haired Chitrali likewise has evolved, from warrior to farmer.

The Chitralis are not Pathans, like their neighbors in Dir District to the south, but the Pathan code of *melmastia*, hospitality, is nonetheless practiced in Chitral, particularly in the rarely visited northern valleys. This Muslim tradition is observed throughout Pakistan's northern areas, but in few places is it offered so genuinely as in Chitral. If someone should invite you to stay in his house, it will be an unforgettable experience. The Chitrali house has a large family room called a *baipash*. In the middle of the baipash is a fireplace with homespun rugs arranged near it, upon which the family and neighbors sit. The mother ladles wheat flour from sturdy wooden chests along the rear wall and cooks tasty round wheatcakes over the fire. At the sides of the room are raised bed areas covered with straw and blankets. Some well-to-do people have a separate room especially for visitors called an *angotee*, in which you would be lodged.

The warm hospitality Chitralis currently accord foreign visitors can be overwhelming. Before the spring wheat harvest several years ago, I was fed and sheltered in four upper valleys for three weeks. Such estimable offerings to the traveler are neither to be expected nor abused. For the individual trekker or couple and their Chitrali hosts, this reception in the home is mutually rewarding; you can carry extra tea or salt from Chitral Bazaar to give any benefactor in appreciation.

The sport of falconry, once widespread, is now rarely encountered in Chitral, but every large town still fields a polo team. Intervillage rivalries are strong. Polo grounds in Chitral are situated on mountain passes (the Shandur and Shah Jinali) and in such other improbable locations as the 10,000-ft. summer village of Lasht Khot in the Khot Valley. Chitral also has a strong musical tradition. The Chitrali sitar, a graceful string instrument, is heard daily at small workingmen's tea-

houses in Chitral Bazaar. The *surnai* and *dol* (oboe and drums) frenet-
ically accompany all polo matches. Taped film music from India and
Pakistan in Urdu, the national language, is played in most Pakistani
towns, but the music heard on cassette recorders in Chitral District is
often recorded by local musicians from small villages in the Turikho
and Yarkhun valleys.

Chitral became a district of Pakistan's North-West Frontier Province in 1969, and only since then have its people been directly affected
by the regulations that accompany central government. The district was
formerly insulated from the national government because of its inaccessibility, north of the Lowari Pass. Now new federal buildings have
been constructed, foreshadowing a larger bureaucracy to come. Near
one new building, by the corner of an unfinished stone wall, a Muslim
religious mendicant, or *malang*, has lived for years in a small mud and
canvas home covered with morning glory vines. If the new stone wall
were completed, the ascetic's dwelling would be destroyed, but his
entreaties halted construction. The malang has successfully resisted a
corner of the future. Yet, like the crockery mender and the camel
caravans from Turkestan, he too may soon vanish.

The Way to Chitral

Chitral can be reached by plane, but seasoned travelers recommend that you enter the district by an overland route. Given sufficient
time, land travel allows you to see the country and more fully appreciate the remoteness of the area to which you are traveling. The ancient
city of Peshawar is the gateway for both land and air passage to Chitral.

First, the air route: the Pakistani airline, PIA, has daily flights
from Peshawar to Chitral Bazaar except on days of bad weather. The
50-minute Fokker flight usually must be booked several days in advance. During the summer, two flights often operate daily. If you go by
plane, try to sit on the left side in order to see the virtually roadless,
self-governed Pathan tribal areas of Mohmand and Bajaur and
beyond, the white, knifelike upper ridges of the Hindu Kush in Afghanistan. Crossing above the Lowari Pass, your plane enters Chitral
District and begins to descend, flying east of the dry lower gorges of the
Kalash valleys. To your right the narrow Shishi Valley slices into the
Hindu Raj Range. Tirich Mir peak, the tallest mountain in Chitral at
25,264 ft., lies ahead to the north.

Bus service north from Peshawar is offered by both the Dir Bus
Service located in Namak Mandi (the old Salt Market of Peshawar)
and the Government Transport Service (GTS) from its terminal on the
Grand Trunk Road near Hashtnagri Gate. Eleven passenger vans
called mini-buses make the run, now that the road is newly graded to
Dir. A mini-bus is the fastest type of land transport anywhere in
northern Pakistan. Peshawar's open-air depot for mini-buses is at the
new bus station on the Grand Trunk Road, 2 mi. east of Hashtnagri
Gate. In 1974, before the road to Dir was widened, two of my sisters and

I groggily took the bus from Peshawar that left at 2:00 A.M. We learned that most of the passengers had arrived the previous evening, sleeping until departure on beds inside the bus station—and on its mud roof. That day the bus had three flat tires on the rough road, and the trip to Dir took 15 hours.

The road northward leaves the hot Peshawar Plain as it snakes up the steep, dry ridge of the Malakand Pass. This is the first geomorphic hint of the great tangle of ranges to the north—the Hindu Kush, Hindu Raj, and Karakoram. On the pass, a large British-built fortress is manned by Pathans in khaki, their shiny uniform insignia reading MALAKAND. From the southerly approach that begins here, the daunting mountain vastness was once well controlled by the three princely states of Swat, Dir, and Chitral. They remained semiautonomous until the early 1960s, when direct federal authority was imposed state by state.

The teeming Malakand Bazaar north of the pass is the last large village encountered before your bus crosses the Swat River, leaving the Swat Valley for the hill district of Dir. On a ridge just beyond the river crossing is a small fortress where Winston Churchill served his military apprenticeship. At an alfresco checkpost near Chakdarra Bazaar, you may be asked to register and present your passport, a custom that remains from the time of Dir State's autonomy. Across the road from the checkpost is a border fort once garrisoned by Scottish Highlanders.

Once in Dir, I have invariably joined others on the roof of the bus for the ride to Dir Bazaar. The absorbing scenery as viewed from the roof is unobstructed, and other passengers who choose the roof like to converse. Once I talked for several hours with a policeman returning to duty in Dir after he had taken a prisoner to the Peshawar Prison. Leaning on our baggage, we discussed Islam, the local penal code, and the intransigence of Dir people, as all the while the tree-covered foothills of the Hindu Raj rose about us.

Beyond the Chakdarra checkpost the road bears to the west, crossing a ridge to the lower Panjkora Valley. When the British were finally able to arrange with the fusty Nawab of Dir to build the road in the 1930s, gunfire from across the river in the nearby Mohmand tribal area necessitated using the ridge route. As you ride along the wide valley with its "river from five districts," you can see into the federally administered tribal area of Bajaur. As recently as 1960, Arnold Toynbee wrote that neither Briton nor Pakistani had ever entered Bajaur, and, even now, few roads penetrate this "free country," as it has been considered by its self-governed inhabitants. When you approach Dir Bazaar, the Panjkora Valley narrows, becoming densely wooded. Such rich timber is still seen elsewhere in Pakistan only within monsoon-facing Swat and Hazara. Vast improvements on the road to Dir were completed rapidly in 1977 after a shoot-out between government troops and Pathan irregulars from Dir over the sensitive issue of timber rights.

Dir Bazaar is a gritty place, formerly an obligatory overnight stop for travelers between Peshawar and Chitral. A GTS booking office is situated in the north end of town. Near it are several small shops that make a Dir specialty: quality pocket knives. The single-blade knives are so well known and the originals produced in such small quantity that imitations are on sale in Peshawar.

The rebuilt road to Dir and the soon-to-be completed Lowari Pass tunnel should enable you to reach Chitral town from Peshawar in one day. In 1959, six days were required for the Italian Mt. Saraghrar Expedition to traverse the same route; the road did not then include such amenities as bridges. Fosco Mariani's informed account of that expedition and the religious and cultural history of Chitral in *Where Four Worlds Meet* remains the best introduction to the region. Crossing the Lowari ridge brings you to Chitral, the land of the Kho, the first non-Pathan people north of the road between Kabul and the Indus River. If you travel far enough in Chitral, you may come to believe with Mariani that the whole region is virtually unexplored.

Chitral Bazaar

In Chitral Bazaar (4,840 ft.), lodgings range from the shoestring-budget small hotels to the Chitral Mountain Inn, an exclusive domain for tourists. When I last visited, my own past favorite, the Shabnam ("Dew") Hotel still served three meals daily to a varied, colorful clientele ranging from visiting officials to local wags. It is located in Ataliq Bazaar on the southern end of town near the Jeep serai. The Chitral Mountain Inn, western in design and fixtures, is situated in upper Ataliq Bazaar, along the street leading to the district commissioner's office. Excellent meals may be ordered there in advance by those not in residence. Most visitors to Chitral will want to stay at other, more moderately priced hotels in Shahi Bazaar.

The Chitral tourist officer can be of assistance with the logistics and planning of your trek. The Tourist Information Center where he works is on the far north end of Shahi Bazaar and is open six days a week. Don't overlook the manager or an assistant at your hotel, who is a mine of information about prices and shops. He will also gladly act as your tutor in Khowar, expanding your vocabulary from this book's Khowar Glossary and correcting your pronunciation. In the bazaar, you can be certain to find most of the basic foodstuffs for trekking: rice, wheat flour, pulses (beans and lentils), vegetables in season, sugar, dried mulberries, apricots, and cooking oil. You should bring canned food and powdered milk with you from Peshawar.

Short Walks from Chitral Bazaar

Two scenic walks begin directly from Chitral Bazaar. A fine but unshaded day hike follows the dry, rocky trail leading from the residential area called Haryankot, just west of the main Shahi Bazaar. This path, which is used mostly by shepherds, will take you 3,800 ft. up to the place called Birmogh Lasht ("Plain of Walnut Trees") where there is an abandoned, mud-walled building that was formerly a summer residence of the mehtars. It has sweeping views of the valley and magnificent Tirich Mir, the broad snowy summit dominating the northern aspect.

An overnight walk leads to the old royal compound of Biron Shal (10,000 ft.). The Biron Shal trail begins behind the deputy commissioner's office, soon entering a scattered *deodar* (East Indian cedar) forest that becomes thickly wooded with pine as you gain altitude. This narrow valley is a game sanctuary, and, owing to its proximity to the civil authorities who enforce its regulations, wildlife can be viewed there if you are a patient, lucky observer. Snow leopards have been seen and photographed in the upper forest. Good luck.

The Kalash Valleys

When the Afghan king Abdur Rahman Khan converted the non-Muslim Kalash tribespeople by the sword in 1895, the name of their locality, Kafiristan, "Land of the Infidels," became Nuristan, "Land of the Light" or "Land of the Enlightened." Since then, three other narrow, well-forested valleys west of Ayun village in Chitral have become the only area populated by non-Muslims in a hundred-mile radius. The Kalash who live in these valleys, called Birir, Bumboret, and Rumbur, have been encroached upon by their Islamic neighbors, anthropologists, and tourists. They seem to have maintained their joie de vivre and unique way of life, but their time as a culturally distinct people is fast ticking away. The traditions of this special people will change greatly within a few years, particularly because tourist-bearing

The pottery mender in Chitral bazaar (photo by Ken Swift).

roads have recently been built into the Bumboret and Rumbur valleys
and because refugees from Afghanistan have flooded into the area.

Kalash women still wear black woolen homespun garments, red
beaded necklaces by the dozen, and an exceptional headpiece that

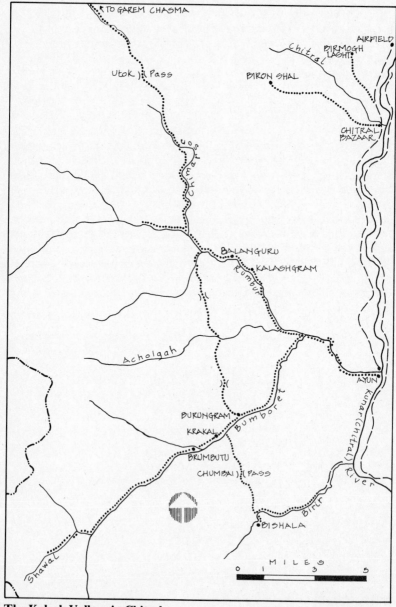

The Kalash Valleys in Chitral

flows down the back, covered in cowrie shells, beads, and trinkets. The Kalash women have an outgoing manner that is disarming, delightful, and unexpected in a region where purdah is generally practiced. Young women have approached me to examine an article of my clothing or equipment and then expressed considerable amusement at my inability to understand their spirited comments.

You greet a Kalash person with *esphad*, the local salutation, comment by saying *prusht* (good, ok) to just about anything, and explain where you are going by using your destination and *parai*; for example, "Brumbutu parai," "I'm going to Brumbutu." Though they have their own language, most Kalash will know more Khowar than you, so you can use Khowar words from the glossary.

Walking into the valleys from Ayun remains the best way to see them. From Chitral, take a Jeep from the serai in Ataliq Bazaar 10 mi. south to Ayun. Depending upon chance and your speed in passing through Ayun, you may be asked to pay a tax of 10 rupees for visiting the valleys. This one-dollar charge is on the level, and you will get a receipt. The shopkeeper who contracts to levy the tax will be glad to sell you any last-minute supplies or to point out the nearby teashop. On your way to or from the valleys, you will probably find that you have to stay overnight in Ayun. Mir Gulab Shah once ran a two-room hotel called Alice's Restaurant just south of the clear river that drains the Bumboret and Rumbur valleys. Mir Gulab is a storehouse of local lore about trade between Turkestan and Chitral, as passed on to him by his grandfather. Ayun was once a major transshipment point on the Silk Route.

From Ayun, follow the sparkling river up a narrow side valley to the west. At the end of a two-hour walk, after you cross many single-log bridges, the river divides. The southern stream fork forms the Bumboret Valley; the northern stream fork is where the Rumbur Valley begins. Bumboret Valley offers side trips to the Birir Valley and Shawal Meadows. The Rumbur Valley leads eventually to a pass and, beyond, a hot springs directly accessible from Chitral.

Bumboret and Birir

Several hours' walk from the river junction along the south fork will bring you to Burungram, the first sizable village in Bumboret Valley. There is a small store here and a teahouse where you can order food to be prepared while you wait beneath the walnut trees. Another mile up-valley, the exceptionally large houses of Krakal will interest you.

The last and largest town in Bumboret is Brumbutu, at the end of the Jeep track. By making advance reservations through the office of the steno (the district commissioner's secretary in Chitral Bazaar), you can reserve a room in the pleasant government rest house at Brumbutu for up to three nights. The manager will provide meals on request and guide you through the small fish hatchery nearby. Imagine having to carry the cement for the fish tanks up-valley from Ayun!

In one very long day you can walk from Brumbutu to the pastures of Shawal and back, but you may want to carry food and stay at Shawal Meadows for the night. To reach them, walk up the main valley from Brumbutu and continue about 4 mi., until you reach the last small grove of pines. Here the trail rises; you pass a last lone pine tree and begin climbing talus slopes. The narrow gorge you have entered divides, with the right-hand path leading to another pasture. For Shawal, stay left; a stiff further climb will bring you to a meandering stream in lush pastureland. This large rocky cirque is called Shawal. When I arrived, hot and tired, some herdsmen were playing a game remarkably similar to quoits that involved the pitching of flat, heavy rocks toward a distant stake. With much good-natured banter, the teammates urged on their own sides and disparaged the efforts of the opposing players.

From Krakal, part way up the Bumboret Valley, the most southerly Kalash valley of Birir may be reached via a trail that crosses the main stream on a typical one-log bridge. Along the south river bank, follow the narrow tributary valley ahead of you steeply upwards 3,500 ft., over the Chumbai Pass. The town of Bishala in Birir sits on the valley floor below. The years-old Jeep road is beyond, down-valley from Bishala, leading out to the main road along the Kunar Valley south of Ayun.

Rumbur

The easiest way to walk into Rumbur Valley is to take the north fork of the river up-valley from Ayun. A harder walk, requiring two days, leads north from Batrik village near Burungram in Bumboret, to the Rumbur Valley. The latter, hilly route is a beautiful one: well wooded and uninhabited, it offers you the opportunity to see the remaining valley of the Kalash. This trail can be confusing at times, however; side paths (used by goats) can take you off course, and an intervening valley must be followed before you reach Rumbur. Hiring a local person to guide you would be best. The intermediate valley is called the Acholgah Gol (in Khowar, *gol* means stream or valley); from it you climb another steep ridge, descend to a small stream and follow it through a narrow rock defile. There you are a mile upstream from the hamlet of Balenguru. This small village is shaded by tall walnut trees and is the uppermost Kalash town in Rumbur. Only 4 mi. of the Rumbur Valley are still populated by Kalash.

An ambitious trek from upper Rumbur takes you over the 15,250-ft. Utak Pass to the popular hot springs at Garem Chashma, also accessible and often visited via road from Chitral Bazaar. For this walk you should definitely take a guide from Rumbur and enough food to last three days. Your route follows the Chimarsan Gol, an hour's walk upstream from Balenguru. The going is tree-shaded at first, as you follow the right bank of the Chimarsan along a typically narrow valley. Several hours up, the trail crosses the stream and begins to rise toward the pass, 4,000 ft. above. This pass should not be attempted before June, owing to its elevation, and after a winter of heavy snow it may not be open until July. The first village north of the pass is Putrik, halfway from the Utak Pass to Garem Chashma. Once at the hot springs you can soak in deliciously enervating water, feeling the aches of the

Kalash woman from the Rumbur Valley, Chitral District.

trek disappear. Jeeps travel frequently between Garem Chashma and Chitral, giving you the option of walking in and returning by road, or vice versa.

Southern Chitral

An interesting trek with several route variations can be made from the southern Shishi Valley over a rarely traveled trail into the midst of the Hindu Raj Range. To reach the roadhead, take one of the readily available Jeeps to Drosh from Chitral Bazaar. Jeeps going south to Drosh, Dir, and Ayun leave from the Jeep serai in Ataliq Bazaar—near the polo field on the southern edge of Chitral Bazaar. Once in Drosh you will have to switch Jeeps, unless you have found one going up the Shishi Valley to Madaglasht. Continue up the valley on foot from Madaglasht, a village originally settled by Farsi-speaking Persians from Afghanistan who made breech-loading muskets for the mehtars. The steep walls to either side of you are reminiscent of alpine valleys, but here—as in most of Chitral District—the trees are few.

From the highest village, Dhaulatabad, the 13,700-ft. Dok Pass at the head of the valley is reached by a recognizable path. Keep to the right side of the gorge and follow the steep upper trail onto the northern ridge. From the pass, the village of Ustur in the Golen Valley is 8 mi. down. At Ustur, three routes are possible:

1. The shortest trail to the main Chitral Valley follows the Golen Valley 9 mi. downstream through a gorge with precipitous sides to the main Jeep road. Walking 2 mi. down the road will bring you to Koghozi, a large town 15 mi. north of Chitral Bazaar. Wait in Koghozi at the main teahouse for a Jeep going south.

2. From Ustur, you can also walk 9 mi. up a different tributary to the summer settlement of Dukadaki. Climbing 4,000 ft. up the steep ridge north of Dukadaki will take you to a 15,000-ft. pass. After you leave Dukadaki, there will be no water until you are well over the pass. A day's walk down-valley on the far side of the pass will carry you to the large village of Reshun, 35 mi. by Jeep from Chitral Bazaar. On the descent to Reshun, the red and violet coloring of the hills is most extraordinary.

3. The most ambitious trek from Ustur leads north to the east-extending Laspur Valley and the large town of Mastuj, near its base. For this walk you must hire a guide from where you start out, in the Shishi Valley, because the distance from the Dok Pass through the Hindu Raj to the village of Rahman—the first settlement in the Laspur Valley—is 29 miles. You will cross the 16,587-ft. Phargam Pass, which lies between an unnamed 20,000-ft. peak and 21,500-ft. Buni Zom, the highest point of the Hindu Raj. From Madaglasht you will probably need six days to reach the road in the Laspur Valley. Follow this road to Mastuj, and there, at the mouth of the Laspur Valley, you can get one of the occasional Jeeps back to Chitral Bazaar.

The Upper Valleys

Treks in the upper valleys begin after a long Jeep ride from Chitral Bazaar. The Jeep serai for all rides north (to the towns of Garem Chashma, Drasan, Warkup, and Mastuj) is located off the west side of the main street, 40 yards north of the Chitral Gol. A Jeep's average speed up- or down-valley is only 10 mi. per hour, owing to the highly circuitous roads. The driver will stop 20 to 30 mi. up-valley for a meal, and you should be certain to tell the innkeeper that you wish to eat, too, before wandering about, or you risk finding the victuals already depleted when you return. More than once I have gone hungry after strolling about to see the village, much to the innkeeper's consternation and my own.

Jeep rides anywhere in northern Pakistan are dusty, cramped experiences, but the country they lead to and through makes them worthwhile. When going up-valley, your pack will be weighed, and you will pay additionally for it based on weight. You will be wedged among your fellow passengers, sitting on several hundred kilograms of goods the driver is transporting. Going down-valley, Jeeps usually carry only passengers. Transportation costs are less then, for the driver makes his money primarily on the goods he takes north. Some words to the wise: arrange your gear very carefully before a Jeep trip; your pack will definitely be sat upon, probably by more than one person at a time. Keep your camera with you in a shoulder bag, cushion all fragile objects, and hope for the best. The front seat in a Jeep is a desirable location but difficult for anyone except a woman or local official to acquire.

The two principal valleys in northern Chitral are named Turikho and Yarkhun, and they run parallel to one another, connected by several passes. We will first discuss the western Turikho Valley.

Turikho and its Tributaries

Turikho Valley south of Shagram village is called Mulikho, meaning Lower Land of the Kho, while above Shagram is Turikho proper, the Upper Kho country. The Kho are the Chitrali people who, legend says, originated in Turikho. Shagram still houses part of Chitral's royal family. I was given kind hospitality by a red-haired polo-playing prince in Shagram while passing through on my spring 1977 trek.

The towns and their surrounding alluvial oases in the Turikho Valley lie high above the river and seem especially well manicured. Rose bushes and flower gardens are abundant and, except for the high relief of the land, you might be walking through English countryside of an earlier age. The poplar trees grow tall in irrigated areas of Turikho, yet the dry wastes between villages are as unsupportive of life as anywhere in Chitral.

To reach Turikho, take a Jeep to Warkup village, the present roadhead. (You could also Jeep to the large town of Drasan, following a slightly different route, but reaching Warkup would then require nearly a day's walk north.) Four miles along the trail north of Warkup, on the northern limits of Rain village, a granite rock with a Buddhist stupa faintly outlined on it recalls the era when this valley supported a Buddhist culture. The rock lies north of the Rain polo field and just above the trail.

From the roadhead at Warkup, a two- or three-day walk up the main Turikho Valley will bring you to Rua, the northernmost permanent settlement in the Turikho Valley, at an elevation of 9,400 feet. Along the way the trail passes many villages and the tributary valleys called, in order, Melph, Tirich, Khot, Ziwar, and Uzhnu. Both the Ziwar and Uzhnu valleys lead to upper-valley glaciers, support no villages, and are known to host scattered herds of ibex in their upper reaches. Fosco Mariani's 1959 Saraghrar Expedition followed the Ziwar Gol on its approach march, and it was this area that he called virtually unexplored. The U502 Army Map Service Mastuj Sheet (NJ43-13) shows all of the Ziwar Valley and most of upper Chitral in perfect detail.

Two miles north of Rain, the Tirich Valley branches off from the main Turikho Valley. The narrow but important watershed of the Tirich curves back to the southwest and rises toward the lower and upper Tirich glaciers on the north slopes of Tirich Mir, the tallest mountain in Chitral. The compact villages in the Tirich Valley have grass-floored groves of apricot trees and mosques with straw-covered entrance porches. People from these villages have worked for the various expeditions climbing Tirich Mir (25,264 ft.), Noshaq (24,580 ft.), Istor-O-Nal (24,269 ft.), and Saraghrar (24,111 ft.). These border summits are the tallest peaks in the entire Hindu Kush Range. In this valley you are apt to see a person wearing mountaineering boots or leading an animal by a length of climbing rope. A two-day walk up the valley will bring you to Shagram, a different village than that of the same name in Turikho. Beyond Shagram, another day's walk takes you to the mouth of the lower Tirich Glacier, directly north of Tirich Mir.

The Tirich Valley parallels Chitral's central valley and is separated from it by a 15-mi. flat-topped ridge averaging more than 12,000 ft. in elevation. The ideal way to reach the ridge, for its unsurpassed views of the high nearby mountains as well as much of central Chitral, is to climb Zani Pass (12,500 ft.). Zani Pass is situated between Shagram in the Tirich Valley and Drasan, the largest town in Mulikho. The pass is 3,000 ft. above Shagram and a mile higher than Drasan. The ridge in both directions from the pass is exceedingly flat, inviting you to stroll along it and view the spectacular Hindu Kush peaks from Tirich Mir to Saragharar and north. To the east, the Hindu Raj, Buni Zom, and a copper-hued area near Mastuj are also visible. The play of light on the Hindu Raj and Hindu Kush is a breathtaking sight as the day progresses. Staying overnight on this ridge would be memorable. A permanent lake on the ridge a short walk southwest of the pass makes toting up water unnecessary. This exceptional viewing area is most easily approached from the Tirich Valley. I climbed Zani Pass in later April with villagers who were going from Shagram to get supplies. We left at 3:00 A.M. so they could reach Drasan on the other side and return home the same night. They walked a total of 8,000 ft. up and an equal distance down that day, carrying loads on the return! As we approached the snow-covered ridge at sunrise, an unforgettable display of rose, gold, then yellow light played on the towering snow peaks.

A grandly scenic, level 5-mi. walk up the Turikho Valley beyond Rua village will bring you to Moghlang, where three upper valleys converge. On inspection, Moghlang itself turns out to be a lone, solidly constructed hut used intermittently by herdsmen and hunters. It rests on a low rise near a large spring and commands an excellent view both down-valley and up the glaciated tributary gorge to the west. Several hundred yards west of Moghlang, the large Rahozan Gol emerges from the north. That valley leads to Bala Bughdu (another shepherd's quarters) and a profusion of glaciers from the Hindu Kush peaks that border the Wakhan Corridor of Afghanistan. East of Moghlang, the large Shah Jinali Gol comes into view between magnificient high buttresses. Twelve miles east of Moghlang up the Shah Jinali Gol is the 13,900-ft. Shah Jinali ("King's Polofield") Pass, a wide rolling meadow. Beyond the pass by 6 mi. is Yoshkist village in the Yarkhun Valley, from which you can return southward to Mastuj. The Turikho-to-Yarkhun circle route makes an excellent trek. If you give yourself at least ten days walking time from Warkup to Mastuj, you will have enough time to explore and enjoy the country and its people.

Another interesting high walk out of the Turikho Valley would be to ascend the Khot ("Cloud") Valley, crossing the 14,000-ft. Knot Pass east to the central Yarkhun Valley. The Knot Gol branches off Turikho 5 mi. north of the Tirich Valley. The best path up the Khot Gol is the one on the northern side that climbs above the valley floor and in 4 mi. passes the town of Lasht Khot ("Cloud Plain") with its polo ground. At Lasht Khot you should consider hiring someone to guide you to the pass, for the trail is less often used than many and misleading stock trails are numerous. As you climb the Khot Valley, you begin to see the Hindu Kush peaks behind the nearby ridges. Walking a long hill is tiring yet invigorating, and as with every high climb there is the reward of nature's unfolding panorama. At the Khot Pass, spires of the Hindu Raj ahead appear extremely rugged. The steep, unmaintained trail from the pass down to the Yarkhun Valley crosses from the left to the right bank of the Khutan Gol some 1,500 ft. below the pass, descending along a ridge. At the Yarkhun Valley floor, walk north to reach the small village of Dizg, by a long green meadow, or trek south 2 mi. and cross the river to the large town of Brep, situated on a wide alluvial fan.

Yarkhun

East of Turikho is the Yarkhun Valley. At the southern extremity of the Yarkhun area, next to the mouth of the Laspur Valley, is the large town of Mastuj with its bazaar of 15 shops, a Chitral Scouts garrison in the old British fort, and a rudimentary, one-room inn. Other rooms are available along the Jeep road nearly 2 mi. down-valley from Mastuj, where the hamlet of Sarghoz has two small inns. In summer and fall, Jeeps from Chitral Bazaar can usually drive directly up to Mastuj Bazaar. Sometimes, however, vehicles are unable to cross the swollen Laspur River, just west of the Mastuj escarpment.

The trail along the wide, 38-mi. corridor of the Yarkhun Valley from Mastuj north to the Gazin Gol sweeps past low alluvial fans, many of them cultivated, and also crosses long stony wastes. The trail is generally level, and long, map-devouring distances can be traversed in a day. The Yarkhun cuts through a succession of precipitous spurs vividly colored in ochre, gold, grey, and rust: a majestic setting. It has more arable land than Turikho, and the large town of Chapali, Brep, and Bang reflect this.

On the southernmost outskirts of Brep, directly on the east side of the trail, is a store and inn run by a pleasant young man. He is often occupied near his home, 200 yards back from the path to the east, but his omelettes and tea are worth waiting for, and his is the last inn as you proceed up the Yarkhun Valley. The rock outcropping in the center of Brep on which the school now stands once supported a Chinese fortress.

The residents of Yarkhun for the most part are Ismaili Muslims, locally called Maulavi. This valley was once a segment of the lawless Silk Route; the Chitrali two-string bow (which shoots rocks, not arrows) and the occasional horseman with breechloader recall that era. Chitralis are great hunters and often tote Afghan-made refles acquired through barter.

In addition to walking west from Yarkhun over the trails described in the preceding section, you can pick up trails leading east to Gilgit. The first three trails described in the next section begin from Yarkhun.

Passes East from Chitral

Four passes can be used to trek from Yarkhun out of Chitral. Of these, one is currently restricted, but it is mentioned in case it later is reopened. The first three lead east to the Gilgit River watershed; the fourth pass leads southeast to the Swat Valley.

1. Perhaps the most tantalizing pass eastwards is 14,760-ft. Thui Pass, offering sheer views upward as you cross between 20,000-ft. peaks. Thui Pass connects the Gazin Gol, near the northern end of the Yarkhun Valley, and the Thui Gol of the Yasin Valley in the Gilgit watershed. In the past, some trekking groups did cross the Thui Pass; unfortunately this fascinating pass is currently in a closed zone. (The glaciated, 14,700-ft. Darkot Pass, farther up the Yarkhun Valley and between it and the upper Yasin Valley is too crevassed to be suitable, and it, too, is in a border area and so closed.)

2. The Chumarkhan Pass (14,200 ft.) is the shortest route to follow between Chitral and the Gilgit River watershed. From the Chitral side the pass is approached through the Zagaro Gol behind Chapali

village, 7 mi. north of Mastuj in the Yarkhun Valley. The main trail through Chapali joins with a wide path leading east to the Zagaro Gol; follow this canyon for 5 mi. until you reach the first large tributary from the southern (left) bank. There you cross the main stream on a bridge and begin a stiff 3,500-ft. climb to the Chumarkhan Pass. All trees are left behind soon after you leave the valley floor, and in the lower reaches of the ascent, several herdsmen's huts are passed. If the hour you reach the stream junction is past early afternoon, consider camping there or within a thousand feet above; water becomes scarce towards the pass. When you descend from the pass, you will be at Barset village in the scenic upper Ghizar Valley.

The Chumarkhan Pass itself is a wide and rolling plain. If you are approaching it from the Gilgit Valley, you may have some difficulty differentiating the pass trail from the various side routes taken by stock in the summer months. Stay toward the center of the wide rocky plain, angling back toward the middle of it if the route you have taken diverges toward the hills.

3. The 12,250-ft. Shandur Pass is the traditional route between Chitral and the Gilgit River watershed. Although the distance from Mastuj to Barset village by way of the Shandur is 32 mi., 10 mi. longer than the Chumarkhan Pass route, the Shandur is 2,000 ft. lower in elevation. A little-used Jeep road connects Mastuj to Sor Laspur, the southernmost town in the Laspur Valley, at the foot of the Shandur Pass. Sor Laspur has a small government rest house whose *chowkidar* (manager and factotum) may be able to help arrange for a porter. A telegraph line, originally constructed by the British, connects Chitral Bazaar with Gilgit town and may soon be accompanied for the entire distance by a road over the Shandur Pass, if work progresses. The pass trail itself is well marked and easy to follow, descending less steeply on the eastern side as it passes a lake. At a locally famous polo ground by the lake, summer matches are played between Chitrali and Gilgiti teams.

4. Accessible by midsummer from the Laspur Valley is the 15,630-ft. Kachhikhani Pass, leading south into the formerly autonomous valley of Swat (described in the next section). From Sor Laspur, the trail continues up-valley for 9 mi. to the first sizable tributary on the right bank of the Laspur River. The little-used route up this tributary, the Kachhikhani Gol, continues an additional 10 mi. to the top of the pass. When you first encounter the lower moraines of the upper-valley glacier, begin to look for a moraine on the east side that joins the scree-covered slope you are following. This is the narrow opening that you take to the pass itself from the Kachhikhani Gol. The route leads through the Hindu Raj range into the Swat Valley's Ushu Gol and south to the trailhead at Matiltan, where a road goes to the large town of Kalam. Hiring a porter-guide is the best strategy for finding your way across this pass, as neither the northern nor the southern approach to it is straightforward. And getting lost is not the only potential hazard: note carefully the caution at the end of the next section.

The Swat Valley

The upper valleys of Swat Kohistan, "Swat's Land of Mountains," teem with steep, pine-covered ridges that rise toward scores of snow-clad 18,000-ft. peaks. Unlike Chitral and the expanses to the north and east, Swat receives monsoon rain and has an alpine flavor reminiscent of the Rockies or Alps. Many of its peaks were first climbed by the British in the days of empire. The Vale of Swat is well touristed during the summer up to mid-valley, but the most scenic northern areas are less often visited. Swat can be the perfect place to walk for the person without weeks of time to pass in the mountains.

Upper Swat is accessible from Islamabad by plane to Saidu Sharif, or from Peshawar or Rawalpindi in a day by mini-bus. The van will take you to Mingora, where you must change to another van or the slower bus for the remaining up-valley ride. Note that in Saidu Sharif, 5 mi. southeast of Mingora and off the main valley road, the venerable Swat Hotel houses a Tourist Information Center (TIC). Also in Saidu Sharif, Swat's traditional capital, you can book rest house rooms for the upper valley.

Thirty miles north of Mingora is the town of Madyan in the last open stretch before a pine-clad gorge leads to Swat Kohistan and, in another 30 mi., Kalam. Kalam Bazaar, which can also be reached by the Kachhikhani Pass described above, is the farthest point up-valley where basic food commodities are available.

The Ushu and Gabrial valleys, north and west of Kalam respectively, are the best trekking areas in Swat. Each of these valleys has a rest house, reservable from the TIC in Saidu Sharif. In upper Swat, look for the unique mosques constructed entirely of wood that are found in most villages. These mosques have a quiet beauty despite their modest size. Three miles south of Kalam is a small village hidden above a bluff with a wooden mosque in its center. A day walk to the ridge line east of that village will take you to grand, Swiss-like vistas.

Upper Swat's many stockades are reminders that the valley and its neighboring districts are Pathan. If you trek north of Kalam in Ushu or Gabrial, you must be absolutely certain to go with reliable porters and a guide. Robberies have occurred in upper Swat, and guns may be used during some chance encounters in these upper valleys. It is best not to trek at all in Swat's uppermost regions unless you have solid assurance from an outfitter who knows local conditions.

5

The Gilgit River Watershed

To travel hopefully is a better thing than to arrive, and the true success is to labor.

Robert Louis Stevenson, 1881

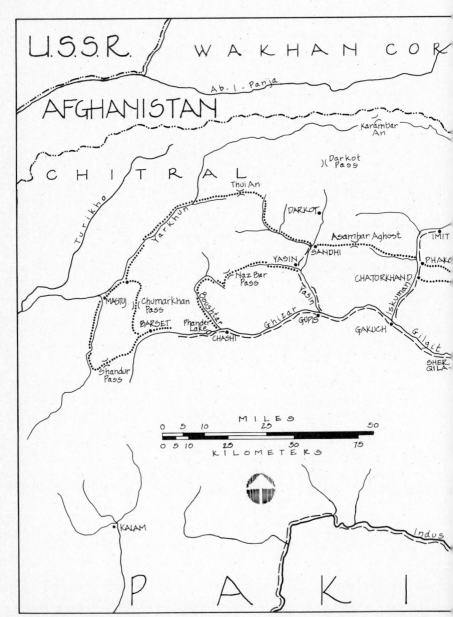

The Gilgit River Valleys

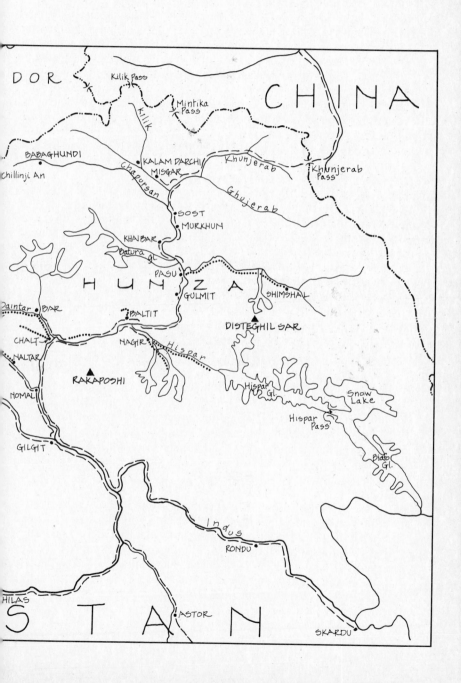

The Unknown Valleys

The four principal valleys of the Gilgit River—Ghizar, Yasin, Ishkuman, and Hunza—each extend into glacier-clad gorges and toward remote, knife-edged peaks. Within the last hundred years, until the British assumed tentative control of these lands, the area comprised seven independent states. Each state had its own ruler whose decisions were law. Ultimate authority lay, in theory only, with the distant Maharajah of Kashmir in Srinagar. Stretching from the Hinju Raj in the west to the Karakoram in the east, and from the lawless reaches of Indus Kohistan south of Gilgit Bazaar to the Pamir on the northern border, these valleys and the few negotiable passes that connect them still are largely places of mystery to the outside world.

The opening of the Karakoram Highway (KKH) along the Indus River to private vehicles means that now Gilgit Bazaar is a 20-hour bus ride from Rawalpindi. Tourism and commerce, once limited in this area, will expand radically; the ancient traditions and customs are being altered by the development of the area and the mentality of the pocket calculator. Let's take a look at each of the four valleys in turn, after describing Gilgit itself. The west-draining Ghizar River and two of the three other parallel valleys are not large, but the Hunza Valley is different. It has many tributaries with hiking routes, and description of this rivershed comprises most of the chapter.

Gilgit

The town of Gilgit (4,900 ft.) remains largely an entrepôt for the visitor. It is—and has always been—a place travelers must pass through and pause at on the way to or from many destinations, but it is not a destination in itself, particularly in the oven-like midsummer months. In the past, the town was alternately fought over, plundered, and ignored. Today the town has an air of growth that does not eclipse its friendliness or swallow its cosmopolitan populace. Although two-humped Bactrian camels led by Turkomen from Kashgar no longer plod into the main bazaar, Gilgit is becoming a key transit point for trekkers interested in Chitral, Hunza, Baltistan, or any place in between.

Planes from the Islamabad-Rawalpindi International Airport arrive daily in Gilgit during good weather, and daily bus service from Rawalpindi up the deep Indus gorge is available. Gilgit's modestly priced hotels change their names and standards over the years, but they are plentiful enough. The Warshikgam Hotel and the PTDC Motel (PTDC: Pakistan Tourism Development Corporation) approximate Western-style accommodations and rates. For these two establishments, reservations by mail may possibly be arranged.

Gilgit has a pleasant small library situated next to the first large irrigation canal running south of the main bazaar. You can reach the library by walking south to the canal from the PWD (Public Works

Department) rest house or from Jaamat Khana Bazaar. Follow the footpath to the west along the waterway until you see the library sign on the north side of the path.

Near Gilgit is a remnant of the area's Buddhist phase, as also found in Skardu, Baltistan, and at Rain in Chitral. To see the carved rock Buddha, follow the main irrigation canal west past the Barmas Nala (*nala* means stream or valley in Hindi/Urdu) above Gilgit, continuing past numerous walled home compounds, green fields, and the village of Napur, to the Kargah Nala. Near the place some 4 mi. west of Gilgit Bazaar where this stream emerges from the ridge, a large niche some 40 ft. above the trail encircles a 10-ft.-high standing Buddha. Amateur archaeologists may wish to compare this unadorned lone figure with the free-standing rock in the Satpura Nala above Skardu, which has a more intricately carved central figure and tableau.

If, on arriving in Gilgit, you want to learn more about the area you plan to visit, ask to be directed to a shop run by people from that area. Such contacts can be most helpful in locating porters, deciding on your itinerary, and practicing local dialects. A restaurant cashier, for instance, will probably speak English and know the clientele. Or visit the local Tourist Information Center at beautiful Chinar Bagh (a *bagh* is a garden); the tourist officer there is very well informed about trekking routes.

Passage on a Jeep going up-country can be arranged at the shops where the vehicles load: Jeeps headed for Hunza take on supplies in Jaamat Khana Bazaar and those bound for Ghizar and Yasin in the westernmost bazaar. The Northern Areas Transport Company, NATCO, is expanding its service to the northern areas and offers bus service to Hunza on the new road. NATCO provides superior service, and its Jeeps are usually booked ahead of the private ones. The NATCO booking office is just east of the Warshikgam Hotel. Jeep drivers, too, are sources of route information and porter contacts.

The Ghizar Valley

This valley is the main link between Chitral and Gilgit and was ruled alternately by the Khushwaqt clan of Mastuj and its own raja in the town of Gupis. When trekking in the opposite direction, from Gilgit, you can hire a Jeep to take you as far west as Pingal or the rest house near Phander Lake, since the long, two-day walk in the valley gorge that separates these areas from Gupis is dry and uninteresting. West of the turquoise-blue Phander Lake, however, the valley becomes more striking and colorful. The rarely used Jeep road continues to the valley's last town, Barset, situated on a barren, windswept plain. Except in Barset, poplar and fruit trees are grown on the village oases and the nalas emptying into the Ghizar River are uniformly silt-free.

The Chumarkhan and Shandur Passes leading west into Chitral were described in the last chapter. From the village of Chashi in the Ghizar Valley east of Barset, a route leads north over 16,300-ft. Naz Bar

Pass to the Naz Bar Nala that flows east into Yasin. This trek will take a minimum of four days, and, especially because it is little traveled and the upper approaches are unmarked from either side, you should take a local person to indicate the way, help carry the supplies, and cook. The path up the stream valley called the Boushtar Gol is plain enough, but when the Ano Gol is reached some 15 mi. upstream, the Ano too must be left—for another northern tributary which leads to the pass. From the time you are an hour north of the Ghizar River until you are within several hours' walk of Yasin, you travel through country that is inhabited only by occasional shepherds. The upper approaches to the Naz Bar Pass itself are rarely used by locals and are unmarked from either side. Views from the Naz Bar Pass stretch from the Darkot Pass area, near the terminus of the Hindu Raj, to Buni Zom in the southwest. Trekking between Mastuj and Yasin over the Chumarkhan Pass and this route makes for a very nice traverse of the Hindu Raj. Allow from 4 to 5 days from Chashi to Yasin, or 8 to 10 days for the entire route.

The Yasin Valley

As we progressed I thought Yasin a comfortable country. Every village had its own glacier and so abundant water, with a sloping plain of good soil, easily worked and irrigated. We found their houses fair, their orchards small but pleasant, their bread leavened and well-baked, and their crops splendid; a very smiling country and very decent folk.

R. C. F. Schomberg, 1935

Like the Ghizar Valley, the Yasin has ties to Chitral that are at least a century old. Running north to south, parallel to and east of Chitral's Yarkhun Valley, the Yasin Valley lies northwest of Gilgit Bazaar. Warshikgam is the valley's name in Khowar, the Chitrali dialect that is understood by some locals. The primary tongue, though, is Burushaski, as spoken in Hunza many miles distant. The town of Yasin has a pleasant rest house with a tree-shaded garden; reservations there must be made in Gilgit. Also in Gilgit, you can book a Jeep to Yasin.

From Yasin Bazaar you can walk directly toward the Naz Bar Pass, as described in the preceding section. If current restrictions are lifted, you can go elsewhere, however. North of Yasin Bazaar, across the mouth of the Naz Bar Nala, is Taus, a village at the southern edge of the Dasht-i-Taus (Desert of the Peacock). Near the desert's northern edge the Thui Gol empties into the right side of the main upper Yasin Valley. The river's sources are the mingled meltwaters of five glaciers, including the Aghost Bar Glacier. At the head of the Aghost Bar, a trail crosses the Thui Pass (mentioned in the preceding chapter), which is closed at this writing. It leads to the Gazin Valley and Yarkhun. At the head of the Yasin Valley, and also closed, is the glaciated Darkot Pass that leads to uppermost Chitral.

The Ishkuman Valley

East of and parallel to the Yasin Valley is the Ishkuman, which has the unique distinction of dividing the most easterly slopes of the Hindu Kush and Hindu Raj and the most westerly peaks of the Karakoram Range. Koz Sar (21,907 ft.), lying to the immediate south of the Chillinji Pass (17,000 ft.) to Chapursan in Hunza, is clearly visible from above the mid-valley town of Imit. Like most peaks in the Karakoram, Koz Sar has steep, grey, sharp-angled slopes above serrated ridges, between which flow glacial torrents. The sienna-colored Hindu Raj has lower slopes of walkable gradient; above the 18,000-ft. level, they too angle sharply. The upper Ishkuman Valley is called the Karambar.

The Ishkuman can be reached by Jeep from Gilgit or by foot from the town of Yasin; walk about 5 mi. north to Sandhi, a town situated near the confluence of the Kurkulti Bar and the Asam Bar on the desert Dasht-i-Taus. At Sandhi, trek east up the valley of the Asam Bar to 14,500-ft. Asambar Aghost (*aghost* meaning "pass"), which is at the valley's head and is south of 19,021-ft. Asambar Peak. Continue east from the pass down the Asambar Gol to the Ishkuman River. An hour's walk south of this junction is a bridge to Chatorkhand, the largest town in the valley. Allow about 3 days to trek from Sandhi in the Yasin Valley to the Ishkuman Valley.

Chatorkhand, which has a small bazaar and a teahouse, is nearly halfway to Imit from the valley's southern terminus at the Gilgit River. Traditionally Chatorkhand is the residence of an Ismaili *pir*, or religious leader. In the valleys of Hunza, Ishkuman, Yasin, and Ghizar, the predominant faith is the reform Ismaili branch of the Shiah sect. Ismailis follow the Aga Khan, said to be a direct descendant of Fatima, the daughter of Mohammed. The Pir in Chatorkhand is the most venerated of that faith in the region. Pir Sayyed Karim Ali Shah, the incumbent, has done extensive work on the grounds of his residence. He is an avid gardener and would surely provide gracious hospitality for any who carry vegetable or flower seed samples. By my recollection, the Pir has one of the best cooks in the northern areas.

From Chatorkhand you can hike east up the Hayul Gol to the 16,000-ft. pass below Khaltar Peak (19,310 ft.). An alternate route from the village of Phakor, an hour's walk north of Chatorkhand, goes up the Phakor Gol to the same pass. Beyond the pass lies a clear lake and the breathtakingly beautiful Naltar Valley. Figure a four- to five-day walk between Chatorkhand, or Phakor, and Naltar. The trail from Naltar is discussed in the section "Nomal to Naltar."

The Hunza Valley

Encompassing the northwestern Karakoram, the Hunza Valley has been accorded effusive praise: "the ultimate manifestation of mountain grandeur," Eric Shipton called it. Lord Curzon noted that "The little state of Hunza contains more summits of over 20,000 feet than there are of over 10,000 feet in the entire Alps." A topographical map of the area has 500-foot contour lines that form many near-vertical solid masses. Glaciers abound, including the 30-mi. Batura. The Nubra, Braldu, Hushe, and Saltoro rivers are born in the Karakoram glacial vastness; the Shyok River encircles the eastern flanks of the range; but only the Hunza River actually cuts through the width of the Karakoram Range.

Hunza, open to visitation by foreigners only rarely in the past and closed in recent times from mid-1974 to late 1978, has again been partially reopened. The wide Karakoram Highway carved through the length of the valley to the long, flat Khunjerab Pass is a fitting testament to the ability of humans to modify their environment. We can only imagine the difficulties faced by those traveling the former Kashgar-to-Gilgit caravan route, which once traversed the length of the valley. Until Hunza was merged with Pakistan in September 1974, no police force had ever existed there. In times past, the large caravans provided sufficient funds, willingly or otherwise, and individual Hunzakuts had never paid taxes to any authority outside the region; until 1975, the only form of taxation was payment by families (in goods only) to the Mir, Hunza's own former ruler, extending a tradition of several generations.

The isolation imposed by Hunza's magnificent gorges led to the wholly indigenous "pure" diet of the people there before they were

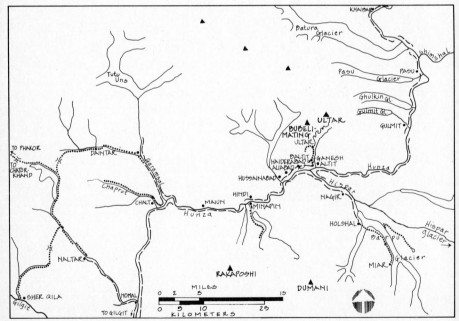

The Lower Hunza Valley

exposed to British "corrupting" influence at the end of the last century. Hunzakuts still talk about the British bringing five substances with them: sugar, spices, tobacco, tea, and *dalda*, or vegetable oil. Many a Hunzakut has bemoaned the passing of pure food in the local diet, all the while puffing on a Folks Own cigarette. With the change in diet and other contaminations brought by outside influence, the longevity formerly ascribed to the populace is now a historical footnote. The strength, individuality, and warmth likewise attributed to the people has not passed from them, but we can expect that as the rate of tourism continues its rapid upturn, the spontaneity of hospitality accorded visitors will become extremely diluted. If you speak a smattering of Burushaski from the glossary, you will surprise people and have experiences denied to the casual tourist.

Before leaving Gilgit for Hunza, stock up on food supplies. Stores and hotels have been only recently introduced in the Hunza Valley. If dry fruit is in season, however, by all means get it up-valley. Previously, all official visitors (which included most outsiders) were housed in one of the numerous rest houses, scattered as far north as Misgar. You may arrange to stay in these rest houses anywhere in the Gilgit River watershed by making application in Gilgit. The tourist officer at Chinar Bagh there can advise which rest houses are available.

The Hunza River has its origin in name at the juncture of the Kilik and Khunjerab nalas, some hundred miles from the river's mouth near Gilgit. Carving a gorge between 25,000-ft. peaks and receiving the waters of scores of glaciers, this is the largest and grandest tributary of the Gilgit River watershed. Most of the Hunza River watershed was once Hunza State, which was semi-autonomous until 1974. Another former state in the valley is across the river from the area of southern Hunza. We will begin at Nomal, near the river's confluence with the hot Gilgit Valley, and note the possibilities for trekking along this route and in the Hunza Valley itself.

Nomal to Naltar

Fifteen miles from Gilgit is the small village of Nomal on the right bank of the Hunza River across the valley from the KKH. This hamlet has a PWD rest house and is the turning-off point for the twisting Jeep track you can follow up to the 10,000-ft. Naltar Valley. Within the valley, the village of Naltar has a large PWD rest house and a PTDC chalet (both bookable from Gilgit) and is the site of the Pakistan Air Force school of mountain and winter survival. The wide valley is grandly scenic and thickly forested with pines in places. Peaks higher than 18,000 ft. and 19,000 ft. rise above the valley. Eight miles beyond the village is an exquisite, clear lake called Pudra.

From Naltar you can walk to Chalt in four to six days via the Daintar Nala and Garamsal Valley. Other routes lead to Chatorkhand and Phakor in the Ishkuman Valley, as mentioned in the previous section; for these hikes, a local villager will be needed to direct you.

Chalt and Bar

Some 10 mi. north of Nomal is the village of Chalt (6,560 ft.), at the place where the Hunza River bends to the east. Chalt is across the river from the KKH, beyond the first series of cliffs and precipice trails traversed by early visitors. In the 1890s, the British defended this far corner of their colonial empire from a small fortress in Chalt. In response to a threat of attack by locals and a breakdown in negotiations, a well-augmented force from the Chalt fort engaged and defeated the Hunza-Nagir army at Nilt, several miles up the Hunza River.

For those who want to explore some rarely visited and readily accessible roadless regions, the PWD rest house at Chalt is an excellent take-off point. (Remember to get a chit to stay at the rest house before leaving Gilgit.) Providing the water for the orchards and fields of Chalt is the Chaprot Nala, of which R. C. F. Schomberg wrote, "The Chaprot Valley is lovely, more beautiful than any other valley in the Gilgit Agency, and it is far more accessible than many better known." A trek high into this valley would make a fine short hike, of about two days' duration.

Just beyond Chalt, the large Garamsal Valley, running north and south into the northwestern massifs of the Karakoram, emerges into the Hunza Valley. As you walk up the Garamsal, the first large tributary you reach is the Daintar Nala, flowing from Daintar, a summer grazing settlement to the west. Bar is the last permanent village up the main Garamsal Valley. Bar's upper summer pastures are beyond, up the left side of the Tutu Uns Glacier at the place called Toltar.

Into Old Hunza

As the KKH rounds a bend across the Hunza River from Chalt, it crosses land traditionally considered to be in Nagir State. The highway remains in Nagir for the distance it continues along the left bank. Beyond Chalt on the northern side of the Hunza River is the customary boundary of Hunza State. The Jeep bridge at Sikandarabad ("Alexander's town"), 7 mi. upriver from Chalt by the old road, gives access to both banks of the Hunza River beyond the Garamsal Valley. After making certain (in Gilgit or Chalt) that the trail is still maintained on this northern side of the river, you might consider walking instead of riding into Hunza. The distance from Sikandarabad to Baltit is somewhat more than 25 mi. and is walkable in two days on both trails and the road. Hindi village is a good midway station, affording a classic, postcard-perfect view of Rakaposhi (25,550 ft.), the "Crown Jewel of Hunza." Entering Hunza on foot is appropriate; dramatic, awesome country, best absorbed at a slow pace, is wedged into the deepest extremities of this gorge separating twin 25,000-ft. ranges. The long walk will give you time to practice Burushaski and to review your notes on the area.

Four tribes live in Hunza; each is originally said to have come from a different region: Kurukutz from Persia, Barataling from Russia, Broung from Kashmir, and Dramatin from Tatary. The famous

"Hunza water" is locally called *mel*: it is a grape wine that can be superb when well made. *Arak*, from the ubiquitous tall mulberry trees, is crystal clear, potent firewater, but rarely made now. Hunzakuts are proud of their heritage, friendly in a taciturn way, and quite individualistic: reminiscent of down-east New Englanders. Before grains and other foods could be brought in, over the Jeep road, Hunza was a food-poor valley, lacking in flat, irrigable surfaces for cropland. Before the spring wheat or barley harvest, it was not unusual for the last of the apricots to give out.

The first village in Hunza proper is Mauin, which is fed by a large nearby nala and lies across the valley from Nilt, where the decisive battle with the British took place in 1891. A bridge carries the KKH to the Hunza side downriver, before you reach Hindi. Rakaposhi towers above you from this perspective; you are now east of the peak with several of its glaciers visible.

A Ridge View

Continuing up the valley, as you round the last ridge top below Aliabad you see the breadbasket of Hunza from its western end. Some of Hunza's numerous garnet mines lie above Murtizabad, although not visible from here, and the vista from the ridge is spectacular.

The five-mile-long fertile area contains 10 or more villages among multi-terraced fields: this is the center of the state. The crops grown here, as in all areas of the Hindu Kush and Karakoram, are made possible by irrigation. In this small section of the valley in particular, the amount of irrigated land is very extensive. The canal (*gotsil*) that provides water to the fields of Aliabad emanates from the Ultar Nala above Baltit, 5 mi. farther on, and crosses intact beneath numerous intermittent streams along the way. The massive amount of labor involved in keeping the canals in repair is shared by all the men equally, and fines are levied on those who do not work. Tempers can flare over water allocation in April and May, when water needed for the growing crops is low.

Before the KKH was built, the Mir, Hunza's former ruler, operated a rest house in Aliabad where incoming visitors were greeted and fed. On arrival by foot in 1974, my brother Ken and I were taken to the property by a young lad and offered delicious apricots (*gzru*). The golden fruit was lying ungathered on the ground and, as we ate, we were told that good luck will befall anyone hit by a falling apricot, according to Hunza lore. Indeed, fresh apricots, unlike most fresh fruit, can be eaten by most people in alarming quantity without dire effects. Hunzakuts believe that for apricots to be digested properly, the seeds (*hanee*) must be eaten after the fruit. Of the more than 20 cultivated varieties of apricots, only 2 types do not have fine-quality, nut-like seeds. During and following apricot season, from Chitral to Baltistan small piles of broken apricot shells lie next to flat rocks upon which the shells are cracked.

Once east of the Hussainabad Nala, you can walk along any of several pathways leading to Baltit, Karimabad, or Ganesh (situated next to the KKH), the three villages on the right bank of the Ultar Nala. These pathways, usually accompanying canals, make excellent routes for day hikes when you are ensconced in the Baltit area. From these paths, you have dramatic views of Rakaposhi, which is seen less foreshortened than at Hindi. From along the upper canals west of Baltit, you can see the lower Hispar Nala, which leads to the capital village of Nagir. Practice your Burushaski; people will enjoy it and you may be asked in for tea.

Baltit

At this large village you will have an estimable view of the fertile basin. Behind the town is a nearly perpendicular ravine, the Ultar Nala, here composed of crumbling conglomerate. Baltit was once a seat of authority, and its 500-year-old castle, which formerly housed the last Mir and his ancestors before him, dominates the town. The old castle lies forbiddingly close to the maw of the steep Ultar Nala. The castle should definitely be viewed—ask for the chowkidar, who will unlock it and show you around for a small fee. The building shows Turkestani influence. Inside, you will see a small collection of fading photographs of former Asian and European monarchs. The rooftop views are unparalleled, and the roof itself is recognizable from old pictures as the site of the Mir's daily court. This castle and a nearby, recently constructed hotel (much out of proportion to all other structures) are the most visible buildings from below Aliabad, where Baltit first is glimpsed. An early Mir chose the castle site well; even today only a white memorial to Queen Victoria that is an hour's scramble above Baltit on the west cliff toward Ultar has a more spectacular position.

Musical accompaniment at a polo game.

In each of the remote valleys, people speak more than one language out of necessity. Hunza is no exception. There, many will know Urdu, and some few will speak good English learned in school. Whatever tongue you use, if you speak a language that is common Hunzakuts will visit with you, unless they have too much work at hand: midsummer will find them hard at work before sun-up, to avoid the midday heat.

Across the Ultar Nala from Baltit is the town of Altit, with its castle built by craftsmen from Skardu centuries ago and, like Baltit's, in a highly precarious setting. The castle appears to be directly over the angry, roiling Hunza River, some thousand feet down. Below, a rope bridge used to cross the river but has been replaced by a newer, Chinese-built bridge capable of supporting vastly heavier loads. The Altit castle has a tower similar to the fortresses of Swat, Dir, and Chitral. At this castle, the Mir would live for several days each spring during Bo Pho, the seed-sowing festival; his "Sunday bungalow" is amidst an orchard garden. In ancient times, the northern boundary of Hunza did not extend beyond Altit, but that was before Hunza gained power and Guhjal, as the upper valley has always been called, came to be part of Hunza State.

Ultar

People in the Baltit, Karimabad, and Haiderabad area like to extoll the healthful qualities of the water they drink from the Ultar Nala. In a proportion greater than in any other stream in the valley, the glacial water issuing from above Baltit carries brightly reflecting flakes, probably mica, that give the liquid a glittering life of its own even as it slips by in an irrigation canal miles away from the steep Ultar Nala. Great nutritive value it has, locals agree. Hunzakuts will also admit that most of the water they take from the nala to drink has been collected in the early morning when the mineral content of the water is at its lowest, or that they let the water settle for hours before drinking it.

The Ultar Nala is a fine example of the kind of ravine often found in the Karakoram, with a few giant axe slices in perpendicular walls, beyond which a severely cold stream thrashes downward, freshly released from its glacial source. From Baltit you can see the narrow Ultar gorge and Bubelimating ("Bubela's Peak"), a granite pinnacle (rounded, 24,700-ft. Ultar Peak is beyond), but the gorge has more that cannot be seen from the valley floor.

Walking into the Ultar Nala makes a fine two-day outing. The trail begins in Baltit at a notch a hundred yards west of the castle. Take cigarettes, tea, and sugar (in addition to your own wheat flour) that can be used to bargain for the milk products of the shepherds. The rich dairy foods that come from those pastures include milk (*mamu*), buttermilk (*dilta*), butter (*maska maltash*), and a white cheese called *broose*. The herdsmen have both busy and relaxed times. If you are interested in how the milk products are made, you can learn a great deal about age-old customs hereabouts by taking a day to observe the men as they make butter and go about their other chores.

The holding pens and stone huts that the men use for their sheep and goats are several hours' vertical walk away from town. Hidden pastures extend to levels well above these shelters. To reach them, climb any of several paths that angle south, back towards Hunza Valley. Wild flowers in vivid color combinations grow beginning near the level of the highest grazing animals. And if you reach the ridge line called Haon you can see the entire crescent of green within Hunza and Nagir and four glacial icefalls on Rakaposhi. The vistas beyond of Nagir's long valley glaciers and the Karakoram Range are spectacular. Sufficient time should be allotted for savoring this rare view. A third day in the Ultar Nala may be passed poking around the upper pastures near the noisy Ultar icefall directly down from the high peaks above Ultar Nala.

Nagir

Of the Pakistani states that were once semiautonomous, Chitral, Swat, and Hunza are most often referred to, but Nagir, a small state in its own right within the Hunza Valley, is equally magnificent. Rakaposhi, Dumani (23,600 ft.), and the 38-mile Hispar Glacier (third longest outside the polar caps) are within the confines of Nagir.

The breadbasket of Nagir is directly across the Hunza River from Hunza's fertile land between Aliabad and Baltit. Nagir's main valley is the Hispar Nala, which empties into the Hunza River opposite Baltit and Karimabad. To reach the Hispar Nala you can cross the Hunza River on a bridge just downriver from Hussainabad and then walk or Jeep up the road. Alternatively, you can take the large KKH bridge at Ganesh (just below Karimabad) and walk or Jeep directly up the parched right bank of the lower Hispar Nala to a bridge connecting with Nagir's main Jeep road that starts near the Hussainabad bridge. Soon you reach the town of Nagir with its unused polo field next to tall poplars. Just beyond, the raging waters of the Hispar River branch off to the east. Continue along the Jeep road among meadows that lie between a steep ridge and a lateral moraine.

Not far beyond the end of the Jeep road is a small rest house at Hoper (also called Holshal), 3 mi. from Nagir town. Two hundred yards before reaching the Hoper rest house, you can walk over the crest of the long lateral moraine you have been following and take a switchback trail farther down to the Bualtar Glacier. Cross the glacier on a route taken by locals that is marked poorly by sporadic cairns. On the far side, ascend a path that leads above the left side of the Barpu Glacier in order to reach the summer settlements of Hapa Kund, Hamdar, and Miar. Here you walk well above the white Barpu Glacier through Nagir's upper pastures, toward towering ice summits east of Rakaposhi. The end of the road near the Hoper rest house is a day's walk from the bridge near Hussainabad. Allow two to four days to explore the upper pastures and hills beyond the road.

Gulmit to Pasu and Shimshal

The Hunza Valley beyond the Baltit-Karimabad area may be restricted. If so, the areas covered in the remaining sections will be closed to you. Check at the TIC in Rawalpindi or Gilgit before getting your hopes up for visiting this dry but exceptionally grand area.

Up-valley from Baltit and Nagir, the Hunza River flows in an arid, V-shaped gorge that is sparsely populated. The riverbed curves to the north, where it has cut through the Karakoram Range. As you proceed the 18 mi. along the KKH from the Ganesh Bridge below Karimabad to the village of Gulmit, you enter the region called Guhjal. Continuing northward through Guhjal, you will see increasing numbers of the friendly Wakhi, people who have emigrated from the Wakhan area.

Several times in recent history, mud and rock slides thundering out of side valleys have blocked the main Hunza Valley in the area of Shishkot Nala, not far south of Gulmit. The KKH has twice been closed by this glacial muck. In 1974, a large mudslide from the Shishkot Nala created a 7-mi.-long lake and entirely covered over a newly built bridge, marooning Gulmit. At one time Gulmit, within a lushly irrigated acreage of orchards and fields, was the summer residence of the Mir. The town has a rest house. The cook once employed there named Ayub is a gem; find Ayub and visit with him, for he is a storehouse of information about any walking excursions you may have in mind.

You can reach the Gulmit Glacier by following the stock trail behind town that leads beyond the cultivated fields. The noisily active glacier descends from an ice-covered 24,000-ft. peak like its larger sibling the Ghulkin Glacier, situated beyond a serrated ridge to the north. Travelers are likely to be struck with a frigid rush of air while passing by the Ghulkin Glacier, 2 mi. north of Gulmit, and the larger Pasu Glacier, 3 mi. farther. Both glaciers are hidden from the road by a moraine. Beyond Gulmit and on either side of Pasu town the valley widens considerably and dramatically.

To the north of the Pasu plain, a ridge comprising scores of pinnacles dominates the view. Its highest point is more than 20,000 ft. and has the name Karun Pir. Unseen from the Pasu town itself is the Shimshal River, entering the main valley at the southern base of the Karun Pir ridge. The Shimshal Valley is the epitome of remote, inhabited areas in the Karakoram: the snow lasts long on the northern slopes, and avalanches occur well into spring. Yet after the snow melts the river rises, owing to the summer melting of the glacier, so the season for trekking is short. The best time is fall.

The November 1975 *National Geographic* contains an article about Hunza by Sabrina and Roland Michaud. In their account of a visit to Shimshal, they tell of Mir Mohammed Jamal Khan saying, "If you want to find our traditions alive, you must travel to more difficult valleys, like Chapursan, or Shimshal." A walk up the Shimshal Valley is not a task to be undertaken lightly: from Pasu town to the village of Shimshal is 40 mi., and the trail is not an easy one. The Shimshal Sheet

(NJ43-15) of the U502 Series is the only sheet for the area from Chitral to Bhutan that has a 1,000-ft. contour interval. Disteghil Sar ("Sheep-fold in the Hills"), the tallest mountain in Hunza at 25,868 ft., is visible from the Shimshal Valley.

Beyond the Batura

The Batura Glacier pushes onto the west bank of the Hunza River beyond Pasu. You can visit summer pastures along both banks of the glacier there, but take a local guide if you go beyond the first few stages. Beyond the talus-covered mouth of the mighty Batura, where the Hunza River squeezes around the western extremity of Karun Pir, the valley narrows again.

Khaibar, a village of 20 Wakhi- and 20 Burushaski-speaking homes, is high on an isolated alluvial fan near the western tip of the Karun Pir ridge. Unlike the villages in most of Pakistan's far-northern areas, Hunza's villages are situated on fans that extend up from the turbid Hunza River, often as much as 700 ft. Khaibar follows the pattern. If you were to climb 5,000 ft. up the Khaibar Nala, you would find that it levels off for several miles above the 13,500-ft. mark. Here you'll have excellent perspectives on Karun Pir and, at the head of the valley, you may glimpse segments of the 30-mi. Batura. The Khaibar Nala pasturing area is used by some villagers, although many local people take their stock to the vast Khunjerab and Ghujerab pastures.

The road continues through a compelling narrow gorge, crosses to the village of Gallapan, and reaches Murkhun 6 mi. from Khaibar. A high trail to Shimshal climbs up the north side of the Karun Pir ridge from the wide nala behind Murkhun. Three miles up-valley from Murkhun is the village of Gircha with a large spring of pure water. From Gircha to Sost village, the valley widens dramatically and you have an increasingly grand view of the northern slopes of the Karakoram.

The Upper Nalas

Like a skewed umbrella frame, the Hunza River north of Sost divides into numerous *nalas*, several nearly parallel, that vary in length from 15 to 60 miles. The first to break away, and, with the Khunjerab, one of the two longest, is the wide Chapursan Valley. It leads ultimately to the tough, glaciated Chillinji Pass (17,000 ft.) above the Karambar River in the Ishkuman Valley, to the west. The Chapursan Valley also was sometimes entered via the Kerman Pass from the west branch of the Kilik Nala, west of the border post called Kalam Darchi. As in Nepal's Mustang Valley, much of the Chapursan region's splendor—particularly in its upper reaches—is derived from the various shades of color in the surrounding hills. Kampire Dior Peak, tall and black, rises north of the valley, and the Yashkuk Yaz Glacier descends from the south. Farther up-valley lies Baba Ghundi Ziarat, the shrine of Baba Ghundi, an important Shiite pilgrimage site.

The Kilik (or Misgar) and Khunjerab nalas join to form the Hunza River 4 mi. north of its junction with the Chapursan Valley. First the

Kilik: 6 mi. beyond the mouth of the Kilik Nala, the town of Misgar is a green oasis astride a side nala on a plain extending well above the valley floor. It is a grand, heroic setting, across from a similar but unwatered plain. During British rule, Misgar was the last outpost of civilization. Once it even had a telegraph wire stretching back to Gilgit. Prior to that, the strategic and well-irrigated town had been fought over by the Kirghiz from the north and the Hunzakuts. Four miles beyond Misgar is Kalam Darchi, the former border fortress and customs post, astride a major stream junction. The western tributary leads to the Kerman Pass trail. Still farther up this western tributary is the 19,000-ft. Delhi Sang Pass, which was crossed into Hunza from the Wakhan Corridor of Afghanistan by Jean and Franc Shor in 1950 as they retraced part of Marco Polo's route across Asia.

Up the Kilik Nala from Kalam Darchi lie the few summer shelters called Murkushi (a Wakhi word for "much rain"), at the junction of the Kilik and Mintika nalas. Each of these nalas leads to a pass of the same name, and each pass has a long, flat top, like the Khunjerab Pass. The Kilik Pass is some 150 ft. higher than the 15,450-ft. Mintika (which means "a thousand sheep"). In former times, the easier-to-ascend Kilik was used more often than the Mintika. The Kilik route provided a single high point separating Kashgar (and China) from Gilgit, unlike the series of five severe passes north of Leh in Ladakh that were all crossed in caravan days. The Kilik Pass is the extreme northerly point of the Indian subcontinent.

The second of the nalas forming the Hunza River is the larger Khunjerab. From its junction with the Kilik, the Khunjerab Pass (15,600 ft.), the present route for commerce, is 50 mi. eastward along the KKH. The rolling Khunjerab and Ghujerab uplands are used to feed vast numbers of sheep, goats, cattle, and yaks; there in the high meadows, Wakhi graze the animals they drive up-valley each year. Formerly, the Mir used vast tracts in these upper nalas for his personal herds. Shimshalis take the direct northern route to the rolling 13,000- to 16,000-ft. grasslands that resemble the Pamir to the north more than they do the rest of the Karakoram.

Balti men making butter inside inflated skins at 13,500 feet.

6
Baltistan

This region of Baltistan contains a larger number of clus-
tered peaks over 24,000 feet than any other area, even in
the Himalayas. Sixty of them are over 22,000. . . . The
Karakorams rather than the Pamirs, to which the title is
usually applied, are the Roof the the World.

Nigel Nicolson, 1975

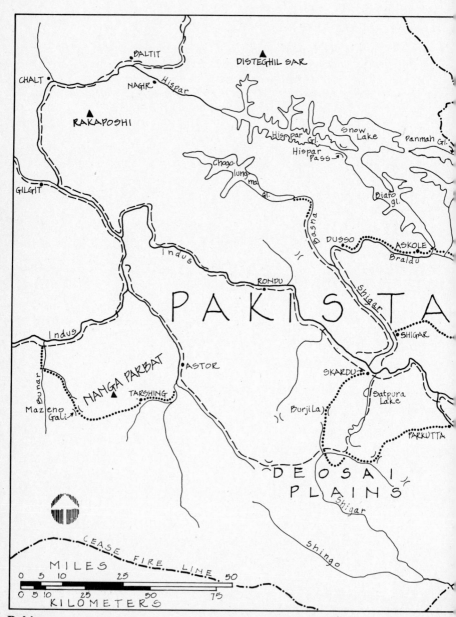

Baltistan

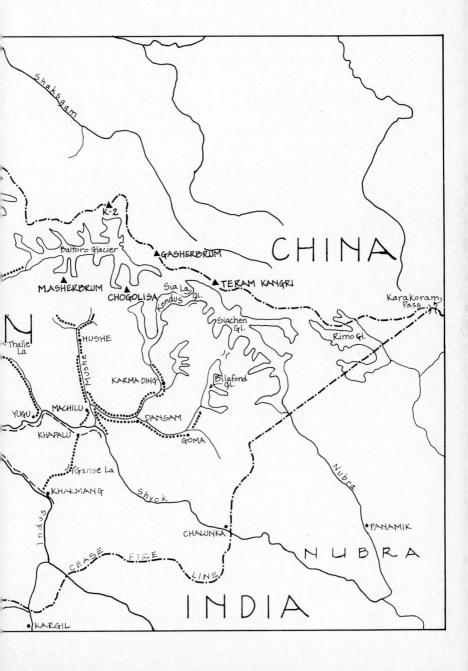

Glaciers and Peaked Caps

From the inaccessible reaches of Karun Pir in Hunza to the spiked pinnacles of K-6 above the Kondus Glacier and beyond, the towering spires of the Karakoram Range are unique in the Himalayan system: these mountains and glaciers lie in a solid mass for 50 mi. north to south. The vast majority of this tangle of incisor-shaped peaks and curving glaciers lie within the area traditionally called Baltistan, now part of what Pakistan has designated its Northern Areas. Closed to commerce south along the Indus River by massive gorges and with no reasonable access to Kashgar in Sinkiang through the Karakoram mass, Baltistan long remained something of a cul-de-sac within the greater region crossed by trade routes to China. Its deeper valleys produced apricots that were dried and then carried south on the growers' backs to be traded in the bazaars of Kargil and Leh, but the trade was small in volume, and only subsistent.

Little known, little studied, Baltistan is a land of endings and beginnings. Here the Tibetan culture has reached its westernmost point, although in Baltistan Islam has replaced Buddhism for more than 500 years. The Balti language bears the same kind of resemblance to modern-day Tibetan that Chaucer's language does to contemporary English. The folds of homespun worn by all and the page-boy hair-cuts of the men in the upper valleys provide another medieval metaphor. The people are of both Caucasian and Mongolian stock, and among the various isolated valleys that Baltistan comprises, people of some highly dissimilar ethnic strains reside in adjoining houses—a mixture of Islamic, Tibeto-speaking people living in villages that edge on the world's most impenetrable mountain mass.

Uncertain historical evidence indicates that the Baltis once were animists, and that the animism in this land gave way to shamanism, then the Bon Po religion prior to the people's conversion to Buddhism sometime between the 4th and 7th centuries. Buddhist practice as taught by Padma Sambhava converted Baltis and Ladakhis before penetrating eastward into Tibet proper. But the Baltis embraced Shiite Islam in the 15th century and have adhered to the Koran ever since. Politically Baltistan was divided into eight usually-squabbling princi-palities owing greater or lesser fealty to the Raja of Skardu. The central marketplace of Baltistan has always been Skardu, with its tenuous southern approaches from the Deosai Plains and the upper Indus Valley. In 1835, G. T. Vigne was only the second Westerner to reach Skardu. He crossed the rolling Deosai Plateau with Ahmed Shah, Baltistan's ruler, and later wrote of the view from the edge of the Deosai:

> I . . . gazed downwards from a height of six or seven thousand feet upon the sandy plains and green orchards of the valley of the Indus at Skardu, with a sense of mingled pride and pleasure, of which no one but a traveler can form a just conception.

Just five years later the forces of Ahmed Shah capitulated to the Dogra army of Kashmir, ending Baltistan's centuries of independence. From that time until the revolt of 1947, when Pakistan assumed control, the area was ruled by Kashmir. Nevertheless, because its remoteness and lack of prosperity made internal control of Baltistan less of a priority than it might otherwise have been, the local rulers retained much of their authority and respect, the latter remaining to this day.

Following Skardu in traditional economic importance were the regions of Khapalu in the Shyok Valley, Shigar (which includes the Basna and the Braldu river valleys) and Rondu, the "District of Defiles" along the Indus gorge northwest of Skardu. Of lesser importance were the areas called Kiris, on the Shyok River, and the three fortress principalities upriver on the Indus called Parkutta. Tolti, and Kharmang (or Khartaksho). Astor, at the base of the eastern ridges of Nanga Parbat, has at times been considered with Baltistan.

The northern boundary of Baltistan is the trackless Karakoram. Baltistan's eastern border is the upper Saltoro Valley. Chalunka is the southernmost settlement along the Shyok River in what is traditionally Baltistan. At one time a cairn of rocks near the town marked Baltistan's actual border with the Nubra region in Ladakh. The southern and western limits of Baltistan usually have been considered to lie within the wide Deosai Plains, although even today some Baltis live in the upper Suru Valley, south of Kargil in Ladakh.

The routes in this chapter begin with those at Skardu and environs, then those through the nearby Deosai Plains, some 6,500 ft. higher. After a description of a typical glacier, we head for Baltistan's glaciated Shigar, Hushe, and Saltoro Valleys.

Skardu

Barring fickle weather conditions, flights from Rawalpindi arrive in Skardu daily. The Skardu airport lies eight sandy miles west of the town's ever-lengthening bazaar; riding slowly from the airport into town may give you time to adjust to the majestic landscape into which you have flown. Your head swivels, eyeing strata of violet, red, grey, ochre, and brown among the 10,000-ft. hills surrounding the 20-mi. sandy plain. On the way, you will be approaching the 2-mi.-long, 1,000-ft. high rock that is a prominent landmark, lying just north of town by a bend in the meandering Indus. You can also reach Skardu by road from Gilgit along the Indus Valley or, rarely, by way of Astor and the Deosai Plains.

The Naya Bazaar, on the westernmost end of Skardu, begins just east of a small school. On the north side of Naya Bazaar's lone street there is a hotel run by Hunzakuts. A barber shop with the only nearby hot-shower facilities is across the street. Eastward along the bazaar, a small trafic island has a memorial statue. North from this intersection, you reach a low-walled *ziarat* (shrine); within are multicolored strips of cloth left by pilgrims. A turn to the south leads you to the old bazaar. Straight ahead on the south side of the street is the K-2 Shop (number 207) run by Ghulam Rasul. Not only is this an excellent, unexpected island of trekking and expedition equipment, but Ghulam is well informed on local contacts in all areas of Baltistan. He formerly oversaw recruitment of expedition porters and, when a sirdar himself, was the best in the region.

Naya Bazaar extends eastward as far as a 15th-century aqueduct, which still works. The aqueduct's base consists of large granite blocks—how these stones were moved to their present position is anyone's guess. East of the aqueduct are the Skardu polo ground and the Askandria Fort, the latter built by Zowar Singh's Dogra forces following their victory over Ahmed Shah in 1840.

Hotel space in Skardu is limited, but as tourists begin to discover this unique land, the usual law of demand will surely be satisfied. The tourist officer at the TIC, situated toward the easterly end of the bazaar a kilometer east of the polo ground, can be of assistance in locating lodging and can help with any other kinds of questions you may have. The PTDC operates a motel at the TIC. Before you contact porter prospects, get a range of opinions on whom to consider. In addition to asking Ghulam Rasul and the tourist officer, ask the local representative of Waljis Travel, who will have information and perhaps also last-minute supplies.

The bazaar in Skardu is not as extensive as Gilgit's, but with the KKH completed and a feeder road up the Indus now open, the bazaar will become more reliably stocked. Basic food necessities are available, although periodic shortages of sugar, milk powder, and the tinned butter that is shipped in have occurred. The local butter is far superior, but also not always sold.

Short Walks from Skardu

From Skardu there are several interesting walking excursions, and they can vary in length as time and energies allow. A stroll around the eastern end of the Skardu rock will take you to the nearby village of Narsok, where you will find a large, pure spring flowing from the base of the monolith. To reach Narsok, walk to the far end of the Skardu polo field and pick up a trail that skirts the rock slopes beneath the fortress. It would be difficult not to feel awe here, as the mighty Indus snakes along below among the silvery white sands. The Indus separates the Karakoram Range on the north from the Himalayan Range to the south, although both ranges are actually part of the same mountain system. This river originates north of Mt. Kailas in Tibet and flows through the west Tibetan plains of Chang Tang before reaching Baltistan. Downriver the braided Indus lazes, before reaching the gorges of Rondu that will drop it to the 4,700-ft. level and its great swing south (near the Gilgit River confluence).

Beckoning you, close to town, is the Askandria Fort. A path follows a convenient wide ledge to its entrance. Once a symbol of Kashmiri rule, the fortress today stands abandoned, its rifle slits guarding only the turgid Indus and occasional grazing sheep.

A climb to the top of the Skardu rock may be undertaken, but this walk is decidedly not for the timid. In 1903 the veteran Karakoram explorer Fanny Bullock Workman reached the top with a porter, but her previously twisted ankle acted up, and 13 scorching hours elapsed before she could descend. To climb the rock, pass the school on the western end of Naya Bazaar and follow a path that diverges from the airport road to the right, paralleling the talus slopes at the base of the rock. Continue past the first slopes to a farther, larger slope that is lighter in hue, with a visible stock trail ascending it. You must keep going up the talus and figure out the difficult route to the left as you approach the top. Several zigzags along exposed ledges require the use of both hands. In the 1830s Ahmed Shah built a well-provisioned fortress on the uppermost knoll, but any easy access route has long since disappeared. Now only the occasional climber or shepherd with his stock will reach the rolling ground above the sheer rock faces. At the top you will see one last wall of Ahmed Shah's demolished fortress here and an intoxicating array of valley vistas. To the north the Shigar Valley debouches into the Indus. Towering above the cultivated land at Skardu, you gain a perspective on the degree to which these lower valleys are the exception to the otherwise extremely high elevations of the Karakoram.

Walking south from Skardu up its alluvial fan takes you to the crystalline Satpura Lake some 4 mi. from town. Follow the aqueduct and its feeder channel above to the Jeep road; it goes directly to the lake, which is well stocked with trout. Reservations for a stay at the lakeside PTDC Motel may be made in Skardu at the TIC. About 1½ mi. south of Skardu on the west bank of the Satpura Nala is a tall rock with a flat, beige-colored northern face upon which was carved, circa 900 A.D., a meditating Buddha framed by Bodhisattvas.

The Deosai Plains and Astor

In front of us lay the Deosai, an absolutely treeless wilderness of comparatively level country framed by minor peaks. It gives a unique impression of desolation. I have never seen its equal in this respect elsewhere. Yet the march was very pleasant with many flowers and streams.

Aleister Crowley, 1929

Besides commenting on the Deosai Plains' apparent desolation, Crowley also said "it has a devilish reputation for inhospitality," and indeed some years it has been snow-covered for nine months of the twelve. Heavy frost near streams may be expected even during summer nights. The Deosai is also noted for sporadic windstorms that would test the stoutest modern tent. Undeniably, though, the Deosai, rarely seen by Westerners, is one of those places with a magic of its own. Nowhere

lower than 13,000 ft., the rolling grasslands support no trees or shrub-
bery, and the ruling denizens are scattered colonies of vocal, Brob-
dingnagian marmots. Extending to some 40 by 50 mi., surrounded by
snow-capped peaks, the Deosai has ultra-pure air that plays tricks on
the eyes: clouds appear just beyond reach, and hills that seem nearby
retreat before the approaching walker. Shunned by most, the plains'
sole human presence today consists of Gujar herders in the summer.

Balti herdsmen from the uppermost pastures.

Moving daily with their sheep, goats, and cattle, the Gujars have some-how solved the problems raised by the lack of wood and occasional windstorms.

A road passable by Jeep from Gilgit extends east from the Astor Valley up the Das Kirim Valley (or Das Kirim *Gah*) and over the 13,997-ft. Chachor Pass onto the Deosai Plains. Continuing in a north-easterly direction, the road crosses Ali Malik Pass at 13,390 ft. and descends the Satpura Valley to Skardu, 155 mi. from Gilgit.

Starting from Skardu, you can take a five- to six-day circle trek that will give you an excellent panorama of the central Karakoram (in-cluding K-2) and allow some walking on the Deosai Plains. The route follows an unnamed valley to the west of the Satpura Nala, debouches onto the plains and circles back, following the little-used Jeep road from Astor and Gilgit. This walking route crosses the spectacular 15,700-ft. Burji Pass (Burji *La*) and is best undertaken after you have already done some walking in the region or at the very least with care-ful regard for the 8,000-ft. rise from Skardu up to the Deosai. In 1912, Ernest Neve wrote of the Burji La that "The view from here looking northward is one of the most magnificent in the whole of the Hima-layas." Personal observation confirms that the great peaks along and at the head of the Baltoro Glacier are visible on a clear day from the pass. They are astounding even 50 to 80 mi. away.

To reach the Burji La from Skardu will take at least two days. The location of the pass may be difficult to determine on the northern side, the direction from which you will probably approach it, and the up-permost reaches of the trail are virtually nonexistent from infrequent use. Look for the true low point above a permanent snowbank toward the Satpura (eastern) side of the bowl at the head of the valley. Those who don't mind melting snow for water may succumb to the great temptation to camp at the pass in order to seek an elevated viewing spot on the ridge to the east. Gypsy Davy, who did just that in 1924, said:

> It was such an expanse of immensity as I have hardly imagined. . . . It seems you cannot talk in a matter-of-fact way in a place like that . . . the eastern down-sweeping horizon brought K^2 into the sun's rays several minutes before Nanga Parbat to the west got any light. I thought the Sierras were large, but here, where we could see three or four score miles north, south, east and west, and see only mountains, and most of them above twenty thousand feet, the Sierras seem like sand dunes . . . .

The Deosai side of the pass gives a first perspective on the rolling plains, their color ever changing with the light. The Pangri Range to the distant south ends in the west with unseen (from the pass itself) Nanga Parbat, the westernmost mountain among those identified geologi-cally as within the Himalaya. Below the pass to left and right are two lapis-blue lakes. The trail from the Burji La cuts back and forth down the pale-yellow south slope, passing the smaller of the two lakes, and merges with a larger valley from the west. Following the gently descending valley toward the open grasslands, you may be surprised to see trout (stocked by the British in the time of empire) darting in small dark pools. This valley lies just to the west of the Satpura Valley, down which the road to Skardu travels; it is the recommended return route.

If you want a more gradual ascent to the Burji La, you could reverse the route and walk up the Satpura Nala. To the south of and visible from both the Burji and Satpura approaches is a hill 800 ft. high, on top of which is a 5-ft. rock cairn. This unnamed hilltop in the northern Deosai commands another unique, clear panorama of both the Himalaya and Karakoram. Walk to this hill as the southern turning point on your circle. As you climb its gentle, grass-tufted slopes, 26,629-ft. Nanga Parbat—the "Naked Mountain"—will come into view west of you.

The Astor Valley, along the once-British-maintained trail from Kashmir to Gilgit, might be the quintessential valley of the Western Himalaya. It is usually reached by Jeep from Gilgit. Astor's dangerous lower gorge of talus slopes is offset up-valley by blissful green meadows beneath towering Nanga Parbat, eighth-tallest peak in the world. Accommodations at Ramah, the splendidly situated rest house 2,500 ft. above Astor village, may be made in Gilgit. So vast are the opportunities for exploring here, the extent of your scrambling on the great eastern ridges and wandering about the meadow at Ramah is limited only by your imagination.

Five miles up-valley from the fort at Astor village is the Das Kirim Valley. (The road up it leads to the Deosai.) Another 6 mi. farther up the main Astor Valley brings you to the town of Rampur on the river's left bank. From there, continue west up to the town of Tarshing, another level 6 mi. toward the vast mountain massif. At Tarshing ask for directions to Rupal and carry on west into that valley, the Rupal Gah, leading along the base of the nearly vertical southern slopes of Nanga Parbat. Several hours' walk will bring you to a point 3 mi. nearly straight down from the highest peak of Nanga Parbat.

The explorative may wish to prearrange food and hire a porter-guide in order to cross Nanga Parbat's difficult 17,000-ft. Mazeno Pass (Mazeno *Gali*), up-valley. Crossing the great southwest ridge of the mountain, this pass route leads to the Diamer Valley, hence to the Bunar Valley and the Indus River 14 mi. east of Chilas. In Chilas, buses are available to Gilgit. From Tarshing above Astor to Zangot in the Diamer Valley is 27 miles. Count on at least a week to reach the Indus from Tarshing.

Glaciers and Dragons

There are no tigers here, but there are ice-dragons which maul the valleys. This valley was mauled by one, not so long since . . . . He's asleep now, at the head of the Braldoh, shrunk to a mere thirty miles. And his helpers sleep up side nalas.

Gypsy Davy, 1926

Outside the polar ice caps, the world's largest system of glaciation occurs in the Karakoram. Nonmountaineers are just now beginning to view the phenomenal mountain formations that accompany these glaciers. Many more trekkers could do this on their own if they choose an accessible glacier and carry sufficient food. Glaciers, like living organisms, have various parts and exhibit predictable curves, slopes, and surfaces along different extremities. And people, like the seven blind men who felt different parts of an elephant in the old parable, have seen differing views of glaciated terrain and have perhaps reached incomplete notions of what it can be.

In some valleys along the Karakoram range, glaciers extend as long as 45 mi., terminating at elevations between 10,500 ft. and 9,500 ft. Initially, as you walk toward a glacier and see the snout of grey ice and piles of randomly sized rocks lying about, your respect may be tempered with disgust at the messy intrusion. But find the headwaters of the river you have been following at the glacier's snout or mouth. There, the thundering accumulation of glacial waters emanates from beneath an ice cavern at a cataclysmic power spot.

You may have to load yourself heavily to start up your chosen glacier. Don't leave before hiring a local who knows the route to carry some weight and cook the food. Engage someone in Skardu, or get names there of prospects in the valley where you will be trekking. Wages have become inflated in Baltistan because of the many recent mountaineering expeditions, but with a little patience and negotiation you can work out an agreeable rate, particularly if you are the only person in the vicinity offering wages at the time. Before leaving Skardu be certain to have enough food and fuel for the period you will be gone. Carefully check that your hiree has adequate protection for snow and ice. He will have a blanket and can use your parka at night, but does he have hat, gloves, socks, and dark glasses?

The Kondus Glacier, in the northern branch of the Saltoro Valley, is typical of all valley glaciers and is an excellent one to walk along owing to its relative accessibility. The Kondus can be reached in about four days' walk from the town of Khapalu in the Shyok Valley, through spectacular country, as described in the last section of this chapter. Beyond Karma Ding, the village farthest up the valley, several hours' walk along alluvial wastes, pastures, and alfalfa meadows brings you to the mouth of the glacier, at the 10,500-ft. level. Willow patches dot this place, called Gronjin; a little farther on the Kondus River makes its unrestrained entrance into the daylight.

A trail will follow one or both sides of most lower glaciers, often alternating between the glacier itself and adjacent slopes, for one or two days' walk. These paths are worn by local stock brought for varying periods of time to graze the intermittent, steep pastures near the glacier. Shikaris, hunters, also use the paths. The trails have stages (*pie-ē* in Balti), each of which is considered a day's journey. A stage may be somewhat shorter in distance than you may be inclined to walk in a day, but be agreeable with your porter about stopping, for there may not be another suitable place to camp for quite a distance. As with sailing for the first time, you quickly realize that on the moraine's rocky, wave-like surface you must adapt to a new, tentative way of walking. In each glacier's lower "ablation zone," it is melting, which is to say that each step may or may not approximate stepping on a wet banana peel.

Chilimski Pinnacle on the Kondus Glacier, Baltistan.

The rocky skin of the glacier is often quite thin, with slippery ice beneath, and you are like a ship traveling up and down along a frozen, rough sea.

Byameparot, the first-stage campground, has a leaky but splendid wind shelter of gnarled cedar trunks with a thick needle floor. The area has views of K-6, K-7, Chogolisa (25,110 ft.), and of the Kaberi Glacier leading toward Chogolisa. This is the farthest that the villagers take their stock. The second stage on the Kondus leads to Rahout Chen, the last named camp, of which the initial view is disarmingly foreshortened. This is the most strenuous part of the glacier walk, but you are rewarded by a continually changing display of unnamed pinnacles, spires, and the subsidiary glaciers—the dragon's wings. Glacial noises range from deep moans and shudders to the ping of a water drop or pebble into a clear pool. Like the ship at sea or the raft in the river, you are on for the ride, and the glacier has you in its grip.

Rahout Chen is a flat, sandy area with tarns (small, steep-sided mountain pools) at 14,000 ft., wedged between the Kondus and a glacier icefall from Sherpi Kangri (23,960 ft.). At this camp, the last green areas above the ice flow begin to fade, and all higher camps will be on the glacier itself. The medial moraines along the glacier's length become more nearly level and easily walkable, while shark-toothed seracs, glacial mushrooms (oval rocks supported by squat columns of ice), and other oddities abound. Unlike most long Karakoram glaciers, which are fairly straight in direction, the Kondus makes three grand bends in its down-valley course. Most of the side glaciers above Rahout Chen meld into the Kondus, which consists of belts of ice alternating with varyingly hued medial moraines that continue for mile on mile. The upper Kondus basin is the glacier's upper snow catchment area; and at the head of the Kondus the narrow, crevassed Sia La (the "Rose Pass," at 18,200 ft.) leads onto the mighty Siachen, longest of the Karakoram glaciers.

Near the 17,000-ft. level on the Kondus, you reach the limit beyond which trekkers should not continue. This limit is not imposed by altitude but by the presence of crevasses. If you intend to step off the rocky medial moraine of an upper glacier, you must have great respect for all crevasses and be able to recognize or find them when they are bridged by unmelted snow. When there is even the slightest question about the surface, you must probe ahead of you forcefully with a long pole. Don't fail to rope up and carry an ice axe. In the cool of the morning, you may cross hidden, snow-covered crevasses unknowingly. Later in the day, the snow layer will be thinner and the same step could land you several hundred feet down in a terrible blackness. The dragon's skin may be deadly. Be forewarned.

The Shigar Valley and the Baltoro Glacier

The Shigar Valley is the watershed for the Chogo Lungma, Biafo, Panmah, and Baltoro glaciers. Along the latter glacier alone cluster 10 of the world's 30 tallest peaks. The wonders to be seen along the Baltoro are described in superlatives by all who have been there. That route, however, is the sweetest fruit on the farthest branches, available to only the most resolute. If you are planning a trek up one of these glaciated valleys, be certain to stock up on all essentials in Skardu. This is not the place to get carried away at the last moment and just start walking, as may conceivably be done in the lusher central and eastern Himalaya. Eric Shipton, a titan of Himalayan exploration, once wrote: "Bill [Tilman] and I used to boast that we could organize a Himalayan expedition in half an hour on the back of an envelope. For my first Karakoram venture, with . . . the immense distances involved, the job was rather more exacting."

To reach the uncharacteristically (for Baltistan) wide and lush lower Shigar Valley north of Skardu, arrange for transport in Skardu with a Jeep driver or a shopkeeper who employs drivers. After leaving Skardu you will cross to the right bank of the Indus, all the while skimming the white sand that is a local landmark. Once Shigar town was the seat of a strong raja. Polo and archery were played, and the fortress was a true seat of power. Before the 1949 war, the Shigar Valley's dried fruits and delectable apricot nuts had a ready market in the bustling Leh Bazaar, but now the border is sealed, and expeditions motor through Shigar town without stopping.

The nala watering the verdant Shigar orchards and fields is called the Bauma Stream (Bauma *Lungma*). That side valley leads from Shigar town to Bauma village in 7 mi., and there the river divides. The southern fork has a trail leading to the high but unglaciated Thalle La and, over it, to a trail down the rarely visited Thalle Valley to the Shyok River. Aside from various routes onto the Deosai, the Thalle La is one of the few unglaciated high passes in Baltistan connecting separate river valleys. This trek from Shigar leaves right from town; you should expect to spend four to six days between Shigar and the Shyok. If this dry but majestic country and its friendly people appeal to you, continue on toward Khapalu from the confluence of the Thalle Valley with the Shyok. That route is noted in the next section.

Four miles up-valley from Shigar town is the small village of Skoro on the Skoro Lungma. At the head of the Skoro Valley is a pass that has suffered the fate of several others in the region over the past 150 years. Once traversable, these passes are now strictly technical ascents, owing to an overall melting trend. Where snow once permanently blanketed a pass, it has melted to reveal a sheer wall; or where a snow bridge crossed a bergschrund,* no bridge now exists, and only the mountaineer may cross. This is the case not only with the Skoro La, but with the Nushik La between Arandu village and the Hispar Glacier and the "Old" and "New" Mustagh passes north of the Baltoro Glacier that may once have been used to reach Turkestan.

The Shigar Valley is formed by the confluence of the Braldu and Basna valleys 17 mi. up-valley from Skoro village. The westerly Basna

---

*Bergschrund: a crevasse between the edge of a glacier and the rock alongside.

leads in 20 mi. to Arandu town, near the mouth of the Chogo Lungma Glacier. To reach Arandu, and the Chogo Lungma, take a road that crosses the Indus west of Skardu at Katchura Lake and continues up the west bank of the Shigar Valley.

Fifty-two miles from Skardu the main Jeep road beyond Shigar village ends at the hamlet of Dusso in the Braldu Valley, seven miles beyond the Basna junction. Past Dusso, the foot trail skirts many ledges and is interrupted by numerous stream crossings. Many accounts have been written about this sometimes dicy trail and the Baltoro Glacier in the upper valley. For the best description of the Baltoro, read *In the Throne Room of the Mountain Gods*, by Galen Rowell. Keep in mind that the upper Braldu Valley beyond Askole village is open only to those who have previously obtained a permit in Islamabad. Owing to logistical difficulties and the inevitable complications involved in obtaining permits, people who expect to reach the upper Baltoro Glacier should make arrangements for going with an organized group.

The sheer rock faces and spectacular peaks along the Baltoro have been called by Fosco Mariani "the world's greatest museum of shape and form." Concordia (15,000 ft.), some 22 mi. from the glacier's mouth, is the remarkable junction where the upper Baltoro Glacier meets the Godwin-Austin Glacier descending from K-2 (28,253 ft.) to the north. To reach Concordia, you walk for five stages from the glacier's snout at Paiju along rugged moraine like that described in the preceding section. Views of the peaks change continually. As in the Khumbu area near Mt. Everest, you will be surprised to see that the tallest summits are not always the most spectacular. Consult Rowell's book for detailed information about and exceptional photography of this "sublime sanctuary of nature."

Khapalu and Hushe

Twenty-two miles east of Skardu, the Shyok River joins the Indus, effectively doubling the latter's capacity during most seasons of the year. The Shyok and its chief tributary, the Nubra River, drain the eastern Karakoram. The lower Shyok Valley comprised the territory of Khapalu's raja and was the largest principality within old Baltistan.

Your Jeep from Skardu to the large town of Khapalu leaves the white Skardu plain at its eastern end and follows a narrow, barren gorge. At the Shyok junction the Indus bends to the south, and you cross it over the Humayan Bridge. Upriver to the south along the Indus lie the old Balti fortress principalities of Parkutta, Tolti, and Kharmang. Heading between Kharmang and Khapalu, you can take a rugged but scenic three-day trek over the Ganse La (16,500 ft.). This high pass, crossed by Tom Longstaff and Arthur Neve in 1908, has no wood for fuel on its approaches but offers marvelous views of Masherbrum (25,660 ft.) and the Saltoro peaks. Continuing east along the Shyok from the Humayan Bridge, your Jeep will traverse the 16-mi.-long former state of Kiris. Eighteen miles from the Shyok's mouth, just beyond Kiris, is the village of Yugu. If you cross a foot bridge at Yugu and continue 4 mi. upriver along the northern riverbank, you will reach the well-populated lower Thalle Valley and a route to Shigar.

Whether approaching by foot from Shigar or in a Jeep from Skardu, you continue a dozen miles up-valley from Yugu past other small oases to reach Khapalu's green alluvial fan (8,400 ft.), 64 mi. from Skardu. If you get a chit from Skardu's tourist officer before you leave, you can stay at Khapalu's rest house, or you can stay in the two-room hotel. The restaurant-cum-hotel is situated in the main bazaar to the east of the nala across from a balconied three-story building. Khapalu's large, fertile alluvial fan offers many sloping, shaded pathways to stroll unencumbered by your pack. In the fan's midst, the large residence of Khapalu's former raja is easily visible, an impressive sight in the remote Shyok Valley.

Continuing up-valley, the Jeep road climbs a high ridge east of Khapalu before descending to the village of Surmo. A climb onto this ridge will provide an excellent view of the Hushe Valley, which cuts a distinctively straight swath south from Masherbrum's symmetrical peak at the valley head. A shorter trail from Khapalu to Surmo covers the distance at near river level; during high water, this trail route will involve one or two easily negotiated short stretches of wading in the chilly Shyok within a mile of town. Also along the way, at landings determined by the river currents, a *zuk* (the Balti-style frame raft buoyed up by inflated skins) ferries goods, stock, and people to the northern riverbank. With each crossing the sheep and goat skins must be reinflated by lung pressure. In 1977, my companions John Mock and Ghulam Hussein and I with our three stout loads were kindly given immediate service and were carried across for a total of 60 rupees.

The trail along the Shyok River continues around the base of the spur east of Khapalu for 6 mi., passing two other villages before reaching Surmo. To the east beyond Surmo, the Shyok valley floor narrows as the river turns to the south. Just around the river's bend is a bridge, passable by Jeep, which can be used by those who don't want to trust the zuk. If you cross the bridge and turn north, you will be heading up the Hushe Valley as if you had crossed by raft, except that you will be miles to the east across the braided stream on the left bank. This is the most direct route to the Saltoro valleys and an alternate route to the path by Machilu up the Hushe Valley, or nala.

Machilu is the usual first stop on the Hushe Nala, and a new rest house has recently been built there. However, unless you have reserved a room at the rest house, don't plan to stay overnight at Machilu; the village children, who have been exposed to mountaineering expeditions, are intrusive. The 17-mi. Hushe Valley is quite gentle, with an elevation rise of only 1,500 ft. from Khapalu. The trail passes many perspectives on verticality that can be seen only in the Karakoram. Tall poplars at a distance resemble ants alongside the towering walls, and Masherbrum is continually visible—you walk directly toward it.

The last town in the valley is Hushe. There, unlike in Skardu and the large bazaars, people wear the traditional round, peaked Balti cap (*nhating*) of white wool for men and black wool for women. In 1974 a party of American climbers and their high-altitude porters surprised the villagers here by descending from a technical col on the eastern ridge of Masherbrum after successfully climbing the mountain. Above Hushe, two glaciers extend off Masherbrum. A third carries the snows of Chogolisa and K-6; a pasture by this glacier is called Chundugero on the Skardu U502 sheet (N143-3) and is locally named Andorrah. The Chogolisa Glacier's meadow is known as Chospah. Accessible pastures along the edges of all three glaciers are grazed in the brief summer season.

The Saltoro Valleys

Across the Hushe Nala from Machilu (on the Hushe's right bank), the Saltoro River appears from behind a beige-colored ridge and empties into the Hushe River. Halde is the village on the right bank of the Saltoro just up-valley from this valley junction. Halde has a small store, and here a bridge crosses the Saltoro River where you begin the flat, 6-mi. walk south to the new Shyok bridge. Stay on the Halde side of the river if you are going up the Kondus valley. If you will be going up the Saltoro Valley, cross the bridge to the south bank, then follow the high trail above the left bank to Dansam Village.

The main trail up the Saltoro Valley continues past Halde on the northern side of the Saltoro River, passing the towns of Tagas and Seeno (Chino on the U502) to the few large estates of Brakhor, situated

Last settlements in the Kondus Valley, below the Kondus Glacier.

directly across the Saltoro River from the large village of Dansam. Here the Saltoro divides with the Kondus Valley going north. Each valley has, at its head, a technical, glaciated pass leading onto the 45-mile Siachen ("Great Rose") Glacier. The last village along the Kondus Valley is Karma Ding, a long day's walk from Brakhor past Lachit, Tahng (called Kondus on the U502), and Chogron. Towering vertical slabs are continually visible for the entire distance above the river's divide. Spires 2,000 ft. high pierce the sky at Karma Ding, and pinnacles visible on K-6 mimic the steep, brooding mountains in Walt Disney's *Fantasia*. The Kondus Glacier, more than 20 mi. long, lies at the head of this valley.

The Saltoro Valley is reached via the left bank of the Saltoro from the Halde, as noted above. The second day's walk beyond Dansam village takes you to the village of Goma, the last village in the valley. From Goma, the glaciated valleys of Chulung and Chumik may be explored. The Bilafond Glacier at the head of the main valley lies within "a narrow rock gorge between enormous granite walls," according to Arthur Neve, who visited in 1908. Beyond the Bilafond lies the Siachen.

These Karakoram valleys present a remarkable landscape, but equally remarkable to those fortunate enough to have visited Baltistan are the strong, cheerful Baltis in their brown-checked homespun, spinning thread and conversing. Whether you go up the Kondus or Saltoro Valley, your return requires retracing your steps back to Khapalu.

7

Kashmir

If there be a paradise on earth, it is this, it is this, it is this.
Shah Jahan, 1640

Though much the largest of the Himalayan valleys it is perhaps the least dramatic. There is none of the savage majesty of Lahul, the Alpine clarity of Kulu or the exotic contrasts of Chitral. Its beauty is more mature and stately. It lies precisely in those "perfect proportions of height to distance" and the "softness mantling over the sublime."
John Keay, 1977

[*"Is there anything Your Majesty desires?"*]
"Only Kashmir."
Jahagir, fourth Moghul Emperor,
on his deathbed, 1627

Kashmir's Imperial Past

Kashmir has been called the "pearl of the Himalaya" since the 16th century when the Moghul emperors began to construct their exquisite formal gardens in the vicinity of Dal Lake. Although the Moghul empire has long since faded into history, the Shalimar, Nishat, and Chashma Shahi gardens remain for our enjoyment. Each symmetrical garden utilizes water from a large spring as centerpiece. Particularly well known is the Shalimar Garden created for Shah Jahan in honor of his Queen Nur Mahal, the woman who inspired the Taj Mahal.

Seventy percent of the State of Jammu and Kashmir (J. and K.) is taken up by the region called Ladakh. Only part of the remainder of J. and K. lies within the Kashmir Valley. This chapter, however, covers only the famous valley, its well-known tributaries, and the passes east to Ladakh.

The oval, 85-mi.-long Kashmir Valley (or Vale of Kashmir) is the largest within the Himalayan chain. Most of its inhabitants are agriculturalists, even if the newly arrived tourist, besieged by touts, believes temporarily that the majority of Kashmiris earn their living with the tourist trade. For hundreds of years Hindu pilgrims from the populous south have flocked to the Vale of Kashmir to reach the ice cave called Amarnath. When Europeans began to discover Kashmir, a law was passed that still remains, forbidding foreigners to own land in the valley. Initially, Westerners were not even permitted to winter in the vale. Undeterred, British vacationers originated the idea of constructing extravagant houses atop local barges as dwellings. Thus was born the thriving modern phenomenon of houseboats, where many present-day visitors reside.

Srinagar, webbed by canals and cut by the meandering Jhelum River, is the principal city; it is said to have been created by the order of King Ashoka in the third century B.C. The more recent history of the vale is as colorful as its gardens in autumn. Islamic dynasties of Kashmiris, Moghuls, and Afghans succeeded each other until 1819, when the Sikh rulers of the Punjab interceded to calm a chaotic situation resulting from Afghan rule. For the next 27 years, Kashmir was administered by Sikh governors. In 1846, the British—desirous of not overextending their direct control in the more remote mountainous regions—signed two treaties with the Dogra Raja of Jammu, Gulab Singh, involving substantial payment to the British government. The Treaty of Lahore ceded Jammu and Kashmir to the British from the Sikhs. The area ceded included all of greater Kashmir from the Chitral border to Lahoul and Spiti, including the Gilgit watershed, Baltistan, and Ladakh. A week later the Treaty of Amritsar recognized Gulab Singh, a Sikh, as Maharaja of Jammu and Kashmir. More recently, the predominantly Muslim Kashmir Valley has been incorporated into the State of Jammu and Kashmir. This chapter next tells you how to reach Kashmir, and gets you started, first in bustling Srinagar, then on the more noted hill trails west and particularly east of the vale. Finally, the various paths to Ladakh from out of or near the Kashmir Valley are noted.

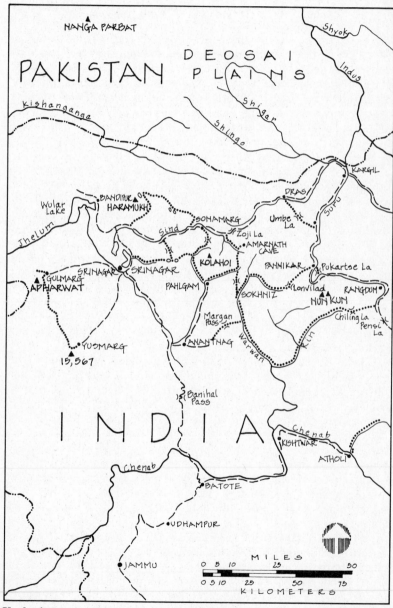

Kashmir

The Way to Kashmir

Daily flights reach Srinagar from Delhi and Jammu, but if you have the time, try going by land. You can always return by air, but if you go by land you'll get a good look at the route in. It is always possible to book an overnight sleeping berth out of Delhi from the seating quota that is set aside for tourists. Go first to Baroda House on Kasturba Gandhi Marg in New Delhi to get your chit and then to old Delhi Station for the ticket and sleeper reservations themselves (see Chapter 3). The train called the Jammu Mail and numbered "33 up" leaves Delhi every night at 8:55 P.M., arriving the next morning at Jammu Tawi Station. Directly on the platform of the station at Jammu Tawi is the booking office of the Jammu and Kashmir Road Transport Corporation. Its bus will leave within the hour of your arrival. You may also go to Srinagar from Jammu by taxi, booking a single seat or the entire vehicle.

Your bus or taxi will quickly leave behind the vast Punjab plains and enter the foothills of the Pir Panjal Range for the twisting, 189-mi. trip to Srinagar. The mountains of the Pir Panjal extend 170 mi., paralleling the Great Himalaya Range from Chamba District on the Ravi River to the Kishanganga River northwest of Srinagar. You will be crossing the ridges and spurs of the Pir Panjal until your bus descends into the Kashmir Valley. Before the road to the vale was paved, the overnight stop en route to Kashmir was the village of Batote (5,000 ft.) on a scenic ridge sprinkled with deodar trees between the Tawi and Chenab rivers. Nowadays, your bus will pause at Batote only for the lunch stop. A side road leads from Batote to Kishtwar, the trailhead for several treks. If you are going to Kishtwar, inquire in Delhi or at Jammu Tawi Station for transfer information.

From Batote the bus descends 2,500 ft. to the deep Chenab River gorge before climbing a mile up to the Banihal tunnel. When you emerge from the tunnel, a magnificent sight greets you: the Great Himalaya Range to the northeast forms a white horizon while deeper green ridges rise from chartreuse rice fields below. There is a sign, "Welcome to the Happy Valley," and you are in the Vale of Kashmir. Once on the valley floor the bus reaches level ground for the first time since leaving Jammu, and for the 40 remaining miles to Srinagar, along a road often bordered with poplars, you feel you are flying. If you arrive in late summer, the air near the town of Pampur will be redolent with the fragrance of saffron from the fields nearby on the Karewas Plateau, to the east.

Within 24 hours after leaving New Delhi, you will arrive at the Tourist Reception Center in Srinagar. The center's complex holds all offices relating to tourism in the valley, including one office specifically for trekking. As you will be tired from the ride, better to find lodging immediately and return to the reception center the following morning for information.

Srinagar and Gulmarg

While you are deciding which area to trek in, you can take several interesting walks in and about Srinagar. The Shankaracharya Hill, also called the Takht-i-Suleman ("Throne of Solomon"), rises a thousand feet high, just east of the Tourist Reception Center. From it you have an excellent view of Srinagar, the Vale of Kashmir, and Dal Lake to the immediate north. The small Shiva temple on the crest of the hill dates from the 6th century, and a nearby Buddhist shrine in ruins is more than 2,000 years old.

To the north is the unmistakable Hari Parbat fortress on the low Sharika Hill. It is said that the hill grew after the goddess Parvati dropped a stone on an offending demon. A wall around the hill below Hari Parbat was constructed by Akbar the Great, Hindustan's ruler, for an Afghan governor in the 16th century. As you approach Hari Parbat, you will pass extensive orchards of almond and fruit trees. Sporadically you may hear loud shrieks and shouting from the depths of the orchards, but resist any temptation to intercede in what you may think is assault and battery. The owners of the trees hire men to shout at birds raiding the unpicked fruit.

At Hari Parbat you are close to the old city of Srinagar, much of which was razed in the earthquake of 1885. Like Kathmandu, Srinagar's older sections appear to be imminently ready to collapse, and many roofs support healthy stands of grass. Srinagar probably tops Kathmandu in its collection of mongrel dogs, although they are only in the old city, not near the posh houseboats. A stroll through the old city's back streets and passageways can make a most interesting morning walk. The pagoda-like venerable Shah Hamdan Mosque rests on the bank of the Jhelum River. Be certain to remove your shoes before entering to admire the papier-mâché work therein. The mosque itself is handsomely constructed of wood. The Sri Pratap Singh Museum in Lal Mandi (closed Wednesdays) has some fine examples of early Kashmiri artwork. The Srinagar Library is next door. The area called Lal Mandi lies on the left bank of the Jhelum River; to reach it, you will have to take a small ferry across the river or walk well out of your way to a bridge.

Kashmir is known for both the quality and variety of its handicrafts and the perseverance with which they are pressed upon you, the prospective customer. You can see finely carved woodwork, leatherwork, embroidery, papier-mâché, carpets, and silver. Be particularly cautious about purchasing anything said to be an antique. Kashmir has been heavily touristed for a long time and it is generally accepted that all antiquities, from coins to Yarkandi shawls, have long since left the valley. Examine the wares offered by several people to get an idea of the qualities and price ranges available; hard bargaining will be in order if you become interested. Because many of the items for sale are made in outlying villages and sold by middlemen, you will find better prices outside Srinagar at the craftspeople's villages. Reach them by taking one of the local buses from the depot near the Lala Rukh Hotel, in the middle of the city.

Gulmarg, the "meadow of flowers," was discovered as a tourist destination by the British in the 19th century. Prior to that, Moghul emperors vacationed in the Gulmarg area. Today, Gulmarg is reached by bus. Lying some 31 mi. east of Srinagar, this settlement is exquisitely situated in a pine-surrounded basin of the Pir Panjal, and it sports a golf course and a ski hill. Nanga Parbat can be seen to the north, from the hills above Gulmarg. This small town at 8,500 ft. makes an excellent base for trekking in the northern Pir Panjal Range. From a distance, the Pir Panjal appears somewhat rounded, but when you are actually walking up its slopes, you will find that its smoother peaks rise above evergreen-clad slopes that seem quite equal in steepness to those of the main Himalaya. West and slightly south of Gulmarg is the 13,592-ft. peak of Apharwat. This peak is, however, on the India-Pakistan cease-fire line, so avoid it.

To the south of Gulmarg, a pleasant trek would be to walk up the Ferozepur Nala and beyond to the hamlets of Danwas, Tejjan, and Tosamaidan. For this you will need a porter who knows the way, because many stock trails intersect the route. The walk from Gulmarg to Tosamaidan is considered to be three stages. You may return by way of Riyar and Khag villages or continue south toward Sunset Peak (15,567 ft.) and then walk into the foothills along the Romushi Nala to Yusmarg, where a road and bus service connect with Srinagar.

Kashmiris like to trek using ponies as beasts of burden. Using ponies is not always easier, however. For one thing, what begins as a low-key trek can rapidly get out of control, unless you are careful to limit the size of your entourage. For another, ponies promised may not in fact materialize. During the busy summer season, many visitors may be riding ponies in the Kashmir valleys; and it is not comforting to find yourself stranded the first night out without your loads because the horses have never actually left with them. Said one agent to a peeved trekking-group leader, in explanation: "Sorry, sahib, not enough horses."

The Sind Valley

Considered the most beautiful of Kashmir's side valleys, the Sind is also the access route to the pass called Zoji La (11,580 ft.), which leads to Ladakh. This alpine valley was thoroughly enjoyed by early travelers to Ladakh: "The Sind Valley, which I was now entering, is perhaps the most beautiful valley in Kashmir . . . a perfect paradise" (Sir Francis Younghusband); "One long succession of grass glades and fir trees . . . a wild fairy loveliness" (M. L. A. Gompertz); "It would be difficult to imagine more ideal conditions for starting off . . . the glory of the valley is its trees" (Kermit Roosevelt). The Sind is not only beautiful in the extreme, but from it you can leave for or return from the best trekking areas to be found in Kashmir.

An excellent base for trekking is the 8,990-ft. "golden meadow," Sonamarg, 52 mi. northeast of Srinagar. In the summer months this delightful meadow area is visited for the day by tourists from Delhi and Bombay who arrive on buses from Srinagar. Pastel saris trimmed with gold shimmer in the daytime breeze, and many of the city people take the 3-mi. horseback ride west to the Thajiwas Glacier. Sonamarg has a small bazaar and some seasonal restaurants, and the Tourist Center is a well of activity. Gaily dressed families arrive by bus and depart for Thajiwas on horseback, led by a tall Gujar. The tourist officer in Sonamarg will be at the center during the day and can be of excellent assistance if you have questions or would like to store some belongings (*saman*) for several days while you are trekking.

Nichinai Pass to Gangabal Lake

A fine walk west of Sonamarg is to climb the Nichinai Pass (13,387 ft.) to Gangabal Lake; at Sonamarg there is a panoramic view of the first wooded ridge to be traversed on this walk. Two miles down-valley toward Srinagar the road crosses the Sind River, below the tightly clustered houses of Shitkari village. It is there on the right bank of the river that you begin walking to the lakes called Krishan Sar and Vishan Sar and, beyond, to Gangabal Lake and Haramukh Peak. From the Shitkari bridge, follow the trail up the ridge into a pine forest

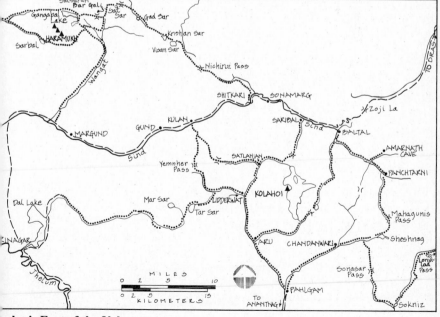

ashmir East of the Vale

and keep climbing the ridge 5,000 ft. up to the barren Nichinai Pass. The trail is well used in the summer and easy to stay with. Two- and three-house settlements appear along the way, and you pass encampments of many Gujar, Bakarwal, or Chopan herders in the forests east of the pass. West of the Nichinai, a green but treeless area slopes toward the Kishanganga River. Many animals are grazed in this large basin.

The western slopes of the Nichinai Pass will have patches of snow into July, attesting to the heavy winter snowfall. Here you are at the head of a tributary of the Kishanganga; to the south lie needle peaks and small glaciers and ahead, across the wide valley floor, are the two unseen lakes: Vishan Sar ("Vishnu's Lake") is at just over 12,000 ft. and slightly larger than the 12,500-ft.-level Krishan Sar ("Krishna's Lake"). From Krishan Sar, the trail toward Gangabal continues via a zigzag route up the near ridge. Do not take the southern trail fork (marked on the U502 map), which goes up a feeder stream between the hills and into a cul-de-sac. Rather, cross the ridge northwest of Krishan Sar, descend to Gad Sar, then rise again to a high ridge that holds the Satsaran Lake, with excellent views northward. The trail crosses the Satsaran Bar Pass and then continues south to Zajibal Pass, where you have a clear view of Gangabal Lake 2,000 ft. below, with Haramukh peak, at the 16,872-ft. level, behind. You might want to attempt one or more of Haramukh's three principal summits, but most walkers will be content to rest by the lake, which is large—5 mi. in circumference. A hundred feet below Gangabal is the smaller lake of Nund Kol, with excellent shoreline views of Haramukh, and the trail leading 2 mi. down to a camping place called Trunkhal at the edge of the forest. Twelve miles down the Wangat Valley from Gangabal, following the direct route down-valley to the Sind, is the spring called Narang Nag. There are ruins here dating from the time of Ashoka. Camping places are nearby. For this alpine trek over the Nichinai to Gangabal Lake and down the Wangat Valley (or the reverse route), you will need at least seven days.

Alternate routes to Haramukh can also be taken. One good approach route begins by bus, from Srinagar to Bandipur; then change for Erin (3 mi. away), and walk up the Erin Valley. At Ishrantar, you must take either the northern fork, keeping Haramukh to your right, or the southern valley to Sarbal Lake. Either way you can get around Haramukh Peak to reach Gangabal Lake.

The alpine hills of Kashmir—its "pearls"—be they the Pir Panjal or the western foothills of the Great Himalaya, are extensively populated in the summer months by nomadic herders. Most are Gujars and Bakarwals, but some of the families are Chopan or Ghaddi, the latter from Chamba. Some herd their own animals, but most care for those of other herders, using traditional grazing rights handed down and known only to them. The Gujars and Bakarwals are indistinguishable to outsiders by sight. They are a very tall people, often using *khol*, a black coloring, around their eyes. They speak their own languages, which are not understood by Kashmiris. The lean men and women are colored like deep milk coffee. Women wear gold jewelry in their noses and ears, but their most distinguishing feature is painstakingly braided hair. Scores of long braids hang from each side of a woman's head (sometimes topped by an embroidered cap); each braid of oiled hair is composed of three black locks. The men are often bearded, and many have the wise, dignified demeanor of those who have long worked in the hills. Everything of size is carried on animals; their retinues include pack horses, chickens, and chained, ferocious dogs. The Gujars usually herd horses, cattle, and water buffalo; the Bakarwals, sheep and goats. Gujars and Bakarwals are found from southern Chitral southeast to the Sutlej River, but most roam south of Nanga Parbat in the hills bordering Kashmir's vale. Like all nomads, they are most friendly, and I have been kindly offered milk or yoghurt for my wheatcakes by hospitable shepherds as I, or they, passed by on the trail.

The Amarnath Yatra Paths

The pilgrimage (yatra) into the Sind Valley to Amarnath Cave, one of the holiest shrines of the Hindu faith, has continued annually for generations. Extending 100 ft. high, the cave is less deep than towering. Inside, behind an open-gated iron fence, an underground trickle of water emerges from a cleft and freezes as it lands to form a tall cone of ice. This cone was originally called "the formless form," but it now has another symbolism. The ice figure is believed to be a manifestation of Shiva's phallus, and on the full moon of Sawan, in July or August, tens of thousands of pilgrims called yatris walk through the gate in the iron fence to view the ice phallus and make offerings of food, sweets, and flowers before it.

This interesting place is well worth a visit, but timing is more important in this short trek than most. The main pilgrimage takes place at the time of the full moon of Sawan, but it is best to visit the cave from mid-June to mid-July when the trails to it should be sufficiently clear of snow to be passable and when the seasonal tent inns, providing both shelter and food, are setting up. Also, the ice stalagmite is tallest then; often by pilgrimage time the ice has been melted by the warmer air to a mere foot in height (despite any claims you may read about the *lingam* [phallus] waxing and waning with the moon).

There are two routes to the cave, which is 1½ mi. up the Amrivati Valley, a small tributary of the Sind Valley. Amarnath is traditionally reached from Pahlgam in the Liddar Valley, 29 mi. away over a 14,000-ft. pass. Since 1971, however, a little-publicized but very serviceable pony track has connected the cave with Baltal, which is down the valley. Baltal is 8 mi. from Sonamarg (described in the preceding section on the Sind Valley) past the Indian Army's Mountaineering School and the meadow-covered, forest-walled valley at the foot of the Zoji La leading to Ladakh. From the few buildings called Baltal, the wide trail climbs 3,000 ft. in 8 mi. to reach the ice pillar of Amarnath: an easy day's walk. This makes a very handy approach. After seeing the cave you can take the pilgrim route out over the longer, higher trail to Pahlgam. Both the Baltal and Pahlgam trails to the cave follow steep gorges with meadows of wildflowers framed beneath snow peaks. For me, the route was as inspiring as the goal. If you trek within three weeks

A sadhu from Madras at the revered Amarnath Cave ice lingam, Kashmir.

before the yatra, you will be able to buy meals along the way at numerous temporary establishments. I found food and tea made by Sri Amarnath Travels to be the best.

The traditional stages of the route from Pahlgam are as follows (distances are one-way):

1. Pahlgam to Chandanwari (the roadhead), 8 mi. (13 km). This is now a Jeep road but is usually walked.

2. Chandanwari to Shesh Nag, 7 mi. (11 km). Shesh Nag is a lake fed by glaciers.

3. Shesh Nag to Panchtarni, 8 mi. (13 km). This stage takes you over 14,435-ft. Mahagunis Pass. At Panchtarni ("five springs") campground, Shiva is said to have performed the Tandava Nritya, the "dance of destruction." Going east off the main trail from Panchtarni leads to a side valley that is off the pilgrimage route; a level plain on this pleasant detour reaches gentle alluvial scree fans across from falling glaciers and additional 16,100-ft. peaks.

4. Panchtarni to Amarnath Cave, 4 mi. (6 km). The pilgrims reach the cave on the early morning of the fourth day, before the evening of the full moon, called Shravana Poornima. Within the cave, some members of the multitudes scrape a white calcium substance, a *vibuti* or blessed dust, from the walls. Outside, the yatris cleanse themselves in the snow-fed Amrivati stream. On the single day of the pilgrims' attendance at the cave, both cave and trail are packed with streams of humanity.

This route from Pahlgam to the holy cave is taken each year by 30,000 or more people. They all follow the Chhari Sahib, the person carrying the gold-plated rod of authority. A vivid cross-section of India's many-faceted societies trudge along the path from Pahlgam to the cave and back in six days. Foreigners also walk along, but if you consider going, please understand that the days will be regimented. No one may precede the Chhari Sahib, and the Indian army is in force to maintain order. There is no such thing as personal privacy during the yatra; rarely, however, can you see such a vivid procession of people, rich and poor, with many ascetic sadhus. You must follow the regimen of the pilgrimage or plan to go before or after. A widely copied advisory for all yatris is published by the government:

Precautions; In view of the cold weather conditions and the hazardous mountain journey, the intending tourists-cum-pilgrims are advised to be fully equipt with heavy woolens, raincoats, umbrellas, waterproof shoes, walking sticks, torches, a thermos containing hot tea or coffee, and tents for shelter. The *yatris* will have to walk on snow.

Three weeks before the Sawan full moon, I walked from Sonamarg to Baltal, ate eggs and biscuits purchased from a lone vendor, then continued to within 3 mi. of the cave before stopping for the night. The next morning at the cave I met a vacationing Californian and a sadhu from Madras who had been walking up the Pahlgam trail together. The man from Madras had voluntarily left the engineering profession to pursue the life of a wandering religious renunciate. We wanted to stay in the holy place; the high cave roof above us dripped water, so we selected our sleeping spots carefully. As I cooked *parathas* (wheat dough fried in butter), the kind, grave sadhu studied my new multifuel stove with a practiced engineer's eye, pointed, and liltingly said in English, "This is all old technology. Only this one part I do not know, for it is new." His words echo when I project a slide of him on the wall: a slim, white-bearded man dressed in white *dhoti* cloth with a grey cotton blanket over his shoulders standing barefoot on the ice next to the 9-ft. ice lingam. He, the Californian, myself, and several other sadhus were the only people sleeping in the holy cave that night.

Pahlgam and the Liddar Valley

Buses leave several times daily for Pahlgam from the Tourist Reception Center in Srinagar. Pahlgam village, 7,000 ft. high in the pine-cloaked Liddar Valley, is the starting point for the Amarnath Yatra, but other treks can be begun there as well. In addition to the route past Amarnath, described from the opposite direction in the previous section, you can cross from Pahlgam to the Sind Valley by foot by several variations. They are some of the most favored trekking routes in Kashmir. Pahlgam itself is larger than Sonamarg, with a touristy bazaar and numerous posh hotels nearby. Check with the tourist officer in Pahlgam for all general information and to make reservations in the rest houses of the Liddar Valley.

You can also take a short day walk from Pahlgam. Follow a pony trail to the meadow of Bhai Saran (7,500 ft.), 3 mi. from town, which offers a valley panorama. An excellent overnight trek would be to continue from Bhai Saran 7 mi. farther, to 12,000-ft. Tuliyan Lake.

For the various trails north to the Sind Valley, the West Liddar River is the funnel. The pleasant trail through the lower valley follows the east bank of the Liddar stream, and there you are apt to meet Gujars, European couples, Delhi walas on foot or horseback, or the Jammu University women's mountaineering team, as I did. The first 7 mi., to Aru, is by a virtually flat Jeep road, and most of the area is wooded. At Aru, you can take one of the popular side trails east to the Armiun Valley beneath Kolahoi (17,799 ft.), the highest peak along the east rim of the Vale of Kashmir. Seven miles up the West Liddar Valley from Aru, the path reaches a major stream junction—beyond to the west lies the rest house of Liddarwat. Rooms for the Rest House can be booked with the tourist officer in Pahlgam. At Liddarwat and 5 mi. farther along the Liddar Valley at Satlanjan village, side valley trails lead west to Srinagar and the middle Sind Valley. These trails are noted below.

The main Liddar Valley jogs slightly east at Liddarwat, and again past Satlanjan for another mile, then bends to the southeast. From this second right-angle bend you can see the valley's end in a grey jumble of steep, rocky slopes near the hidden Kolahoi Glacier. Another 2 mi. up-valley, the first trail ascends the ridge on the northern side. Following this steep trail up the ridge for 3,000 ft. takes you to a 14,000-ft. pass that leads to the Sind Valley town of Saribal. Saribal village in the Sind Valley is 4,500 ft. below the level of the pass and 5 mi. up-valley from Sonamarg. Whether or not you climb the pass from the Liddar Valley, a walk of 1,000 ft. or so from the valley floor gives you a superb, close-in view of the pyramid-shaped peak of Kolahoi and a remarkable perspective on the Kolahoi Glacier as it snakes its way down the mountain's precipitous rock slopes. This glacier resembles a writhing dragon that breathes not fire but the freezing Liddar River headwaters.

At Liddarwat, the Sekiwas stream valley descends from the west, dividing 4 mi. upstream at a fork called Dandabari. The southern branch leads to Tar Sar Lake, which is separated from another lake, Mar Sar, by a low ridge. The trail down into the Vale of Kashmir from the Mar Sar outlet enters the Dagwan Valley, passing through Dachigam village to the roadhead near Dal Lake, just northeast of Srinagar. Alternatively, from Tar Sar or from the northern fork at Dandabari, you can loop back by a more northerly route over the popular Yemnher Pass (13,300 ft.) to the Sind Valley town of Kulan, 9 mi. below Sonamarg.

The ridge area between the Liddar and Sind valleys has other picturebook lakes and passes as well. The best way to pick a path through the meadow-strewn byways is to have a good map before you reach the trailhead. The AMS U502 Map Sheets named Srinagar (NI 43-6) and particularly the one named Kargil (NI 43-7) are very helpful for these trails in the eastern hills of Kashmir. The Anantnag Sheet (NI 43-11) is necessary for any area south of Pahlgam; for example, for most of the passes east that are described below.

The Passes to Ladakh

Zoji La

The principal pass between Kashmir and Ladakh, though no longer the best for trekkers, has always been the 11,580-ft. Zoji La. For centuries, the Zoji La was the only trade route to cross the Himalayan system between the Hunza Karakoram path in the northwest to the trail up the Sutlej Valley 400 mi. southeast in the Punjab Himalaya. The pass is not high, and experienced mail runners have crossed it in every month of the year, but it is completely snowed in five or six months yearly. This is a uniquely formed pass: the western slopes of it, in the Sind Valley, are steep, pine-clad hills, while the pass area on both sides is an almost flat, U-shaped basin jutting away from the Sind Valley to the northeast. The meadows in the pass area are treeless but green, the first change toward the dry Ladakh atmosphere. The road up Zoji La from Baltal in the Sind Valley was built in 1960; as it zigzags up the pass, you have a postcard view south along the beginning of the

Amarnath trail up an alpine valley to the east of Kolahoi. Only the Gujars and Bakarwals with their herds cross on foot into Ladakh by the Zoji La, now that the road has been built.

Umbe La

The Umbe La is a pass south of Dras village, situated beyond (east of) the Zoji La in Ladakh. Local buses for Dras leave from Srinagar, passing through and stopping at Sonamarg. Dras is 26 mi. beyond Baltal and 34 mi. east of Sonamarg. At Dras, you should hire someone to lead you south to the 14,000-ft. Umbe La, with its excellent northern view of the mountain mass called Nun Kun. Umbe village is the first settlement reached on the other side; as you descend on the Ladakh side, the people you see are Central Asian, distinct from those in Dras or Kashmir. Continuing down, you reach the large Suru Valley at Sankho village. As many as two buses a day pass along the Suru Valley road going north to Kargil, 23 mi. from Sankho. Daily buses leave Kargil for Leh in central Ladakh. Or, once in Sankho, you could also plan to trek or bus south 14 mi. to Pannikar village, then walk back into Kashmir via the Lonvilad and Sonasar or Margan passes. (See next paragraph.)

Routes through the Warwan Valley

The favored trekking route from Kashmir into Ladakh, now that the Zoji La is paved, crosses the Lonvilad (or Bhot Kol) Pass leading to Pannikar village. The approach is from Pahlgam, but first let's stop and note that there are actually two passes from the Liddar to the Warwan Valley, and another pass paralleling the Lonvilad as well. From west to east, you can take either the Sonasar Pass (14,500 ft.) or the Margan Pass (11,500 ft.) from the Liddar Valley to the Warwan. Then you can take either the Lonvilad Pass (14,400 ft.) or perhaps the more difficult one called Morse Pass or Spang La (15,500 ft.) to reach the Suru Valley in Ladakh.

An alpine trail follows the pilgrim route from Pahlgam to Amarnath for the first 10 mi. to a point 2 mi. beyond Chandanwari, the roadhead. There, a pair of steep, narrow side valleys veer off to the south. The easterly (up-valley) branch leads to 12,500-ft. Sona Sar, the "Lake of Gold," 2,000 ft. below the snow-covered Sonasar Pass. Crossing this pass you see Kolahoi and the easily recognizable vertical strata that form the peaks above Panchtarni. The trail into the Warwan Valley descends more than a vertical mile before reaching Sokhniz village, the highest in the valley.

The Margan Pass is not approached from Pahlgam but rather from east of Anantnag, a town situated near the base of the Liddar Valley. Take a bus to Anantnag (where you will find pandemonium at the bus station). Once there, change for a taxi or local bus to the roadhead below the Margan Pass. The trail from the 11,500-ft. Margan Pass drops into the Warwan Valley about a day's walk south of Sokhniz. At

Sokhniz, the Sonasar Pass and Margan Pass trails join and continue up-valley in the direction of both passes to Ladakh.

The Lonvilad Pass is favored by trekking groups. Its 14,400-ft. col is reached from the (northern) right side of the Bhot Kol Glacier at the head of the Warwan Valley. The trail on the far side of the pass rapidly drops down to Pannikar village through a sere Ladakh landscape like that of all Ladakh-side approaches to the Kashmir passes. The different, more difficult route that parallels the Lonvilad is called the Morse Pass, or Spang La. The Spang La is reached from the Morse River, which joins the Warwan Valley at a shepherds' summer quarters called Kon Nag that is down-valley from the Lonvilad. The walk from Pahlgam or the Margan Pass to Pannikar by either route will take most people about a week.

At Pannikar village, you have crossed from the rain-drenched Kashmir Valley to the dry, sculpted landscape of Ladakh. From Pannikar you can climb directly to the Pukartse La and a sweeping, glacier-filled view of Nun Kun's 23,410-ft. peak, the highest Himalayan peak in the 450-mi. stretch from Nanga Parbat to Nanda Devi.

Chilung La

The Chilung La is another rarely crossed pass from the Kashmir side to the Suru Valley. This difficult, glaciated pass southeast of Nun Kun is more than 17,000 ft. high. It connects the upper Suru Valley with the Rin Valley, which has a large stream that joins the Warwan River. To reach the Chilung, cross the Margan Pass and follow the Warwan Valley 18 mi. down-valley, south, to its junction with the Rin. For this pass you will need a porter. If you already have one and he doesn't know the Chilung La, change porters in one of the several villages near the Rin and Warwan river junction. On the other side of the Chilung Pass, the Ladakh side, the trail leads to a road linking Kargil and Padum in Zanskar. Continuing trails are discussed in the Zanskar section of the next chapter. Down-valley from the Chilung La is Rangdum Gomba, the westernmost bastion of Buddhism in the greater Tibet area.

Umasi La

North of the Chenab Valley, southeast of the Warwan, several named cols have been crossed from Kashmir to Zanskar in Ladakh. None of these routes are easy, and they are rarely if ever crossed by locals. The one possible exception to this is the Umasi La, approached from Kishtwar. To reach the rolling green Kishtwar plain, take a train from Delhi to Jammu or fly from Delhi to Jammu or Srinagar. At Jammu or Srinagar take a bus to Kishtwar: a long day's trip. Be sure you are fully provisioned at Kishtwar for a trek that can be expected to take between 9 and 11 days, to Padum in Zanskar. At Kishtwar take a bus up the Chenab Valley road, which is presently under construction, to the roadhead. Depending how far the road has been completed by the time you arrive, you will reach the village of Atholi with its small shops in somewhat less than a single day's walk from the roadhead. Kishtwar porters are not the best. You could get a porter there or at the trailhead; probably you will change for a porter who knows the pass, once up-valley. At Atholi, leave the deep Chenab gorge for the Bhut Nala that strikes northeasterly into the Great Himalaya Range. Up this valley you pass villages, an occasional waterfall, and many meadows before reaching the village of Machail, the last large Hindu town. Machail has some interesting temples; and above town sapphires were once mined. Beyond Machail ascend a northerly side valley to the first village inhabited by people of Tibetan origin. Farther on you will reach the Zanskar Nala, below the Umasi Glacier. The ascent up the glacier on moraine debris and ice is not readily apparent; depend on your porter. Do not attempt this pass before midsummer. The Umasi La (about 17,300 ft.) offers great views into Zanskar and is steeper on the Ladakh side than on the southern (Chenab-side) snow approaches. Crampons are helpful but not essential for this pass. A day-and-a-half walk down the Bardur Chu Valley past the ancient Dzong Khul Monastery will bring you to the wide Doda Valley, where you will be a day's walk west of Padum.

8
Ladakh

*[The Nubra shikaris] were real "jungli wallahs," moun-
tainmen, born and bred in the high Himalayas. They were
tough as old leather. They had eyesight that would shame a
telescope. Their clothes were voluminous folds of drab
homespun. They ate a curious grain compound. Their skin,
garments, and food were all of varying shades of brown.*

Theodore Roosevelt, 1926

One pen. One pen. One pen.
Modern Ladakhi mantra spoken by children to tourists

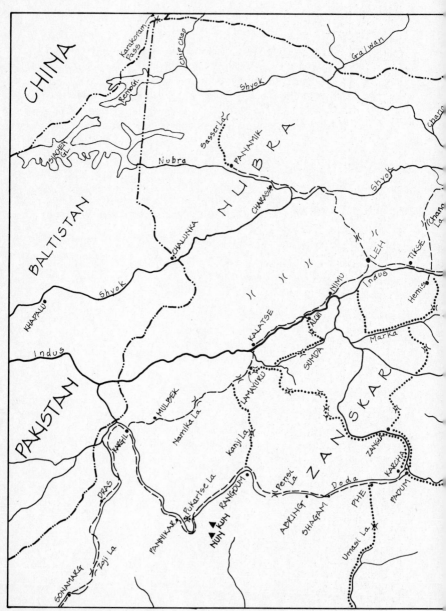

Ladakh

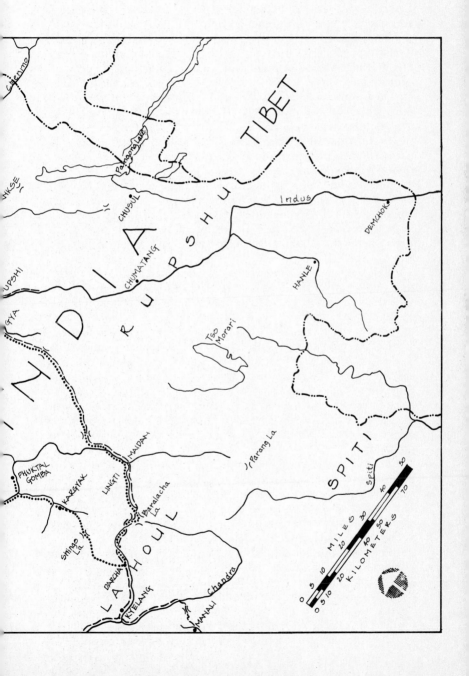

A Living Tibetan Museum

Ladakh, with its Buddhist culture, is much akin to Tibet. And its high, dusty landscape is also like Tibet's. The lowest elevation in all of Ladakh is above 9,000 ft., where the Indus flows north into Baltistan, and nowhere else is the Himalayan mountain system's northwest-to-southeast plunge more rift with parallel ranges. The Karakoram and Kailash ranges form the north and east borders of Ladakh: the main Great Himalaya Range isolates it from the south. A majority of the countryside is covered by the Ladakh and Zanskar ranges, each crowned with scores of 20,000-ft. peaks. The lowest passes of the northern Ladakh Range divide the Shyok and Indus valleys at the 17,000-ft. and 18,000-ft. levels, and the Zanskar Range's many sharp ridges and torrent-filled defiles limit access for summer pasturage to the hardy Chang-Pa nomads forced from their former grazing areas in the central Tibetan plains.

Ladakh has sandy plains, but only along certain portions of the major valley floors, where the majority of its inhabitants live. Foremost among these is the Indus Valley, but there are clusters of communities in the Nubra, Shyok, Padum, Dras, and Suru valleys as well. Flat land is also found in Ladakh adjacent to several large lakes in Rupshu, its highest area.

Leh, Ladakh's 11,400-ft. capital, receives a scant three inches of rain yearly, and agriculture is conducted only where irrigation is possible from glaciers or the Indus River. In Ladakh, a row of poplar trees is a sight to be enjoyed. Animals in use there were traditionally sources of income and transport, packing in food from Kashmir during the summer. Great caravans once converged on the serais of Leh from Turkestan, Tibet, and Kashmir. The route from Srinagar to Yarkand crossed the Zoji, Namika, and Fotu passes before it even reached Leh. This part of the journey took two weeks, and beyond Leh five still more perilous passes remained to be crossed. Ladakhis still make essential trading excursions across mountain passes that most foreigners would refuse to cross without undertaking an extensive physical-training program.

The caravans continued until the 1950s. In October 1951, the passes north were closed by the authorities, halting the vital north-south trade to Yarkand, trapping a number of Yarkandi merchants in Leh, and effectively paralyzing the town commercially. Since that time, events have brought first the Indian army and, in 1974, tourism, providing new sources of income and a new veneer to Leh.

Presently, in Ladakh, Muslims form a bare majority of the population; and many Ladakhi Muslims are beginning to use Urdu learned from religious use and the radio, instead of speaking traditional Ladakhi. Ladakh's current population of less than 200,000 is increasing rapidly, as the polyandry of the Buddhists (which tended to inhibit fertility) is replaced with monogamy and polygamy. The old ways and new coexist: here is another Himalayan land where the grandparents dress in traditional fashion while those in their midtwenties wear clothes that would not be out of place in New Delhi. The attractive buttoned, woolen gown called a *coss* remains in style as standard Ladakhi dress for Buddhist or Muslim. And the *tibi* or *sahru* remains popular. This is a top hat cut out on the front with upturned ear flaps, worn by men (often flaps akimbo) and women. The *pyerack* headdress, with rows of turquoise and a charm box, has been standard fashion for married women, but today is seen less often in the bazaars. At festivals, the pyerack is usually worn by older women. Contrast the existence of the modern clothing seen in Leh bazaar today with the fact that in 1951 there were fewer than five radios in all of Ladakh, as Justice William O. Douglas was told then. He was also informed that no crime of violence had ever been reported in Leh.

For more than a thousand years Ladakh was considered to be west Tibet, part of the vast Tibetan cultural and religious tradition. Ladakh has retained the monastic Buddhism that was forcefully terminated within Tibet in the 1950s; in fact, the image of Tibetan culture that many of us share is now more appropriate to Ladakh than to Tibet itself, as the monasteries and temples—the gombas—of Ladakh have not been systematically closed down as they were in Tibet following the Chinese takeover. Large Buddhist monasteries, many sculpted from rocky prominences, continue to operate in the Indus Valley and within side valleys hidden among saw-toothed ridges. The Ladakhi people living in these dry but heroic mountains are of Mongolian extraction and speak a dialect of Tibetan.

Ladakh was an independent west Tibetan kingdom prior to the 14th century. It was ruled by a theocracy, which was beneficent or self-serving, depending on one's point of view. There was and is a royal family, and the ancient monasteries continue to survive, prospering to varying degrees. During parts of the 14th and 16th centuries there were periods of Islamic rule, and conversion to that faith began, but by the latter half of the 17th century Ladakh's power was declining. Late in the century, a deal was struck between the rulers in Srinagar and in Leh whereby, for protection from invasion, a mosque would be built in Leh. The same mosque (with a handsome Yarkandi carpet) continues to sound with the call to prayers in Leh's central bazaar.

In the early 19th century Ladakh was one of several west Tibetan states that were associated. (The largest, then named Guge, contains two hidden, magnificent Sutlej Valley cities, Tsaparang and Tholing, each a repository of exquisite but decaying fresco-lined temples.) In 1834 Ladakh fell to a Dogra army led by the one-eyed Gulab Singh. Since then, this mysterious mountainous land has formed some 70 percent of the total area of Jammu and Kashmir, while remaining quite separate from it economically. The first recent jolt to Ladakh's dusty, museum-like atmosphere occurred in 1962 when the 272-mi. road was completed from the Kashmir Valley to Leh. The Indian government quickly established large garrisons near Leh and elsewhere, bringing in tens of thousands of troops and changing the economy drastically.

Then, in the autumn of 1974, Ladakh was opened to tourism. In 1978 civilian airflights began. The ancient Wheel of Existence on view at the entrance to each Ladakhi gomba must have creaked once again.

Following the Caravan Routes

The new road from Kashmir to Leh closely parallels the ancient 15-stage (15-day) trail, and thousands of visitors have begun to bus across the mountain ranges that hide Ladakh's towns from the outside world. Here are some glimpses from along the road to Leh.

A 737 jet designed for high-elevation landings has made scheduled flights since late 1978 from Srinagar to Leh, but don't even think of flying round trip—the sights along the way should not be missed. If you rent a Jeep, you can take your time getting to Leh or cover the distance in a single exhausting day. Or, take one of the buses leaving daily from the Tourist Reception Center in Srinagar; it traverses the 127 mi. to Kargil, then after you have a night's rest, proceeds the remaining 145 mi. to Leh.

While you wait for the bus at Srinagar to load, try the fresh *puris* with *halwa* sold by vendors who cook them at the depot. A puri is a thin wheatcake cooked in oil, often eaten at breakfast with the sweet farina topping called halwa. Thus fortified, take your seat and watch the Kashmir Valley recede as the bus enters the beautiful wooded Sind Valley (see the section about it in Chapter 7). Early lunch will be taken at Sonamarg before the bus proceeds over the 11,580-ft. Zoji La into Ladakh.

In the Zoji La area, private vehicles have to wait while military convoys pass, and your ride to Leh may be interrupted for an hour or so, but the bus drivers know when the road is to be closed and arrange their schedules to minimize delays. When I rode to Leh, we were stopped 20 mi. east of the pass near Dras by an approaching convoy. I climbed an embankment near the road and emerged near the mess tent at the edge of a military base. I had turned to leave when I was hailed from a nearby tent: "Sahib, come and take tea!"

When your bus reaches the top of the steep Zoji grade and enters a green, U-shaped valley, it will be approaching the actual pass; you will have crossed it when you see a stream flowing eastward, the direction you are traveling. This crossing into Ladakh's desert brings one of the most abrupt climatic changes you will ever see. The Sind Valley pines are gone, and the lush meadows will likewise evaporate before many miles are passed.

East of Dras, the road enters a narrow gorge that eventually merges with the Shingo River, which drains the Deosai Plains. For the next 7 mi. where the road hugs the Shingo River, it parallels the cease-fire line with Pakistan along the ridge to your immediate north. The Shingo empties into the Suru River 3 mi. north of Kargil; here, you are nearly halfway to Leh. Kargil itself was the crossroads of travel to Baltistan until partition of India and Pakistan in 1947, and some Baltis still reside here on the India side of the border. The old, stone-paved Kargil bazaar angling down toward the river is well worn but reeks pleasantly of antiquity. A visit there after the bus ride will stretch your legs. Kargil is the chief town of the Dras, Suru, and Wakka Chu valleys, known collectively as the Purig region.

The small village of Mulbek, 25 mi. east of Kargil, has some of the first indications of the Buddhism of this land; here you will find a stupa (reliquary shrine) and, above on the ridge line, a small monastery. Just beyond the telephone wires and a new white temple on the south side of the road stands a large relief carving of Maitreya, the Buddha-to-come, chiseled from the rock outcropping. This is the largest of the several rock carvings in Ladakh. There are, in fact, three stone pillars east of Dras carved with 7th century figures and mandalas.

From Mulbek the road rises to cross the Namika La (12,220 ft.) and then descends into a tributary valley of the Indus River. The valley floor is fertile and green from irrigation, but the hills on either side are so barren that even a small herd of sheep would have to graze quickly to fend off starvation. Moving up this valley, you pass several small communities, including Hiniskut, where a trail from Rangdum *Gomba* (monastery) in the Suru Valley emerges into the valley you are ascending. (This side trail is described in the Zanskar section.) Southward, toward the head of the dry valley you are following, you can see clearly the old caravan trail that proceeds up from the valley floor. Trail and road alike cross the third and highest pass between Srinagar and Leh, the 13,430-ft. Fotu La. At the pass area the earth appears bleached. The ancient caravans must have hurried past such inhospitable surroundings.

At the Fotu La you cross the Zanskar Range and begin to drop toward Lamayuru, one of the oldest and most spectacularly situated monasteries in all of Ladakh. Perched precariously astride a narrow spur, its buildings are the picture of an exotic Himalayan monastery. Just inside the entrance gate the monks have established a plain, one-room inn, where you can roll out your sleeping bag and eat the meals provided, gazing at recently painted frescos of Buddhist divinities. Not far beyond the guest room is the monastery's main kitchen, recognizable by the pile of furze (a low-growing bush) for fuel just outside the door. The large cauldrons inside are sometimes half-hidden in billowing smoke. The *Du-khang* (main assembly hall) in the central building has new wall paintings of excellent quality that can be photographed without a flash attachment. This is a rarely encountered situation, for nearly every monastery you will see (away from the Indus Valley road and its electric wires) all the way to Bhutan is poorly lit inside.

A hike up the parched hill north of the road gives an excellent view of the monastery in its dry valley. If you climb for about a half hour, you will see grey pinnacles south in Zanskar, a breathtaking background for Lamayuru, sequestered below. A more level walk would be up the old caravan trail leading toward the pass. This path is easily visible from the monastery, gently curving upward past long *mani* walls

(5-ft.-high stone walls topped with stones inscribed, "om mani padme hum"), rows of stupas, and the upper limit of bewitchingly colorful wheat fields.

Toward Leh from Lamayuru, the nearby valley becomes a phantasmagoric place of wind-eroded rock, leaving no doubt why Ladakh is often called the moonland. Rapidly descending in hairpin turns, the road reaches and crosses the Indus River near the town of Kalatse (or Khalsa), where your bus will stop for lunch. Seven miles east of Kalatse the Indus Valley widens, and you enter central Ladakh, the middle of this vast region. An additional 25 mi. past scattered settlements and larger towns takes you by the village of Nimu, where the Zanskar River joins the Indus. This confluence is a remarkable sight: although the Indus headwaters rise more than 400 mi. away, to the southeast, the river is dwarfed here by its so-called tributary. The slate grey Zanskar River is fully three times the size of the languid, brown Indus. At this point you are within 20 mi. of Leh, the capital of Ladakh.

Leh

Many outsiders approach exotic Leh still with something of an ancient traveler's ardor. Excitement mounts in the bus as it turns away from the Indus by Spituk, a small hilltop monastery, and begins to churn up the wide, dry alluvial plain for Leh, 5 mi. straight away. High above the town, the 16th-century Temple of Guardian Divinities perches on Namgyal Peak, and well below, not far above Leh, is the equally old fort-like royal palace built by Senge Namgyal, the most powerful of Ladakh's kings. The palace is nine stories tall, five less than the famed Potala in Lhasa. Unlike in present-day Lhasa, however, long streamers of prayer flags flutter in the breeze from stupas beside both the imposing castle and the temple above.

Ladakh was opened to tourism when the Indian government wisely removed many of the areas along its northern border from the Inner Line restrictions that had been enforced prior to 1974. Ladakh's opening had been lobbied for by many Ladakhis, and within three years of it more than 35 hotels sprang up in Leh. Many people utilized spare rooms in their homes, built additions, and later added hotel names to their premises. If you have any question about where to stay, you can stop first at the Tourist Office, which has a chart of all Leh hotels. The Tourist Office is west of the main bazaar, on a side street at the Tourist Bungalow near the school.

For those who feel comfortable in modest surroundings, the Palace View Kidar Hotel in the Kidar area of Leh (east from the southern end of the long bazaar street) is recommended for one important reason: its dining room is actually the kitchen of the Ladakhi family that operates the hotel. Guests are served meals while sitting on cushions along two walls at a *chog-tse*, a low table. The hotel kitchen-dining-family room is in traditional Ladakhi style, with a handsome arrangement of cooking pots, bowls, and plates hung about the log walls. Family friends come and go. One day during a breakfast of eggs, tea, and *taigee* (sourdough wheatcakes eaten with local butter), a metalsmith from the Zanskar town of Sumda arrived carrying a made-to-order copper teapot with ornate brasswork.

Leh's L-shaped bazaar runs directly toward the royal palace above on the ridge. The city's 300-year-old mosque sits just north of the right angle of the bazaar street; in the summer, women in *sahru* caps sell green vegetables nearby. Before the road in was built, when the bazaar was unpaved, merchants would close their street-facing doors to permit bazaar-long polo games. Now the town has changed focus, become cosmopolitan. In fact, these days you will now find more Tibetan refugees and foreigners along Leh's bazaar street than Yarkandis and Baltis. Auto parts, consumer goods, and tourist souvenirs have replaced the pashmina, carpets, and silk of yore, but such necessities as grains, tea, spices, and textiles are still carried in the shops. Dawdling over tea in a second-story restaurant with journal or aerogramme will permit impressions from the bustling bazaar to linger.

Beneath Leh's castle, the old city's narrow, twisting lanes and underpasses are reminiscent of any medieval town. More shops line a street along a diverted stream behind the mosque; following that street, the walker is soon north of the city, following centuries-old paths past stupas and mani walls. While you test how it feels to walk slowly uphill at the 12,000-ft. level, you can glimpse traditional country scenes along trails that extend miles up the irrigated terracing north of Leh. Leh's castle on the ridge above is a scene of disrepair: the building has been abandoned for more than 60 years and, while the front of it is un-affected, the interior is unliveable and the side walls need reconstruction. The smaller temple high on Namgyal Peak is reached from a trail that diverges upwards behind the windowless Avalokitesvara Temple. From its prayer-flag topped ridge, there are excellent views of Leh and the Spituk Monastery in the distance on the Indus Valley plain. You can also see the area of the Khardong Pass to Nubra, some 18,400 ft. high and now crossed by road, which lies to the north.

The Monasteries of Central Ladakh

Within the wide Himalayan desert of the Indus Valley lie the palaces of Leh, Shey, and Basgo, and numerous remarkable monasteries. The monasteries and palaces of Ladakh are its most visited sites, yet few visitors have any meaningful sense of what they are seeing in these places: the ritual implements, *tangkas* (scroll paintings), books, murals, mandalas, and images of guardian divinities. It is not within the scope of this book to give more than a brief introduction to Vajrayana Buddhism, the picturesque monasteries and palaces, and the region's chief festival. To fully understand the meaning of the rich religious panoply, one would have to undertake a great deal of concentrated study. Most local monks and certainly most Ladakhi Buddhists have only a limited understanding themselves of the Tibetan Buddhist divinities. If the cursory discussion here whets rather than sates your interest, peruse *The Cultural Heritage of Ladakh*, volumes 1 and 2, by David L. Snellgrove and Tadeusz Skorupski, and *Peaks and Lamas*, by Marco Pallis.

The monasteries were established for the propagation of the *dharma* (the doctrine or path), as stated by Lord Gautama Buddha. The basis of the doctrine is the Four Noble Truths: suffering, its cause, its suppression, and the Eightfold Path leading to its suppression. All else is but commentary upon the Four Noble Truths, but there has been much to say. Consider that the Tibetan Canon—the Kanjur—contains 108 books, and that its commentaries—the Tanjur—are longer yet. The Vajrayana or "Diamond Vehicle" of Tibetan Buddhism has four schools or orders: the Nyingmapa, Sakyapa, Gelugpa, and Kagyupa. Every monastery you will visit in the Himalaya belongs to one of these schools or a subsect. In central Ladakh, the Kagyupa and the Gelugpa (the branch to which the Dalai Lama belongs) control all but two of the monasteries. The Gelugpa order, sometimes called the order of "Yellow Hats," was established by Tsong Khapa, while the lineage of the Kagyupas includes Naropa, Marpa the Translator and Milarepa.

The monks' Du-khang is a monastery's most important meeting place. It is typically reached by a row of steps from a courtyard in front of the main building. Most Du-khangs, on the wall of the porch at the entrance, have a painting of the Wheel of Existence.* Inside the Du-khang you will see a central image, often Buddha in one of his manifestations, between smaller figures of attendants, guardians, or disciples. Rupee and even hard-currency offerings are left before the central image in a barley-filled dish. In all large monasteries, seven or more butter lamps burn continuously. Two rows of the low tables called chog-tse (but more ornate than those at the Palace View Hotel) are arranged for the monks to sit at for *puja* (prayers or worship) and other ceremonies. Drums hang from the ceiling, *chenai* (instruments like shawms) lie on the tables, five-color Buddhist flags drape low, and the walls are covered with shelves of books, small images, tangkas, and wall paintings that portray myths of the order governing the monastery. Other rooms in the central building and outbuildings contain images, paintings, the monastery's stores, its kitchen, and the monks' quarters.

Everyone traveling to Ladakh visits some of the monasteries. Most people reach their quotas between the second and fifth, but some remain fascinated and continue to see more. The experience you have at a monastery may be different from that of someone next to you, and

---

*Grasped by the claws and fangs of Yama, Lord of Impermanence and Death, the wheel is a complex pictorial metaphor of human life. On the wheel's rim are pictured the phases in the cycle of rebirth, and in the middle are a snake, pig, and cock symbolizing anger, stupidity, and greed, the three vices. The mass of the wheel is divided into six slices, divided by spokes. The top and bottom slices portray heaven and hell; those remaining represent the worlds of animals, humans, titans, and a purgatory. The Buddha sits outside and above the wheel.

the reception you are accorded today may be quite unlike tomorrow's welcome. If you like a gomba and return more than once, you will learn much more about it. Your demeanor, the people you meet there, shared language ability, the circumstances under which you meet, the time of day—these variables and more contribute to what will or won't happen. Unless prayers are being said in the Du-khang, you may not even see anyone immediately. The monks go to their rooms, leave to work on their ancestral property, and perform various religious ceremonies at homes or related monasteries, and thus they are not always about when you arrive. Someone will soon be along if you are patient, perhaps walk about outside the buildings. When people visit a monastery, whether devotees or tourists, the custom has always been to leave a gift of money. The amount given varies entirely with the visitor's means and feeling for the situation. Some gomba complexes are relatively well touristed (at least in certain rooms), such as Alchi, Spituk, Shey, Tikse, and Hemis, while others are visited much less often.

The following list describes most monasteries and palaces outside Leh along the Indus Valley. West to east, they range from Kalatse to Hemis. (The list does not include Lamayuru, which has been covered, nor Hemis, which is discussed below.) All but Ri Dzong are connected with the main Indus Valley road by Jeep roads, and most are within a 45-minute walk of the principal valley bus route.

Tingmo Gang. Seven miles east of Kalatse on the main valley road is Nurla village. An hour's walk north of Nurla takes you to one of the old palaces that were held by minor rulers before Ladakh was unified. Tingmo Gang rests in a pleasant setting amongst poplar trees. Although much of the original castle is in ruins, several more interesting shrines can be visited. People from this valley used to hire out as porters for foreign sportsmen and explorers.

Ri Dzong. An hour's walk north of the main road from Uludrokpo village, Ri Dzong is the newest Gelugpa monastery in Ladakh, built just over a hundred years ago. The Du-khang has an image of Tsong Khapa (as do most Gelugpa monasteries) and other statues, primarily of Buddha in his different incarnations. Ri Dzong means "mountain fortress."

Alchi. Most monasteries cling defensively to steep ridges or top low outcroppings, yet Alchi, which is the oldest and most iconographically important building complex in Ladakh, sits in a low valley. The side road to Alchi Gomba leads across a bridge over the Indus just west of Saspul. A half-hour walk takes you first to the larger village of Yul Khor, then in another mile to Chos-Khor, where buildings rest above the Indus but out of view of the main road. This collection of buildings and shrines collectively known as Alchi "represents an extraordinary survival from the past," according to David Snellgrove. Alchi, like Hemis, is nearly a thousand years old, and has never been touched by invading armies.

Likir. Likir Gomba is an extremely well kept Gelugpa monastery with many small chapels, a mile and a half north of the main road on the ridge between Saspul and Basgo villages. Within the last century, the Likir Monastery has taken responsibility for the temples several miles away at Alchi.

Basgo. This palace (now largely in ruins) and its still-utilized shrines were once the center of the largest Indus Valley state, before the unification of Ladakh under Leh's authority. Basgo also has a Kagyupa temple, near the road, 5 mi. west of Nimu. It is the second oldest in Ladakh after Alchi.

Phiyang. Twelve miles west of Leh, Phiyang is just north of the main Indus Valley road on top of a small hill. A Kagyupa gomba, it is affiliated with Lamayuru.

Spituk. Atop a sheer outcropping near the Indus south of Leh, Spituk Monastery overlooks the airport—an anachronistic touch. This is a Gelugpa monastery with a new Du-khang. It is built on several levels of the solid rock crag above Spituk village. A large image of the protector deity Bhairava (as seen also in Kathmandu's Durbar Square) in the gomba has often been misnamed Kali (a goddess associated with destruction) for the benefit of locally quartered soldiers. Pujas are performed here specifically for tour groups.

Stok. East of Spituk and a few miles south of Leh is Choklamsar, a village with a new Buddhist Philosophical School and a Tibetan refugee camp. Across the wide Indus Valley from Choklamsar is Stok, the only royal residence that has been maintained and lived in since the 1842 Dogra invasion. The present ranking family member, the Rani of Stok (named Gyalmo Diskit Wangmo), was elected to Parliament in New Delhi for one term.

Shey. Seven miles east of Leh, the ruined palace of Shey sits on a knife-edged ridge with the main Indus Valley road running along its base. The flat valley floor near the palace has scores of stupas. Inside a temple near the road is a two-story image of Buddha. Another temple contains a Buddha that has been gilded in bronze by eight Nepalese craftsmen.

Tikse. Since the 15th century, monasteries and palaces have been built on hilltops or in unassailable positions so as to be immune from attack. Tikse, about halfway from Leh to Hemis, is one of these, a beautifully situated, multistructured monastery complex best seen from the east. The penultimate story has a roof with a sweeping view overlooking both Shey and Stakna monasteries, above the same wide, irrigated stretch of valley bottom.

I visited Tikse after the Hemis Festival, arriving late in the day and sleeping outside by a large entrance stupa under brilliant moonlight. In the morning I found a monk doing puja (prayers) in an upper room dominated by a large black image of the dreaded Yidam protector deity named Yamantaka. On either side were Kaladrupa and Mahakala the Great Black God. Like Yamantaka, these gods are so fearsome to human eyes that their faces must be kept covered. When the puja was finished, I was kindly invited to have sattu with the monk. We each ate several bowls of the nut-like toasted barley flour moistened with rich Ladakhi *solja* (tea with milk and butter). For a while, I felt I was touching a very real part of Ladakh. About midmorning, when I left, the first tour bus was arriving, billowing smoke as it climbed the hill.

Stakna. Four miles up the Indus Valley from Tikse, the white buildings of Stakna perch on an isolated, razor-back outcropping north of the Indus. In the Du-khang of this small Kagyupa monastery there is a large, silver-gilt stupa built since 1950.

Ma-Tro. This gomba is south of (across) the Indus from Stakna and slightly upriver. It is the lone Sakyapa monastery in central Ladakh and is well known for its yearly festival, in which two monks (who have previously been in solitary meditation) become possessed by a god that temporarily gives them certain powers called *siddhis.*

Chendey. This small Kagyupa monastery is connected with Hemis Gompa and sits across the Indus Valley from Hemis, south of Sakti village.

Trakthok. The name of this monastery means "top of the rocks." It is the only Nyingmapa monastery in this part of Ladakh and is situated near Sakti on the way to the Chang La. Trakthok has a small cave in its base said to have been associated with Padma Sambhava, the founder of the Nyingma school and the destroyer-transformer of Bon Po worship in Tibet.

The Hemis Festival

The festival at Hemis is held each year about late June. Always well attended, it now attracts foreign visitors as well as locals and pilgrims,

Tikse Monastery, near the Indus River, Ladakh.

for almost all other Ladakhi festivals and extended religious ceremonies take place in the winter months when outsiders have left. Hemis Monastery is part of the Kagyupa's Brugpa branch of Buddhism that is dominant in Bhutan. Hemis is Ladakh's largest monastery and the richest, controlling a vast amount of choice farm and grazing land. West of Karu village and not visible from the floor of the Indus Valley, Hemis has been bypassed—like Alchi—by several invading armies.

For 72 hours the sloping, poplar-covered valley floor near Hemis Monastery sprouts a city of canvas and nylon tents, noodle stalls, and people selling meat *thupa* (soup), *dalbhat* (rice, lentils and vegetables), souvenirs, and tambolo games. Rajastanis sell medicine, Sikh salesmen offer dentures, puppeteers perform, and of course many tea shops operate. You'll see older women wearing pyeracks, with fur-inward lambskins draped over their shoulders. Nomads from Rupshu, Leh shopkeepers, Tibetan Drok Pa, Zanskaris, network broadcasters, journalists, tour group members, and others mingle as they eye the wares of the ready-made bazaar. The people are part of the show at Hemis, whether you are watching the performance or ordering chow mein in a busy restaurant tent beneath the Lombardy poplars. The blend of new and old is striking: a mod-haired boy in bell bottoms converses with his mother, dressed Ladakhi style, while a polyester-clad Frenchman strides ahead of the members of his group, who exchange amused glances with a Chang-Pa family.*

The heart of the festival is a two-day performance by monks in costumes and masks who are surrounded by an audience that covers roofs, balconies, steps, and the courtyard. Western-born Lama Anagarika Govinda, who visited Hemis before wheeled vehicles had reached Ladakh, saw these "mystery plays," which were then three days in length. He said of them that "they were far from being merely theatrical performances: they were the coming to life of a higher reality through magic rites, in which . . . performers and spectators are welded into one and have both become active participants. . . ."

The festival's ceremonies are always attended by a selected lama. When the officiating lama is seated, the first play begins. Performers descend from the Du-khang between rows of spectators to the music of drums, and 8-foot-long horns. The courtyard becomes a Globe Theatre. The lamas present a series of symbolic scenes from Padma Sambhava's life; most dramatic is a scene depicting the destruction of the ego, which is symbolized by a dough figure that is splattered and kicked into the audience.

During the performance, two Tibetan traditions are carried on: those of the *Shirimba* and the *Chabo*. The former is an older monk,

---

*Also at Hemis Gomba, you can hike to a shrine and monastery not directly connected with Hemis. At daybreak, about 5:00 A.M., you may join scores of people walking up the valley behind Hemis to a small side valley on the south where a small gomba has been built above a sacred cave. The ceiling of the cave slowly oozes a firm, sticky black substance called *shialajit*, said to have curative properties and also found in other Himalayan locations.

perfectly typecast, who patrols the perimeter of the performing area. He carries a long whip, which he uses to scatter spectators from areas needed for imminent scenes. He never uses the whip with real force, but older women smile widely as they make off, much to the evident surprise and delight of the crowd. The Chabo are two young, energetic monks dressed in red and yellow robes, red masks, and long false pigtails. Their duty is to dun people for contributions to the monastery. One Chabo throws a *kata* (prayer scarf) over someone's head while the other monk claps his hands to draw playful attention to the victim, who must pay or continue to be pestered. The two Chabo also go beyond the monastery courtyard during the dances, becoming the most familiar masked faces of all.

Treks Out of Ladakh's Indus Valley

Ladakh District is one of the four regions remaining to old Ladakh after 1846, when the Treaty of Lahore separated off Spiti and Lahoul. Central Ladakh, which is limited to a 60-mi. stretch of the Indus Valley below the Ladakh and Zanskar ranges, is majestic beyond imagination, the kind of country where one wants to walk into the sunset. Trekking there, aside from walks of a few days around the countryside, means trekking out of the central region to the three other areas of today's Ladakh: Zanskar, Nubra, and Rupshu. The latter two regions are closed to foreigners and Zanskar is difficult to walk through, so trekking has been slow to develop out of Leh. If you decide you want to trek, you will surely be able to find someone to porter, but don't count on arranging it your first day in Ladakh. Check at the Tourist Office in Leh

Masked dancers at Hemis Gomba, Ladakh.

for names of people who might be willing to porter for you. Some Tibetan refugees porter, and they are usually good, hard workers. Most people from Ladakh will not porter, however, but rather rent themselves and their horses. The new trekking agencies in Leh can help.

The trails leading from central Ladakh will be discussed in the following three sections—on Zanskar, Nubra, and Rupshu, which include the majority of Ladakh's area.

Zanskar

Aside from the Karakoram glacial vastness, no place in the Himalayan system is so wide and impenetrable as Zanskar Tehsil (an administrative area) in Ladakh. Zanskar lies south and east of Leh, comprising some 3,000 square miles. Only since 1978 has a rough, dusty road connected Kargil to the small bazaar of Padum, Zanskar's district headquarters; and the wide, flat valley near Padum seems to be the only horizontal surface in Zanskar. Unlike the narrow Ladakh Range, the Zanskar Range is wide and complex; and it is a long range, reaching all the way to Nepal. Most of Zanskar's area is rent with high, sharp-edged ridges that catch enough snow to make the steep gorges below very difficult to ford in the short summer months. Alexander Cunningham, Ladakh's first chronicler, tells us that Zangs-kar means

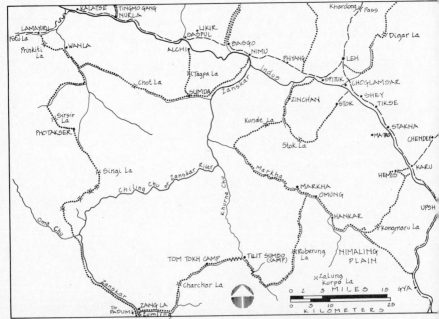

The Indus Valley and Northern Zanskar (*Note*: Trail locations in Zanskar are not exact.)

"white copper." No trading routes of note transect Zanskar, and the region's inhabitants formerly traded only with neighboring Baltis, Ladakhis, Chang-Pas, and Lahoulis.

Some routes can be trekked in Zanskar—several will be mentioned—but no currently available map will give you more than a rough estimate of the jagged terrain. Maps that will correctly depict the difficult landscape are much to be desired. The "reliability diagrams" that accompany the U502 Series sheets covering Zanskar (principally NI43-8, Leh, and NI43-12, Martselang) indicate that the region is not accurately represented. So it takes a hardy, adaptable trekker to strike out along trails far into Zanskar, and all hikers going there will need a local with horses who knows the way, to be guide and cook. Your best sourcebook for information on Zanskar is the second volume of *The Cultural Heritage of Ladakh*, by Snellgrove and Skorupski.

Zanskaris are engagingly friendly for the most part, although some have learned to beg vociferously. As everywhere, the amount of begging is in direct proportion to the prevailing degree of tourism. The sure way to recognize a man from Zanskar and other outlying regions is by his unique hairdo: traditionally, a man shaves the hair on his head completely off to a line running ear to ear over the top of the head, permitting the remainder of his tresses to fall loose to below his collar. The sahru with its upturned flaps is preferred headgear for older Zanskaris.

One trekking route into Zanskar begins at Pannikar village, picking up from the trails that connect with Kashmir. Pannikar village is approached by bus from Kargil or by foot from the Lonvilad Pass. (See Chapter 7.) South of Pannikar is a magnificently situated 12,500-ft. spur called the Pukartse La that can be reached only on foot. Of this pass Arthur Neve (the British physician and explorer) said, "One of the grandest views of the world is that from the Pukartse La, on the first march from Suru to Rangdum." At the pass, you can see closely the rarely viewed double-topped peak of Nun Kun—the 23,410-ft. Nun overshadowing 23,250-ft. Kun. Also visible is the Ganri Glacier, as it descends towards the Suru River, 2,400 ft. below. South of the Pukartse La you can either walk along the flat valley—expect this to take two days—plan to catch a bus at Parkachik village for Rangdum Gomba.

Rangdum Gomba and the small monastery in Mulbek currently are the westernmost extensions of Tibetan Buddhism in the Himalaya. Rangdum rests upon a low hill at the foot of a wildly striated ridge of the Zanskar Range. The monastery puts up hikers and is not particularly isolated now that the Kargil-to-Padum road passes by. Just north of Rangdum is a tributary valley leading eastward. You can walk up this valley to the Kanji La and, beyond, to Hiniskut, on the Srinagar-to-Leh road, some 28 mi. in all. Combining this walk with a trek from Kashmir to Rangdum makes a fascinating hike of at least 2½ weeks. The walk from Rangdum to Hiniskut takes four to five days. Be sure to go with a porter. At Hiniskut you will be 17 mi. west of Lamayuru by road and 9 mi. from Lamayuru by the parallel caravan trail.

Lamayuru is the trailhead for a trek into Zanskar that goes not far from and parallel to the Indus Valley. As you cross the Prinkiti La (2 mi. from Lamayuru) to the village of Wanla, you begin to enter traditional Zanskar. A tributary leading to the southeast rises to the Chot La, from which you descend toward the small village of Sumda with its ancient gomba, some four days' walk from Lamayuru. Sumda lies at the base of a north-south path that will lead you to Alchi, near the Indus. The trail from Sumda crosses the Tagpa La (16,200 ft.) to reach Alchi. Sumda village is the home of the craftsman who made the copper and brass teapot for the family at the Palace View Hotel. Alternatively from Sumda, you can continue eastward along the trail that ascends and descends in erratic fashion along the Zanskar Valley. Friends who have done this trek emphasize that the actual trail from Lamayuru through Sumda and along the Zanskar Valley does not at all resemble the path as shown on the Leh U502 sheet.

Another walking route through Zanskar follows the Marka Valley, an eastern tributary of the raging Zanskar River also called the Chiling Chu; chu means "water," often designating a river. The lower Marka Valley is reached from Spituk, 5 mi. southwest of Leh, by taking a trail west over the Kunde La (16,200 ft.); parts of the valley you've entered, the Marka Valley, have a deep reddish hue. In the middle of the 35-mi. valley is a gomba, upriver from the 30 homes of Marka village (12,600 ft.). At a point a half-hour's walk up-valley from the village a difficult path leads up a side valley from the river's left bank to the Ruberung La and thence southward into the rugged heart of Zanskar; this route is described two paragraphs farther on. Continuing up the main Marka Valley, there is a handsome gomba some 600 ft. above the river at Omung town. Near the head of the Marka Valley is the Kongmaru La (about 17,000 ft.) on the shortest route out of the valley. The Kongmaru, which permits views northward into the Indus Valley, leads to Martselang village by the Indus. Taking this route, you will need about nine days to walk from Spituk into and out of the Marka Valley. Another path out of the upper Marka crosses the Lalung La and descends to the Leh-Manali road a few miles north of Gya village. From there, walk the 15 mi. to Upshi village on the Indus, where buses are available.

Two long north-to-south routes also lead through Zanskar—from the Indus River to Padum (about 11,500 ft.) Of the two paths, the westerly trail from Lamayuru to the Zanskar river and south to Padum is relatively less difficult, but only by Zanskar's forbidding standards. Leaving Lamayuru, a three-hour walk over the low Prinkiti La takes you past wild rose bushes to Wanla village. You continue from Wanla on the path to Chot La but soon leave it and head south through a narrow canyon with sheer sandstone walls and many stream crossings. In the next few days you cross six passes over 15,000 ft., descending little between some of them. The convoluted, multicolored strata is remarkable, south of Photakser in particular. During the week's hike between Lamayuru and the Zanskar River, the trail is sometimes nearly nonexistent, sometimes inches wide next to sheer precipices, and often involves fording ice-water streams. You will pass villages where people ask for "bon bon"—sugar—and request writing pens: although the area is isolated—no doctors practice here, for example—trekkers are now well known. Once you reach the wide, turbid Zanskar River the going is generally easier to Padum. Eventually you arrive at well-touristed Karcha Gomba, the largest monastery in Zanskar. Karcha's many buildings are situated above a village that is a dusty walk north of (and across the Doda River from) Padum. Without question, take a local guide on this trek, and do not expect to be able to resupply food until you reach Padum. Your guide will bring horses (each costing in excess of 50 rupees, more than 6 dollars, per day), without which you could not make the trip.

The second route between Padum and the Indus is extremely difficult. For starters, the route has more than 65 river crossings. If you go before midsummer, the streams will be too high, but if you leave after the middle of September, you risk being caught in early snows. This trek through the midst of jagged Zanskar requires you to have an experienced guide and be completely self-sufficient in food. From the north, the shortest route enters the Marka Valley by the Kongmaru La above Martselang in the Indus Valley. South of the Marka Valley, little forage is available for your guide's horses during three days of rough travel. The trail out of the valley leaves downriver from Omung village and goes up a nala that is dry until about the 14,400-ft. level, above the point where the canyon's creek goes underground. Continue upward to the Ruberung La (about 16,100 ft.) and follow a twisting route into the Kurna Chu gorge. (The correct route up this nala is virtually impossible to find without a guide.) Proceed to a place called Tilit Sumdo, then head west up a narrow canyon involving scores of icy fords to the 16,200-ft. Char Char La, the last pass you cross before reaching Zangla village on the Zanskar River. This oversimplified sketch of the seven- to nine-day walk from Martselang to Zangla may make the hike sound straightforward, but that is not the case. The route cannot be followed by someone who does not know the way; and there is no easy path out if you become lost. Most likely you will not see other people for as much as five days during the middle of this trek.

Once near Zangla, you will recognize the typical flat-roofed Ladakhi village with its whitewashed gomba. From Zangla, the ancestral king of Zanskar's home, Padum is a short two-day walk south along an easy trail, or you can take a bus. Look hereabouts in the Zanskar River Valley for wolf traps: circular, waist-high rings of stones with the topmost layer of rocks cantilevered inward. A lamb is placed inside the 15-ft.-wide trap as bait, and any wolf unfortunate enough to jump in cannot leap out. Perhaps you will also see billy goats with wool or burlap aprons tied below their rib cages. These strange garments are used as birth control devices!

Padum villagers are a mixture of Ladakhi Muslims and Buddhists, their number augmented by a few flatland civil servants who must feel they have been banished to Siberia. Padum even has a tourist officer. A few stores carry food necessities and kerosene, so Padum can be a supply point for basics. Be prepared to encounter vicious midday dust storms in the wide valley upriver and down from Padum.

The stark but spectacular route from Padum south to Lahoul over the Shingo La has become popular with trekkers. Most people make this walk to the roadhead at Darcha village in Lahoul (or the opposite course) in about a week. From Padum, the trail begins by following the Tsarap Lingti Chu southward past Burdun Gomba on its huge rock promontory. Next comes Mune, a hamlet below a small monastery that houses about 15 monks. At Pune, farther to the south, you should definitely take the side trip (three hours each way) to Phuktal Gomba. Phuktal, said to have been founded by Naropa, is a large, fairy-tale monastery built into a cave's mouth on a cliff. Nearby is a tiny spring. Take your flashlight in order to see the gomba's intricate frescos, most of which are hidden in darkness. The walk between Phuktal and the main trail follows the Niri Chu, a dazzling turquoise stream that drains some of Zanskar's most remote hinterland. On your return from Phuktal, recross the main stream at Pune and continue toward the emerging peaks of the Zanskar Range. A long day's hike or more from Pune lies Kargyak, the last village in the valley. Kargyak has numerous mani walls, many stupas, and large, full-blooded yaks. Ask for the excellent yoghurt often available in town. Beyond Kargyak you may have difficulty finding the trail through the rocky glacial debris—keep to the west forks as you ascend. A spectacular if chilly campsite will be found at about 15,000 feet. The remaining two-hour climb is occasionally steep; at the top, a prayer-flag–topped cairn caps the Shingo La (about 16,800 ft.). The continuation of this route is noted briefly at the end of the Lahoul section in Chapter 9.

Nubra

Nubra, which has been restricted to outsiders prior to this writing in mid-1981, lies north of Leh across the 18,400-ft. Khardong Pass, the first of the five passes crossed on the Leh-to-Turkestan route. This area had always been Ladakh's largest district until part of its land—the wintry, 17,000-ft. plateau called Aksai Chin, the "Desert of White Stones"—was lost to China. Nubra's remaining territory consists of two long, low valleys beneath the eastern Karakoram, the highest peaks within Ladakh. These are the upper Shyok Valley, which skirts the easternmost spurs of the Karakoram, and the Nubra Valley, at the head of which glacial water from the Terong Glacier and the great Siachen emanates.

The Nubra Valley was once glaciated as far south as Charasa village and so is U-shaped with steep granite walls along much of its length. Its slate-colored river rises at the mouth of the 45-mi.-long Siachen Glacier and merges with the Shyok River at the 10,000-ft. level some 60 mi. south. At this river junction you are due north of Leh, across the Khardong La over the Ladakh Range. The Nubra snakes back and forth across the 2-mi.-wide Nubra Valley floor, glancing off the ridge walls and making passage difficult during the high summer waters, particularly in the upper valley. In the side valley east of Tigur village is an old fortress with Buddhist wall frescos, and beyond that is Santanling Gompa. On the right bank of the Nubra, across the river from Tigur, is Charasa with its rock-anchored fortress.

On the east side of the valley are the town of Panamik (more than 50 mi. by bus from Leh) and its nearby springs: red-colored, sulphurous, and, at more than 150 degress, too hot to immerse oneself in directly. Teddy Roosevelt, who visited the springs in Panamik, mentioned seeing a green algae utterly unlike anything seen elsewhere in Ladakh. Panamik village has always been a kind of Ultima Thule—the last place where caravans of yore or today's trekkers (if permitted) would see any green vegetation for at least nine days.

Six miles north of Panamik the old caravan route turns east, up a narrow gorge with mile-high walls, for the dicey Sasser La, a glaciated pass (18,000 ft.). This is the most treacherous of the five Leh-to-Yarkand passes. Early travelers who climbed the hairpin curves traversing its slopes tell of bones alongside the trail—not just a few bones but bleached piles of them, from the animals that could not make the climb or were caught in summer storms.

Once over the Sasser Pass the caravan route descends into the upper Shyok Valley near the border. There, the rare visitor is not far from the Shyok River's origin, at the place where the water from the Rimo Glacier meets the Chip Chap River. Just to the north is the Karakoram Pass, now the oficial meeting point of Pakistan, India, and China. The trekker returning from the upper Shyok would have to retrace the path taken, over the pass.

Although the entire Nubra region remains closed to outsiders, there is now a road across the Khardong Pass, and other paths as well. The Leh U502 sheet suggests no fewer than five other high-pass routes that cross to Nubra: trails north from Tingmo Gang, Saspul, and Basgo, as well as the Digar La route up the valley just east of Leh. On a typically brilliant Ladakh day, a person would have fine views of the eastern Karakoram from most of these passes. But if you are allowed in, go prepared. The Ladakh Range is high; these passes are mostly snow-covered and over 17,000 ft. There can be vicious storms at those elevations any month of the year.

Rupshu

Rupshu is an ideal trekking location for those who have no difficulty in acclimatization, for it has majestic terrain, high passes with distant Tibetan views, and a fascinating, hardy, nomadic people. The inhabitants of Rupshu are the Chang-Pas, said to be the world's highest dwellers and some of the last wide-ranging nomads of central and south Asia since the Powendas (Koochies) were officially barred in 1972 from crossing the Pakistan-Afghan border.

Topographically, Rupshu is an integral part of Chang Tang, Tibet's 600-mi. wide, 15,000-ft. northern steppes. East of Zanskar and the Manali-Leh road, Rupshu is Ladakh's highest area. The lowest point in all of Rupshu is at 13,000 ft. along the Indus River near the town of Chumatang. Within Rupshu's 5,500-square-mile area are the peaks of the Ladakh and Zanskar mountains, and several high, crystalline lakes framed in wide basins between the two ranges. The large size of Tso Morari and Pangong Lake, among other lacustrine jewels, distinguishes Rupshu from any other Himalayan area outside Tibet.

The 14,000-ft. and 15,000-ft. plains of Rupshu, the extreme western part of the Chang Tang region (or Zhang Zhung as it is called in Tibet), support the totally nomadic Chang-Pa. The Chang-Pa economy is geared to the yak, a creature that dislikes descending lower than a 12,000-ft. elevation, and which provides food, fuel, shelter, and wool for clothing. The Chang-Pa live in black yak-hair tents called *rebu* and traverse a land so high that, as in Nepal's Dolpo District, one of the first requirements for anyone living there is an animal-skin bellows to keep a fire going in the thin air. Chang-Pas have traditionally subsisted on a hearty but unvarying diet consisting almost entirely of roasted barley flour (here called *phe*), tea, *chang* (grain beer), meat, salt, milk, butter, and cheese. The menu most days is phe with *solja* (tea with butter and salt) and various kinds of soup. The women wear their own version of the Ladakhi pyerack and, like all Bhotia women (women of Tibetan origin), they appreciate coral and turquoise. The Chang-Pa are Buddhist. Like most ethnic Tibetans, they celebrate Losar (the Tibetan New Year) with fervor and gladly travel long distances for celebration.

Although the once-massive herds of speedy *kyang*, the Tibetan wild horses, are greatly depleted in Rupshu, the marmot colonies have not visibly suffered from poaching. In Rupshu, as in the sweeping Deosai Plains of Baltistan the sizable, sleek marmots—larger than the groundhogs they resemble—appear to be the true homebodies of the mountain desert.

The traditional path across Rupshu is the first stretch of the Leh-Gartok-Lhasa caravan route, now a paved road. It diverges from the Indus at Karu village, climbing the Ladakh Range (across the Indus Valley from Hemis) to reach the Chang La (18,300 ft.), passing several villages and the Chendey and Trakthok monasteries. This route now reaches Tankse (Tangtse) within 20 mi. past the Chang La. Tankse is a summer village 14 mi. south of the Shyok River's southern bend. It used to house Ladakh's easternmost customs post and was the effective limit of Ladakh's territory. At Tankse, the road continues south to Demchok village, near the current political border. Rudok in Tibet lies beyond. Another nearly level valley leads east from Tankse. Cradled by marble cliffs, this route crosses a low, lake-topped pass and, 25 mi. beyond, reaches Pangong Lake (13,917 ft.).

The vivid blue Pangong Lake, meaning "great cavity" in Tibetan, is continuous for nearly a hundred miles as it crosses into Tibet, almost touching Rudok. Pangong evokes wonderful images to the desert-fancier: a solitary, tranquil camp near a glacial stream; drinking tea with a Chang-Pa family; and, come evening, tracking the shy kyang through low lakeside hills. In *The Way of the White Clouds*, Lama Anagarika Govinda tells how on first approaching the lake he inadvertently walked into it: "The water was as invisible as the air!" Along the straight eastern shore of the lake, the glacial tributaries can supply drinking water—the lake is sterile and incapable of supporting bacterial life. The water of the Pangong may be invisible near its shore, but in the middle of the lake it assumes a deep, lapis-lazuli blue—the blue that is seen over high passes as one approaches Tibet.

Rupshu, like all of Ladakh, abounds in myth and legend, most of it based on fact. Some say that Jesus passed the "lost" years of his life in Hemis Monastery. Lama Govinda received his second initiation while resting on the approaches to the Chang La. And Gypsy Davy and Lady Ba camped for three weeks at various places about Pangong Lake in the early 1920s. Once, along the northern side of the lake, Lady Ba's horse, Tomar, disappeared with a herd of kyang. The best shikaris were sent to track him, and they did, across two ranges and a valley. On the third day, Tomar returned "seven years younger than he went out on *shikar*."

Tibetan woman wearing a prayer box charm (photo by Linda Liscom).

9

The Himachal Pradesh Region

The solitude of the mountains had given me back to myself.
Unknown

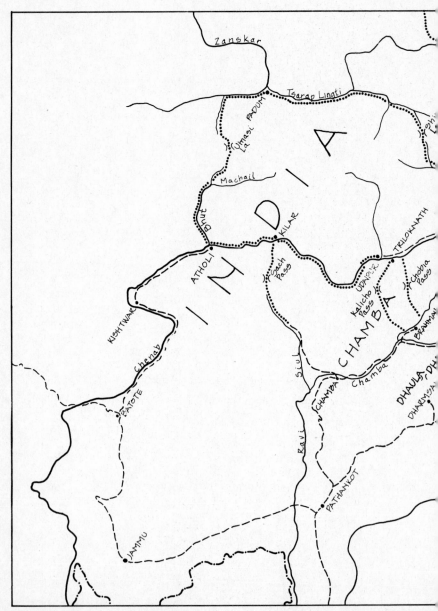

Chamba, Kulu, Lahoul, and Spiti

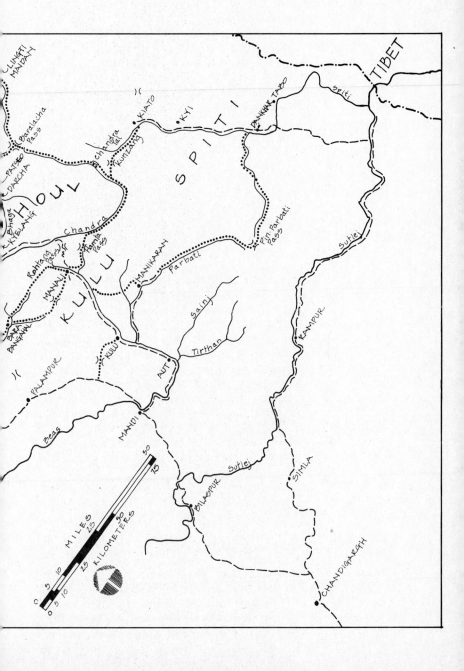

The Districts of "Himalaya State"

Four rarely visited west Himalayan areas form the grist for this chapter—Chamba, Kulu, Lahoul, and Spiti. These valley systems lie south of Ladakh's Zanskar and Rupshu regions, to the northwest of the deep Sutlej River gorge, and entirely within the Indian state of Himachal Pradesh, "Himalaya State." They are, respectively, the upper watersheds of the Ravi, Beas, Chenab, and Spiti Rivers. Chamba and Kulu, in the southerly draining Ravi and Beas valleys, offer lush, monsoon-drenched vistas ribbed with ancient paths that are rewarding for experienced rainy-season hikers. Their people are Hindu, whereas Lahoul and Spiti, in drier land to the north, are Buddhist.

Before the British defeated Gulab Singh's army in the mid-1840s, Chamba and Kulu were two independent middle-Himalayan kingdoms. These small states were insulated from the southern plains by the adjacent hill principalities called Kangra, Mandi, and Kinnaur and from the north by their inaccessibility through the Chenab River gorge and the walls of the Great Himalayan Range. As this west Himalayan region was demarcated by the British, neither Chamba nor Kulu was included in southernmost Jammu and Kashmir, Maharajah Singh's domain. Kulu, small in size but strategic with its direct north-south valley, was an important link in a trans-Himalayan trail used by officials and merchants traveling to or from west Tibet. The main path from Kulu to Lahoul over the Rohtang Pass has always been vital to the Ghaddi shepherds, who move their throngs of animals north every verdant spring and south in the windswept autumn.

The Buddhist areas of Lahoul and Spiti, north of Chamba and Kulu, were once the farthest reaches of southwestern Tibet. While the kings of Ladakh were in power, Lahoul and Spiti were united with the Indus Valley by lengthy paths northward through the rugged Zanskar and the Rupshu uplands, which required two weeks to walk. Later, the English recognized that Lahoul and Spiti could provide trade routes to transport the prized pashmina shawl wool and bypass Kashmiri taxation; until 1946, these areas were still part of Ladakh. Today, Lahoul and Spiti districts remain linked culturally with Ladakh, although they are administered and approached from the south. As of mid-1981, Spiti remains closed to visitors.

The relatively few Westerners who have walked in Kulu or Lahoul know the pleasures of walking little-known paths through valleys that are as scenic as other, more crowded trails, just less publicized.

How to Reach These Four Areas

Chamba is reached in two stages from New Delhi. Take a bus or, for a more comfortable ride, a sleeper train to Pathankot, not far from the Jammu Tawi Station on the way to Srinagar. (Note how to book trains from New Delhi in Chapter 3.) Change at Pathankot for the 75-mi. bus or taxi ride to Chamba town, passing through the attractive hill station of Dalhousie. Many visitors like to stop and cool off in Dalhousie, at an elevation nearly three times that of Chamba bazaar.

The Kulu Valley is approached directly by bus from the Inter-State Bus Terminal in New Delhi, or by taking a train from Delhi to Chandigarh and there switching to a bus for Mandi (which is en route) or Manali. Vouchers for reserved seats on the daily bus to Manali, the chief town in the Kulu Valley, can be purchased in New Delhi at the Haryana Emporium on Baba Kharak Singh Road near Connaught Circus. Buses into Kulu are often delayed long hours during the summer monsoon, as I found out one warm night at the Mandi Bus Depot: the overnight express was forced to halt, doubling its journey time to Delhi, while ochre-colored avalanche debris 6 mi. away was bulldozed from the road. The 14-to-20-hour bus ride from Delhi to Manali brings on what one exhausted traveler called "inevitable sleeping-position weirdness." There is a small airstrip at Bhuntar, 7 mi. south of Kulu town, but flights into the airfield are few.

In order to reach Kyelang, the largest village in Lahoul, you must first travel to the Kulu Valley. There, from either the depot at Manali or Kulu town, take the morning bus over the Rohtang Pass. Many hairpin turns, knee-cramped hours, and mind-boggling glimpses later, you will arrive in Kyelang. From there, a bus road extends along Lahoul's main Chenab Valley to Udiapur, but the Chenab Valley highway continuing west from Udiapur to Kishtwar and Kashmir will not be completed before 1990.

The barren Spiti Valley is connected by road with both Lahoul's upper Chandra Valley (an extension of the Chenab) to the west (and to Manali via the Rohtang) and with the deep Sutlej gorge to the east. North of the Rohtang Pass, the main Kulu-to-Lahoul (Kyelang) road twists, descending through pastures and boulders. At a place called Gramphu, the narrow Jeep road to Spiti diverges up-valley, crossing the barren Kunzang Pass. The lower and more accessible bus approach to Spiti is from Simla (north of Chandigarh) through Kinnaur, in the Sutlej Valley. When Spiti and Kinnaur are derestricted, you will be able to take a bus from Simla to Kalpa in the Sutlej Valley and there change vehicles to reach the Spiti Valley.

Chamba

Hidden behind the Kangra region's 15,000-ft. high Dhaula Dhar ridge, Chamba lies between Jammu to the west and Lahoul and Kulu to the east. A mountainous, rectangular tract 60 mi. by 70 mi. across, Chamba includes the easternmost peaks of the Pir Panjal Range and a stretch of the deep Chenab gorge downstream from Lahoul in the Himalaya. Few areas in the Himalaya (excepting far western Nepal) as large and climatically favorable have so long remained virtually unknown to trekkers.

The town of Chamba (2,380 ft.) lies on the south bank of the Ravi River, 25 mi. east of Dalhousie. This is the principal village in the area, with hotels, a tourist's rest house, a large bazaar, and transportation to upper valley trailheads where paths lead to Lahoul, Kulu, and Kangra. Chamba has been Hindu for two millenniums. This enduring faith is symbolized by the six tall stone temples dedicated to Vishnu and Shiva in Chamba Bazaar, near the half-mile-long marketplace and promenade. Every August, a fair celebrates the ripening of the valley's corn, and it is widely attended by hill people who come as much for the grand bazaar and the sociability as for the colorful procession of religious images that climaxes the festival.

The most intriguing and best-traveled denizens of Chamba and Kangra are the Ghaddis, a clan of people who are usually seen high on green mountain meadows during the summer with their mixed herds of sheep and goats. Their well-trained dogs help move the animals. The Ghaddi men annually travel long distances from their warm, monsoon-blessed southern valley up to the dry mountain deserts of Lahoul and even as far as Rupshu; the Ghaddi women and children stay at home in the summer to work the fields. When I walked in northern Lahoul during the second week of July the Ghaddi shepherds were there, fanning out in the tributaries of the upper Bhaga Valley. Another clan of seminomadic herders, the Gujars, whom I had seen in Chitral and Kashmir, resemble tall, long-striding, mocha-colored Pathans; but I was in for a surprise when I first saw Ghaddis walking near their flocks. These short, deep-brown-complected men are dressed like mountain sprites in woolen homespun clothing, and when they move they seem to float. While talking with them, I admired their smoke-white woolen robes, which are worn gathered at the waist by many loops of black wool cord. In daytime the garment hangs to the knees like a Muslim's shirt, but at night the robe is let out, providing the warmth of a blanket. If you are invited to tea and warmth by their fire, giving some extra matches or tea is a good way to express appreciation.

Trekking Possibilities from Chamba

With thousands traveling the favored routes in Nepal each year and countless more seeking other places to walk, it is reassuring that places such as Chamba can be departure point or destination for people who want to hike in the mountains yet lack the herd instinct. From three areas in Chamba, treks can be undertaken to Lahoul, Manali, Kangra, and Zanskar.

The first of these three areas surrounds the two upper branches of the Ravi River. The town of Brahmaur, formerly the capital of Chamba State, lies on the large Budhil Nala 40 mi. east of Chamba Bazaar. Here, as well as in the main Ravi Valley to the south, you are in the Ghaddis' homeland, a country with Hindu temples 1,500 years old. From the beautifully situated town you can walk north over the high Chobia or Kalicho passes to western Lahoul, or south over the Chobu or Nikora passes to Bara Bangahal. Check with locals regarding pass conditions, particularly if you are going to Lahoul: those cols are high, and some are glaciated. If you are going to Triloknath in Lahoul via the Kalicho trail, or to Bara Bangahal over the Nikora Pass, figure a three- to five-day walk, depending on weather conditions and your pace.

Bara Bangahal, like Chamba, Kangra, and Kulu, is the name of a region and of its largest town. The town of Bara Bangahal is some 60 mi. southeast and upriver from Chamba Bazaar, near the headwaters of the Ravi River, the smallest of the "five fingers" of the Indus. The town of Bara Bangahal may not yet be connected up-valley with Chamba by road. The bazaar is used by Ghaddis and, by following their trails, you can walk over high passes southward to Kangra or eastward to the Kulu Valley towns of Solang, Manali, Katrain, and Baragran. The passes to Kulu cross the easternmost ridges of the Pir Panjal Range, which sweeps northwestward past the Vale of Kashmir. South of the Ravi Valley approach to Bara Bangahal Bazaar are various trails that connect Chamba with the towns of Dharmsala, Palampur, and Baijnath in Kangra.

The third area, centering on the Siul Nala and its tributaries north of Chamba Bazaar, contains trails of greater length than the paths in eastern Chamba. Several relatively low-level trails lead into the Chenab Valley below Kishtwar in Jammu, where when you descend to the main valley floor, you reach the Kishtwar road. Farther north up the Siul Nala, however, are higher passes to the currently roadless Chenab Valley area called Pangi, between Jammu and Lahoul. The 14,480-ft. Sach Pass caps the best-known route to the Pangi region and leads directly to its main village, the remote town of Kilar. From Kilar a trail descends the Chenab Valley to the roadhead; in 1981, this was near Atholi. A high, rarely used path departs Atholi for the Umasi La, a glaciated pass to Zanskar. (Note the description of the Umasi La in Chapter 7).

A Few Notes on Kangra

Kangra formerly was one of the most important west Himalayan hill states, occupying a wide area west of the Sutlej. Now the area called Kangra reaches only from the ridge line of Dhaula Dhar, south of Chamba, to the Siwalik Hills bordering the Gangetic plains. The Kangra region is replete with ancient temple architecture, but most Angrezi who travel there today are not antiquarians: they are usually tea-house habitués or students of Buddhism who stay in Dharmsala. As previously noted, hikers going north can take trails from Dharmsala, Palampur, or Baijnath over Dhaula Dhar to Bara Bangahal in Chamba. In eastern Kangra, a lovely side valley called Chota Bangahal, Ghaddi trails lead as well to the Kulu Valley.

Kulu

Of the four areas, the Kulu Valley, called the valley of the gods, has received the most tourism by both Indian and Angrezi, for it was open to foreigners prior to 1974. Kulu is known for its pine forests, its lively autumn festival, and its network of hill trails.

Treks from Manali

The upper Kulu Valley town of Manali (on the Beas River, at 6,300 ft.) is the most popular place to begin or end a brek in Himachal Pradesh. Trails out of Manali lead to passes connecting with Chamba and with Lahoul's Chandra Valley. Manali's tourist officer can advise you about the region's most frequented paths, and if you need a porter or crew he can also direct you to one of the several trek outfitters in town.

Manali is not a hill station for the gentry like Dalhousie or Simla. The long bus ride from New Delhi and lack of abundant luxury hotels limit the number of people going to the Kulu Valley. Still, Manali has grown—from a few shops 20 years ago to an eclectic hodgepodge of new and newer stores, hotels, and lodges. During the summer season the bazaar teems with Pahari-speaking Kulu walas. Lahoulis, Nepali laborers, Tibetan refugees, and foreign downcountry tourists. The people of Kulu, slightly built and congenial, raise excellent fruits of many varieties in addition to the valley's renowned, succulent apples. Men from this valley and from Lahoul wear distinctive pillbox hats, which have changed in recent years; the front-facing material of the hats was formerly subdued velvet but now is cloth of a bright, multi-colored pattern. In winter when the valley is snow-blanketed, people stay at home spinning and weaving wool for the costly, elegant Kulu shawls of pashmina and Angora, and Manali sleeps.

Manali is the trailhead for many walks and excursions. The pagoda-roofed Hadimba Temple housing an image of goddess Hirma Devi is sheltered in a grove of gargantuan deodar on a low spur just northwest of the bazaar. A road out of the upper bazaar leads to a trail up through this cedar forest, but the 400-year-old temple can also be approached from the south. To do so, take the trail out of Manali bazaar that goes to Sial village, situated on a knoll just west of town. At Sial you'll see typical Kulu homes with one or two lower stories of mud plaster topped by an upper story cloaked in wood from roof to porch. In Sial ask for the way to Sonoghee, the next village up the path. Sonoghee lies on the north bank of a small ravine, a 15- to 20-minute walk from Manali. Rest and take tea at Sonoghee, or continue on the wide trail, heading up-valley within the evergreen-clad folds of the vail. Ten minutes away is the tall, daunting Hadimba Temple.

Many people, arriving in Manali after a trek or the long ride from Delhi, will at once hire a taxi or walk 2 mi. to the hot baths at Vashist. To reach Vashist from Manali, cross from the bazaar to the left bank of the Beas River, where large signs announce the commencement of the 295-mi. Manali-to-Leh road (which in Ladakh is little more than a wide, rocky path). Continue northward along the road, then up an easterly path to the place where the Tourism Department has erected bathing cubicles and a cafe. If you wish to use the old baths in the village, carry on along the paved road to Vashist bazaar. These original baths, where locals go regularly to wash, are less antiseptic than the newer spa and not for those who dislike an occasional floating green waterplant.

Solang, one of the last settlements up the Kulu Valley, can be reached directly by Jeep or by taking a bus from Manali to Palchan village and then continuing up-valley by foot. Solang has a rest house that can be booked with the Manali tourist officer. From here, you can take a day hike to Beas Kund (a mountain lake) or begin your trek westward over the high pass to Bara Bangahal in Chamba.

Beyond Palchan on the road to the Rohtang Pass is the turnoff for Kothi village, its rest house the accommodation closest to treeline in the pass area. The stretch of road from Kothi on up to the settlement of Mahri offers scenery reminiscent of the Swiss Alps. During the monsoon summer, snowfields above pour cascades of water over slate faces framed in tall pine forests. Tourists from the industrial Punjab who have never been into the mountains take taxis or the special daily round-trip bus to the top of the nearly 13,000-ft. Rohtang Pass, a full 30 mi. by road from Manali but barely out of sight above the town. A separate pathway up the Rohtang remains in use for the tens of thousands of animals and their Ghaddi herdsmen who yearly cross and recross the wide, rolling pass. When William O. Douglas traversed the Rohtang, near the end of July in 1951, he encountered a torrential rainstorm on the approach to Kothi and the next day on the pass saw cattle and horses killed by a freak snow. Beyond the Rohtang Pass are road connections along the Chandra Valley to Spiti (on the east), Kyelang, and Udiapur.

A hike lasting several days involves walking east from Manali to the Hamta Pass (about 14,500 ft.). The Rohtang has a vehicle road, but the Hamta Pass will continue to be negotiated exclusively by the occasional donkey train going to Spiti, a few Ghaddi shepherds, and the occasional group of trekkers. From the top of the pass, 19,690-ft. Deo Tibba in Kulu is visible, as are other, higher peaks in the vast, uninhabited mountain mass of Lahoul. One route on the other side of the pass is described in the section on Lahoul.

Kulu's Side Valleys

Most visitors to Kulu, like visitors everywhere, follow particular roads and only to the well-touristed places. It is as though seeing Kulu's pine-covered ridges beneath meadows fed by snowmelt is so grand that one shouldn't dare to further intrude. But once you have made the journey to the Kulu Valley, you are amid the scenery, not regarding the view from afar as you would at a hill station. Grazing trails in profusion thread the slopes, and the plucky walker who wants to tramp through the hills may want to explore one or more crossings between Kulu's idyllic side valleys.

The Sainj and Tirthan valleys debouch near Aut village in southern Kulu, some 50 mi. below the headwaters of the Beas at the boundary with Lahoul. Between the Rohtang Pass and those two valleys in lower

Kulu are nearly 20 tributary valleys, all leading to passes or snow-covered summits of the Pir Panjal and Himalayan ranges. These feeder valleys generally enter the Beas Valley at right angles, like the branches of an evergreen tree, with the southern streams longer than those to the north. If you have time for a trek of several days, take a bus or walk into a southern valley and begin heading northward, crossing ridges as you go. If, on the other hand, you want only one or two nights out, you may decide to leave from a northern town and return to it through a nearby nala.

Due partly to the beauty, ambiance, and relative accessibility of Kulu, small colonies of foreign travelers congregate there for the local *charas*. In English we call charas by its Arabic name: hashish. Serious aficionados, whether local or Angrezi, call themselves *charasi*; they use considerable effort preparing their own charas or they purchase it only from trusted friends, because adulteration has increased in recent years. Charas is often used by long-distance walkers and mountain climbers in the Himalaya to relieve fatigue, increase flagging appetites, or aid the onset of sleep at high elevation. It was a cash crop for the hill people who collected it long before Westerners began buying in quantity during the late 1960s, although its value has increased greatly since then. Note, however, that the Kulu Valley has no monopoly on charas. In virtually all regions discussed in Chapters 4 to 13, the wild cannabis plant is either rubbed for hashish or cut for *ganga* (marijuana) despite its illegality.

Lahoul

The unprepared traveler might imagine Lahoul, remote and isolated by high ranges, to be economically bereft or scenically desolate. The latter impression is quashed first, as soon as the visitor reaches the far, northern side of the wide Rohtang Pass. Across the Chandra Valley an entire glacier is visible, from its white upper snow chutes to its grey snout belching a frothing stream. Shortly thereafter the new arrival comes across large homes and well-dressed Lahoulis, and realizes that people in Lahoul are often more prosperous than their neighbors.

Lahoul has three principal valleys. The area called Pattan is in western Lahoul's deep Chenab River gorge. Upstream, the Chenab divides into two more valleys, called the Bhaga and Chandra. These gorges, emanating from their respective sources near the Baralacha Pass, resemble the thumb and forefinger of the upturned left hand touching, where the thumb is the Bhaga and the forefinger the Chandra.

The districts of Lahoul and Spiti have been allied by both geographic locale and their common Buddhist culture. Ancient upland trails from Leh and Lhasa crossed both regions. Today only ruined buildings remain of what were once vast wholesale bazaars at Patseo in Lahoul and Losar in Spiti. The barren plains of Patseo and Losar were resting places for great caravans while their goods were bartered by traveling merchants from Kulu, Ladakh, Yarkand, and Tibet.

Some Lahoulis continue to transport goods by mule into upper Spiti and over the Baralacha Pass to the high plains of Rupshu, but most people in Lahoul are farmers or work for the government. Seed potatoes grow well in Lahoul's bracing climate, and from that crop alone some Lahoulis have become wealthy enough to buy choice tracts of land in Kulu for winter residences. Another unlikely but profitable source of income for Lahoulis is the harvesting of wild herbs. The plant called *kut* is a fine example: oil extracted from its roots is valuable as a perfume base.

Traditionally Lahoul has been divided into six regions, and there are also five or six local dialects. The keeper of the one-room restaurant cum hotel at Sumdo in the Bhaga Valley remarked that he has difficulty understanding the Lahouli dialect of people from Gondla in the Chandra Valley, fewer than three hours away by bus. Irrespective of locality, the women of Lahoul wear an embroidered, pleated maroon or brown dress that reaches to within a foot of the ground. To this may be added large, old-style earrings of turquoise and brass, nose rings, and heavy leggings, though some prefer modern silver earrings and stockings. The younger women wear various styles of necklaces, while their mothers prefer neckpieces of alternating coral and turquoise. Each woman uses a scarf to provide sun protection and color. All ladies have a single braid of hair, and the old-style hairdo of married women involves removing hair above the forehead in an area the shape of a V, with the apex of the V at the part.

The green oasis of Kyelang in the Bhaga Valley has been the administrative capital of Lahoul for enough years now to warrant having constructed a second generation of utilitarian government buildings. During the months of May to December, buses run daily to Kyelang from Manali and Kulu bazaar over the weather-lashed Rohtang Pass, when it is clear of snow for road travel. Kyelang's modest bazaar, dating to the caravan days, offers basic necessities at regulated prices. The large PWD rest house maintains extra tent lodgings in the busy summer season, and several plain restaurants serve meals. Kyelang's square, stolid houses are three or more stories tall, Tibetan style. There is a gomba high above town and a larger one named Kardong across the deep Bhaga Valley.

Trekking in Lahoul

People who like walking in high mountain desert will appreciate Lahoul, but they must choose their season. The upper valleys and passes are not clear of snow before the Ghaddis bring their herds in during July, but by that time the monsoon has begun, and the hiker needs to be prepared for the possibility of rain. The summer months are good ones for walking, nonetheless, as the rain that does reach Lahoul tends to fall at night. Note that the Rohtang Pass road may be closed by late October, so that if you are not back in time you will have to walk over it to get south to Manali.

In the Pattan area of the Chenab Valley in western Lahoul, the town of Triloknath (with its ancient temple containing a white marble Buddha image) sits at the base of a nala leading to the glaciated Kalicho Pass. Both the trail from Triloknath and the path over the high Chobia Pass beginning at the nearby village of Bima lead to Brahmaur in Chamba. Check with locals to be certain the pass you want to cross is open, before you attempt it. These paths to Chamba are usually not passable until mid-July.

A good trek for the hardy walker would leave from Manali, cross the Hamta Pass and, after descending, follow Lahoul's long upper Chandra Valley northward to its head at the Baralcha Pass, continuing over the pass and down the Bhaga Valley to the roadhead at Darcha. A day's walk out of Darcha I met an English couple who had nearly finished this walk. They were tired, having walked without a porter and carried all their food, but they were also most satisfied. The 8,000-ft. climb from Manali to the Hamta was the most difficult part, but their muscles firmed up along the Chandra Valley, where they waded many glacial streams, communicated by sign language with Ghaddi herders by the evening fires, and found Chandra Tal ("Moon Lake") to be the most beautiful spot on the trek. With their heavy packs, they went slowly at first, then sped up, taking 11 days from Manali to the road-head at Darcha. With a good porter and no trouble at streams, you might do the same trek in slightly less time.

A shorter walk that takes you through sere ochre- and magenta-splashed mountain desert can be made by traversing one stretch of the previous route, up and back from Darcha to Baralacha. To reach Darcha, you can take the 4 P.M. bus from Kyelang. Before leaving Kyelang, however, stop at the SDO's office behind the PWD rest house and request a chit that will allow you to stay at the Patseo rest house; 8 mi. beyond Darcha, this two-room structure with a tiny chowkidar's hut in back is the only building north of Darcha for at least a week's walk.

Leaving Darcha on the deserted road to the Baralacha Pass (about 16,100 ft.), you enter a land populated in summer by shepherds and their scattered herds of sheep and traversed by infrequent mule trains from Manali going to Rupshu. Geographically you could be in Tibet: there are no trees or bushes, and locals must carry wood or use dung chips for fuel. This walk from Darcha to the Baralacha and back will take about four days.

Finally, there is the horse trail over the Shingo La (about 16,800 ft.) that most trekkers follow to reach Zanskar from Lahoul (or the reverse). This path, from the Darcha roadhead to Padum in Zanskar, takes about a week to traverse. The initial unforgettable spot along this trail is an icy river crossing a short day's walk beyond Darcha. The valley becomes progressively drier as you proceed upward, and the scraggly trees along the canyon's walls eventually disappear. The frigid stream must be recrossed, and you make two especially steep, rocky ascents before the pass is reached about two days' walk from Darcha. Look for wild horses in the upper valley. The continuation of this route from the Shingo La to Padum is described in the Zanskar section of Chapter 8.

Spiti

Visiting the Spiti Valley as recently as 1956, David Snellgrove wrote that "Spiti has completely preserved its Tibetan character"; however, that was before the road was built into Spiti from the Sutlej Valley. A 1977 newspaper squib related that regular bus service was due to begin from the Sutlej Valley to Tabo in Spiti, "known in archaeological circles as the Ajanta of the Himalayas." There is great curiosity about this district because of the artwork in Spiti's gombas, the few photographs published of its dry canyons, and the lure of the unvisited valleys, but as of 1981, all of Spiti remains restricted to foreigners. Good sources of information on Spiti are Snellgrove's *Buddhist Himalaya* and G. D. Khosla's *Himalayan Circuit*.

Until 1630 the Spiti Valley was the westernmost province of the west Tibetan kingdom called Guge that stretched to the village of Taklakot near the present Indo-Nepalese border. In those times, Spiti people practiced polyandry and all married women wore the *perag*, a local version of the Tibetan headpiece of coral and turquoise. Befitting the valley's high elevation, the principal crops were and still are barley, buckwheat, and peas. When Guge disintegrated, Lahoul and Spiti came under the suzerainty of Leh's royal family. The Spiti Valley has not been prosperous since the days of the great trans-Himalayan trade caravans, when one branch of the ancient Hindustan-to-Tibet route utilized Spiti's high valley as a connecting link from Tibet to Kulu and the southern path to Kashmir.

All passes into Spiti from the south are snowed in for an average of eight months yearly; now, however, the road that has been built into Spiti from the south would remain open. But if Spiti is ever derestricted, any of several routes could take you in. A Jeep road over the Kunzang La goes from Gramphu to the head of the Spiti Valley, and bus service connects the lower valley with the Sutlej road. There are also a few footpaths into Spiti from the south, although they are rarely used now except by herders. The principal trail into Spiti south of the Kunzang La crosses the Pin–Parbati Pass (about 15,000 ft.). Named for the valleys it connects, the Pin-Parbati Pass is approached from the west by taking a bus from Kulu Bazaar to Manikaran or as far beyond Manikaran as the bus continues up the Parbati Valley. From there, it is about a 25-mi. walk to the pass and an equal distance along the Pin Valley before the main road near Spiti's old capital of Dankhar is reached. (You can go just as far as the pass at present.) Spiti's borders with Lahoul, Kulu, and Kinnaur are marked by a concatenated strand of white, 20,000-ft. peaks. The few additional recognized routes into Spiti originate in Kinnaur, between those summits, but they too are restricted.

As with many gombas and temples throughout the Himalaya, the artistic heritage that remains in the monasteries of Spiti is only the portion of the past that remains unthieved. Nonetheless, four gombas in Spiti are said to merit attention, as much for their spectacular settings as for the images and paintings within them. Proceeding upriver from the lower valley, the four best-known gombas begin with the temple of Nako, built over a rock that has an imprint alleged to be of Padma Sambhava's foot. The small building is important only because of this footprint, which is similar to the indentations in rocks at Luang Prabang, in Laos, and at Adam's Peak in Sri Lanka. Farther along is the most important gomba in the valley, a Nyingma-sect temple in Tabo with excellent early frescos and a beautiful, many-armed image of Avalokitesvara (the Buddha), of whom Padma Sambhava was a human manifestation. The third temple in Spiti is at Dankhar, two small buildings containing 16th-century frescos. Above the Dankhar monastery sits the old fortress capital of Spiti. Some 25 mi. beyond Dankhar is Kyi Gomba, situated just as you could hope to find the highest monastery in a remote valley: the small white buildings of Kyi rest on a knoll above the trail and seem to float before the high, stratified escarpment like a miniature lost city.

Spiti's upper valley is splashed with deep reds and browns. In caravan days, travelers through Spiti knew they were nearing Lahoul and the green vale of Kulu when they passed the maroon canyon where the valley turns due west at Kiato. Spiti has many serpentine side valleys tending either to the southwest or northeast. These southwest valleys are usually culs-de-sac, but several tributaries heading northeast from upper Spiti lead to the Charap Valley, which connects with the Lingti Maidan (*maidan* means "plain") on the Manali-to-Leh Road north of the Baralacha Pass. Maps show a trail going north just east of Kiato and another better-known path over a pass called the Parang La to the valley of the Para Chu. The Parang La trail is the direct Spiti-to-Rupshu route—the kind of trek that inveterate hikers like to dream about in front of the home fire. The Para Chu Valley leads onto Rupshu's high plains—to the great salt lake of Tso Morari and the trail to Hanle and Tashigang in the upper Indus Valley. All of these treks, however, will have to wait until the areas are derestricted after an international border is negotiated.

10

The Yatra Trails and Garhwal

A hundred divine epochs would not suffice to describe all the marvels of Himachal. As the dew is dried up by the morning sun, so are the sins of mankind by the sight of Himachal.

Skanda Purana, 5th Century A.D.

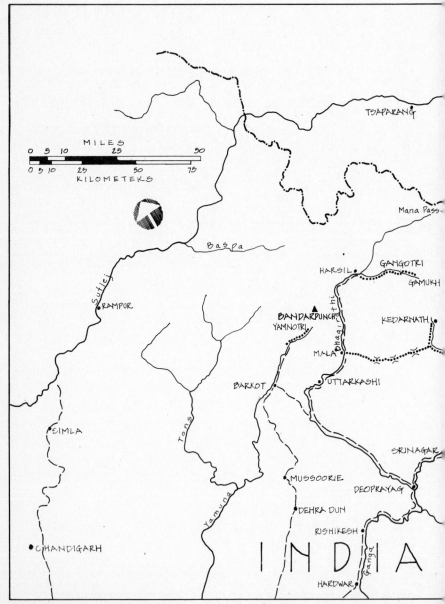

The Yatra Trails and Garhwal

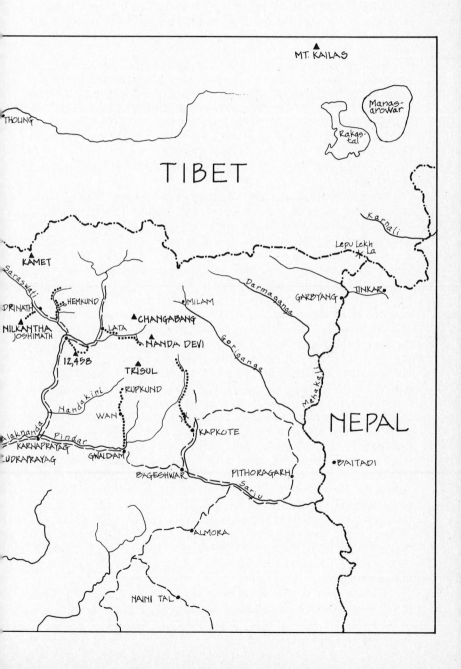

The Sacred Mountains

This chapter covers the central Himalaya for two hundred miles, from the deep Sutlej River gorge east to the Mahakali River, which forms the border between India and the Kingdom of Nepal. In going from the Sutlej to the Kali, as it is known, we cross from the watershed of the mighty Indus to the drainage of the holy Ganges River, a cultural basin stretching 700 miles to the Sikkim border.

The upper stream valleys of the Ganges and Yamuna rivers contain hundreds of shrines sacred to devotees of Krishna, Vishnu, and especially Shiva. The upper Ganges also has a Sikh pilgrim path to Hemkund Lake. Trails east of Nanda Devi's summit lead toward the forbidden Tibetan Plateau, Lake Manasarowar, and Rakas Tal (*tal* means "lake"), near Mt. Kailas—the "Crown Chakra of the Earth," holy of holies to Buddhist and Hindu alike. The pilgrim, or yatra, routes to the principal shrines will be described, but first some geographical background.

The previous four chapters taken together have covered a vast oval area layered in ranges, including the Pir Panjal, Zanskar, Ladakh, Kailas, and Karakoram in addition to the main range, the Great Himalaya. From the Karakoram Pass, that marks the junction of Pakistan, India, and China, to the ancient land of Poo, where the Sutlej River leaves Tibet for India, the disputed Indo-Chinese border caroms in a basically north-to-south direction. East of the Sutlej, the border between India and China bends to a southeasterly slant for a couple of hundred miles more, to the point where Nepalese territory faces the Tibetan frontier. The area where the Sutlej enters Tibet means more to the map reader and trekker than a border shift to the southeast, however. To the north and west of the Sutlej, the area of the Western Himalaya, Karakoram, Hindu Kush, and their subranges form a wide jigsaw mosaic of ridges and valleys stretching into infinity. East of the Sutlej, however, the mountainous areas south of Tibet include only the central and eastern extensions of the Great Himalaya and its southern protectors, the Mahabharat and Siwalik ranges; most of the high mountain terrain falls south of the Tibetan border.

The valley kingdoms south of the Himalaya and east of the Sutlej receive more rain and have more vegetation than the lands to the northwest. These central and eastern Himalayan valleys are folded into steep, narrow gorges that can be traversed by people but not, in the main, by pack animals. The valleys generally run from the mountains in the north to lower hills in the south, and up-valley they lead toward the forbidden frontier rather than to neighboring valleys. The Tibetan border either demarcates the Himalayan crest or parallels it just north of the main peaks.

Those who have seen the upper areas of the Yamuna and Ganges river valleys, described in this chapter, are astonished at their unheralded beauty. Few of us now interested in Himalayan trekking can remember the era in the 1930s when Shipton and Tilman were having what Shipton called a "Himalayan Heyday," exploring and climbing in the Garhwal area. Since then, excepting Heim and Gansser's epic 1936 sojourn, the 1950 Scottish Expedition, and very few others, India's central Himalaya has been closed north of the hill stations. In 1974, when the Inner Line was relocated and many new areas opened to visitors, public interest focused mainly on Ladakh. Few people knew then or know now that the 200-mi. stretch from the Sutlej to the Mahakali, an area equal in scenic grandeur to any in the Himalaya, is open for trekking. In Uttarakhand, as the Ganges headwater area is traditionally called, are paths leading to vistas unsurpassed for mountain scenery. And in the many holy places of this region, India's legions of pilgrims practice traditions that are millenniums old.

In the 18th century, this area was divided into two hill states. Kumaon lay between the Mahakali River on the east and Nanda Devi; its capital was the ridge-straddling town of Almora. The other, much larger, hill state within Uttarakhand was Garhwal; its capital, named Srinagar (different from Srinagar in Kashmir), is still on a flat plain by the Alaknanda River. West of Garhwal were two groups of small princely states, the Bara ("Twelve") and Attara ("Eighteen") thakurai. These 30 states must have been vest-pocket size compared to Garhwal and Kumaon, for they did not extend beyond the Sutlej and together comprised a strip of territory roughly 30 mi. wide from the Tibetan frontier to the Punjab plains. In the beginning of the 19th century, the Nepalese Gurkha army defeated first the forces of Kumaon, then Garhwal, moving the western border of Nepal to the Sutlej. By the time the tough Gurkha forces reached the last ridge before the Sutlej, however, their supply lines were so long and their cumulative injuries so debilitating that their campaign began to run aground against the motley forces of the 30 princely states. The border of Nepal remained at the Sutlej until the conclusion of the British-Gurkha War in 1816, when the Treaty of Sagauli established the boundary at its present location along the Mahakali River.

The people of Garhwal and Kumaon are descended from both Aryan and Mongol stock, and many villages still have families with distinct racial heritages. Most villagers you will meet speak local dialects, but they also know as much Hindi as you will have learned from the glossary. Dotials (like those who portered with the Scots in 1950) and other Nepalis often migrate to the Garhwal and Kumaon hill country for summer work, and you may be able to speak Nepali with them. A Nepali will not likely have a good knowledge of local trails but may be better than a porter from Garhwal. Some of this area's most interesting denizens are the Tibetan-descended Bhotia villagers from the upper valleys, who resemble their brethren in Nepal but who, unlike other Bhotias, are Hindu and usually worship Shiva, the Lord of Himachal, whose throne is atop Mt. Kailas.

The majesty of the central Himalaya is in its ruggedness: the juxtaposition of monsoon-drenched valley floor with soaring rock buttresses dusted in snow is repeated like a fugue in Garhwal. But when the summer monsoon strikes in June these fantastic gorges can become as difficult to reach as mythical Shangri La. So walking in spring and fall is the rule in Garhwal and Kumaon unless you are entirely prepared for weather and are experienced in the Himalaya.

The Holy Yatra Trails

Much of Hinduism's myth and tradition stem from the Vedas, sacred writings compiled between 3,500 and 4,000 years ago. Many of their lively legends about Vishnu, Krishna, and especially Shiva speak of places in the Himalaya. The oldest text, called Rig-Veda, describes the veneration of rivers in terms of their physical and spiritual properties. Shiva, one of the three principal gods worshipped as a manifestation of Atman (the Ultimate Essence), is considered to dwell in the Himalaya. His throne is atop sacred Mt. Kailas and from the strands of his long, matted hair flows the holiest of rivers, the Ganges. Since prehistory the natural wonders of the Uttarakhand area in particular have been identified by Hindus as manifestations of the gods themselves, or of places where mythic events took place. When you trek in Uttarakhand (or visit Amarnath Cave in Kashmir, or Muktinath in Nepal, or a Buddhist gomba), you too will be a yatri, "going around places," a pilgrim of your own kind.

With the passing of centuries, six Himalayan sites have come to be of undisputed importance for Hindu yatris. Of these, four will be discussed at some length in this section, for they lie in Uttarakhand. Another, Mt. Kailas, is mentioned because it is nearby, important to both Buddhist and Hindu, and is traditionally visited from Uttarakhand, although because Mt. Kailas is in Tibet it is inaccessible to

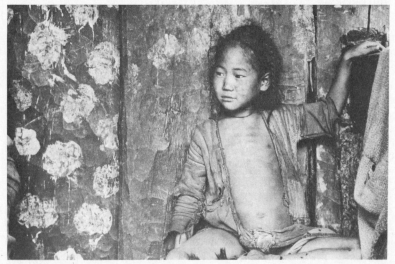

Bhotia child at the front door of home, in one of Garhwal's upper valleys (photo by Kevin Bubriski).

trekkers and even to most Indians. The sixth is Amarnath Cave in Kashmir, covered in Chapter 7. The four *tirths* ("sacred places") that we can visit are called Yamnotri, Gangotri, Kedarnath, and Badrinath. Yamnotri and Badrinath are associated with Vishnu the redeemer and preserver, a force who shakes his fist at time; Gangotri and Kedarnath are shrines for Shiva, the destroyer and transformer.

In the summer the four accessible tirths are visited by thousands of yatris from all parts of India. Devotees approach the holy shrines to perform puja ceremonies that involve recitation of scriptures and the ritual sacrifice of grains, oils, spices, or other substances or precious objects. These ceremonies, evolved over hundreds of generations, are important both to assure the soul's future life and to honor those now dead. The ritual cleansings that preceed the puja are designed to wash away the sins of the past and are performed in sacred locations on the Yamuna and Ganges adjacent to the temples. Both the bathing rituals (which you may also see in Varanasi and elsewhere) and the puja ceremonies (some of which can continue for hours) seem quite different from Western practice, until you consider Christian multitudes in church kneeling for the weekly blessing, or a congregation receiving communion. And the baptism ceremony of Christians is not at all unlike bathing purification rites that Hindus practice in traditional, unselfconscious fashion throughout their lives.

I had been reluctant to bathe in Varanasi on the Ganges plain due largely to the turbidity of the water. When I visited Badrinath, however, I saw steam rising from the hot spring called Tapta Kund and realized that before me was the perfect spot to first immerse myself in India. Leaving the *bhavan*, the pilgrim rest house, I walked to the hot spring early in the morning when the bathers were few, left my clothes in a pile by the side and, wearing briefs like the other male bathers (women bathe in a nearby enclosure), enjoyed a warm, neck-deep soak in the large covered pool. There is nothing like participation to remove the "us-them" feeling, and as I walked away from the ancient bathing tank, returning the smiles and nods of the nearby sadhus, I too was a Badrinath yatri.

Until roads were built into Garhwal in the 1950s by order of the Indian government, yatris needed to walk for weeks to reach a single tirth. Nowadays paved roads lead to within at least 13 mi. of each of the four spiritual places, and Badrinath can be reached by road directly. The order in which the four tirths are discussed here is from west to east: Yamnotri, Gangotri, Kedarnath, and Badrinath, followed by a note on Mt. Kailas.

Yamnotri

Yamnotri Temple is 8 mi. beyond the road that is at the base of a spur below a glacier-fed lake—the lake considered to be the headwaters of the Yamuna River. This is the smallest and least-visited of the four holy places, but it has the special characteristics of these shrines: a *shila*, a large rock with mythic associations—here connected to Vishnu, the temple deity—and a spring hot enough to boil rice (which then becomes *prasad*, consecrated food). A second hot spring is diverted into a tank for bathing. Yamnotri sits at the base of sacred, 20,720-ft. Bandarpunch, the "Monkey's Tail"—the peak was named for Hanuman, the monkey that was Ram's faithful servant in myth. These holy shrines all have *pujaris*, Brahmin-caste priests, and *pandas*, Brahmins who assist pilgrims in performing the appropriate rituals. At the modest Yamnotri Temple, the pujaris and pandas all come from Kharsali, the uppermost village in the valley, 4 mi. away. The roadhead for Yamnotri, at the village of Hanuman Chatti, can be reached from the Ganges River towns of Hardwar or Rishikesh by taxi or bus, or you can take a shorter route from Mussoorie through the middle hills once ruled by the Maharaja of Tehri.

Gangotri

The temple of Gangotri (10,000 ft.) was built in the 18th century by the Gurkha General Amar Singh Thapa near the sacred shila called Bhagirath. On that same large boulder, King Bhagirath had meditated intently for years and, by doing so, the king caused the holy waters of the Ganga to descend from heaven into Shiva's piled hair. After the king's further meditation, Shiva was pleased and allowed the most sacred river Ganga to appear on earth in the heart of his Himalayan abode at three sources. The principal source of the Ganges River is up-valley from Gangotri Temple. The temple is reachable by road (although several times you must change buses and walk around road breaks), but beyond Gangotri you must walk to arrive at Gamukh, the mouth of the 25-mi.-long Gangotri Glacier, which is revered as the "Cow's Mouth," the font of the holy Bhagirathi tributary. Gamukh is a beautiful place, within sight of the peak called Shivling ("Shiva's Phallus"), a place where sadhus come to meditate each year, finding for themselves the meaning of the tribute by Marco Pallis (the experienced Tibetologist and author) to Gamukh: "It is useless to try to describe the grandeur of the scene: there are perfections about which the only eloquence is silence."

Kedarnath

The next holy place to be visited is Kedarnath, "Shiva's Abode." Pilgrim buses with their fuming exhausts began plying newly built roads through these sacred mountains a quarter century ago, but before that time all yatris who visited the temples followed specific trails and stayed at the pilgrim's rest houses called *chattis* that are along the way. You can reach Kedarnath from Hardwar or Rishikesh via the Alaknanda River Valley, but the ancient pilgrim trail from the Bhagirathi River town of Mala (more than 40 mi. south of Gangotri) is an excellent way to walk to Kedarnath. The 46-mi. walk from Mala to the roadhead near the temple crosses three ridges. On the trail along the last, northernmost ridge, the scenery is beautiful enough to lift the heart of any mountain walker.

Kedarnath Temple (11,700 ft.) is reached after a 9-mi. walk from Gaurikund, the place where Shiva found his consort, Parvati. She, characteristically, had meditated in such an auspicious place to win Lord Shiva. The stolid Kedarnath Temple is composed of large, moulded blocks of rock and was built 800 years ago over a stone considered to be the remains of a "selfborn" manifestation of Shiva as Nandi the bull. This rock (believed to be the bull's hump) is worshipped daily by pilgrims infused with *bhakti* (adoration for the godhead). In the morning the image is honored in its natural or unadorned form with offerings of ghee and milk. In the evening the image is adored in its ornamental form; under a gold canopy it is covered with flowers and brightly colored offerings.

Badrinath

Badrinath, like Kedarnath, is reached from Hardwar and Rishikesh via the Alaknanda River valley. Forty miles upriver from Rishikesh is the confluence of the Alaknanda and the Bhagirathi, which at Devaprayag, form the Ganges, or Ganga (its Hindi name). Continuing upriver along the twisting Alaknanda Valley, your bus will plow its way past other towns with names ending in *-prayag*, which indicates that they too are sacred river *sangams* ("confluences"). All buses halt at the large town of Joshimath (6,500 ft.), magnificently situated a thousand feet above the river. From the gate at Joshimath, the pilgrim-packed buses set out daily at an officially appointed hour. The buses roar down to the bottom of the gorge on the one-way road, then race each other several thousand feet up the other side and 30 mi. beyond to Badrinath in a spectacle that must be undergone to be wholly appreciated.

Badrinath Temple (10,300 ft.) is the most-visited tirth. It lies just across the Alaknanda from vehicular traffic and is reached by a walkway. You follow the cement path past meditating and alms-seeking sadhus, cross a bridge and continue to the centuries-old shrine through narrow, winding lanes called *galis*, past restaurants, souvenir and puja-accessories shops, and more sadhus. Proper pilgrims will have taken a holy dip in the hot Tapta Kund before entering the temple or taking part in one of the numerous pujas offered morning and evening. "Reserve Your Pujas Here," reads one sign in English. Unlike the custom with the stone at Kedarnath, the image of Lord Badrinath (Vishnu) is worshipped adorned for the entire summer season here, and worshipped unadorned during the winter when it resides in Joshimath.

In all directions from Badrinath the trekking possibilities are excellent, although currently those trails north of Badrinath are beyond the Inner Line and so can't be traversed. Directly west of town is a side valley that extends, rising, toward the white spire of Nilkantha, or "Blue Neck" (21,640 ft.), which the British climber Frank Smythe called the "Queen of Garhwal"—reversing the mountain's ascribed sex, but no matter. Take a day hike up this tributary from Badrinath village toward Nilkantha's base; you will have excellent views from a series of steep talus slopes beneath towering buttresses that are layered like massive snowcakes, the peak more than a neck-craning mile (2 km) above. Walking thus directly from Badrinath you approach glacial features quickly; within hours of leaving the village you are on morainal debris, leading toward the snows of a Himalayan cirque.

East and south of Badrinath are the Bhyundar Valley and the lake called Hemkund (covered in the next section): north, in the area now restricted, are other extremely sacred locations along the Alaknanda tributary. Vashudhara Falls is in the Alaknanda Valley on the way to Satopanth Lake, where the divine trinity of Brahma, Vishnu, and Shiva are said to meditate beneath 23,420-ft. Badrinath Peak (Chaukhamba) and the peak called Swargarohini, the "Path to Heaven." Swargarohini divides the glacial source of the eastern Alaknanda from the western side's Gangotri Glacier, source of the Bhagirathi. Since the time of the Hindu epics, only Shipton, Tilman, and their porters have crossed the Badrinath Range (which requires both special permissions and technical aids) from the Alaknanda to the Bhagirathi. At the Tibetan frontier due north of Badrinath is the 17,900-ft. Mana Pass, crossed by Krishna in the "Age of the Gods." North of Mana Pass is the ancient temple city of Tsaparang, where early Christian missionaries "discovered" a thriving regional center. But as most recently documented, by Lama Anagarika Govinda and Li Gotami in 1948, Tsaparang had been virtually deserted, its water supply from glacial melt having previously run dry. They saw its irreplaceable frescos and buildings crumbling, like those of the equally remote city of Tholing to the east, another museum from the past.

Mt. Kailas

The most sublime "throne of the gods," "the crown chakra of the earth," and "Shiva's throne"—Mt. Kailas (19,910 ft.) is revered by Buddhist and Hindu alike as the physical and metaphoric center of the world. Kailas is situated north of the sun and moon lakes—Manasarowar (called "Mapham" in Tibetan) and Rakas Tal. Pilgrims traditionally approached Mt. Kailas by no fewer than 12 yatra routes, reaching the mountain from an area spanning Kashmir and Ladakh in the west and beyond Lhasa, hundreds of miles to the east. In the days when people walked to Kailas, they performed the obligatory Parikrama, a 32-mi. circumambulation of the mountain, in which they meditated on the full cycle of life and death at the appropriate locations along the difficult course. Virtually no yatris approach Mt. Kailas now, and few Westerners have ever made the trek. We can console ourselves, or whet our appetites, by reading some of the excellent accounts by those who have gone: Lama Govinda, August Gansser, and Herbert Tichy tell excellent tales of pilgrimages to holy Mt. Kailas.

Hemkund and the Valley of Flowers

Twelve miles north from Joshimath in the Alaknanda Valley on the Badrinath road are the unpretentious teahouses of Govind Ghat. From this stopping place you can walk into the midst of the central Himalaya at its most precipitous, following a path that leads to the Sikh pilgrimage spot called Hemkund, a cobalt-colored lake at 14,200 feet. The path to both Hemkund and the beautiful vale that one climber called the "Valley of Flowers" crosses the Alaknanda River at Govind Ghat and rises into the Laxman Ganga Valley. Before you lengthen your stride in anticipation and cross the new footbridge at Govind Ghat, register with the police at the *chaulki* (post), telling them you will be three nights up-valley. A few yards beyond the police chaulki is a Sikh-run *gurdwara*, a rest house freely provided for all pilgrims. If you have arrived during the hours when meals are offered, you will be served gratis delicious Punjabi food (offerings appreciated), a heartening prelude to, or reward after, the walk.

From Govind Ghat, at 6,000 ft. in elevation, the trail rises for 10 spectacular, green miles. The constantly ascending path passes seasonal teahouses, for many pilgrims on this trail are Delhi-walas or live in the flat plains of the Punjab. The tea sellers along the warm lower trail do a good business during "the rush," August and September. Along the way, 6 mi. from the roadhead at Govind Ghat, is the small, neat village of Bhyundar at the junction of the Laxman Ganga Valley and a tanta-

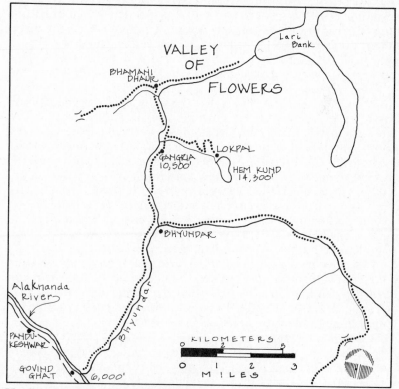

Hemkund and the Valley of Flowers

lizingly beautiful, tree-cloaked tributary called the Kak Bhusandi Valley. Later, when you return by way of Bhyundar, you could hire a porter-guide to show you the little-known way back to Joshimath via the Kak Bhusandi and a high ridge trail beyond.

Ten miles from Govind Ghat, at 10,500 ft., is another Sikh-operated gurdwara called Gangria (also called Govind Dham, "Govind's Holy Place," after the guru who is connected with Hemkund). At the gurdwara, accommodating volunteers provide meals at fixed times and lodging (donations accepted). Nearby, private tea shops dispense the brew any time of day, in the cool of the pine-shaded valley floor. Just beyond Gangria, trails divide. Those going to Hemkund take the well-maintained zigzagging trail 3 mi. and nearly 4,000 ft. up to the lake. This dham is sacred to the memory of Guru Govind Singh, the tenth Sikh guru, who created the Khalsa Order, the "Pure Ones." A new gurdwara dedicated to Govind Singh has been constructed lakeside.

The large circular building was partially completed when I walked up in early June, 1977. Inside the gurdwara I observed two Sikh brethren complete a ceremony that involved chanting and the draping of Govind Singh's holy volume with layers of cloth. Outside, the trail had just been cleared of snow by an army platoon, which was then departing; soon the soldiers were followed by the two Sikh worshippers, who had kindly given me fistfuls of sweet prasad. Thirty yards from the large, unfinished gurdwara I found a tiny, low-roofed chatti dedicated to the deity Laxman. I happily settled for the evening in this rest house made of stone, cooking tea to drink with the sugary prasad.

The alternate route from Gangria is a wide trail that leads up by the Laxman Ganga stream and through a rocky defile into the upper valley. This is the "Valley of Flowers" that Frank Smythe crossed into after he made the first ascent of Kamet (at 25,447 ft., the third tallest mountain in India). Smythe also called the valley "a place of escape from modern civilization." The spring I saw it, 46 years later, it was in much the same pristine splendor: a narrow, U-shaped vale with terraces the green of early spring growth, washed with narrow waterfalls, one after another, draining snowfields unseen above. I was fortunate to visit early in the season, for during a full day's time in this exquisite place I saw only a single herdsman with his sheep, far across the way. My only other companions were several hawks floating far aloft.

This uninhabited valley has been well studied by botanists, who have found hundreds of wildflower varieties. Local legend tells of Bhaman Dhaur, "Bhaman's Cave," where a saint once meditated, sanctifying the vale. The cave is there—a massive slanting rock with walled entrance and a dry, straw-covered floor. Looking toward the rock cave from the trail, you will see a pasture angling steeply upward beyond the rock. If you follow the animal paths 1,500 ft. up, you will reach a shepherd's camp. An additional 1,700-ft. rise will take you to a col 7,000 ft. above Hanuman Chatti on the road to Badrinath.

From Joshimath to Nanda Devi
Short Treks from Joshimath

Yatri and mountaineer alike rest in Joshimath en route to their destinations farther north. The pious Hindu pilgrim will visit some of the many shrines in Joshimath, particularly the Durga Temple and Jyotirmath Temple, the latter connected with Badrinath Dham. The mountaineer or hiker will send or collect mail, purchase provisions, and will yearn to be off for the hills; Joshimath, the northernmost large bazaar in the valley, is very busy in the summer season. The town is scattered about on many levels, both above and below the main bazaar. In the midst of the bazaar, the road divides like the river does far below. One fork of the road follows the Alaknanda River to Badrinath and the areas covered in the two previous sections. The other branch of the road goes up the Dhauliganga Valley, east of the Alaknanda, toward the Nanda Devi area. Along the Dhauliganga Valley are remarkably beautiful scenes of the lush forest and high granite typical of Garhwal's untrammeled wilderness.

If you have limited time or want to warm up for a longer trek, hike for a day or make an overnight camp on the ridge line up from Joshimath. It has some of the best view points in all of Garhwal. As you walk up from Joshimath Bazaar, you'll see farther up both the sacred Alaknanda Valley and along the Dhauliganga to the tributary Rishiganga gorge that drains the vast Nanda Devi sanctuary. Good trails take you from Joshimath up to the *bugyal* (grazing meadow) called Auli and on to Gorsin Bugyal. If you are walking up for the day only, take water, lunch, and an umbrella to divert sun or rain. For a superb overnight hike, carry shelter and camp where you wish: there are many sites. With a good start from Joshimath one morning, you can walk up and camp, then leave the next day to walk toward the triangulation point at 12,458 ft. on the Nanda Devi U502 Sheet (# NH44-6). From that remarkable spot, you have a 360-degree view. You can see Kamet, Nilkantha, the Badrinath Temple area, the 20,000-ft. peaks above Hemkund, Lata Peak, some of the renowned summits that encircle the Nanda Devi sanctuary—Hanuman, Dunagiri, Bethartoli (unclimbed until 1977), Trisul—and Nanda Devi standing majestically apart.

These lovely meadows above Joshimath may entice you for a leisurely walk of several days. Beyond Auli and Gorsin are a web of trails leading from pasture to pasture, with dramatic, changing vistas throughout. Three miles south of the 12,458-ft. point is the well-traveled Kuari Pass (12,140 ft.), once crossed by Lord Curzon and, in 1950, by the Scots with their Dotial porters. An additional 3 mi. from the pass to the east is the high summer village of Delisera, another gently rolling grazing area, frequented by herds from the south that are driven over the Kuari Pass. More than 6,000 ft. down from Delisera and the pass is the small town of Tapoban with its sacred hot springs. A circle route can be followed from Joshimath to the grazing areas and a high point or two, then down to Tapoban, a walk that takes three to five days. Continue by bus from Tapoban, a short ride from Joshimath through the precipitous lower Dhauliganga gorge.

Into the Nanda Devi Sanctuary

The wide, rolling, inner meadows of the "secret shrine," the Nanda Devi Sanctuary, lie 18 air miles from Lata village up the once-impenetrable Rishiganga gorge. The sanctuary had not felt human footsteps until 1934, when Shipton and Tilman, with Sherpas and Dotials, forced a precarious route up the primeval valley to the vast meadowlands inhabited by herds of *bharal*, the blue sheep. The trail to the Sanctuary is barely discernible in places but is nevertheless readily traversed: the route was established by the groups and expeditions between 1974 and 1977, when the lower Rishiganga Valley emerged from behind the Inner Line. However, poaching of musk deer, concern for the Sanctuary's untrammeled aspect, and the flap over a nuclear-powered sensing device hidden on the slopes of Nanda Devi resulted in the closing of the Rishiganga gorge beyond Lata and Peng villages to both trekkers and locals in 1978. It may be reopened after evaluation.

In mid-May 1977, with only the scantiest information about the Nanda Devi Sanctuary and the route to it, I found myself with a new friend and a porter on the local bus from Joshimath to Lata, little expecting what the next 18 days would bring. We hoped we had enough

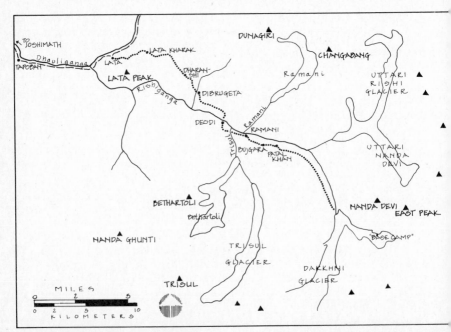

The Nanda Devi Sanctuary Trail

food, we thought we might be ahead of the groups going into the valley, and we expected a real trail—not the frail paths connecting ledges that we were about to find. The unlikely route is divided into eight stages: eight days' travel with laden porter between Lata and the sanctuary. Half the stages are less than 2 mi. in straight-line distance, but compensating for their brevity these stages have steep inclines or narrow ledges that make walking difficult, and hazardous in places.

In the future, if the area is opened for general use, a stage-by-stage description of the route will be added. Meanwhile, there is plenty to see between Nanda Devi and the Nepal border.

The Pindar, Goriganga, and Darmaganga Valleys

The Pindar Valley

On the well-traveled pilgrim road to Joshimath and Badrinath, at the sacred confluence of the Pindar River and the Alaknanda, lies the town of Karnaprayag. The Pindar Valley begins 50 mi. east of Karnaprayag, cathing runoff from such summits as Trisul and Nanda Kot that form the southerly bastions of the mountain ring about Nanda Devi. Two destinations of interest to trekkers can be reached from the Pindar Valley: Rup Kund, a small, high mountain lake on the slopes of the Trisul massif; and the Pindari Glacier, at the head of the Pindar River.

Rup Kund, at the 15,670-ft. level, actually drains into the Nandakini Valley to the west, but it is usually approached from Pindar Valley to the south, along an old pathway through Debal village and Wan Bazaar. To reach this trail, take a bus from Karnaprayag up the Pindar Valley to Gwaldam with its lovely orchards. The route continues northward from Gwaldam through beautifully terraced country on a path that was followed by pilgrim and mountaineer before roads were built into these hills. Plan to walk for a total of 10 to 15 days in this area if you intend of reach Rup Kund, whether you return by the Pindar Valley or the Nandakini. You will be able to find staple foods as far along as Debal, so don't lug everything from the roadhead. The trail up from Debal and beyond, through high meadows, is spectacularly scenic. Some landmarks along the way have names, such as the "Petrified Dancers," a series of rocks associated with the ill-fated Nanda-Jat, a pilgrimage of ages ago, when ecstatic yatris who ignored the prevailing caste, sex, and age restrictions angered the gods, provoking catastrophes. Legend (but not fact) tells that bones from these yatris remain scattered about the shoreline of Rup Kund.

Of the many glaciers in Garhwal, the Pindari is the most accessible and the one known best to Westerners. A series of six PWD bungalows are available at stages along the Pindar and Sarju valleys, beginning with a bungalow at the roadhead of Kapkote in the Sarju Valley, south of the Pindar and reached from Almora. The Pindari Glacier, like most in the central Himalaya, is strictly a falling glacier (one that is steep, with broken chunks of ice) that requires ropes and ice equipment for climbing. It has no interminably long moraines like those of the Karakoram glaciers, but instead a massive tangle of ice chunks seemingly frozen in free-fall that extend only a few miles from the catchment area to the glacier's mouth. At the top of the Pindari Glacier is a highly technical 17,700-ft. col named Traill's Pass for the British administrator and explorer who first crossed over it into the Goriganga Valley.

The Goriganga and Darmaganga Valleys

The Goriganga and Darmaganga valleys are tributaries of the Mahakali River, which demarcates the western boundary of Nepal. Along with the more northerly Kuthi Yankti Valley, these deep, parallel gorges are walled by high peaks and crested with caravan passes leading toward the ancient entrepôt of Purang town and holy Mt. Kailas. The upper regions in these valleys (including the entire Kuthi Yankti Valley) lie north of the Inner Line and have rarely been visited. Fine accounts of travels in these valleys have been published: by two members of the 1936 Swiss Expedition to this area, and by W. H. Murray of the four-person 1951 Scottish Himalayan Expedition. Both of these groups were notable for their small size, for their members' wide-ranging interests, for their good rapport with locals, and for their "discovering" the advantages of eating the local diet and traveling lightly as possible. Murray tells us that close to the village of Mapong (on the Goriganga River very near today's Inner Line) at the base of the deep canyon between Nanda Kot and Panchchuli's summit, there was once a stone marker inscribed, "All land north of this stone is Tibet."

The forested mid-level valleys south of the restricted area are particularly colorful during the harvest season, when Bhotias from the upper villages move southward on their annual migration from the snows. Perhaps the best-known Bhotia to come from this area has been Nain Singh, who was from Milam village on the upper Goriganga. Known as "Number 1," he was the most accomplished of the early pundit surveyors, having reached Lhasa after traveling and keeping clandestine observations through 1,200 mi. of unmapped Tibetan territory. Today Milam-walas and others attend local autumn harvest fairs, such as the Jouljibi Fair at Miansairi in November, but for now the days of wide-open travel to Tibet by the Garhwal Bhotias are over.

For cognoscenti of the remote (and politically unreachable), here are several notes on the far northeast corner of this area of the Himalaya, around the Mahakali. The snowfields that feed the Mahakali's source lie below the 16,800-ft. Lepu Lekh La, once the busiest summer pass to the Purang area and holy Mt. Kailas. The Lepu Lekh La is still shown on the one-rupee maps you can buy of the yatra routes through Uttarakhand. An upland tributary of the Mahakali that exceeds it in size above their confluence is the Kuthi Yankti. The Kuthi Valley includes two other passes to Tibet, and Kuthi village, at 12,300 ft., is said to be the highest town in the central Himalaya.

Finally, there is the Tinkar Valley, which is not within India at all but inside Nepal. Tinkar is only reachable from the Garbyang trail in India's Almora District, or by the Tinkar Lepu La connecting the valley's headwaters in Nepal with Tibet. Heim's account of twice entering the Tinkar Valley in the early 1930s, when Nepal was still forbidden land, presents the thoughts classically experienced by anyone who suspects he is breaching a restricted area. Tinkar village with its gomba and lama is a quite fitting prelude to Nepal.

The Hill Stations

During the British raj, large hill towns were built in English resort style, with hotels, villas, cottages, restaurants, and cinemas; each town also had a mall. Until the early 1960s, successive generations of civil servants, British and then Indian, moved the state seats of government to the various hill stations seasonally, to avoid administrative paralysis in the early summer premonsoon oven. The most accessible and representative of these (aside from Murree, north of Rawalpindi, and Darjeeling, north of Calcutta) are in the hills of this chapter's area, north to northeast of Delhi. These islands of old Angleterre bear as much relation to the surrounding villages as Disneyland does to Orange County, but they remain popular, enjoyed today by city families on holiday to escape the summer heat. And for some whirlwind tourists, a quick taxi ride to Mussoorie (or to Ranikhet near Almora) will be the entirety of their fling with the Himalaya.

These quasi-Elizabethan, neo-Indian hill towns are buzzing throughout the busy spring and summer seasons, but off-season—especially during a clear midwinter full moon—a hill station offers mountain hikers a quiet, comfortable place to stroll and reflect while regarding the snow mountains. In Simla, Mussoorie, and Almora, all manner of eastern and western cuisine is available in restaurants adjacent to the hotels and lodges. Each of these hill towns is situated on a ridge-top, and each offers its own lookout point with a wide Himalayan panorama.

From these towns, paths for day, overnight, and weekend-long walks extend into the nearby hills. Many people overcome their initial reservations about trail walking with a hike to the nearby hilltops, or *tibbas*, as they are locally called. Simla, "the queen of the hill stations" with its Jakoo Hill overlook and large mall, is more removed from the trekking areas of Garhwal, farther east, than is Mussoorie or Almora. Simla was once the summer home of the central government. Not far from Mussoorie is Benog Hill; 8,570-ft. Top Tibba and 9,915-ft. Nag Tibba are overnight treks. Almora's hills are known for the temples that top them, harking to pre-British days when Kumaon was ruled by the Chand dynasty from Almora.

Mussoorie's 7,026-ft. Gun Hill viewing point is approachable from the mall below by walkway or suspended gondola. I stood on the deserted Gun Hill observation deck late one January afternoon, trying to discern a few summits not entirely cloud-hidden and reflecting on a recently completed Himalayan sojourn. The peaks from Bandarpunch to Nanda Devi were cloaked in grey stratus, but, to the west, glowing clouds graced the beginning of a glorious sunset.

Man in western Nepal (photo by Kevin Bubriski).

11

Nepal's Wild West

Nepal is very hilly country.
Chhetra Bahadur, in Jumla,
commenting on the trail to Humla, 1974

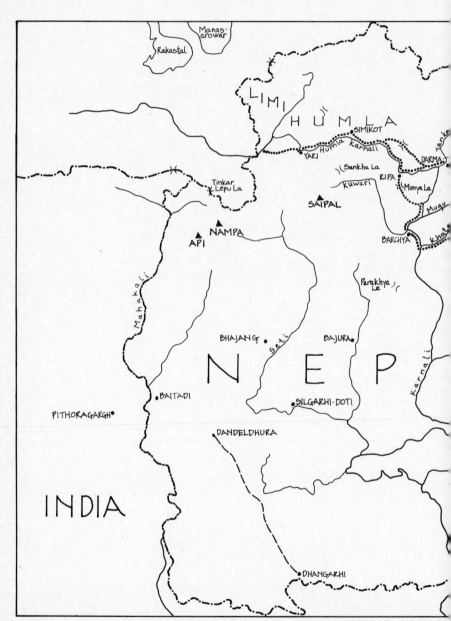

Western Nepal

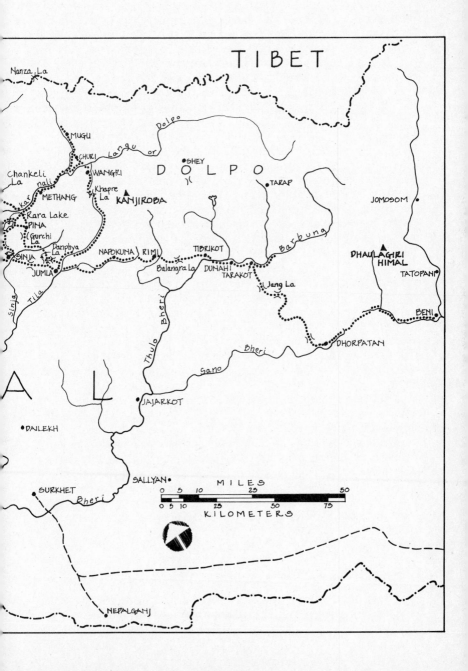

The Karnali Watershed

The mountainous region of Nepal, a jumble of valleys, ridges, and snow mountains, appears to culminate in a solid barrier of high peaks and vertical ice walls along the length of the northern border. But in fact Nepal's northern frontier is pierced in six places, from Humla in the far west to the Arun Valley near Sikkim, by rivers older than the Himalayan Range. Chief among the river systems that drain Nepal's mountains are the Karnali, the Gandaki, and the Sapt Kosi. These three watersheds generally correspond to the regions covered in the next three chapters, which outline, respectively, the main trekking routes in northwestern Nepal; in central Nepal; and in eastern Nepal and Sikkim.

The Karnali River and its tributaries drain the least studied, least trekked, and most remote area of Nepal: its far west. The area discussed in this chapter is bounded on the west by the Mahakali River and on the southeast by the Dhaulagiri massif. This western third of the country is half again as wide from north to south as are Nepal's central and eastern regions. The large and sparsely populated Karnali basin contains vast forested areas and high, winding ridges that are peculiar to the west of Nepal. These long ridges, called *lekhs*, rise to between 12,000 ft. and 17,000 ft., extending from the westernmost spurs of the Saipal to the southern ridges of Dhaulagiri in the east. There are lekhs across all of Nepal south of all the main peaks, but the lekhs in western Nepal are larger, more numerous, and less precipitous, offering good pastureland. The north-facing slopes of many of these western lekhs are covered with aging coniferous forests of blue pine, hemlock, fir, and 150-ft.-tall spruce. Western Nepal's himals (one Nepali word for "snow peaks") are not as high as peaks in the country's central and eastern areas.

Experienced walkers, tired of the relatively crowded trails in the Annapurna and Everest regions, have enjoyed the differences in Nepal's west: trails that Westerners rarely see lead past rude, widely scattered villages (many of them each housing a long-haired shaman); rice fields extending up to the 9,000-ft. level nourish the hearty red rice that used to be carried hundreds of miles across the hills to Kathmandu for use by the kingdom's epicurean rulers; traders walk the paths next to the sheep, goats, or yaks that carry their homespun side packs of grain or salt. If you trek here, you'll feel you are discovering new country.

Short Walks from Jumla

Jumla, on an eastern tributary of the Karnali called the Tila, is the best place to begin trekking in much of western Nepal, but Jumla is not easy to reach. At the moment no roads extend north of the southern hill bazaars of Dandeldhura and Surkhet. Because of the high temperatures in this area, walking to Jumla from Surkhet, the closer of the two hill towns, should be attempted only in autumn and spring. You can also fly there from Surkhet although the packed-earth STOL (short take-off and landing) airfield near Jumla is usable only if monsoon rains or winter snows do not cover the field. And reservations are usually needed long in advance. You may also fly to Jumla from Kathmandu, by way of Surkhet or Nepalganj; be sure to inquire about these flights if those direct to Jumla are booked. In addition, such other small airfields in the far west as Baitadi and Silgharhi-Doti offer service sporadically.

Jumla (7,700 ft.) is the largest upland hill town in Nepal's west, but Jumla's bazaar appears large only to the trekker or local approaching town after weeks in the hills. There may be a few bicycles in Jumla now, but the 200-yard-long stone-paved street has never really known the wheel. The Tila River just south of the bazaar runs crystalline most of the year, and Jumla's flat valley is often traversed by horsemen. Jumla and its nearby villages are populated primarily by the dark-skinned people of the Chhetri, Brahman, and Thakuri clans. The most visible denizens are the *latos*, the smiling, buffooning "half-wits" who, on further observation, appear to be wise fools mimicking the society they reject. For all Jumla's frontier-town roughness, however, it is acquiring a tinge of respectability with the arrival of government employees who work in the whitewashed administrative buildings west of the main bazaar. The most striking departure from the drab, flat-roofed one- and two-story buildings along the main street are four tall bamboo poles flying sienna and white tricornered standards. These banners adorn Jumla's main temple, dedicated to the mythical saint Chandan Nath, whose accomplishments included emptying a lake that once covered the valley, defeating two serpents that threatened Kalangra (as Jumla was once called), and bringing the tasty high-altitude rice from Kashmir.

If you arrive by plane, bring all but basic grains and pulses with you. Until a road from the south reaches Jumla, temporary shortages of sugar and cooking oils may continue, and the available gas and kerosene will not be of the best quality. Do supply yourself with the delicious local rice, which may have to be purchased in a nearby village, rather than the bazaar. Excellent Tibetan porters can be hired in Napokuna, a day's walk east of Jumla.

While you are arranging supplies and porters, several warm-up hikes can be taken from Jumla. A half-hour walk from town, downstream along the north bank of the Tila Valley, is the small village of Micha, 300 ft. above and out of sight of the main trail. Next to a house in Micha is a walled burial ground with stone grave markers that were constructed during the Malla dynasty. The powerful Malla kingdom controlled much of what is now western Nepal from the 11th to 14th centuries, interweaving Buddhist and Hindu art, architecture, and religious practices. Time's sediment has partially buried the lichen-covered totems in Micha, but these outsized stone stelae resembling chess pieces are unlike any of the other stelae that remain from the Malla period.

Two high, grass-covered promontories near Jumla are good to scale for acclimatization. Directly northwest of the bazaar is Malika Dara, an 11,510-ft. hill with scattered pines for shade along its lower flanks. From the top of Malika, you have a fine view of west Nepal's nearby lekhs and Kanjiroba Himal. The Chaudabise River enters the Tila a 30-minute walk east of Jumla; just beyond the Chaudabise confluence, an unforested ridge called Chimara Lekh rises to 12,220 ft. On its top is a small shrine, and from there on a clear day you will enjoy a view that spans the distance from Saipal Himal in Humla to Dhaulagiri. Take head covering, water, and lunch.

The Trails to Rara Lake

Oh master divine!
Have you stripped beauty of all her gifts
And poured them down the shores of Rara. . . .
                          H. M. Mahendra Bir Bikram Shah, 1964

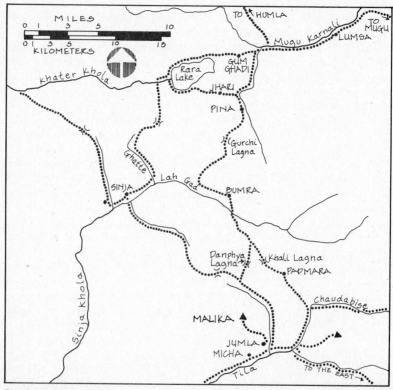

Jumla to Rara Lake

Rara Lake, a clear oval pool 3 mi. in length, is the largest body of water in Nepal. Rara is situated 9,780 ft. high between two forested lekhs, a three- to four-day walk north of Jumla. The deep-blue lake, also called Rara Daha, is the centerpiece of Rara Lake National Park, established in 1975. Surely this is one of the least-visited national parks in the world. The inhabitants of both villages on the lake's north shore were moved to Nepal's southern terai, and guard's quarters have been built on the main trails into the area in order to enforce the park's status as a game sanctuary. If you want to get away from the hordes, go to Rara Lake (supplied with all foodstuffs you need) and you will not be disappointed.

The view from lake level on Rara's grass-covered southern shore is reminiscent of the Rocky Mountains: the highest point visible is a 13,250-ft. ridge, to the south, and evergreens dominate the tranquil landscape. A faint trail encircles Rara, passing through a dense forest of blue pine at the lake's western end and by several chest-high Malla stelae above the north shore. An anachronistic element at the lake is the handsome dwelling used by the park's warden. This Western-style log cabin with its deck, shuttered glass windows, and skylight in a shingled roof was built by an American. When the incongruous building was completed, locals would walk for three days just to gaze at it.

Two principal trails reach Rara Lake from Jumla; each route involves two passes, and the one-way trip requires three to four days of walking. Take porters to make the hills go easier. The more easterly of the two paths is slightly shorter in distance and has lower passes, but it is more up and down along the way. This eastern path also has trails over two initial passes; these then join for the rest of the way to the lake. The longer and lower of these two trails of the easterly route—and the less likely to be snowbound—ascends the Chaudabise Khola (*khola* means river valley in Nepali) east of Jumla, then continues up the narrower Ghurseni Valley to the village of Padmara. Not far above Padmara is the grass-covered, 11,630-ft. Khali Lagna (*lagna* means pass), and shortly beyond, this trail and the higher one join. The higher route crosses the 12,000-ft. Danphya Lagna, named for the iridescent monal pheasant, Nepal's national bird. This pass offers a sweeping view of Jumla's valley and the flat-ridged Thakurji Lekh to the south, but don't attempt the Danphya Pass in snowy weather, as the southern slope is steep and the pass is exposed to strong winds. The way to the Danphya Pass lies up the left bank of the tributary valley north of Jumla, but the route is not always readily apparent. Let your porter guide you past Charya Chaur, the wide horse pasture below the steep climb to the pass. Here at Charya Chaur, on our first walking day, my companion and I learned the hard way that "you may be the sahib, but your porter knows the country." We elected to monopolize route finding and got side-tracked onto a herder's trail that disappeared on top of a snowy lekh.

North of the Danphya Lagna (which is a very long day's walk up from Jumla), the trail emerges from a low forest to join the Padmara track along a gentle meadow. Soon the path angles out on a ridge and drops 2,000 ft. to the Lah Gad Valley. At the bottom of the V-shaped gorge, a wooden bridge rests beneath a pine-studded rock face. Along the Lah Gad, the right-bank trail rises toward two villages with a heartbreaker drop into a side valley between the towns. Beyond the second village, follow the Chautha Valley northward through a narrow gorge studded with evergreens to a wide upper pasture where the valley branches. Just below this large meadow, a substantial spring issues forth, begetting the stream you have been following. Where the pastureland branches, take the western valley to where it forks again, and this time bear right along a distinct trail that rises through grasslands to the 11,340-ft. Gurchi Lagna. From the pass itself you can see little, but if you climb the steep, grass-tufted slope to the north, you will reach a place above the pines where you can gaze on intersecting ridges that plow into the lower Humla and Mugu valleys, the valleys of Nepal's westernmost inner Himalaya, which from here are within several days' walk. Rara Lake is not visible from this ridge line, but now the snowy peaks north of it appear distinctly closer.

From Gurchi Lagna, the trail drops into a pine forest, passes a small brook, and descends in short, steep switchbacks to the village of Pina at 8,000 ft. At Pina, paths divide; you can either take the route north, down-valley, to the Mugu Karnali River and trails to Mugu or Humla, or you can ask for the upper track ("*maati baato*") to Jhari village—Jhari lies along the most direct route to Rara Lake. The half-day trail from Pina to Rara follows a tributary valley west, passes Jhari, then leads up 2,000 ft. over a gently sloping ridge that rolls away to Rara's southern shoreline.

The second route from Jumla to Rara is a few miles longer than the first; it also passes through forested country typical of western Nepal. Like one of the first route's exits from Jumla, this trail follows the valley north of town, but instead of climbing to Danphya Lagna it enters a forest of tall conifers beyond the meadow at Charya Chaur. Continuing some 20 mi. over an unnamed, grassy pass to the village of Sinja, the path goes by many pleasant camping spots beneath immense gnarled pines. Locals accomplish the Jumla-to-Sinja trek between morning and dusk, but Westerners usually require two days. When you see the distinctive Kankasundri Temple on its steep low knob, you will know that Sinja lies just beyond. The trail passes south of the peaked, white temple and descends to the main river, crossing a thick plank bridge at a place where the water has cut a deep, narrow furrow through bedrock.

Sinja village rests upon a small alluvial plain on the west bank of the clear Lah Gad River, here called the Sinja Khola. Four stelae beside the main path south are the only standing reminders of what was once the thriving Malla winter capital. The now-ruined town actually stood on the east bank of the Sinja Khola at a place known as Kotgaon where you can poke amongst the sculpted, overgrown stones.

Just north of Sinja, stone-bound aeries once used by meditating renunciates are visible along the rock walls. The trail to Rara passes beneath those austere nests as it enters a narrow gorge that continues for several miles to the junction with the Ghatte Khola, which enters from the north. Follow the Ghatte up its left bank past Botan, the last village before Rara. The Ghatte is a beautiful miniature valley that doglegs northeastward past the Rara Lake National Park guard's house at a place called Ghorasain. The Ghatte Khola path toward Rara travels through much wilder country than the eastern route through Pina. Above the guard's huts, the path leaves the stream and continues toward Rara, rising onto the Chuchemara *Danda* (Chuchemara "Ridge" or "Pass"); here the exposed, narrow trail skirts the west-facing Khater Khola basin. The views toward Humla are superb. Eventually you come out onto the last ridge line before Rara, at 12,500 ft., where you have an excellent prospect of both Rara Lake and the valley leading to Mugu.

From lakeside, this same route taken to the south initially follows the northern bank of the Khater Khola, Rara's outlet. One and a half miles from the lake, take the side path up the hill south of the Khater. This track climbs 3,000 ft. past moss-draped trees to the just-mentioned Humla-Rara-Mugu view point on the Chuchemara Danda.

Nepal's Far Western Hills

Before continuing with four sections that describe the northern high country of west Nepal's snow-covered lekhs and old Tibetan trade routes, let's briefly note Nepal's wide-reaching 4,000-ft. to 8,000-ft. hill areas to the south and west of Jumla—the "middle hills." This region amid the Mahabharat Range lies between the himals to the north and, to the south, Nepal's flat terai, its largest rice-growing area, the far reaches of the fertile Ganges plain. Not much rain falls in these western hills, and the land cannot support a population as large as that in Nepal's central and eastern middle hills. This aridity, plus an increase in the average lifespan, the slowing of border trade to the north, and inflation have combined to force many Nepalis from the Mahakali and Seti valleys to seek summer labor in the hills of India as far west as the Chenab Valley road project near Kishtwar.

The hill people of this region are Dotials. Members of this clan portered for Shipton and Tilman into the Nanda Devi Sanctuary in 1936 and 14 years later proved to be excellent porters and companions for the Scots in Garhwal.

To head into Nepal's unvisited far western hills you should be both experienced and adventurous, for you will be in valleys that Angrezi rarely enter. You should probably hire a porter familiar with the area you will be walking in. Get copies of the relevant U502 maps, which are helpful particularly with village names. There are virtually no inns or English-speaking Nepalis on these trails. Choose a place to begin walking that is appropriate to the time you have or the season of year. (Go low only in winter.) Flying into Jumla, Silghari-Doti, or Baitadi is easier than going all the way to the trailhead by road. From Jumla, you can follow the Tila River down-valley to reach Chuli Lekh, where trails lead to the area called Doti, north of Silghari Doti. Alternatively from Jumla, take the westerly Humla trail by way of Sinja to the Karnali River and enter northern Bajura on the path crossing the 9,000-ft. Parakhya La. Continuing on from there, you could walk to the upper Seti Valley south of Nampa (22,160 ft.) and Api (at 23,400 ft. the highest himal in Nepal west of Dhaulagiri), or you could trek south into the rolling lower hills. You are definitely on your own in far western Nepal.

From Jumla to Humla

In the rain shadow to the north of Nepal's main Himalayan peaks in the central and and western areas are perhaps eight high valleys populated by clans of people who speak various Tibetan dialects. The most renowned of these Buddhist clans are the Sherpas, in the Everest area. As you traverse the inner Himalayan valleys of western Nepal, you will meet the hospitable, trade-oriented people of these clans. The westernmost such valley is known as Humla, situated along the Humla Karnali gorge northwest of Rara Lake. Reachable from Jumla at the end of a 10-day walk, Humla is definitely not on any circuit of trekkers. When Chris Wriggins and I arrived with our Tibetan porters in the springtime of 1974, two days before the end of the Nepali calendar year, we were the third and fourth foreigners to register for the year just ending at Simikot, Humla's district capital. The two people before us were anthropologists doing extended field studies. Now an airstrip has been built at Simikot, but because flights are infrequent and liable to be cancelled owing to the elements, the trail from Jumla is the more likely route. Humla is a food-deficient area, and once there, you may have difficulty, as we did, in purchasing food essentials. So stock up well on supplies before departing Jumla, and replenish your grains before crossing the last pass into upper Humla.

The most commonly traveled path to Humla begins along the already described trail to Sinja. (Another route that leads east of Rara Lake, over the Chankheli Lagna will be referred to later.) From Sinja, walk a mile downriver to Lurku village and turn west up the side valley. A steep climb leads to a low pass; on the other side, descend to a tributary of the Khater Khola, the river that drains Rara Lake, and follow it to the 4,400-ft. Karnali River Valley. Along the Khater Khola you will pass lush rice fields, banana trees, and thatched houses quite unlike anything seen in the higher areas you have come from. Descend the Khater Khola to the Karnali itself. Some people here wear vests or necklaces of old Indian coins. The men smoke pungent *tambakoo* (tobacco) in their clay *sulpas*, pipes they light by striking stones with strips of steel to ignite dry, sage-like tinder.

Once on the west bank of the Karnali, after crossing a bridge near the Khater's debouchment into the Karnali, you will reach a main north-south trail with connecting paths to the south and to the far western areas called Bajura, Bhajang, and Doti. This main trail along the Karnali is used by numerous Thakuri and Bhotia traders who roam from Tibet to the southern hills. The current economic plight of these long-distance food haulers since the strict regulation of trade with Tibet is recounted by Christoph von Furer-Haimendorf in his thorough book, *Himalayan Traders*. Like the American cowboy, these traders have a fanciful reputation in contrast to their hard day-to-day lives.

To reach Humla, however, continue up the Karnali Valley for a day's walk. The trail intersects the narrow, wild Kuwari Khola, which offers a very difficult alternate route into upper Humla. The Kuwari is a deep, forested gorge leading northwest via a summer pass called the Sankha La (15,400 ft.) or Rani Kharka ("Queen's Meadow Pass"). South of this pass, the icefall on Saipal Himal's eastern face is a brilliant early-morning sight. Before you leave the Karnali Valley trail for this route, however, check at the village of Barchya on the main trail to be certain that the pass is open. With the decrease in the salt trade, the alternate Kuwari route is seldom used, but its uninhabited upper reaches make a great walk.

The main Karnali Valley trail drops to cross the Kuwari Khola and continues along the Karnali's right bank, passing scree slopes and scattered cacti to a place about a mile below the junction of the Humla Karnali and Mugu Karnali rivers. These two main tributaries of the Karnali drain a 150-mi.-wide area north of the Himalayan chain, reaching from the Humla Karnali's headwaters south of Mt. Kailas in Tibet to the upper reaches of eastern Dolpo above Dhaulagiri, where the Mugu Karnali originates. Near a small stream on the Karnali's right bank, the path rises 2,000 ft. directly up a dry spur and angles northward to the fields of two small villages that mirror other terraces across the vertiginous Humla Karnali gorge. Ask in the villages for the trail to the Munya La; the path slants gently upward into the next forested side valley. Cross this tributary and, on the other side, climb the northerly ridge to the Munya La (about 12,500 ft.) on the southern border of Humla's traditional boundary. Looking to the south from the top of the Munya La, you see low, forested lekhs and have an overview of the way you have walked from Jumla. In contrast, the northern aspect is topped by snow peaks. From the pass, the trail descends steeply for the most part, to Ripa village.

Before trekking on north, note that from Ripa a route leads downvalley to lower Humla, a good way to return eventually. The alternate route south from Humla crosses the lower Tanke Valley near Darma village and continues south over the Chankheli La (11,700 ft.), which is north of the Mugu Karnali Valley. Once at the Mugu Karnali, you take the trail to Pina village and return to Jumla along the eastern path to Rara Lake.

Continuing north from Ripa, the main Humla Karnali trail will follow the left or right bank (depending on the river's water level), passing through groves of rhododendron and bamboo. (Ask locals to show you the trail junction with an alternate upland route leading south to lower Humla, over the high Margor La.) The Humla Karnali River flows generally southeast from its point of origin south of Mt. Kailas. Except for a few stretches, the Humla Karnali plows away at the bottom of a V-shaped gorge from lower Humla right on up to the last few miles before the Tibetan border. When you are in the Humla Valley, be sure to ask for the honey that is produced in hollow log hives. Humla's honey is some of the best in Nepal, but be prepared to pay well for it.

Humla's most important village is Simikot, situated at about the 10,400-ft. level on a spur high above the north bank of the Humla Karnali, a two- to three-day walk from Ripa. A STOL strip adjacent to town has been fashioned from the village wheat fields on a gently sloping shelf. Administrative buildings in neat rows sit just back on a nearby knoll that commands excellent views of converging gorges beneath snowy saw-toothed ridges. Simikot village is largely composed of Thakuris, the same clan found in Jumla. The Thakuris living in and about Simikot are virtually the only Nepali Hindus to conduct trans-border trade in Tibet; Nepal's traders are mostly Buddhist highlanders whose ancestors migrated earlier from various Tibetan regions.

At several junctures along the lower trail up the Humla Valley beyond Simikot, side paths lead steeply east to two summer settlements. These villages—Dhinga and Yakba—are along an upper trail that continues onward, still steeply, to a 16,100-ft. pass called the Nyalo La or Ninyan La. From this pass, sacred Mt. Kailas is visible. The region beyond the pass is called Limi: a high, isolated valley with three villages whose Bhotia inhabitants raise animals and engage in trade that once

At the Munya La, with Humla's peaks in the background, western Nepal.

extended as far as Lhasa and still reaches to Kathmandu.

Back on the main route through Humla, the frequently restricted trail up-valley from Simikot leads into more steep country, inhabited in the first part by Buddhist Bhotias and Hindu Thakuris and farther up by Bhotias only. Beyond Simikot this trail passes several villages near the narrow gorge bottom, eventually reaching Kermi, the first all-Bhotia village. Kermi has a 20-ft.-long prayer wall and its own gombas of the Nyingma and Sakya orders high above the town. West of Kermi, look for the vertiginous Khawa Lungba ravine leading south to Chala village and the Sankha La. Chala was once a thriving trader's rest stop, in the days of unrestricted transborder trade. Crossing several small meadows, the once heavily traveled valley route in northern Humla continues by Yangar, Munchu, and Yari. The former and latter towns once held large summer trade fairs with their neighbors across the Tibetan border. Near Munchu the valley widens, and beyond Yari the trail negotiates the Nara La, on a high ridge. Not far up-valley, but beyond the Tibetan border, is a track leading south to the Tinkar Lepu La, the pass at the head of Nepal's nearly inaccessible Tinkar Valley (see Chapter 10).

The Mugu Valley

The narrow Mugu Valley lies east of Humla and the practically uninhabited Tanke gorge. Mugu's inhabitants have been strictly limited to trading for a livelihood, because their own valley has little room

Tying up provisions for herders in Humla (photo by Kevin Bubriski).

for fields and its upper headwaters lie beneath a good pass that leads to Tibet. We will meet the Mugulis, as they are called, but first let's look at the two principal routes to the usually restricted Mugu Valley.

From Jumla, both a high and a low path lead to Mugu. Each route requires at least a week's walk to reach Mugu village, although the upper trail following the Chaudabise Valley may be snow-covered for more than five months of the year. If you are going in the autumn and want to try the upper trail, do so on the outbound leg of your trek, for the Khapre Pass at the head of the valley may be snowed in by the time of your return.

To take this route, walk east from Jumla along the Tila Valley to the Chaudabise confluence. (Ask for honey at homes along the lower stretches of the Chaudabise, especially near Talphi village.) Many Mugulis have built houses in the flat bottomlands near Talphi and they will know if the Khapre Pass is being used. At Talphi, a lesser used alternative trail branches north through Maharigaon. This secondary trail crosses three passes and is open slightly longer than the approach over the Khapre La, owing primarily to the Khapre's steep northern slope. Along the Chaudabise route, a two-day walk through a heavily forested and unpopulated valley brings you north past the final birch trees to a narrow upper gorge below the 16,600-ft. Khapre La. Do not be guided by the U502 Series maps of this area, which indicate that the Chaudabise does not connect with the Khapre, for, in fact, below a scree-covered 1,500-ft. drop north of the pass, the trail reaches a side valley that leads directly to Wangri village. From gritty, rough Wangri, continue to the bottom of the river gorge. This major tributary of the Mugu Karnali is called the Langu or Namlang on most maps, but the locals call it the Dolpo Chu; it drains the entire area of northern Dolpo. To reach the Mugu Valley, you can take a near-vertical track 3,000 ft. over the high ridge to the north, but an easier if slightly longer trail traverses downstream along the northern face, a thousand feet above the Dolpa River. In several miles, this trail drops to join with the lower trail from the south.

Since Wangri and Dalphu villages are the last towns up the valley for many miles, game is sometimes seen up the Dolpa River to the east of the two villages. One of the most interesting endangered species in the Himalaya lives in this area: the Himalayan musk deer is a 30-pound animal that is pursued by hunters living in Wangri and in Dalphu village (situated across the deep Langu gorge). This unique animal has wide-stranded wavy hair that is shiny like plastic and longer hind legs than forelegs. Always secretive, the musk deer becomes nocturnal if its ways are threatened, as indeed they are, for the *kasturi*, as it is called from Kashmir to Bhutan, is hunted with ardor virtually everywhere it lives. The male deer has the misfortune of carrying a subcutaneous gland near its stomach that holds an average of 35 grams of yellow-grained musk, which also is called kasturi—and the best of which is called *beautay* in west Nepal. Like rhinocerous horn, this beautay or kasturi is believed to have near-miraculous aphrodisiacal and curative properties. Until gold exceeded $500 an ounce in Kathmandu, even its price was exceeded by kasturi's. Rodney Jackson, the author of the natural history chapter of this book, studied the hunting patterns of men from Dalphu and Wangri in the winter of 1976–77 and estimated that more than a hundred animals were killed for musk in this remote area alone. The toll throughout the Himalaya must be staggering. The Himalayan musk deer will unwillingly continue along a path to extinction in the wild unless it can be protected in sanctuaries like Rara Lake National Park.

The second, lower trail from Jumla to Mugu follows the eastern path to Rara Lake as far as Pina village. A half-day's walk near the river bottom down-valley north of Pina takes you far below Gum Gadhi, Mugu's ridge-straddling district headquarters, and down to the Mugu Karnali gorge. At this junction the trail to Mugu takes an easterly course, into an area known as the Karan Hills. This Karan region is separate ethnically from the villages of Churi and Mugu in Mugu proper. There are a dozen Karan villages—some, like Lumsa and Methang (also called Mangri), scattered at around 6,500 ft. near the main trail, others half hidden at the 10,000 ft. level on the slopes of northern side valleys. Replenish grains and ask for yoghurt (*dahi*) and eggs (*phul*) at the lower villages, as there is little fresh food in Mugu beyond Methang.

Eight miles east of Methang is the confluence of the Mugu and Dolpo branches of the Mugu Karnali River. Several old stupas rest above the vertex of the two streams, as if to announce that all upriver lands are protected by the dharma. Just above the river junction, the trail from Dalphu and Wangri connects with the main trail up the Mugu Valley.

The first of the only two villages in Mugu itself is Churi, 1,700 ft. above the river along the rarely traveled upper ridge trail from Dalphu. The valley trail passes well below Churi and continues along the base of the steep valley around two bends where the gorge, now not so narrow and U-shaped, aims directly north to the Nanza La at the Tibetan border.

Mugu village sits at the 11,000-ft. level on the left bank of the river, a tight collection of a hundred three-story homes constructed of stone, wattle, and timber. The village is windswept and windows are small, but each roof has a protected, open porch, and each home has a well-used family room on the third floor. The white Nyingma gomba in its grove of evergreens above town offers a pleasant contrast to the upper valley's study in brown and ochre. The deserted town of Purana Mugu (Old Mugu) lies a two-hour walk up-valley from Mugu near the last groves of trees.

Mugulis, whether met in Jumla, along the trail, or at home, have a vivacity and buoyancy all their own. Ethnically they are Tibetan, with round, bronze faces. The older generation has clung to its ways: the men are often away trading or grazing animals, while the women clean, spin, and weave woolen homespun for clothes, blankets, and animal packbags. Until blue Chinese sneakers became popular, men made and wore the *somba*, a shoe with legging in the Tibetan style that is ingeniously made from leather and wool. Women from Mugu wear distinctive, circular, 3-inch-wide silver earrings.

Trading between Mugulis and the nomadic Drok Pa north of the political border has been strictly circumscribed by the authorities to the north, and as a result Mugu has lost regional influence. In 1976 a Muguli trader who owned 15 yaks told me that the border was legally open only during September and October. During that time, he and his neighbors made as many trips as possible with their yaks over the high Nanza La to Pong Dzu in Tibet. Taking grains, they returned with salt, wool, dry cheese, butter, and the Tibetan tea, which is moulded into bricks. These goods were stored in the second stories of their homes until the season was completed and travel southward with yaks or sheep could begin. In winter, many Mugulis make at least one trip to Surkhet. 10 days south of Jumla. Song Bu, a 25-year-old Muguli who had traveled as far as Calcutta, amazed Chris and me by observing our 1:506, 880 "West Sheet" of Nepal and, without being able to read the English words, naming off towns, rivers, and passes.

The Eastern Track to Dhorpatan

It is possible to walk between Jumla and Pokhara, scores of miles to the east, in 2½ to 3 weeks if you don't take side trips or run into bad weather. The route follows the old path that was used by people carrying Jumla's red rice to Kathmandu during the rule of the Rana family. We will look now at the western two-thirds of this trail, as far as Dhorpatan; the Dhorpatan-to-Pokhara stretch will be noted in the next chapter. Though this trek is rarely undertaken due to Jumla's relative inaccessibility, the walk is most varied, traversing well-populated lowlands near Pokhara and passing through primeval forests and spectacular gorges west and south of Dhaulagiri.

Stock up at least five days of food at Jumla, and expect to replenish basic supplies in Tibrikot and Drikung to the east. The trail begins along the gentle Tila Valley, passing initially through terrain reminiscent of the Colorado high country. In the afternoon of the first day's walk, after climbing a low ridge, you will reach Gothi Chaur, a sheep-rearing station in a rolling meadow. Just east of the long buildings, a small spring emerges beneath a stone Malla shrine. Across the meadow lies an anachronistic, faintly marked STOL landing strip. A short half-day's walk beyond Gothi Chaur in the upper Tila Valley is the recently built settlement of Napokuna, populated by hospitable formerly nomadic Drok Pa from Tibet. Good porters who are used to high passes can be found at Napokuna, a frontier-spirited community. If Nepal's refugees from Tibet should ever follow the Dalai Lama en masse into Tibet, then Napokuna's Drok Pa will leave their homes and disappear northward.

Several hours' walk east of Napokuna, a low pass brings the trail out of the Karnali River watershed and into the Bheri drainage. (The Bheri is technically part of the larger Karnali system, joining the

Karnali just north of the Siwalik Range.) A forested lekh looms ahead, but first the Jagdula River below must be crossed. The path descends to the hamlet of Chaurikot, then proceeds through a large notch and on to the interesting village of Rimi. On either side of Rimi are Malla stelae, but the most intriguing objects in town are the ubiquitous wooden *dok pa* figures, human-shaped protector deities.

Throughout much of Nepal west of Tibrikot are small buildings called *khotans*. The dok pa figures in Rimi and the town's khotan represent prehistoric traditions that continue alongside the veneration of Hindu gods and goddesses. Next to the khotan, during ceremonies performed four times yearly in the full moon, oracles known as *dhamis* speak in trance with the voice of a local god. Dhamis are often older men with long, roughly braided hair twisted atop their heads who initially gained their position by manifesting *siddhis* ("powers"—often of divination) and performing "impossible acts," such as rubbing kernels of rice to produce small green plants. Despite the many carved figures, khotans, and dhamis that the trekker can see while passing through, it is the rare foreigner (aside from an occasional Peace Corps volunteer or anthropologist) who ever witnesses a dhami in trance during the full-moon ceremony.

Angling down from Rimi, the path crosses the Jagdula River and continues toward Kaigaon village. Less than a thousand feet above Kaigaon, the trail divides: the path south toward Jajarkot heads directly uphill, while the track to Tibrikot and Tarakot goes somewhat more gently to a false pass at 10,800 feet. Sometimes there are restrictions on trekking in the upper Bheri Valley (because the trail crosses through the southernmost part of the Dolpo District), and the roundabout southern gorge trail to Jajarkot must be taken down the Bheri Valley as far as the Sano Bheri turn-off to Dhorpatan. If your Jumla-to-Pokhara trekking permit lists Tarakot, you will be able to continue, through Kaigaon, over the 12,590-ft. Balangra Pass, reaching Tibrikot. With its Gurkha-built temple above town, Tibrikot rests in a rugged gorge on a spur 700 ft. above the Bheri River. The area called Tarakot lies two days' walk east; from Tibrikot, the low river trail passes the Dunahi airstrip and, farther on, Dunahi Bazaar, the headquarters and southern tip of Dolpo District.

You can find Tarakot on maps, but Dzong is the name used by locals. A prominent fortress town on a knoll south of the Bheri, Dzong is one of four south-bank villages in the region formerly called Tichu Rong. Dzong's residents once supervised toll collection on caravans traversing Tichu Rong via the Bheri. Above and slightly west of Dzong is Ba, a large village whose inhabitants have the distinction of speaking their own language, a dialect called Kakay. Still higher above Dzong is prosperous Drikung village, populated by Tibetan and Magar Buddhists. From the roofs of Drikung's solid homes, you have a grand, 360-degree view of this deep, awesome gorge. North rises a 20,000-ft. ridge, which is west of Dolpo's Tarap Valley. To the south are the westernmost summits of the gargantuan Dhaulagiri Himal, a snow-cloaked series of peaks 40 air miles in length that reach to Dhaulagiri I. The Bheri River below you disappears down-valley to the west, but within eyesight the gorge divides upriver to the north and east, where its paths are known as the Tarap and Barbung valleys respectively. The Barbung makes up part of the direct route north around Dhaulagiri, noted in the next chapter.

Trails south leave Drikung and Ba villages and rise more than 4,000 ft. to the Jang La (about 14,900 ft.). This route from the Tarakot area to the meadowland and village at Dhorpatan takes four to six days (longer if you encounter snow). The path rises and falls consecutively as it crosses three barren passes and a few low ridges while passing only two impoverished villages. This is very impressive ridge and gorge topography, much of it very wild, although some upper meadows are well grazed in the summer. Difficult though the route is, it gets good use in spring and fall from trading caravans that often include pack-carrying horses. Trekking between the Tarakot area and Dhorpatan should be undertaken only with a porter cum cook who is familiar with the way. Several pages would be required to describe the route precisely. This is tough, rewarding country—for days you traverse the western flanks of Dhaulagiri. Look for bharal in the upper meadows. Once at Dhorpatan you can replenish supplies from homes that are a half-day stroll from the Kali Gandaki watershed and less than a week's walk from Pokhara.

Dolpo

With sweeping, windswept vistas and a traditional Tibetan culture, the high valleys of Dolpo are some of the most remarkable Himalayan gems. A guide that did not immediately emphasize Dolpo's excessive remoteness, however, would be remiss. Most villages in Dolpo are removed from the rest of the world to the south by one or more difficult passes. Dolpo must import grain, and any outsiders who enter should be completely self-sufficient in food. This is important—treks to isolated places anywhere are perhaps most often curtailed because of low rations. Any person planning to walk into one of Dolpo's valleys north of the extensive Dhaulagiri Himal must have a permit valid for the area, enough food, and a porter-cook who knows the trails and camping places. This can be a nearly impossible order to fill.

The name Dolpo remained unknown to the rest of the world until David Snellgrove and three Nepali companions began to hear the word used in conversation when they reached the region in May 1956. *Himalayan Pilgrimage* is Snellgrove's account of his seven-month journey largely within Tibetan-speaking, inner-mountain areas of west and central Nepal. The book remains one of the most knowledgeable, compassionate, and well written of Himalayan journals. It also contains a wealth of information about trails in Dolpo. Snellgrove found that valleys of the upper Bheri and Langu (Dolpo) watersheds have been divided into subregions called Tarap, Tsharbung, Namgung, and Panzang. These four areas compose Dolpo. Tarap and Tsharbung are valleys of the upper Bheri; Namgung and Panzang comprise several of the uppermost tributaries in the Langu watershed. Namgung and Panzang are considered to be "Inner" Dolpo, for they lie to the north of Tarap and Tsharbung, beyond additional high passes.

The few hundred people who reside year-round in Dolpo's upper villages near 14,000 ft. are among the world's highest dwellers. The only grain that can grow in the highest valleys is barley, the area's staple food, which is served roasted and ground as tsampa. Although Dolpo has long been part of Nepal, its villagers have looked to Tibet for their culture and commerce, and are of different south Tibetan clans. Most people are either Rung Ba, valley farmers, or Drok Pa, semi-nomadic yak herders.

People in Dolpo wear homespun clothing that is sometimes dyed maroon, and they favor Tibetan-style somba for footgear. Men and women often wear both religious amulets and strings of coral and turquoise about their necks. Women plait their hair in various styles. Older men wear braided hair wrapped about their heads or hanging down their backs, leaving a swath of grease on their wool shirts.

As if to emphasize Dolpo's seclusion from the rest of the world, some villages still practice the pre-Buddhist Bon Po religion. This early sect was almost entirely replaced when Buddhist doctrine spread across Tibet. Now, in Nepal, only a few small remnants of Bon Po believers remain: they are largely in and near Dolpo and in the upper Arun Valley to the east. The ideography of Bon and the ritual implements employed during Bon ceremonies are so similar to those of Buddhism that practically anyone approaching a Bon Po building will believe it is another Buddhist gomba. Some Bon paintings or gombas are easily identified, however: look to see whether any swastikas are pointing counterclockwise. Swastikas, the ancient Indian symbol for good fortune, always point clockwise on Buddhist iconography but are often reversed in the Bon Po tradition. Less obvious but likewise contrary to Buddhist practice is the way Bon prayer walls are skirted. While Buddhist mani stones are meant to be passed on the left, people proceed to the right of Bon Po walls. The Buddhist mantra *Om Mani Padme Hum* often carved on prayer stones has various levels of allegoric meaning, but the traditional Bon Po invocation—*Om Matri Muye Sa Le Du*—is largely enigmatic. Other differences exist, but nowadays Bon Po is effectively a branch of Tibetan Buddhism.

How to reach Dolpo? The fact is that very few people will be able to summon the energy, time, and permissions required to set foot upon this extremely isolated area. *Himalayan Pilgrimage*, an unintentional but excellent Baedeker, is your best sourcebook for this region. It was reprinted in 1981 by Prajna Press of Boulder, Colorado. If you seriously plan a trek to Dolpo, study that book. If you go, carry the book with you. This chapter, however, will tear no more rents in Dolpo's veil.

Marpha village on the Kali Gandaki River.

12

Around Annapurna, Dhaulagiri, Manaslu, and Gosain Kund Lake

Such houses and such men, ragged, tough and cheerful, both alike reeking of juniper smoke, speak of high valleys upon the threshold of great mountains.
H. W. Tilman, in the Marsyangdi Valley, 1949

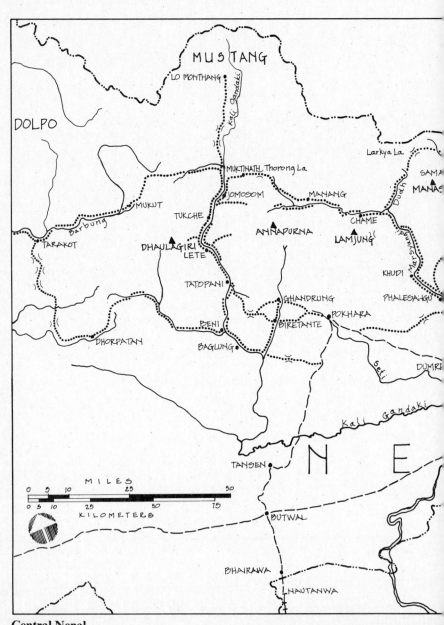

Central Nepal

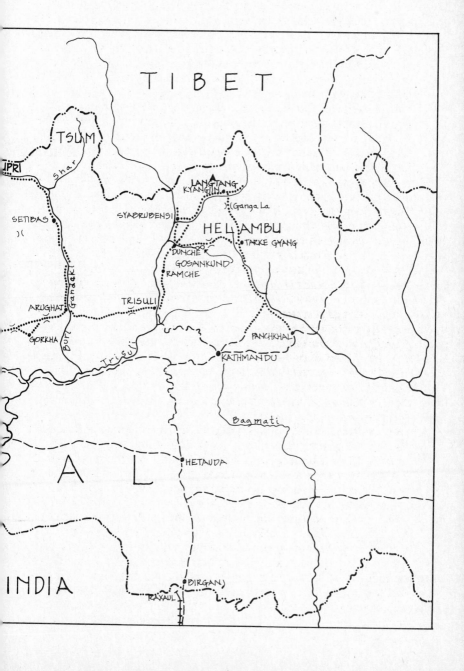

Nepal's Amazing Gorges

In central and eastern Nepal the Great Himalayan Range rises abruptly north of the middle hills. Deep, V-shaped gorges—among the deepest on the face of the earth, and swathed in stone and greenery—carry streams and rivers rapidly into the lower, more southerly Mahabharat Range. Hikers on the roller-coaster paths along these valleys are often surprised by the rapidly changing sequence of culture, climate, and landscape as the trail passes from the warm middle hills to the dry upper valleys. With the exception of the streams in the Kathmandu Valley, virtually all those from the kingdom's mountains empty into one of Nepal's three river systems before penetrating the low hogback ridges of the Siwalik Hills to reach the flatlands of India. Lying between the drainages of the western Karnali and the eastern Sapt Kosi, Nepal's central watershed is called the Great Gandaki. The Gandaki river system includes four gorges that have their origin north of the main Himalayan Range. These four trans-Himalayan valleys—the Kali Gandaki, the Marsyangdi, the Buri Gandaki, and the Trisuli—comprise much of the terrain covered in this chapter.

The valleys of both the Great Gandaki and Sapt Kosi watersheds share a distinctive topography, natural history, and culture. Slowly, roads are being built north along some of these valleys, for the middle hill areas are bounded only by low slopes, without steep gradients. Once you have reached the valley you will ascend, you are in subtropical country 1,000 ft. to 4,000 ft. in elevation, where banana and papaya trees shade water bufflalo, rice is the principal crop, and the people are Hindu. As you walk up-valley, the ridge lines are replaced by higher and steeper spurs of the Great Himalayan Range. Farther north begins a narrow gorge with stretches of sheer rock walls; depending on which valley you follow, the gorge requires from one to two days to negotiate on trails that seesaw frequently. While you are passing through the gorge, the river is your roaring attendant, morning temperatures stay cooler, and villages are small and scattered. The path skirts and crosses ribs of the himals above, and in spring and summer the gorge has many waterfalls. Once you are into the Himalaya the valley floor rises quickly, and the inhabitants you meet are usually Buddhists living near evergreen-forested slopes. Beyond the villages and the last silver birch trees are summer huts in the middle of high grazing meadows. Paths into other valleys continue over rock fields and often through snow toward high, prayer-monument-topped passes.

The greater part of this chapter describes four circular treks involving three to four weeks' walking time (depending on your pace) and mentions a few of the many side-trails en route. Each of the four circle routes follows a main valley or tributary valley upward from its southern trailhead or a connecting path. Using these routes, three of the world's ten tallest peaks and the sacred lake called Gosain Kund can be encircled. Remember that you must get a trekking permit before you leave on any walk in Nepal and that permits are difficult to obtain for areas north of Dhaulagiri and Manaslu.

In addition to trekking the circle routes, you can make a number of lower-elevation hikes in the central midlands, as the following brief section suggests.

Trekking in the Middle Hills

Central Nepal's lush and well-populated midlands are some of the country's most accessible areas, owing to the roads among the middle hills that connect Kathmandu with both Pokhara to the west and Kodari on the Tibetan border to the north. From April through September, the hills lower than 5,000 ft. are first quite warm and then offer the rains and leeches of the monsoon; however, from November through March the hills are neither hot nor muddy. The midlands hill walks suggested here are only a few of the myriad hikes possible in central Nepal. Depending on your time constraints or whim, these treks can be taken in part or full or can be extended, and they can be followed in either direction. Some routes are described sketchily, others only suggested; you may devise better ones as you trek or after map perusal. However, trails are so many that, without a guide, unless you have a good map and are proficient in asking directions in Nepali, you will have difficulty keeping to any planned course. So do take a porter-guide who knows the area. Also, the U502 map series is helpful for the middle hills in Nepal, although some large villages are misnamed or omitted.

Remember that Nepal's middle hills are largely Hindu and that you will not be aware of many local customs, particularly with respect to the preparation and consumption of food and in the matter of sleeping arrangements. Review the section on acculturation in Chapter 3. If you ask shelter from a Chhetri or Brahman family, you and your porter may be politely directed to the porch or a nearby outbuilding. Your clan (Angrezi) or your porter's may not be considered sufficiently refined! Ancient Hindu principles from the Vedas, dating back thousands of years, determine what is and is not considered pure. The Nepali word *jutho* indicates the concept of something being rendered impure by contact alone. If you touch any piece of unoffered food, it may become jutho food, which must be fed directly to the animals. People's bodies are believed to decline in sanctity from head to feet. Thus, patting people on the head or stepping over them is not done. When interrelating with locals in or near their homes, watch and follow the lead set by others.

Paths lead to the midlands from the Kathmandu Valley, but nowadays most people take one of the routes in by vehicle. Hikers often bus to Panchkhal and continue to the Helambu region (see the last section of this chapter). Others walk via the first few days' segment of the trail from Lamosangu toward Mt. Everest (see the next chapter) or take the bus to Trisuli Bazaar. Buses to Trisuli leave northwestern

Kathmandu's Pakanjol area (on the way to the Balaju Water Gardens) in early morning and early afternoon for the 43-mi. trip. Treks of a week or more can be conveniently undertaken from Trisuli Bazaar.

With someone to porter and guide, you can take a 10-day or longer loop walk from the town of Trisuli. Follow the main trail west and then, branching off, head up the terraced Ankhu Valley, cutting back across two southeastern spurs of Ganesh Himal. The farther north you cross these high ridges dividing the Ankhu and Trisuli valleys, the closer you will be to the main range and to the upper grazing pastures on Ganesh Himal, populated by Tamang herders. A high jungle route farther up the Ankhu Valley crosses two 12,000-ft. passes that are on the way to Gatlang and the Trisuli River.

West from Trisuli up the Samri Valley lies the beginning of the old Kathmandu-to-Pokhara trail, which leads to the Pokhara Valley in a walk of about a week. Lodging along this main trail is traditionally available in homes that take in travelers for the night, but you will not know which are the correct houses unless you ask. From the ridges on this ancient track, you will have panoramic views of snowy peaks. The historically important town of Gurkha (or Ghorka) lies on one branch of this trail east of the Marsyangdi River.

Some of the best middle-hill trekking can be found along the southern spurs of the Annapurna-Lamjung massif. This region is approached most easily from Pokhara. From Pokhara Bazaar, take day walks north to temple-capped hills or to Batulechaur, the home village of a clan of *gaine*, or minstrel singers, who wander for weeks at a time performing in different locales. Scenic overnight hikes from Pokhara reach Naudanda with its magnificent Himalayan panorama; or, along the same trail, spend two or three nights out to reach Chandrakot's view point of Annapurna South and Machhapuchhare. Route descriptions of the trail to Naudanda and Chandrakot are given in the next section.

In the leech-free dry season you can walk north from Pokhara for two to four days and go beyond the villages in the lush Mardi or Seti valleys that drain Machhapuchhare's vertiginous south slopes. If you follow the Seti Valley far enough on the rough trail, Machhapuchhare will be southwest, towering 12,000 ft. above you.

Longer walks of a week to 10 days lead along tracks east or west of Pokhara where you will have excellent exposures to hill life. With a porter who knows the way, walk northeast out of the Pokhara Valley floor to a large town populated by Gurungs such as Siklis or Ghanpokhara. You will traverse thick jungle and terraced fields and probably meet English-speaking former Gurkha soldiers along the way. On the return you can trek to Pokhara by a different hill route or go south along the Marsyangdi Valley to the roadhead at Dumre. Another loop route, this one west of Pokhara, begins south of town at the roadside bazaar of Naudanda (a different Naudanda from the one previously mentioned), which you can reach by taking the cramped bus from Pokhara for the 1½ hour ride—or share a taxi. From Naudanda this lowland course follows the hot Andhi Khola to Karkineta along the trail noted in the first part of the "Around Dhaulagiri" section of this chapter. On the second day of that walk, just before reaching Kusma, turn north along the Modi Khola trail to Biretante, and return on foot to Pokhara by the main trail or the more circuitous but scenic jungle track through Ghandrung and Landrung.

Around Annapurna

The complete 3–3½-week Annapurna circuit is best undertaken counterclockwise, up the Marsyangdi Valley and down the Kali Gandaki. Most trekkers walk up the Marsyangdi Valley to the Kali Gandaki rather than the reverse for several reasons: although the time required to walk in either direction is the same, there is only a 3,200-ft. climb to the pass from the last camping place on the Marsyangdi side; the walk along the Marsyangdi Valley is more gradual in elevation gain, which makes acclimatization easier; and going toward the Kali Gandaki Valley you have the good Thakali inns to anticipate. But given the attractiveness of the Kali Gandaki Valley as a destination in itself, the great gorge of the Kali Gandaki deserves first mention. The Annapurna circuit is being mentioned out of the west-to-east sequence because it is popular, it is not restricted, and the Kali Gandaki is part of the Dhaulagiri circle.

The Kali Gandaki Valley

The ancient trading route from Pokhara that ascends the Kali Gandaki gorge west of Annapurna Himal has probably introduced more hikers to Himalayan trekking than any other trail in the range. Pokhara's accessibility to Kathmandu by air and road, the region's scenic majesty, and the area's well-established inns run by Thakalis from the Kali Gandaki all help to ensure the replacement by trekking of the lost business along the old salt-trading route to Tibet. *Bhattis*, traditional inns adapted slightly to Western tastes, are found in most villages between Pokhara and Jomosom, a week's walk away.

The Kali Gandaki trail begins at the far end of Pokhara's Bagar Bazaar (about 2,800 ft.) where donkey caravans with jangling bells still enter town led by Loba clansmen from Mustang. More likely, however, you will see there the porters, Sherpas, and sahibs of a trekking group as they begin or end a trek. Leaving Bagar Bazaar through a gauntlet of new shops, the main path meanders by rich rice lands near Hyangja village, then rises after several hours' walk to Naudanda, a ridge-straddling chain of homes and inns. A less-traveled alternate route diverges near the teahouses at Suikhet (located before Naudanda in the flatlands), angling northward through the villages of Dhampus and Landrung to Ghandrung, almost three days away. The main trail passes through Chandrakot ("Moon Town," 5,100 ft.) with its bhattis and a sweeping prospect of green hills rising to meet Annapurna South (23,680 ft.) and Hiunchuli (21,135 ft.). The distinctive, sharp double

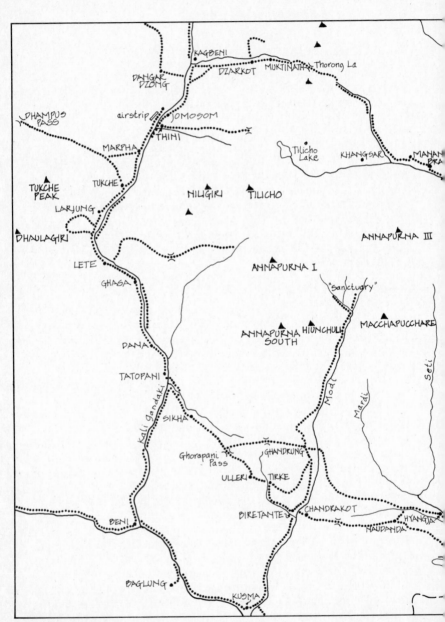

Around Annapurna

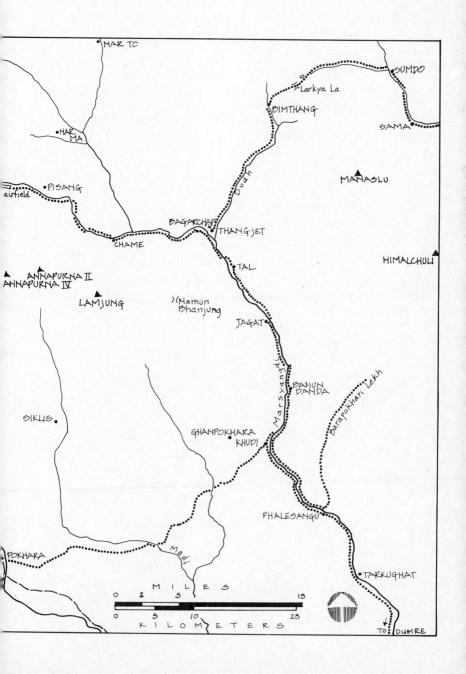

peak of Machhapuchhare (22,940 ft.), the "Fishtail," is first seen from Chandrakot.

Below Chandrakot to the west sits Biretante (3,400 ft.), astride the Modi Khola, a glacier-spawned torrent that drains the peak-encircled Annapurna Sanctuary. Well-provisioned mountain walkers can reach the Sanctuary after a three- to four-day walk up a side-trail north of Biretante. The going is easy as you climb wide stone steps to the large Gurung town of Ghandrung and follow a good trail to Chumro, the last village. The path becomes increasingly difficult as it then winds through a bamboo forest that is subject to severe avalanches in winter and spring. The trail leads into the narrow gorge wedged between Hiunchuli and the nearly vertical west buttresses of Machhapuchhare, and eventually provides entrance to the inner meadows. This Annapurna Sanctuary, at 12,000 ft. and higher, receives little sun because of fickle weather and the nine encircling summits higher than 20,000 feet. Walk up the north side of the west glacier for views of Annapurna I (26,545 ft.) and an intimate experience with a towering rock face. Carry a copy of Chris Bonington's *Annapurna South Face* for a good description of this view. Heavy-duty trekkers with adequate rations and technical climbing gear like to attempt 18,580-ft. Tent Peak north of this glacier.

The trail west of Biretante rises and falls nearly 6,000 ft., crossing the wooded Ghorapani Pass (9,300 ft.) to reach a tributary of the Kali Gandaki River. The sunny toil involved in climbing endless midvalley flagstone steps is offset by a cool rain forest draped with Spanish moss, particularly on the eastern approaches to the pass. If you meet a donkey caravan on the narrow forest path, step back or you may be brushed aside. An early dawn hike up from Ghorapani Pass on the side trail to

Rug weaving, a cottage industry in Nepal.

Poon Hill (about 10,100 ft.) will, in clear weather, give you a sweeping perspective of Nepal's central Himalayan peaks.

Far below Ghorapani, just north of the suspension bridge across the Kali Gandaki River, is Tatopani (3,800 ft.), a village with three clusters of houses. By the northern group of lodges and stores in Tatopani are the hot springs that give the town its name. Pilgrims from India and Nepal on their way to the shrine at Muktinath pause to bathe away sins at the spring, while trekkers from many countries wash away earthly grime at the well-used, stone-lined basin of hot water.

The 10-mi. walk from Tatopani north to Lete (8,300 ft.) takes you up through a narrow gorge from tropical rice fields to long-needle pine forests in the lower reaches of the area called Thak Khola. This region is populated by the industrious, congenial Thakali clan, once the controlling power of the salt trade. Now, Thakalis operate businesses in Kathmandu, Pokhara, and Butwal and run most of the bhattis along the Pokhara-to-Muktinath trail. Across the river from Lete on the east bank is Chhoya village, from which a rugged forest trail climbs steeply to cross a 14,500-ft. ridge on the tricky route to Annapurna base camp, near the headwaters of the Miristi Khola. The trek to the ridge will take most of two days; continuing down to Annapurna base camp and back to Chhoya will involve at least six to seven days of hard walking.

Annapurna I and the striking peak called Fang (unclimbed until 1981) are visible from along 2 mi. of the main trail beyond Lete. Beyond Lete along the main valley's west bank trail near the Ghatte Khola tributary, other herders' trails diverge upward to meadows at 12,500 ft. near the noisy terminus of the east Dhaulagiri icefall where rocks fall off the steep glacier as it melts. You will probably need a local to guide you onto either of these side trails—but what diversions they are! From the valley floor at about 8,300 ft., Dhaulagiri and Annapurna, both more than 26,500 ft., loom on either side, and the gorge below is nearly 3½ mi. down: the deepest valley on the face of the earth.

Back on the Kali Gandaki trail, from a bridge at Kalopani north of Lete, you can walk up either the east or west side of the flat, rock valley floor to Tukche. The east-bank trail is quicker but passes few villages, and in times of high water the log bridge near Tukche leading back across the river to the primary up-valley path will be washed out. The west-bank trail passes several interesting Thakali villages, including one town you walk beneath, between logs that support the buildings above. From either Tukche or Marpha, you can pick up high side routes following herdsmen's trails. Assuming you stay on course (easier in good weather) or go with the guidance of a local, or if you stay high on the ridge and use good trail sense, you will emerge onto the 17,000-ft. Dhampus Pass. West of the pass is an upper basin aptly dubbed Hidden Valley by Marcel Ichac during the French exploratory reconnaissance in 1950. Descend into this high valley only if you are well supplied with food. If you reach Hidden Valley, you will be north of Dhaulagiri and can try slogging up snowfields to reach French Col (17,500 ft.) for a look-see of the Mayagdi Glacier. The walk up to French Col from the north is non-technical, but you *must* be experienced in glacier walking to traverse the dangerous, heavily crevassed Mayagdi Glacier that descends south from French Col west of Dhaulagiri I.

The main route along Kali Gandaki Valley emerges north of the main range beyond Marpha village (8,760 ft.). Within a few miles the forested landscape is transformed into a dry inner valley with scattered villages of flat-roofed homes adjacent to fields of wheat and barley. Be prepared for the unusually strong wind that is likely to blow either up- or down-valley between about 11:00 A.M. and 4:00 P.M., from Kalopani to Kagbeni. This daily gale results from unequal air pressure between the lowlands and Tibet. You will find yourself walking quite slowly if the wind is not at your back.

An often discussed but rarely attempted high side-trail is the route east from Thini village (Thini is north from Marpha on a low ridge above the east bank) that leads to a col overlooking Tilicho Lake, also called "Great Ice Lake" (16,140 ft.). As for the hike to Dhampus Pass, you should pack minimally three days of food if you want to reach the pass and must take more rations if you plan to explore the high plateau beyond. The path above Thini divides in several places, so you may need a porter-guide to keep you on the direct trail. The low point of the ridge (16,790 ft.) is a technical glacial icefall, so instead you must scramble up a 1,500-ft. scree slope to the north that reaches a higher but negotiable col. At the top you will have a spectacular view of Tilicho Lake and the Great Barrier (a long, high ridge ending in Nilgiri Peak) of Annapurna.

The village of Dzong Sam (or Dzong Sarba) was misinterpreted as Jomosom by early surveyors, and so it retains that name today. With an airport, government offices, and new hotels, the dusty town is growing rapidly, but it does not have the charm of many other towns along the valley. However, it has excellent views southward to Nilgiri and the great Kali Gandaki gorge. North of Jomosom, trails divide: a difficult route west to Dolpo's restricted Barbung Valley from Dangar Dzong is noted in the "Around Dhaulagiri" section; a large trail leads north to medieval Mustang; while to the east a well-trod path climbs to Muktinath and the Thorong La.

For years the rumor has circulated that Mustang will be derestricted. For the time being however, this intriguing, parched region that protrudes northward into Tibet will remain tantalizingly close but unreachable. When entry to Mustang is permitted, you will be able to hike about three days' distance from Jomosom, past villages with multistoried houses, forlorn monasteries, and crumbling castles, to reach Lo Monthang (12,400 ft.), the walled capital of this once-autonomous kingdom. The most striking element of Mustang, as described by those who have been there, is its landscape: sandstone pillars rise near old moraines, and time and again the trails angle up and down over barren, eroded ridges and high terraces. Mustang's pastel shadings, hues of red, yellow, sienna, tan, and grey, undergo dramatic changes in lighting throughout the day. On the Nyi La (12,600 ft.), north of Geling and on the second day's walk from Jomosom, you cross the traditional boundary from the region called Baragaon into Mustang. At Tsarang and Gemi villages, tall castles remind you that, as in Ladakh, here you are in a region of Tibetan culture. As greater numbers of people come to walk the shortest route, to Lo Monthang and back, you can seek out for yourself the small, untouristed villages and shrines off the main path.

By a small teahouse three miles north of Jomosom, take the trail east to Muktinath and the Thorong La slanting up a dry, dusty slope. Up the hill, you will round a bend to a bleached side valley with six villages and several abandoned fortresses. The towns begin at 10,500 ft. and extend to Muktinath's small cluster of shrines at 12,400 feet. A ridge that blocks views to the north extends to 17,240 ft.; a day hike along its sere crest offers fine views both into Mustang and toward the himals to the south. You will also be able to find large ammonites (locally called *saligram*) remaining from the era when this region was an ocean floor. Saligrams have important religious significance for Hindus. These fossilized black rocks from the upper Kali Gandaki are displayed in temples as far away as Varanasi on the Ganges River. Aside from Pashupatinath near Kathmandu, Muktinath is the most sacred place in Nepal, and noteworthy for its trans-Himalayan location. But do not confuse sanctity with splendor. The small Hindu temple dedicated to Vishnu is well maintained, along with the 108 spring-fed brass water spouts in the shape of cows' heads behind it, but the Buddhist temples nearby are badly in need of repair. The holiness of Muktinath dates from antiquity and arises from the small flame of natural gas within a small Nyingma Buddhist shrine close by. Beneath the flickering bluish glow a small rivulet of water emerges, producing a "miracle" conjunction of fire, air, and water.

The trail to Nyeshang, as the upper Marsyangdi Valley is called, departs from Muktinath and rises more than a mile to the 17,770-ft. Thorong La. Be advised that water is rarely found past the stream that is a 20-minute walk beyond Muktinath.

The Marsyangdi Valley

The Marsyangdi Valley is usually ascended from Dumre village (about 1,350 ft.), roughly two hours' drive east of Pokhara on the Kathmandu-to-Pokhara road. A road has been built from Dumre as far as Besisahar, and if transportation is available you may decide to ride that far (about a day-and-a-half walk). You can also reach the Marsyangdi trail farther north, at Khudi, by walking from Mahendra Pul (a bridge) in Pokhara along trails that rise and fall through the middle hills. This route, I can affirm, requires the assistance of a local who knows the way. The hilly, usually unshaded track should not be tried during hot weather, but it does provide excellent views of Annapurna II and IV and of Lamjung Himal (22,740 ft.). However you begin the trek up the Marsyangdi Valley, prepare for warm going; carry an umbrella and get early starts. As you proceed, you will have fine perspectives of Lamjung, Himalchuli (25,895 ft.), and Bauda (21,890 ft.). For the first couple of days you walk from Dumre, as the trail slants toward the high, white mountains through low terrain, you will not see a breach in the massifs.

A scenic side trek through wild country lasting three to five days (depending how far you go) can be taken out of the lower Marsyangdi Valley along Bara Pokhari Lekh, a spur of Himalchuli. Numerous trails lead onto the flank of this giant ridge, which is east of the Marsyangdi. The most direct route, from the south, branches off the valley trail at Phalesangu, where you can buy last-minute supplies. The key to correct routefinding along the numerous stock trails on this lekh, or high ridge,

Two Magar women on a high lekh in western Nepal. They wear necklaces of musk teeth and old coins (photo by Kevin Bubriski).

is to go with a local who knows the paths, for no habitation is permanent above 6,500 feet. Most of the way you will be walking on the crest, which makes water difficult to find. Bara Pokhari, at 10,200 ft., is a holy lake with a two-story pilgrim's rest house on the shoreline. The farther you proceed along this spectacular ridge, the closer you will be to Manaslu, Himalchuli, and Bauda Peak, the southern outlier. If you go before May, expect to encounter snow on the upper stretches, where Himalchuli's snowfields appear to be at arm's length.

From Phalesangu on the main Marsyangdi Valley trail, you can proceed north on either the east or west side of the river valley. The eastern side's trail is higher and more direct, but you will not likely find lodging for a full day's walk beyond Phalesangu. Not far beyond the west bank town of Khudi, the two paths join at Bhubhule near a new suspension bridge. The track follows the river into its gorge and soon crosses a large tributary. Then it climbs a terraced bowl to the ridge-straddling village of Bahun Danda ("Brahmin Hill") with its stores, tailor shop, and shady square. North of Bahun Danda, corn begins to replace rice cultivation, and waterfalls drain snows unseen above. The narrow Marsyangdi gorge continues for more than a day's walk between Bahun Danda and the few houses of Dharapani. Across the valley from Dharapani is the large Dudh Khola, discussed in the "Around Manaslu" section. At the Dudh Khola confluence the valley turns westward, north of Lamjung Himal. Dense mixed forests blend into stands of pure conifers beyond Bagarchap village, where the valley's lowest gomba is situated. Between Bagarchap and Pisang the narrow gorge is a pine-carpeted delight, with the clear stream thrashing below.

Before the district headquarters of Chame is the narrow entrance to the forbidden Nar Valley, flanked on both sides by vertical rock walls. Nar is another quintessential hidden valley, restricted to the point of having a checkpost that controls the place where its stream issues into the Marsyangdi. Although the valley is currently off limits, we know that trails enter it from several directions: over a pass reached from Ghyaru and Ngawal villages up-valley; from Tange in Mustang (over the Mustang La, a difficult pass probably unused now that is described well by H. W. Tilman in *Nepal Himalaya*); over a pass leading from Tibet; and directly from a trail along the valley floor that is said to cross the Nar River 15 times. Only two villages exist in this valley: Nar Ma (Lower Nar) above terraced fields and Nar To (Upper Nar) wedged atop an eroded, scalloped promontory. Nar's populace is of Tibetan descent: here the primary occupations are growing buckwheat, barley, and potatoes, and preparing yak butter to trade. Like Dolpo, Nar is a place far removed from time.

In the main Marsyangdi Valley near Chame (8,710 ft.), with its jumble of offices and a bank, you begin to have fine views of fluted Annapurna II high above and to the south. The trail above Chame crosses and recrosses the river, finally rising through pines on the south bank. The path then passes small, ancient stone memorials across from a wide stone slab that descends thousands of feet on the northern side of the valley. Soon, a wall of prayer stones appears and a panorama of the 15-mi.-long upper valley floor opens out.

Here you enter the region that is known locally as Nyeshang but has generally come to be known as Manang. (Strictly speaking, Manang is only the largest village in Nyeshang.) Since 1790, Nyeshangbas—as the locals are called—have been granted special international trading privileges by Nepal's king, although these rights could someday be terminated. Bell bottoms, portable radios, and golf hats emblazoned with "Thailand" are de rigueur for many. Traders set out their goods by the trail or come to your camp bringing gem stones and other merchandise from Burma and Bangkok, along with local wares. Soon the outside world will be brought to Nyeshang directly; a paved airstrip has been constructed in full view of Annapurna II, III, and Gangapurna. No words written here can describe the awesome beauty of the Annapurna Himal's northern spurs plummeting directly to the upper valley floor. Near Pisang, Braga, or Manang, walk up off the main trail 1,000 or 2,000 ft., make camp, and enjoy an entirely fresh perspective of this valley and its surrounding peaks.

The town of Manang (11,500 ft.) with its large gomba is the penultimate village on the principal trail. To the west, Tilicho Lake can be reached up the main valley in two days, but routefinding is difficult (particularly on the talus slopes toward the end) without a local who knows the way. As you leave Manang village, you will see a large and often noisy glacial icefall on Gangapurna and, to the west, Annapurna's Great Barrier, which is also visible from the Kali Gandaki side. The trail bends northward, at first rising well above the Jhargeng Khola, then dropping to cross the Jhargeng amid overgrazed yak pastures. The last camp below the Thorong La is a gently sloping piece of ground at 14,570 ft., hemmed in by talus and vertical rock walls. An alternate camping area exists 300 ft. above the bottomland; a trickle of water is sometimes found just below this upper site. Bharal are often sighted in this vicinity.

The steepest section of the 3,200-ft. climb to the Thorong La is encountered at the outset, but you are compensated for its difficulty by the ethereal sights that emerge as you rise. Twin 21,270-ft. peaks flanking the pass come into view, and simultaneously you have your last glimpses of the Annapurna summits that have been familiar sights for days. Do not attempt this pass in uncertain weather. Our group crossed on a mild May day; however, a month later scores of animals were killed and several groups of trekkers had to turn back owing to a freak snow. Some years the pass is snowed in by November. The level, 17,770-ft. Thorong La is often swept by penetrating winds, but pause as you cross long enough to toss a stone onto the large cairn, to propitiate the gods.

Around Dhaulagiri

West of Annapurna is the 40-mi.-wide Dhaulagiri Himal. The high difficult track north of Dhaulagiri has long been restricted, so you cannot presently complete the circuit; however, as with other restricted areas, this part of the trek is described briefly. The remainder of the section covers, first, the walk from Pokhara to Dhorpatan village south of Dhaulagiri. (The continuing path from Dhorpatan to Tarakot, northwest of Dhaulagiri, was noted in the last chapter.) The second part of the section describes the remaining portion of the trek to the north of Dhaulagiri from the east side, the Kali Gandaki approach.

Pokhara to Dhorpatan

Several trails from the Pokhara vicinity lead to Beni (2,200 ft.) at the junction of the Mayagdi Khola with the Kali Gandaki Valley. You will have to pass through Beni in order to reach Dhorpatan and the high, roller-coaster track to Tarakot and western Nepal. For the southerly route to Beni (all of which is very warm between April and October), take a bus or taxi south from Pokhara to the roadside bazaar of Naudanda. From there, follow the well-used track west up the Andhi Khola to the ridge-top bazaar of Karkineta (5,500 ft.). At Karkineta, with its sweeping views and Nepali style bhattis, descend to the Modi Khola by angling northward, asking for the trail to Kusma at or near trail junctions, for there are many paths hereabouts. From Kusma, high above the west bank of the Modi Khola, continue through warm country on the left bank of the Kali Gandaki River past a bridge leading to Baglung. Climb up to Baglung's large bazaar if you desire lodging or supplies; otherwise continue on by the river to a suspension bridge near Beni. An alternate and slightly longer way to reach Beni is by following the main trail out of Pokhara toward Tatopani as far as Biretanti (see the section on the Kali Gandaki Valley earlier in this chapter), then walking south to Kusma and on to Beni.

At Beni the trail to Dhorpatan diverges west along the low, green valley bottom of the Mayagdi Khola to Darbang. During two months of trekking in western Nepal in 1974, Darbang's stores were the largest I had come across. If you head up-valley to Darbang from the fleshpots of Pokhara and Beni, however, you will not likely be as impressed. Just above Darbang, cross a bridge to the right bank where, after crossing a tributary several rough miles upstream, you will rise on switchbacks up a jagged ridge through long-needle pines. If you carry ropes and ice axes and have experience on crevassed glaciers, you may wish to locate the path north up the Mayagdi Valley and attempt the Mayagdi Glacier to French Col (noted in the previous section).

To reach Dhorpatan, keep on a high trail through several villages past Muna, where the valley turns to the west. On a clear day along this stretch, you will enjoy views of Churen Himal and Dhaulagiri II and III (the latter two higher than 25,000 ft.). Muna is the last large village in this valley. Several hours later you will leave all habitation behind and begin the steep ascent through forest to Jaljala Pass (about 12,000 ft.), which divides the Kali Gandaki and greater Karnali watersheds. A gentle, long half-day's walk west of Jaljala Pass through meadow and forest takes you to Dhorpatan's stolid houses and wide meadows, approximately a six-day trek from Pokhara.

North of Dhorpatan lies the virtually uninhabited path to Tarakot that is described briefly in Chapter 11 under "The Eastern Track to Dhorpatan." This path definitely requires the services of a porter-guide familiar with the route. Once at Tarakot, you can join the route next described (if you have a permit for the walk) to complete a circle around the world's sixth tallest peak.

Jomosom to Tarakot

Once it is derestricted, the following route should be considered only by experienced trekkers, for beyond Jomosom you will be in rugged, high terrain with little chance to replenish supplies. The closest approach for circling north of Dhaulagiri is from the upper Kali Gandaki Valley. Following the route in the "Around Annapurna" section of this chapter, trek to Jomosom and walk 5 mi. north to Dangar Dzong village, which sits above and hidden from the river's west bank. From the tightly packed houses of Dangar Dzong, the trail angles up to a 14,100-ft. ridge line. At this waterless vantage point you have excellent views toward Mustang, Muktinath, and the Annapurna Himal. The path then continues in a westerly direction, into the rugged gorge of the Keha (or Cha) Lungpa, a route that should not be attempted without a local who knows the trail.

From the village of Sandak in the Keha Lungpa Gorge, your guide will lead you either by the gorge route or onto the high trail toward the wide, flat, 16,810-ft. pass at the head of this grey, impossibly convoluted valley. But this is only the first divide to be crossed. Another pass, the 18,200-ft. Mu La, leads you to a tributary of the Mukut Khola. You will have to camp between the two passes and hope that no storms occur. The weather can be fickle: Christian Kleinert (who wrote *Nepal Trekking*) told Chris Wriggins and me of crossing the Mu La two years in a row on the same date, April 19th. The first year a flash blizzard swept his camp; the next April fields of wildflowers smiled beneath a deep blue sky.

Between Sandak village and a point about a day's walk outside Dzong (Tarakot), this trek takes you through territory that is considered part of Dolpo. In this desiccated country, yak-dung fires urged on with leather bellows have traditionally sustained life.

West of the Mu La lies Mukut village. Downstream, the Mukut Khola joins the upper Bheri River, here called the Barbung. Descending the Barbung for several days from Mukut takes you to the Tarakot area, where you can connect with either the trail south to Dhorpatan or the path west to Jumla. Expect that the trek from Jomosom to Tarakot will last at least a week and perhaps longer; the entire circle of Dhaulagiri will take minimally four weeks from Pokhara and back again. What a trek this is—you leave the green lowlands for deep gorges and remote fortress villages recalling Tibet of a century ago, then walk once more into the tropics.

Around Manaslu

Manaslu (26,760 ft.), the world's ninth tallest peak, and its high outlier Himalchuli can be circled to the north by crossing the 17,100-ft. Larkya La, a pass that connects the head of the Buri Gandaki Valley (which lies east of the massif) with the Dudh Khola, a tributary of the Marsyangdi. The upper Buri Gandaki is usually restricted, so you cannot be certain of receiving permission to walk there. However, let's begin with the Buri Gandaki Valley and then describe the Dudh Khola approach to the Larkya La. The entire circle trek will take a minimum of three weeks.

The Buri Gandaki Valley

The best roadhead for reaching the Buri Gandaki River is at Trisuli Bazaar. From Trisuli, take the main trail west up the Samri Valley. In about 2½ days you will arrive at Arughat Bazaar, on the Buri Gandaki's west bank.

Up-valley from the shops and teahouses of Arughat, you will walk for some four days through the increasingly narrow gorge of the Buri Gandaki, which, like the Marsyangdi Valley, turns in a westerly direction once north of the wide himal it drains. The Buri Gandaki's gorge is longer and more intimidating than most: during several days of walking, you pass steep rock ridges that plunge to the valley floor. You have to climb and descend many of these spurs on hand-hewn stone steps as you progress north between the Manaslu and Ganesh himals. Within the sheer gorge are a few scattered bhattis, where Gurung women with velveteen blouses serve food. Along the way, you may see both plastic and old-style wooden water containers being used, and men knitting sweaters for winter with knitting needles of old umbrella ribs.

As tropical vegetation diminishes in the midst of the gorge, you reach the low, stone buildings of Setibas village with its checkpost and stupa. A half day's walk north of Setibas is Bangshin, a Gurung village where you will get tantalizing glimpses of precipitous slopes above the Shar Khola ("Eastern River"), a major tributary of the Buri Gandaki. The Shar Khola leads to the restricted area called Tsum, a small valley dominated on either side by high peaks, which projects into Tibet like a miniature Mustang. This would be a wonderful side trip if it were not restricted. In the 1950s many Tibetan refugees entered Nepal over a high pass south of Jongka Dzong that leads into Tsum. Nearly 900 years ago, the revered Tibetan mystic Milarepa is said to have meditated in a cave high above Tsum's valley floor.

In the Buri Gandaki Valley beyond Bangshin, just before reaching the point where the Shar Khola issues into the main valley, is the mouth of the glaciated Chulung Valley. At about this point, the valley usually becomes restricted. This western side valley drains Himalchuli's eastern flanks. On the high southern ramparts of the narrow Chulung Valley is the mysterious Rupina La, a snow pass (like the higher Namun Bhanjang over Lamjung Himal to the west) that is dutifully noted on most maps and discussed by veteran trekkers, but invariably left for someone else to cross.

At the Shar Khola junction, the Buri Gandaki turns westward. Your perspiration will flow less readily when you have entered the area locally called Kutang, a narrow, shaded stretch of valley serenaded by the thundering river. The valley trail crosses to the northern bank below the barely glimpsed upper town of Bih, where another high track leads east to Tsum. Continuing through mixed forest and corn fields, the main path recrosses the river and rises past several villages to Namdru checkpost and the upper valley region known as Nupri. During our rapid traverse of the valley, my friend Pancho and I found Nupri's inhabitants to be most congenial. At Li village an older man with a mala (the Buddhist rosary of 108 prayer beads) showed us the 10-ft.-tall prayer wheel in the local gomba and smilingly turned the giant cylinder as we looked over its small room.

Near Lo hamlet, the valley becomes U-shaped, and snow peaks to the south emerge as constant companions. A stupa by the trail above Lo appears in a flat meadow, where the sweep of summits from Himalchuli to Manaslu opens up. Manaslu appears quite foreshortened from this point among pine, birch, and rushing streams. The valley's last large village is named Sama on the maps, but locals know it as Ro. The town is guarded on the east by a large mani wall of flat stones; to the north across the deeply cut river lie flat village pastures.

For the last couple of days from Lo and Sama to the pass, the trail continues rather gently upward. Just beyond Sama the valley turns north to the last hamlet of Sumdo (or Babuk), situated near an intersection of trails: south lie Nupri and Tsum and, west, the Larkya La leads to the Marsyangdi Valley and Nyeshang. Additionally, from both east and north are other border passes that connect with the trading village of Riu in Tibet. The high, northern Gya La is the route most often taken by traders to Tibet.

Beyond Sumdo the trail to the Larkya La (17,100 ft.) curls to the west past a valley glacier and then jags to the north side of a long lateral moraine. Hours later, passing a small lake near the pass, the path meanders toward the topmost cairn with its faded prayer flags. Here you are between high snow slopes that descend from the Manaslu and Larkya himals. Allow at least 11 days without stopovers or side walks to reach the Larkya La from Trisuli.

The Dudh Khola

To reach the Larkya La from the west, you must trek up the Marsyangdi Valley to Dharapani village, as described in the section on the Marsyangdi Valley. At Dharapani, cross the river to Thangjet (also called Thonje) and begin the climb up the wild Dudh Khola, the "Milk River." This region near Thangjet is called Gyasumdo, the "Meeting of Three Highways." Here, trails meet from both up-valley and down-valley along the Marsyangdi, and the Dudh Khola path joins in as well, leading to the Larkya La and to the passes beyond, which connect with Tibet. The only town above Thangjet along the Dudh Khola is Tilje. Beyond Tilje, a few homesteaders have begun to build log fences around fields hacked from the more gentle slopes, but most of the valley remains uninhabited. The two- or three-day walk from Thangjet to the Larkya La leads higher and higher, through shaded glens and past two large, snow-fed tributaries, to a place where the valley turns to the north and offers your first view of Manaslu's west-facing flanks. As you proceed through a pine and rhododendron forest, the eastern aspect opens out and you must cross the rubble-coated glacier that begets the whitish waters of the Dudh Khola.

Set between the glacier and a birch forest 5,000 ft. below the Larkya La is Bimthang, an idyllic oval meadow belied by its name, "Plain of Sand." A small prayer wall and several tumbledown stone structures are all that remain to remind us of a former era when salt, wool, and turquoise from Tibet changed hands for the grains, tobacco, and textiles of the south. All these goods were bartered at Bimthang under the eyes of government-authorized tax collectors, for this was the lone trading point between Riu in Tibet and the populace of the upper Buri Gandaki and Marsyangdi Valleys.

The path's final ascent from Bimthang to the Larkya La continues on moraine past a few last camping spots, then steepens, following rock- and snow-covered slopes to the top of the pass. The hearty will find the 18,000-ft. snowfields north of the pass excellent to explore for views of several himals.

Around Gosain Kund Lake

Treks in the Langtang and Helambu regions north of Kathmandu can be combined by crossing a pass sometimes called Laurebina Pass near Gosain Kund (*kund* means lake); or, if you are experienced, by the difficult Ganga La. Both routes connecting Helambu and Langtang proceed north of sacred Gosain Kund, allowing you to take an easily approachable walk of 2–2½ weeks through varied countryside. This is the only circular trek in this chapter that does not involve walking north of the main Himalayan Range. First, the main paths to the high, narrow Langtang will be noted, then both the ridge and river trails to green Helambu. Keep in mind that, due to ease of access, each of these areas sees many, many trekkers.

The Langtang Valley and Gosain Kund

Trisuli Bazaar (about 1,700 ft.) is the closest trailhead for the Langtang Valley. Get an early start from Trisuli: the initial day's walk uphill from the humid valley is often an ordeal by sweat. From the town of Betrawati, almost two hours beyond Trisuli, the trail ascends fairly steadily through scattered villages. If in doubt at trail junctions during the first day's walk, take the upper forks. By the time you reach the

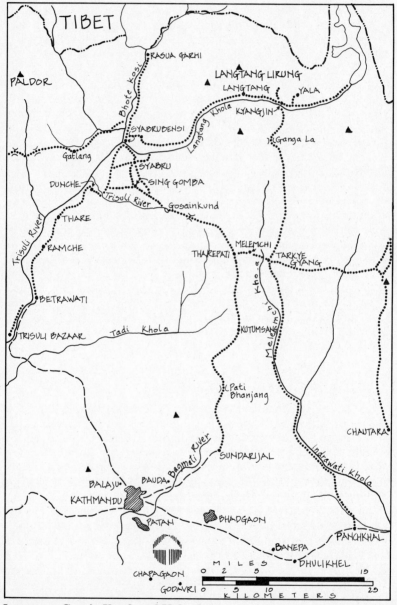

Langtang, Gosain Kund, and Helambu

bhatti at Ramche (5,870 ft.) in the evening, you are well up from the steamy valley floor and will have passed the first two grass-covered stupas. At Ramche you have a last view of the lights back at Trisuli Bazaar and can see the main Trisuli Valley disappearing ahead around a ridge line. Along this path are villages inhabited by Tamangs, Buddhists who usually add "Lama" as their last name. The stone homes of the Tamang hamlet called Grang have roofs of wooden shingles anchored by rocks, like villages in eastern Nepal and Bhutan. The path up-valley contours in and out of forested ridges and crosses places where landslides have occurred, before reaching the large town of Dunche.

The eastern tributary north of Dunche is called the Trisuli Khola. As with the Alaknanda River in Garhwal, a side stream here gives its name to the main valley, due to the importance of a mythical event: Shiva is said to have created Gosain Kund and its two smaller lacustrine neighbors by jabbing his *trisul* (trident) into the ground to form the Trisuli River's headwaters. North of the Trisuli, the main river valley is known as the Bhote Kosi (the "River from Tibet"). The trails to Gosain Kund will be noted, but first let's continue north to the Langtang Valley.

From Dunche, angle eastward to cross the Trisuli Khola; take the northwesterly trail toward Barku, not the eastern track to Gosain Kund. At Barku village you may either take a longer route down through Syabrubensi village (at the junction of the Langtang River with the Bhote Kosi) or a shorter path that leads over the ridge from Barku to Syabru. From Syabrubensi (at the bottom of the gorge), the path to Langtang climbs a long, steep hill, passes two villages, and descends into forest. Syabru, a north-slope village of homes built centipede-like in a single line facing east, obviously has an industrious resident woodcarver. Each house is decorated with wooden filigree; some homes have flowerboxes. The trail from Syabru angles downward to cross the Langtang Khola and soon thereafter joins with the Syabrubensi path. The single trail then rises through the thick forest, emerges from the V-shaped gorge, and enters a formerly glaciated upper valley. You are now well within Langtang National Park; at some point down-valley a fee will have already been collected for entry. Langtang village is the uppermost town in the valley.

Beyond Langtang village is Kyangjin (about 12,500 ft.) with its small gomba and cheese factory. This summer settlement is the usual base of operations for trekkers in the upper valley. Here you have fine views of the snow peaks north and south of you. Ask the local herders (whose cow-yak crossbreeds called *tsauries* provide milk for the cheese-making operation) to point out the hill trail east of Kyangjin that leads to another cheese-producing location at Yala. Yala, Tibetan for "up," sits some 3,000 ft. above Kyangjin. A peak above Yala named Tsergo Ri can be climbed for even better views of the Langtang peaks, including Langtang I (23,770 ft.).

East from Kyangjin you can take day or overnight hikes to the interesting upper valley. Continue past the STOL landing strip and the five shepherd huts collectively called Nubmathang. You should stay on low ground to not get caught in the high moraine protruding from the north, as I once did. It is exciting to stride onward and see new stretches of the valley come into view as you proceed around further talus slopes. The upper valley glacier begins beyond the single hut named Langsisa. If you want to explore the glacier and surrounding high country, take food and a tent with you from Kyangjin, as the distance is too great to be covered in a single day. You will see the beautiful fluted peaks of the Jugal Himal in the eastern end of the valley to best advantage if you climb up a south-facing valley slope. The uppermost part of the glacier, although many maps do not show it, is narrower above and extends from due north like a crooked little finger parallel to the Jugal Himal.

The 16,800-ft. Ganga La south of Kyangjin leads to Tarke Gyang village in Helambu. A perennially snow-covered pass, the Ganga La is mostly used by trekkers. Some mountaineers have successfully made their own way across the pass and others have found the path, but the approach route by trail is not easy to locate (particularly on the southern side), so you should definitely hire a local to guide you. Take shelter and enough food for three or four days. This is not an easy pass and should only be attempted by people who feel comfortable on steep, snowy slopes. The descent to Tarke Gyang on the south takes at least two days, following a route that is not always easily discernible.

A lower pass, east of Gosain Kund Lake, also connects the Trisuli and Langtang valleys with Helambu. To reach Gosain Kund and the pass beyond, you can either walk up from Syabru village, if you are returning from the Langtang Valley, or you can ascend from Dunche. From either Syabru or Dunche, you have more than a day's walk up the long ridge to Gosain Kund. Beyond the halfway point en route to the lake is Sing Gomba, where you can obtain food and lodging overnight (when it is open), and nearby, a cheese factory. Gosain Kund (14,200 ft.) is the third and largest lake you see. At monsoon time during the full moon of July-August, a large pilgrimage called Jani Purne is made to Gosain Kund in honor of Shiva.

To reach the 15,100-ft. pass (sometimes called Laurebina Pass) that connects with Helambu, take the trail along the north side of Gosain Kund. Follow this path as it slowly rises to the southeast in view of several other small lakes that feed into Gosain Kund. When I took this route alone, toward the end of October, I was glad for the tracks of those who had preceded me the previous day. The trail was snowy, and the unobvious route would have been difficult to follow without marks of some kind. Beyond the pass cairn, the path drops precipitously at first and then contours down rocky slopes, eventually passing a couple of streams and two separate overhanging rocks that are good for overnight shelter. The track then gently ascends to several shepherds' huts at Tharepati (11,400 ft.), a waterless notch with splendid views of nearby ridges and the dusky valley below called Helambu.

Helambu

The region called Helambu (or Helmu) is situated about three days' walk north-northeast of the Kathmandu Valley. Helambu is popular with those having severely limited time to trek, being quick of access and quite picturesque. The area is populated by people called Sherpas, but although they have the name in common with the well-known clan of the Khumbu area near Mt. Everest, the two clans have different language, dress, and family lineage. Most inhabitants of Melemchi and Tarke Gyang, the two large villages in upper Helambu, are well-to-do and have homes decorated with copper and brass cookware, like the prosperous Thakali bhattis west of Pokhara. Handsomely maintained gombas, particularly the large one in Tarke Gyang, are additional evidence of Helambu's thriving economy.

The hotter, quicker route into Helambu begins at the roadhead of Panchkhal on the Kathmandu-to-Kodari road, the road to the Tibetan border. You can reach Panchkhal by bus from Kathmandu or by private taxi, which can be shared. The trail north of Panchkhal is actually a rarely used Jeep road for the initial day's walk along the valley bottom. At Melemchi Pul village, you enter the Melemchi Khola, the valley in which Helambu is located, and you continue past Talamarang, finally gaining elevation. This path takes you past several towns to Tarke Gyang (about 8,500 ft.), the largest village in Helambu and the starting point, from this approach, for the walk over the difficult Ganga La. A trail leads from Tarke Gyang down to the river and up again to Melemchi village across the valley, but before you leave Tarke Gyang consider making a side trip overnight onto the ridge extending east, to take in the excellent view of Nepal's central Himalayan peaks. If you are here in fall or winter ask whether the excellent local apples are available.

The higher trail to Helambu leaves from Sundarijal in the Kathmandu Valley. Much of the capital's water supply reaches the valley floor by means of a large pipe that descends from a reservoir above Sundarijal. Hire a taxi to Sundarijal, or take a bus from Ratna Park in Kathmandu to Baudnath, and walk from there or hire another taxi to Sundarijal. Stop for a cup at the local tea shop before you start on your way up. The 3,500-ft. ascent, initially along the large water pipe, takes you to the point on the rim of the valley called Burlang Bhanjang (*bhanjang* is yet another word meaning pass) at about 8,000 ft. Beyond Burlang Bhanjang you can follow a ridge trail for two days to reach Tharepati; from there, either drop down to Melemchi in Helambu or climb to Gosain Kund. Or at Pati Bhanjang, not far from Burlang Bhanjang, you can take a rocky trail leading off the ridge down to Talamarang in the Melemchi Khola. There are several villages along the ridge during the first part of the walk, but from not far beyond Kutumsang you will encounter only temporary shepherds' quarters. The path rises and falls, often passing through rhododendron forests, and reaches 12,000 ft. in places. This ridge marks a significant divide: it is the boundary between the Great Gandaki watershed, which extends west to the southern slopes of Dhaulagiri, and the Sapt Kosi river system, which drains Nepal's mountainous regions all the way to the country's eastern border with Sikkim.

The ridge route ends at Tharepati, on the trail between Gosain Kund and Melemchi to the east in Helambu. Melemchi village (8,500 ft.) is reached from Tharepati by a forest track with many side paths that is used by shepherds and woodcutters. If in doubt, take the northerly trail forks. Melemchi's large homes are scattered on a level shelf at about the same elevation as Tarke Gyang, across the valley. The ridge route takes about three days to reach Melemchi; the valley route to Tarke Gyang is a day shorter. Wealthy tourists are often deposited in Melemchi by helicopter for 40 minutes in order to give sweets to children and see "the real Nepal."

13

Eastern Nepal, Sikkim, and Bhutan

I turned to the intricate terrace fields that represent the honest toil of farmers. Mechi to Mahakali they are the stuff and substance of the country.

Harka Gurung, 1979

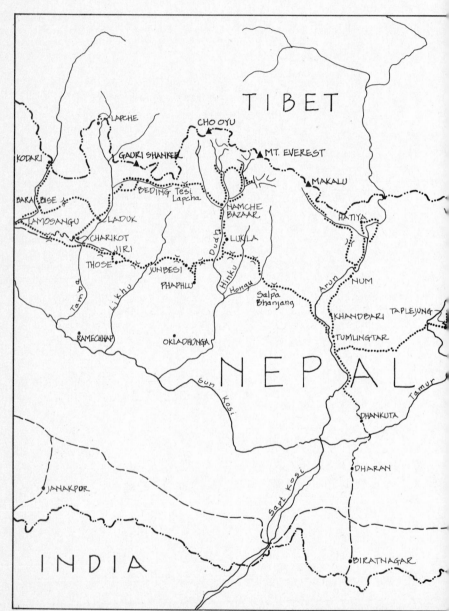

Eastern Nepal, Sikkim, and Western Bhutan

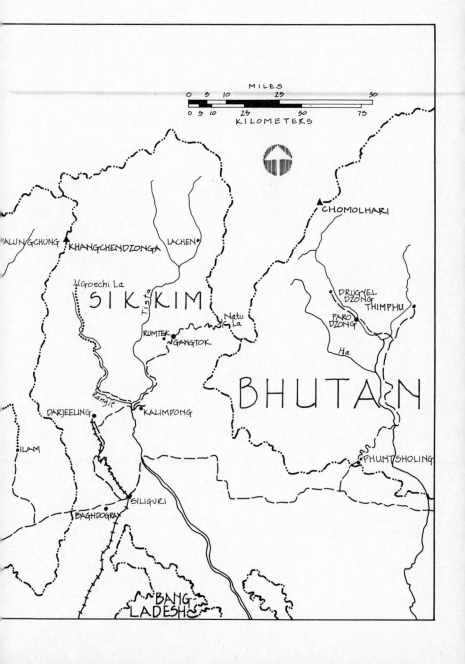

The Verdant Eastern Himalaya

Excepting the southern slopes of Dhaulagiri and Annapurna, the area encompassing Nepal's eastern valleys, Sikkim, and Bhutan reaps more of the monsoon's life-giving rain than any other portion of the Himalaya. During late summer here, the seven large tributaries called the Sapt Kosi (the seven Kosi) rivers in Nepal and the Tista River in Sikkim resound with the thunder of runoff. Thanks to this abundance of rain, terraced, irrigated cultivation is especially widespread in eastern Nepal, and these hills are the most densely populated in the kingdom.

The weekly or biweekly market days called *haat* bazaars are unique to the region of these fertile hills. Haat means "hand," signifying trade from hand to hand. Stretching from Dolakha by the Tamba Kosi to Pashupati near the eastern border, the haat bazaars are a bright, multi-clan spectacle. Most bazaars are held on the edge of towns, but in some places, like Ilam, they take place in the central square. Usually people travel no longer than a day with goods to trade, but sometimes they travel up to five days to trade or sell a single *doka* (basket) load of grains or produce; *kukris* (the curved Gurkha knives); or manufactured goods from roadhead towns to the south. Other goods exchanged often include local fruits in season, butter, pulses, salt, spices, raw tobacco, cigarettes, sugar and candy, chickens, piglets, brassware, plastic bracelets, combs, beads, and other trinkets.

A haat that is atypical but far better known than most others occurs every Saturday above the 11,000-ft. level near the principal Sherpa town of Namche Bazaar, south of Mt. Everest. Due to the prosperity wrought by tourism thereabouts, it is often said that the Sherpas have learned to mint their own money. With this in mind, people often walk for several days to sell or trade goods at Namche Bazaar. As the morning sun first reached the trail leading to Namche one December Saturday, I climbed to an overlook and watched as scores of people walked up the valley with loads to be sold in the market. Simultaneously, Sherpas descended on three paths from above town. Later, at the two level haat grounds just south of town, I watched Sherpas (dressed in both traditional clothes and the latest in down wear) buy from and barter with the thinly clad vendors of the Rai and Chhetri clans. As the goods were sold, the down-valley people left in groups on the homeward trail and the Sherpas gravitated toward Namche Bazaar, which was redolent of *chang* (beer). Like all markets, which are social as well as commercial, Namche's involves an exchange of both goods and the weekly news.

We will look at some of the principal trekking routes in eastern Nepal's vast Sapt Kosi watershed and then briefly note opportunities in Sikkim and Bhutan.

The Rolwaling Valley

Rolwaling is a sparsely populated, east-west valley near the Tibetan border that is west of the Khumbu region and just south of the magnificent Gauri Shankar Himal. You can walk into this valley and return in a minimum of just over two weeks. If you have sufficient equipment and experience, you can attempt the difficult Tesi Lapcha Pass at the valley's head, reaching Namche Bazaar in the well-trekked Khumbu region a day and a half later. Because the route has no inns, you should probably take along a porter who is familiar with the region.

To reach the trailhead for this trek, take a bus from Kathmandu to Barabise village, not far beyond Lamosangu (the trailhead for the full trek to Khumbu). If you are with several people, halve the driving time by renting one of the vehicles for hire that are parked near the Paras Hotel on Dharma Path in Kathmandu. On the way to Barabise you will ride through terraced middle hills along the first few-score miles of the Arniko Rajmarg, the road linking Kathmandu with Lhasa, Tibet. Barabise (2,700 ft.) is in the Bhote Kosi gorge just beyond a bridge where the road crosses to the river's east bank. Take tea in Barabise and purchase any final supplies you need before beginning your walk south along the river's east bank. Soon you reach Sun Kosi Bazaar, a town that has lost its former commercial importance to Barabise, which is on the road.

At Sun Kosi Bazaar, begin walking to the east up the Sun Kosi Valley on the north side of the stream. Passing through several hamlets and crossing feeder streams, you will reach Dolangsa, the valley's last village, with its small gomba above town. Above Dolangsa, you pass

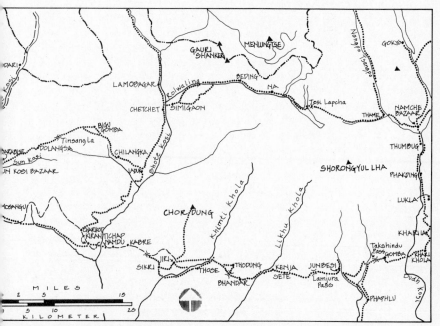

lwaling and the Trail to Khumbu

through a mist-filled forest with many rhododendrons before reaching the Tinsang La (10,900 ft.). Below, near Ruphtang, the first town beyond the pass, you may continue down-valley, or climb a thousand feet to see the convent called Bigu Gomba (8,240 ft.). Its white gomba is fronted by a long, low, whitewashed dwelling that serves as a sleeping quarters for the nuns.

You pass scattered white houses, terraced landscape, and three large tributary streams as you descend, still well above the northern bank of the Saun or Sangawa Khola. Several hours' walk beyond Chilangka, above the village of Laduk, you round a ridge line and have excellent views to the north. Here you are some four days' walk from the roadhead. Begin asking for the trail to Chetchet as you start walking along the Bhote Kosi Valley. Like the other Bhote Kosi, to the west where you began the trek, this river is so named because it originates in Bhot: Tibet. These rivers take on different names (Sun Kosi and Tamba Kosi, respectively) when each is joined by a large *cis*-Himalayan tributary (a tributary that enters from the Nepal side, south of the main crest).

To the north, farther than you will go, is Lamabagar with its checkpost and wireless station. Beyond Lamabagar, near the tip of a tiny finger of land belonging to Nepal, lies the small Lapche Gomba. For an interesting account by an extremely observant scientist who was allowed into that restricted area surrounded by Tibet, read the "Kang Chu" chapter in *Stones of Silence,* by George B. Schaller.

Just north of Chetchet, cross a suspension bridge (3,500 ft.) to the east bank of the Bhote Kosi. Here you climb steeply for thousands of feet, passing only the village of Simigaon (6,600 ft.) and the two shelters called *Shakpa* (the Sherpa word for soup). The main trail continues up and over a ridge; however, you might take an upper path that divides from the main trail above Shakpa and ascends to cross the Daldung La (about 13,000 ft.), passing through several high summer pastures. This upper path has an excellent view of Gauri Shankar's double peak (23,439 ft.) where you reach the first ridge above the Rolwaling Chu and begin traversing eastward into the Rolwaling Valley.

Two long days from the Bhote Kosi bridge, you reach Ramding, one of several closely spaced winter villages used by the valley's Sherpa inhabitants. The lone community of Sherpas in this spectacular, narrow valley move up to Beding and, farther along, to Na, depending upon the season. Up-valley from Ramding, the stone houses of Beding (12,000 ft.) rest on a hill around the village gomba, which contains an 8-ft.-tall prayer wheel like that found at Li in the Buri Gandaki Valley. If you walk on to the summer settlement of Na (13,700 ft.) and take a day hike up the valley's southern slopes, you will have an excellent view of Gauri Shankar and its northeastern face in Tibet. Numerous side excursions will become evident if you have a copy of the 1:50,000 Rolwaling Himal Sheet (see Appendix A).

One possible way to leave the valley is by the long route that crosses the Yalung (17,420 ft.) and Honobu passes, eventually reaching Jiri on the main east-west trail, which is south. For this out-of-the-way route, you will need food for at least six days, a strong porter who knows the way, and the Rolwaling Himal Sheet. Sometimes locals will claim to know a rarely traveled route such as this one, then admit along the way that they do not. Having a definitive map can help avoid difficulties.

Attempt the Tesi Lapcha Pass (18,875 ft.), which separates the Rolwaling Valley from Khumbu, only if you are a well-acclimatized hiker or a mountaineer equipped with ice axe, crampons, and rope and are adept at cutting ice steps. The best help you can obtain for crossing the Tesi Lapcha is a Sherpa from Rolwaling who has already been over the pass. He can guide you past the rock falls and other dicey spots along the way.

For the pass route, from Na, walk past the last pastures at Sangma to the north side of the Trakarding Glacier. Near Tsho Rolpa Lake (Chu Pokhari) rockfalls are a real danger, and you must walk the lower portion of the glacial moraine beginning at dawn, before the sun's heat loosens the rocks above. Continue along the Trakarding Glacier past the Drolambao Glacier's icefall that descends onto the Trakarding from the north. Just beyond the Drolambao icefall, climb onto steep rock, then onto the Drolambao itself. You may have to cut steps here. Be very alert for falling rocks, particularly in the afternoon. Take a last look at Gauri Shankar as you ascend. After you are above the Drolambao icefall, walk north along the glacier's eastern side, then continue to the pass east of you up a snowy diagonal ramp. Be careful as you climb toward the pass; there are some crevasses along the way. The views toward Khumbu are superb at the pass. A steep descent east of the pass leads into the upper Thame Valley. Stay to the north side of the valley, pick your route carefully, and again be alert for falling rocks. Once below the rock fall and the permanent snow line, you are one long day's walk from bustling Namche Bazaar.

The Trek to Khumbu

Since 1953 when descriptions and photographs began to circulate about the British Expedition to Mt. Everest, many people have been fascinated by the thought of walking to the base of the world's highest mountain. By now, thousands of trekkers have discovered for themselves the steamy, many-hilled trek to Khumbu, the region south of Mt. Everest that is inhabited by Sherpas. This section briefly describes the walk to Namche Bazaar, the entrance village in Khumbu; the next section discusses the principal high-elevation walks you can take in Khumbu itself.

This trek can be done with a porter to carry gear or, staying at the small inns called bhattis along the path, you could trek alone here. (Women in particular should see the section on trekking alone in Chapter 1.) In Kathmandu you can get a locally produced trekking map that will give a good approximation of the distances involved. But the best maps for this route are the 1:50,000 Schneider Sheet named

Tamba Kosi-Likhu Khola (covering the route from Kirantichap to Junbesi) and the Shorong/Hinku Sheet that covers from Junbesi to Namche Bazaar. (See Appendix A.) Most people take from 10 to 14 days to reach Namche Bazaar from the roadhead at Lamosangu, although some have made the walk in much less time by hiking very long days. You could avoid the first four days or so of lowland walking by booking a Royal Nepal Airlines Corporation (RNAC) flight from Kathmandu to Jiri and beginning the walk there. Or, if you fly all the way to Lukla still farther east, you will be only a full day's walk from Namche Bazaar.

The trek begins in Lamosangu ("Long Bridge," at 2,525 ft.) on the Sun Kosi River. To reach the trailhead at Lamosangu, take an early morning bus from Kathmandu in order to get a good start on the trek. If you want to halve the five-hour bus ride, rent one of the vehicles for hire near Kathmandu's Paras Hotel. A Jeep road to Jiri now branches east from the main road through Lamosangu not far south of town, paralleling the foot path you will take east; you may find yourself following this narrow road along some stretches of the route. To begin on foot, cross the Sun Kosi River by the suspension bridge beyond Lamosangu's bazaar and begin walking up the first long hill. This trek is characterized by up-and-down crossings of five major ridges before you reach the Dudh Kosi Valley below Namche Bazaar. Use an umbrella brought from Kathmandu for sun protection, and plan your uphill walks for the cooler morning hours if at all possible. Backlighting is beautiful in the mornings as you walk east through country that appears increasingly vast as you progress.

The first hill seems interminable; you pass Kaping, Perku, and Pakha villages among terracing and scattered trees. On your second day out, at the hamlet of Muldi (more than 6,000 ft. higher than Lamosangu), you will have a brief but tantalizing glimpse to the distant Himalayan Range. Here, along the top of the ridge, you can either follow the new road that contours along a fairly level course to the north, or you can take the trail. By either route, you then descend to Surkhe and follow the northern bank of a tributary to Shere (also called Serobesi). Cross another bridge to the northern bank of the Charnawati Khola and continue down-valley. Then climb slowly through terraces, using your umbrella for shade, until you reach the small, pleasant bazaar of Kirantichap. The road, too, passes through Kirantichap, but whichever way you have walked thus far, you will probably want to take the shorter route, the trail, down to the suspension bridge over the Bhote Kosi River. At the Bhote Kosi, you have descended nearly to the elevation of Lamosangu, where you began.

Climb steeply onto the ridge line east of the river, then pick up the Jeep road as it gently rises through Namdu and Kabre villages south of the ridge. You may see a cluster of villagers approaching: is it a wedding or a funeral? If people are dressed in white (the color of mourning) and carrying a swaddled body, they will be going to a burning ghat—a cremation platform—beside the river. But if there is singing and one well-dressed youth walks bedecked in flower chains (the bride may not be present), then you are watching a *bibaha*, a wedding procession.

Beyond Kabre, leave the road for the trail and cross the Yarsa Khola, then begin climbing the wooded ridge you have been approaching. Above the small village of Chisopani ("Cold Water"), ascend to the pass at 8,240 feet. From here you can see the impressive summits of Gauri Shankar (23,439 ft.) on the border and Menlungtse (23,554 ft.) just inside Tibet. Follow the trail down to the village of Sikri 2,000 ft. below, or, if you wish, follow the road as it contours northward to its terminus at Jiri. If you have taken the path to Sikri you can continue on one of two trails: the shorter path goes down-valley, crosses the southeast ridge, passes through Kattike village, and then goes up the Khimti Khola to Those, the largest bazaar between the main road and Namche Bazaar. At Those, iron was once produced for locks and bridge chain links, but the town's output has now declined greatly.

To reach Jiri (6,200 ft.) from Sikri, cross the upper bridge northeast of town and climb a ridge where you will pass a flat area used for the haat bazaar on Saturdays. Not far below lies Jiri, with its airstrip, hospital, lodge, restaurant, and large agricultural project. From Jiri, you may want to take a side trip north to Chordung, a 12,105-ft. high point, for excellent views of the main peaks. Allow a day and a half for this dry-ridge walk. To continue to Those from Jiri, where the Jeep road ends, walk among fields south along the east bank of the river to Kune. Then climb slowly through pine groves to meet the trail from Sikri, where you turn east and reach Those by way of Kattike. After exploring Those's bazaar with its whitewashed homes, continue up the left bank of the Khimti Khola to a suspension bridge beyond Shivalaya. A different eastern path from Jiri climbs in a southeasterly direction over the ridge called Patashe Danda, descends through Mali village, crosses the Yelung Khola, and joins the main trail at the suspension bridge over the Khimti Khola.

At the suspension bridge (5,905 ft.), climb past Sangbadanda village to an 8,850-ft. pass with double mani walls. Alternatively, you could continue along the crest of the spur from Sangbadanda through the town of Buldanda to a small cheese factory near the ridge top (10,250 ft.). In summer and fall you may be able to purchase milk, yoghurt, butter, and cheese at the factory. Not far south of the cheese factory is Thodung Gomba. The gomba and cheese factory are connected with the pass by a trail that closely follows the ridge line. East of the pass, descend to the large stupas and small gomba at the Sherpa village of Bhandar (also called Changma) on a shelf less than halfway to the valley floor. Ask for the hotel in town. High on the eastern ridge you can see the Lamjura Pass, which you will cross. From Bhandar, descend gently, and then steeply eastward beside hulking ridges and cross the tributary Surma Khola to reach the Likhu Khola. Pass over the Likhu Khola on a suspension bridge, and continue along the east bank to the small village of Kenja (5,350 ft.) with its several modest bhattis, on the northern bank of the Kenja Khola.

This village marks the beginning of the 6,200-ft. ascent to the trek's highest point prior to Namche Bazaar. Break up this climb, if possible; stop overnight at Sete (8,450 ft.), a small settlement with a gomba. To reach Sete, take the right-hand trail fork several hours' walk above Kenja. From Sete you need an early start for the next day's long hike over the pass. Be certain to stock up on water, because none will likely be found above town. Climb to the top of an east-west spur above Sete and continue to a trail fork; take the northerly path through rhododendrons to the cairn- and flag-bedecked top of 11,580-ft. Lamjura Pass. Two hours away, at 13,160 ft., is a magnificent view point north of the pass.

Since reaching Bhandar you have been in Sherpa country and will continue through land populated by this hardy clan as far as the last pastures beneath Mt. Everest. Sometime in the mid-16th century, the group of people that have come to be called Sherpas ("People from the East") migrated to their present homeland from Kham in eastern Tibet. Buddhists of the old Nyingma sect, Sherpas speak an unwritten Tibetan dialect that is often translated directly into spoken English with a delightfully scrambled word order.

Sherpas—like all uplanders—were once exclusively agriculturalists, animal breeders, and transborder traders; today their livelihood depends largely on visitors to their homeland. The men of the clan first became known to English visitors in 1907 as strong, reliable mountain porters and guides. Once Sherpa porters were paid five rupees (about half a dollar) a day plus food. Now the average porter earns more than five times that amount, and some high-altitude porters have been paid hundreds of rupees for carrying loads up a single stage high on Mt. Everest. Until recently, every recognized sirdar in Nepal was a Sherpa. Many of the clan who work for trekkers and mountaineers are young men, and some are young women (called Sherpanis), but you may still see older Sherpa men with turquoise earrings and the traditional long braid who look at photographs or maps through curled fingers as if scrutinizing the printed image with a magnifying glass.

The trail on the eastern side of Lamjura Ridge descends through evergreens that hug plunging slopes. Here you enter the region called Shorong, by Sherpas, but the area is more widely known as Solu. Until trekking became big business, the Sherpas of Solu were better off than those in Khumbu, for the crop land in Solu is lower and its pastures are more verdant. Solu butter is still carried to the market at Namche Bazaar and commands a good price. The first village reached in Solu is Tragdobuk. Another 2 mi. takes you to Junbesi (8,755 ft.) with its gomba, new school, and large homes typical of the prosperous Swiss-like houses found hereabouts. Above the head of the valley is the peak called Shorong Yul Lha (22,826 ft.), the "Country God of Solu"—also called Numbur. Two miles north of Junbesi, near Mopung village, is Thupten Choling Gomba under the direction of Tulshi Rimpoche, who formerly was one of two abbots at Dzarongphu (Rongbuk) Gomba in Tibet north of Mt. Everest. If you visit this gomba, approach with caution. Tibetan mastiffs protect the grounds.

From Junbesi you can walk southward to reach Phaphlu's rarely used STOL airstrip, its busy hospital, or Chiwong Gomba high on the ridge northeast of Phaphlu. Further south—off the main Khumbu trail—is the large administrative town of Salleri. To continue toward Khumbu from Junbesi, cross the Junbesi Khola and take the upper trail heading

Sherpa women from upper valleys of the Arun in eastern Nepal (photo by Kevin Bubriski).

southeast and up the ridge. As you round the grassy ridge line 1,200 ft. above Junbesi, you have your first view of both Mt. Everest and Makalu. Descend through Salung, cross the main river below, and walk up through Ringmo village. The direct southern trail from Phaphlu and Salleri joins the trail at Ringmo. Above Ringmo is a one-building cheese factory. Not far beyond along the gentle slope, cross Takshindu Pass (10,075 ft.) marked by a large stupa, here called a *chorten*, with prayer flags. This is the last east-west pass on the trek, but you still have one more high spur to cross before Namche. Proceed on the middle trail east of the pass for the 15-minute walk to Takshindu Gomba; here you can stay the night in an attached inn with views of nearby snow-topped peaks to the east and north.

When leaving Takshindu Gomba, take the trail toward Manidingma that angles southeast—not the northeast path, or you will end up in a cul-de-sac below several villages. Continue down 2,400 ft. through Manidingma, where bhattis are available, and another 2,300 ft. to cross a bridge over the Dudh Kosi (5,100 ft.), the "Milk River" (a different Dudh Kosi than in the preceding chapter). You have glimpses of the bridge as you approach this large river, which drains all of Khumbu. On the eastern bank, angle northeasterly through scattered terraces past several villages and a notch to reach Kharikhola village, with its few shops and an inn, just south of the valley known as Khari Khola. The lower branch of the trail to the Arun Valley leaves from the village. This region, from Kharikhola to Namche Bazaar, is called Pharak by its Sherpa inhabitants. Steeply up from Kharikhola are the few scattered homes of Kharte (8,800 ft.) also with a small bhatti. The upper branch of the Arun trail leaves from Kharte; this route is noted in a later section.

Beyond Kharte the trail angles up to a large bhatti on the ridge line at a place called the Khari La. Here you have imposing views up and down the precipitous gorge. Go slightly down to a stream valley, then directly onto another spur past the small village of Phuyan along a gentle trail to another ridge line at 9,660 ft., some 450 ft. below the Khari La. Up-valley you will see some large hotels and Lukla airstrip, which lies on a perceptible slope.

Once you have descended from this ridge to the hamlet of Surkya (7,520 ft.), you will be on relatively level ground until you climb to Namche Bazaar, a long day's walk northward. Now you enter country between permanently snow-clad ridges. You see the first snow peak, to the east, beyond Chaunrikharka, the next village. It is not necessary to climb east to Lukla as you walk north; just continue on the main trail.

If you are arriving at Lukla (about 9,200 ft.), on a flight, avoid looking at the two abandoned airplane fuselages south of the runway; merely smile unconcernedly at your neighbor and tighten your seat belt. Once down, grab tea and perhaps *dalbhat* at a small bhatti by the airport and start north along the trail. The track from Lukla meets the north-south path some 40-minutes' walk north of the airfield. Waiting for flights out of Lukla on the return to Kathmandu is an oft-discussed travail, particularly for those on a tight schedule. If the weather is poor, you may have to wait for days. Be patient but persistent with the RNAC agent in charge. When the skies clear, several flights will probably be arranged to reduce the backlog of passengers. Planes usually land only in midmorning: to be available for one, be at the airfield by 9:00 A.M. When I flew out, the liftoff was accompanied by the spontaneous applause of the relieved passengers.

East of Lukla is the 16,215-ft. Chhatara Teng Pass, which connects with the upper Hinku Valley, the 17,765-ft. Mera La, and the upper Hongu Valley. Only attempt this route if you are experienced, well provisioned, and with a knowledgeable porter-guide. The Schneider Shorong/Hinku map shows all of this area, which is uninhabited.

North of Lukla the going is easy and the trail fairly obvious. If you have flown into Lukla, you may feel the altitude, but if you have walked from Lamosangu or Jiri, you will be an old hand and this will be the easiest part of the trek thus far. The path continues near the bottom of the steep, forested gorge on the east bank of the Dudh Kosi to just north of Phakding, where you cross to the west side of the river. Within an hour, after passing over a large tributary, recross the river just beyond a small settlement called Benkar. In the midst of delightful forest, cross a large stream that drains the Kyangshar Glacier at the base of the mountains Tamserku and Kangtega. After the bridge is Mondzo village, where you descend through a narrow notch to a bridge that takes you to the west bank. Here is Thumbug (also called Jorsale) with its two-story inns, the last village before Namche Bazaar.

Less than a mile beyond Thumbug, cross the Nangpo Tsangpo River and begin the 2,100-ft. climb to Namche Bazaar. At a ridge line not far up, you can catch a glimpse of Mt. Everest behind the Lhotse-Nuptse wall. Hereabouts you may begin to pinch yourself and say, "I have arrived in Khumbu."

Khumbu: Sherpa Heartland

Namche Bazaar and Vicinity

Namche Bazaar (11,270 ft.) consists of several-score buildings—homes, stores, hotels, and a gomba—built in a wide semicircle above a large spring. At Namche ("Nauche," in the Sherpa dialect), you can acclimatize while stocking up on pricy food, fuel, or warm clothing. Remember the bustling Saturday market for buying bulk food or fuel. Namche is the last town with stores, although you will be able to find canned expedition food and hot prepared meals at least as far as Lobuche, several days up-valley. If Namche is too crowded for you, try the nearby villages; walk for an hour straight up the hill above town toward the Shyangboche airstrip; pass it and continue over the ridge to Khumjung and Khunde (about 12,500 ft.). These villages do not have numerous stores and hotels like Namche, and you may only be able to find lodging in a home. Some people prefer these towns to Namche's commercialization, while others welcome the array of food and amenities available in Namche.

Wherever you stay, rest a day to help yourself acclimatize before proceeding up-valley. West of Namche Bazaar you might take a day or overnight walk to Thame village. The path to Thame is mentioned later in this section. The sacred mountain Khumbila (from its full name, Khumbui Yul Lha, which means "Country God of Khumbu") has a climbable spur above Khunde, the smaller village just west of Khumjung. As you ascend, you will have excellent perspectives on the peaks of Kwangde, Thamserku, Kangtega, and Ama Dablam, all higher than 21,000 feet. Also up from Namche Bazaar you might visit the Everest View Hotel, nearer town. This twelve-room hotel is a 20-minute walk northeast of Shyangboche airfield, near the edge of a 12,800-ft. shelf. The posh and little-patronized hotel offers its guests oxygen in each room. From the lounge, you can see the uppermost peak of Mt. Everest above the Lhotse-Nuptse wall, a long face of rock and ice that averages 9,000 nearly vertical feet.

The remainder of this section on Khumbu describes first the direct route to the base of Mt. Everest and then, briefly, several side treks you can take in this well-visited region. Your best possible guide to this area is the 1:50,000 Khumbu Himal Map noted in Appendix A. With that sheet, you can pick routes and embark on numerous climbs or side hikes on your own. Remember that, like all maps, the Khumbu Himal Sheet shows only the main trails.

The most important precaution about trekking in Khumbu is to avoid going too high too fast, particularly if you have flown into the

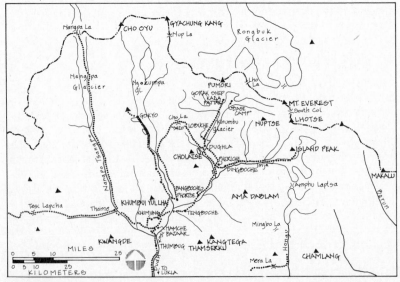

Khumbu

region at Lukla or Syangboche. Unacclimatized people have become very sick and a very few have even died from walking too rapidly into the upper valleys. If you begin to develop symptoms of altitude sickness (see Appendix B), descend immediately and rest before attempting to trek higher.

The Direct Trail to Mt. Everest's Base

From Namche Bazaar, the up-valley trail ascends briefly east of town, then begins a level traverse with sweeping mountain views high above the river to the point where you continue along the track from Khumjung. The path descends through trees and passes a few scattered houses at Trashinga, then crosses the Dudh Kosi just below Phunki (10,700 ft.) which has an inn and several water-powered grain mills. Watch for the many iridescent Impeyan (or monal) pheasants, called *danphe* in Nepal, which roam the underbrush between Khumjung and Tengboche (the "Great High Place").

The square, red Tengboche Monastery (12,700 ft.) sits on a spur at one of the most picturesque locations along the main trail in Khumbu. Forty monks resided at Tengboche when the first western mountaineers reached the monastery in the fall of 1950. Presently, with tourism in full sway, you will not likely find ten maroon-robed monks. Tengboche rests beneath the spreading arms of Ama Dablam (the "Mother's Charm Box," at 22,494 ft.), considered by many people to be the most striking peak in the area. Here you can also see the tip of Mt. Everest peeking from behind the formidable Lhotse-Nuptse wall. At Tengboche, you may either stay in a room provided by the monks or in a modern, New Zealand–built, glassed-in dormitory.

Beyond Tengboche, the trail contours through a moss-draped forest that in the mornings is often coated with frost. After passing near Deboche Convent, you drop to the level of the thundering river and cross to its west bank. Soon Pangboche village comes into view with its upper gomba, red and squarish and with a pagoda-style roof like the one at Tengboche. Three miles from Pangboche the main river forks. You can follow either the left or right bank of the western tributary, the Khumbu Khola, to reach Pheriche (14,000 ft.) on the stream's northern bank, a mile beyond the river junction. Here you are in the wide, U-shaped Khumbu Valley. Pheriche consists of several low stone buildings and is considered a *yersa*—summer settlement. Trekkers often halt a day here for acclimatization, and while here visit the Imja Valley, to the east (noted later), or climb the northern ridge to visit the small, usually locked Nangkartshang Gomba. This gomba offers excellent views of Ama Dablam and Makalu. A Trekker's Aid Post at Pheriche is usually staffed in the spring and fall by a physician belonging to the Himalayan Rescue Association.

From Pheriche, walk across the wide bottom land toward Lobuche Peak. Alternatively, you can climb the northern slope behind Pheriche and take a higher trail past the few buildings of Duga, another yersa. Either way, you begin to climb the Khumbu Glacier's terminal moraine, where you have a fine view of Cholatse's sheer north face. At the two small buildings of Duglha (15,150 ft.), you will welcome a cup of tea. The altitude slows your step on the trail to Lobuche (16,200 ft.), another yersa with one or two funky and often crowded "hotels." Climb the low hill above Lobuche for excellent perspectives of the tan and grey granite webbing on Nuptse and the beautiful tower of Pumo Ri ("Daughter Peak," named for George Mallory's daughter). Most people take three to four days (allowing acclimatization time) from Namche Bazaar to reach Lobuche. Don't count on being able to buy cooked food above this point.

Above Lobuche, follow the path as it winds alongside the Khumbu Glacier's lateral moraine and crosses moraine rubble of the Changri Glacier. After some rocky scrambling, you can look ahead and see Kala Pattar ("Black Rock"), a spur of Pumo Ri and, below, the sandy basin called Gorak Shep. At Gorak Shep (17,000 ft.) a small tarn provides water, but you may have to use a nearby rock to break the ice covering it. Be sure to drink enough liquid to avoid dehydration at this elevation. Sometimes tea and pancakes are available from a small hut here.

Beyond Gorak Shep are two principal places of interest. Walk slowly for an hour and a half up the slope to the west to reach Kala Pattar (18,190 ft.), where you have the classic view of Mt. Everest. If you want to see Everest's South Col, keep going along the ridge toward Pumo Ri beyond the first high point. Here on Kala Pattar, you are directly below Pumo Ri's light granite and slanted snow channels. The surroundings have an awesome, unnatural brilliance. To the south, the Khumbu Glacier sweeps below you; northward rise several border peaks and the vertical Lho La, reached from the Tibetan side by Mallory and Bullock in July 1921, the first time foreigners had seen the Khumbu Glacier. Stolid and monumental, Mt. Everest (29,028 ft.) rises above all. Known as Chomolungma ("Lady Goddess of the Wind") by Sherpas and Tibetans and named Sagarmatha ("Churning Stick of the Ocean") by Nepalis, the mountain was initially called Peak XV by surveyors, when it was first identified from the plains. In 1852 it was recognized as the highest peak on earth and four years later was given the name Everest in honor of Sir George Everest, the early surveyor general. The mountain was first climbed on May 29, 1953, and since then its summit has been briefly surmounted by more than 110 people of more than 25 expeditions. Some scientists have determined that single-celled organisms live atop Mt. Everest.

The second walk from Gorak Shep takes three to five hours to complete. This hike to the area called "base camp" on the Khumbu Glacier can be done round trip from Lobuche in a day, by the fit, but it will be a long, tiring trek. Beyond the memorial stone at the far end of Gorak Shep, a narrow trail leads onto the Khumbu Glacier. Once on it, your route may not be readily apparent: keep heading along the moraine toward the Lho La past tall seracs. After you reach the area across from the base of the Khumbu icefall (the scene of most of the fatalities that expeditions have suffered) you see trash piles and other discordant signs of human use. You have reached the area called Everest base camp, where you are out of sight of but as close as you can get to Mt. Everest.

The Nangpo Tsangpo Valley

The first side walk in Khumbu angles to the northwest from Namche Bazaar up the Nangpo Tsangpo Valley (also called the Bhote Kosi). This trail is the last portion of the path that leads from the Rolwaling Valley over Tesi Lapcha Pass. To begin this walk, follow the wide trail that angles out of Namche's basin from the village gomba. In less than two hours you will reach Thomde village; its gomba rests above town somewhat down-valley. Beyond Thomde the path descends and crosses to the Nangpo Tsangpo's right bank, then rises, crosses the tributary stream draining the basin below the Tesi Lapcha, and ascends again to the small village of Thame. Thame is three to four hours from Namche Bazaar and the farthest you are permitted to proceed up the Nangpo Tsangpo Valley. In the restricted area at the head of the long valley is the wide Nangpa La, an 18,750-ft. pass providing Khumbu's traditional access to Dzarongphu (Rongbuk) Monastery and Lhasa in Tibet. A few traders still use the glaciated Nangpa La with official permission, but the pass is far less frequented than it used to be.

At Thame you can see the town gomba on its hillside above a few stunted conifers. The Mani Rimdu masked drama, which depicts the introduction of Buddhism into Tibet by Padma Sambhava, takes place at Thame Gomba during the full moon of May. (The same scenes are enacted at Tengboche during the November-December full moon). Tenzing Norgay, one of the first two people to climb Mt. Everest, grew up in this village. A trail above Thame Gomba leads up the westward side valley toward the Tesi Lapcha Pass (18,875 ft.); information about this difficult pass crossing is in the Rolwaling Valley section.

The Dudh Kosi or Gokyo Valley

Many people consider trekking up the Gokyo Valley to be the high point of their experience in Khumbu. This upper valley has only one large permanent village, Phortse, at the valley mouth. If you plan to walk up this valley, you will have to take food and fuel for at least four days—and for up to six days if you plan to climb high or to try the pass leading eastward to the main Everest trail. Stock up on essentials in Namche Bazaar, and ascend to Khumjung village—an hour's walk straight uphill past the airstrip and then over the ridge. At Khumjung, the trail toward Gokyo slants upward from the eastern end of town and rises to a stupa at 13,030 feet. The path then descends more than a thousand feet to the Dudh Kosi River, where it meets a trail leading downward from Phortse. From this junction the trail begins the long traverse up-valley.

As you begin the ascent up the Gokyo Valley, you have excellent views behind you of Kangtega ("Snow Horse Saddle") and Thamserku, two summits over 21,500 ft. that rise above Tengboche Monastery. Soon you will see Cho Oyu (26,750 ft.) emerge at the head of the valley. Note any signs of altitude sickness among your party as you proceed; it is easy to climb too quickly up this high valley. Make camp near water at night, and if you question how well you are acclimatizing, halt early in the day or take a day's rest. You pass several small yersa as you proceed. One of the most beautifully situated summer settlements is Machherma, which you will probably reach at the end of your second day out from Khumjung. After Machherma is the yersa called Pangka, near the terminal moraine of the Ngozumpa Glacier, the longest glacier in Nepal. Soon the path leads up rock west of the glacier's lateral moraine.

The few buildings and walled pastures of Gokyo (15,700 ft.) are on the eastern shore of Dudh Pokhari, the third lake you will reach. Start early from Gokyo to reach one of Khumbu's most spectacular viewing locations: the peak above Gokyo, marked "5483" on the Khumbu Himal Map. From this point you can see the vast Ngozumpa Glacier, Cho Oyu with its neighbor Gyachung Kang, Mt. Everest rising above a fluted ridge, Lhotse, and Makalu: four of the world's highest peaks. Some call this the finest mountain panorama in Nepal. Also, you can walk up-valley beyond Gokyo to reach two more remote lakes.

A 17,780-ft. pass variously called the Tsho La or Pass 5420 (referring to its elevation in meters on the Khumbu Himal Map) connects the Gokyo Valley with a secondary path that emerges near Duglha in the Khumbu Valley. You can guide yourself best here with the Khumbu Himal Map or the services of a Sherpa who knows the way. To reach this pass from the Gokyo side, walk through Na (mislabeled Tsoshung on the Khumbu Sheet) and ascend the trail above the small settlement of Dragnag. After two hours' walk on rolling pasture and moraine, climb steeply on scree to the low point in the eastern ridge, the place marked "5420." The eastern descent follows a nearly level glacier at first, but you must keep to the right (south) side of this glacier and cross onto the rock before too long, for the lower part of this small glacier is crevassed and impassible. Traverse to the left (here east) of the streams you meet and walk to the yersa of Dzonglha, situated on a low knob. From Dzonglha, you can follow a trail down-valley past Cholatse's steep, leaning face and the lake of Tshola Tsho, continuing to the main Khumbu Valley path.

If you try this pass from the Khumbu side, carry supplies for at least four days. On the ascent from Khumbu, keep left on low ground beyond Dzonglha and, as you approach the glacier, angle to the left on moraine. Remember to ascend on rock at the near (south) side of the glacier; then, where the rock becomes too steep to climb, cross onto the snow.

The Imja Valley

This fairly level valley lies to the east of Pheriche and the Khumbu Valley. You can reach the Imja Valley by walking over the ridge east of Pheriche or, when walking up from Pangboche, by following the Imja

Khola's right bank to the east at the point where the Imja and Khumbu rivers join. The first habitation in the Imja Valley is the spread-out village of Dingboche (about 14,200 ft.), where potatoes are raised in abundance. A trail leads up from Dingboche to Nangkartshang Gomba, which can also be reached from Pheriche. The Imja's unique allure is visible in the views of steep walls as you proceed up the slowly rising trail along the main valley. To your right are perspectives of Ama Dablam's northern face. As you continue walking in an easterly direction, the Lhotse-Nuptse wall comes into view, towering 2 mi. high. The last settlement you pass through about 3 mi. beyond Ding-boche, in the Imja Valley, is Chhukung (15,250 ft.). You reach it after crossing many streams from the Nuptse, Lhotse Nup, and Lhotse glaciers. From Chhukung, the view of the Lhotse-Nuptse wall is excellent, and you can also see the 20,305-ft. Island Peak to the east-northeast. This summit can be climbed from the south if you are equipped with rope and ice axe and have some mountaineering experience. Walking beyond Chhukung, you continue south of Island Peak, from where you can see the Amphu Laptsa, a steep-sided, 18,962-ft. col that connects with the upper Hongu Valley.

These are only some of the main trails in Khumbu. Using the Khumbu Himal map, strike off for a distant high place you can call your own.

From Khumbu to the Arun

A rarely trekked route, mentioned earlier, leads from Kharte (a day's walk south of Lukla airfield) in the Dudh Kosi Valley to the deep

The Nuptse–Lhotse wall behind Tengboche Monastery, with Ama Dablam to the right.

gorge of the Arun River. This route was first negotiated by Westerners when the 1950 Mt. Everest reconnaissance expedition walked it from the east. In 1951 a group that included Eric Shipton and Edmund Hillary walked the trail and explored some of the passes at the head of the Hongu Valley. Even today you might walk the entire distance to the Arun Valley without seeing another Westerner, as you cross high, forested ridges and pass isolated Sherpa, Rai, Chhetri, and Brahmin villages. Take a local as porter and guide unless you are somewhat familiar with spoken Nepali, for you will often encounter confusing trail junctions and have difficulty finding your way through the sprawling Rai villages. No bhattis are maintained here, so you must either camp or seek accommodation in the rude dwellings that are scattered en route. Primarily, this trail is used by people transporting grain to Namche Bazaar from the neighboring eastern valleys. Expect to walk just less than a week from the time you leave the main trail at Kharte until you reach the Arun River. You should carry enough food for this period unless you plan to buy grains along the way.

Note the route description in the section on "The Trek to Khumbu"; diverge at Kharte village (8,800 ft.), below the Khari La. Walk the contour east to the Sherpa village of Pangum. Here, the decrepit gomba contains a brilliant 7-ft.-tall prayer wheel, and weeds grow on the village roofs. Pangum can also be reached from lower elevations, by a trail from Kharikhola village below. Take the trail to the Pangum La (10,405 ft.), a thousand feet above the village; beyond this thin ridge, the narrow path descends very sharply to the east in switchbacks to the Hinku Valley (or Inukhu Khola, 6,090 ft.). Following a trail that is barely discernible at times, climb the eastern slopes on the other side of the Hinku Valley. Walk past the village of Gaikharka ("Cow's Meadow") and past rhododendrons with trunks so thick you cannot wrap your arms around them. You reach high pastures, then make the steep climb to the Sipki Pass (10,120 ft.). On the other side you are in the Hongu Valley, and most trekkers will head south.

Well-equipped, adventurous groups with experienced Sherpas have trekked north into the upper Hongu Valley, departing from the regular path described below, not far east of this pass. To walk north, you should go with a well-provisioned, organized group or be extremely capable in nearly trackless Himalayan terrain. Only a few Sherpas have experience in this region; and they will likely be already engaged with a Kathmandu-based trekking outfitter. Another difficulty is that if you want to trek into the upper Hongu Valley, you must carry food for two weeks. If you go there, however, you can see Mt. Mera (21,245 ft.), Chamlang (24,010 ft.), and, from a distance, the tip of the rarely seen east, or Kangshung, face of Mt. Everest. From the upper Hongu, a trail leads west over the glaciated Mera La (17,765 ft.) to the upper Hinku Valley and the Chhatara Teng Pass above Lukla. As already noted, you must be experienced and in the company of a local who knows the route to make a success of the Chhatara Teng route.

Continuing on the main route from the Sipki Pass, descend southward through a mossy oak and rhododendron forest to reach Kiraunle, an isolated Sherpa village. Continuing southward above the Buha, a tributary of the Hongu, you pass by the widely scattered Rai homes of Bung village, situated on a large shelf. At the base of the V-shaped Hongu gorge (4,310 ft.), expect to cross the grey, glacial waters on a bamboo bridge that is replaced each year following the high water. (When one trekker reached this torrent farther north on his way to the upper Hongu basin, he crossed the river on a dilapidated bridge that lacked many planks and railings. On the far side, he met a toothless old gentleman who motioned silently toward the skewed bridge and broke a twig between his fingers.)

The steep hills west of the Arun River are the homeland of the Rai clan, the largest ethnic group in eastern Nepal. Rais are easily recognizable by their distinctive almond-shaped eyes; they are of Mongolian extraction. Most Rai live between 3,000 and 6,000 ft. in elevation, but many have migrated to flatter land. This large clan has eighteen divisions called *thars*, and the dialects Rais speak number nearly as many as these subgroups. Although primarily agriculturalists, many Rai men have bravely distinguished themselves in Gurkha regiments of the British or Indian army. Strictly speaking, Rais are not Hindu but worship local deities according to ancient custom. Unlike Hindus or Buddhists, they bury their dead, often beneath stone memorial platforms. Many Rai women wear nose rings, large, round jeweled earrings, and necklaces of old coins.

Ascending out of the Hongu gorge, climb steeply—more than 2,200 ft.—to the subtropical village of Gudel, then rise steadily to Sorung (7,110 ft.), a Sherpa village. Farther is another Sherpa settlement, called Sanam, where you can often purchase excellent milk products. In the middle Hinku and Hongu valleys, the Sherpas, who raise wheat and potatoes and have cattle, always live higher than the Rais, who grow corn, millet, and rice. After Sanam, the track continues in a steep pine- and rhododendron-forested side valley with all shapes, sizes, and colors of green. After the path crosses the last available drinking water, it rises to the stupa-crowned Salpa Bhanjang (about 11,200 ft.). This pass marks the watershed between the Dudh Kosi and the mighty Arun River. North of the pass 1½ mi. is the small lake called Salpa Pokhari, where fairs presided over by shamans are held twice yearly.

Descend first east from the Salpa Bhanjang on a ridge and then down farther through oak forest to the village of Phedi (about 7,300 ft.). You are now approximately 10 humid miles west of the Arun River. Continue by following the Irkhua Khola, crossing and recrossing it on bamboo bridges. At a bridge called Lamsangu (2,600 ft.), begin to angle southwards up the ridge called Chhange Danda toward the village of Dangmaya. Here, walking through scattered sal trees and terracing, the sweat will pour every time you walk uphill. Continue beyond Dangmaya to Dandagaon and hike down to the Chirkhuwa Khola, a tributary that flows south of and roughly parallel to the Irkhua Khola. South of the Chirkhuwa Khola is a high ridge topped by the large town of

Dingla, but you need not walk the several thousand feet up to it; continue instead down the right bank of the river. Ask here for directions to the village of Katike Ghat, where you will find a hollowed-out tree trunk that serves as a ferry across the wide Arun River (980 ft.). If you don't find the boatman there, you can cross the Arun on a bridge less than two hours' walk south, at Turkay Ghat.

Once on the Arun River's east bank, walk south to the wide red terrace where Tumlingtar airstrip is situated. At Tumlingtar, you reach the main north-south Arun River trail, which is discussed in the next section, and you are a hot two-day walk north of the roadhead near Dhankuta.

The Arun Valley

The Arun River originates in Tibet southwest of Shigatse, where its mysterious northern headwaters are called the Phung Chu. This mighty waterway predates the Himalaya and carves a deep gorge where it cuts through the range on its way to the Ganges plain. The Arun is one of Nepal's two largest rivers, along with the Karnali, and it flows rather directly from north to south. Near Nepal's northern border, the Arun passes through country that is sparsely inhabited by Bhotias called Lhomis who practice Bon Po. The river descends through deep, thickly forested gorges and continues for many miles through low hills that are thickly populated by Rai, Limbu, Chhetri, and Brahmin villagers. This valley is a naturalist's delight, supporting an abundance of flora and fauna. *The Arun*, by Edward Cronin, is a good natural history source book for the area.

Bon Po shaman in the upper Arun Valley (photo by Chris Wriggins).

The Arun Valley is not often visited by hikers for several reasons: it is little known; not readily accessible; very hot in its lower areas; it contains several steep portions of trail; and permits to visit its most interesting northern regions are granted infrequently. Still, request permission to trek as far as Chepua or Hatiya: if you must return from as far south as Num, or thereabouts, you will miss the Arun's most fascinating areas. Alternatively, you can diverge from the main valley at Sedua and cross an alpine pass into the upper Barun Valley to the northwest near Makalu (27,805 ft.). Plan to take minimally 2½ to 3 weeks from the southern roadhead if you want to trek into the Lhomi-populated northern area. You will need more time if you take any side treks or plan to walk to the base of Makalu. Since the southern part of the valley is extremely hot during much of the year, you may prefer to trek here between November and March. In midwinter, however, the upper pass areas will be closed. Let's begin in the lower Arun Valley and head north.

The best place to begin walking up the Arun is from Tumlingtar airfield. Owing to the low number of flights scheduled there, however, you may start this trek from Dhankuta, which is two to three days south but more easily accessible. The first leg of a trip to Dhankuta from Kathmandu is either a dawn-to-dusk express bus to Biratnagar or one of the numerous 40-minute RNAC flights landing there. Biratnagar, in the terai near India, is Nepal's second-largest city: a steamy place teeming with rickshaws and lorries that has many jute mills and other industries rarely found elsewhere in Nepal. Once at Biratnagar by either means, take the first available bus to Dharan (1,350 ft.), which is situated on the southern slopes of the Siwalik Range, here called the Churia Hills. At Dharan you should be able to continue directly north to Dhankuta. After you cross the ridge line north of Dharan, look for a view of Khangchendzonga (or Kangchenjunga, 28,168 ft.) on Nepal's northeastern border with Sikkim.

Dhankuta (3,800 ft.) lies on the first ridge to the north of Dharan, across the Tamur River. The weekly haat bazaar continues to be held, on Thursday, even though the road has now reached town. Astride a narrow spur, Dhankuta is a large town with scores of shops and offices and several schools. Ride or walk on north to Hile (6,200 ft.), which has a gomba in the southern part of town. Hile's population increased considerably when Bhotias from Walungchung in the upper Tamur Valley moved into town after a disastrous landslide ruined part of their prosperous village. Beyond Hile, proceed on the Jeep track, passing Pakribas and its large agricultural demonstration and experiment station. The last good views to the north for several days are on the descent to the torrid Arun Valley floor.

Continue near the eastern bank of the Arun, where porters carry all manner of goods for the large bazaar towns to the east and west. Tangerines (*suntala*) are plentiful in the lower Arun during fall and early winter. You will cross several tributaries as you walk toward Tumlingtar's red-earth airstrip. At night, in this area, you may hear jackals howling. North of the Tumlingtar airfield, start climbing to the last bazaar town of Khandbari with its small hotel, whitewashed houses, cobblestone main street, and its own Saturday haat market. Stock up on food in Khandbari; many basic rations will probably be difficult to purchase in any quantity farther north. Continue ascending as you draw parallel to the Irkhua Khola across the Arun, where the trail to Khumbu (described in the preceding section) disappears westward. From here north into Tibet, the Arun gorge is particularly deep; enjoy the cooler air and, in response to the children who say "whaat ees zoor name?", ask where you can get drinking water, for streams are few on this ridge. Spectacular views of the northern peaks are seen through the rhododendrons, especially at the Sherpa town of Munche (or Munde).

Descend to Num, then continue steeply down through jungle to the Arun. Once the trail reaches the west bank of the river, it climbs again. To the west is the tributary valley of the Kasuwa Khola and the beginning of the alternate route north: with a local who knows the way, you can descend into the Kasuwa and trek up through Sedua village to the nearly 14,000-ft. Barun Pass, which provides entrance to the upper Barun Valley. Five to six days' walk from Sedua through rugged terrain takes you into the Barun Valley and past the lower Barun Glacier to the place known as Makalu base camp. If you have the determination to reach this isolated place, you will be rewarded with the sight of Makalu's 8,000-ft. "pink" granite south face and a great deal of solitude.

On the main west-bank trail of the Arun, continue past the permit checkpoint at Hedangna and through scattered Rai villages as you plow along near the base of the valley's deep furrow. Beyond Uwa, climb to a notch, then descend to the valley floor. (At a nearby bridge across the Arun, you can cross on the way back, having made a circle walk in the upper valley.) North of the bridge is the hamlet of Lamobagar Gola and the mouth of the Barun Valley, its pine-forested lower gorge too steep to negotiate. Now you are beginning to reach the area populated almost exclusively by Lhomi Bhotias, many of whom are Bon Po. Here, about four days' walk north of Tumlingtar, most nearby villages have both Bhotia and Nepali names. Beyond the village of Sempung, you cross a high spur that has dramatic close-up views of the border peaks. Clinging to such spurs high above the Arun are the few villages hereabouts—Hatiya, for example, the next right-bank town after Sempung.

Hatiya (5,200 ft.), locally called Damdong, is a large Lhomi village set above a bend in the river and ringed by high, forested ridges. Most houses are stone-walled, with woven bamboo roofs from which many homes have five bamboo wands spread in a fan shape and topped with prayer flags to protect against malevolent spirits. Small yarn cages called spirit traps are also in evidence. People wear homespun, vegetable-dyed clothes, silver jewelry, necklaces of coral and turquoise, and some have squarish pillbox hats or Tibetan-style hats with large ear flaps. Hatiya is Bon Po like most nearby villages: prayer wheels are turned counterclockwise, and prayer walls are passed on the right.

When Chris Wriggins arrived in Hatiya, he was just in time for an inebriated three-day marriage celebration. Millet beer called *tungba* that is drunk through bamboo straws (a favorite beverage in east Nepal) and distilled rakshi taken in bamboo cups were flowing freely. Unrestrained dancing continued for hours, some of the participants wearing masks depicting animals, skulls, or demons. Later in the day, an intoxicated priest wearing a bandolier of bone carvings and a round black fur hat began a ceremony. The finale involved an exorcism that ended with the shooting of an arrow into a small pile of burning straw decorated with small symbolic figures.

Crossing the Sursing tributary just up-valley from Hatiya, you can continue to the large village of Honggaon (Pangdok) high above the Arun. From this town of nearly a hundred houses a path leads through dark, vine-tangled jungle up to the border pass, which is called the Popti (or Ponti) La. If, with your permit, you have been able to pass the several checkposts and get this far north, you can walk to the pass and back—it will take a very long day or more from Honggaon.

On the return from Honggaon, you can make a small loop by taking the path below town to the east; traverse crudely terraced fields to a bridge across the Arun River. At the bridge you begin the walk down-valley by climbing a steep, 4,000-ft. ridge cloaked in pine and eerie damp jungle of rhododendron and bamboo. Beyond a 9,100-ft. pass, descend sharply to Namoche village. Some of Namoche's homes and all its granaries stand on bamboo poles. Chickens and eggs will probably be available. South of Namoche, a relatively gentle downhill trail carries you back to the Arun River bridge south of the Barun Valley. From the bridge crossing, the path down-valley to Tumlingtar or Dhankuta is the same path you took north.

Sikkim

Sikkim, on Nepal's eastern border, measures only 40 mi. by 80 mi. and is isolated from both Tibet and the rest of India by high ridges. Smaller than Yellowstone National Park, Sikkim was joined to the British empire by treaty; its northern boundary was demarcated in 1890. Sikkim became an Indian protectorate in 1947; recently, it was made India's newest and smallest state. Its area is composed of the Ranjit and Tista river basins. These two river valleys are immensely luxuriant, with thick forests ranging from sal in the deep southern gorges to conifer in the upper tributaries. Sikkim's varied vegetation includes literally thousands of plants, among them magnolia, tree fern, lily, wild strawberry and raspberry, woody creeper, primrose, bougainvillea, crimson and yellow rhododendron, poinsettia, and hundreds of orchid varieties. Sikkim's "endless diversity of green" is best seen during the monsoon. Also in the wet summers, both butterflies and leeches abound. Cardamom plants provide Sikkim with one of its largest export crops. Tiny and black, cardamom seeds are popular in Asia, Europe, and North America, and the spice has become a luxury item.

Sikkim's population of just under a quarter million is largely ethnic Nepalis. Nepalis were urged to emigrate to Sikkim by the British, who required administrators and cultivators. Until Sikkim became an Indian state in 1975, it was ruled for five centuries by the Buddhist Namgyal dynasty. The Namgyals are Lepcha, traditionally the region's most powerful clan. More than 50 Buddhist monasteries are scattered across Sikkim, primarily in the more densely populated south. Rumtek is the area's best-known monastery, situated high on a ridge not far southeast of Gangtok, Sikkim's capital. This monastic community was home to the late Gyalwa Karmapa, leader of the Kagyupa branch of Tibetan Buddhism. Each May at Rumtek, masked ritual dances are performed that reenact events from the life of Padma Sambhava. These dances are similar to those that take place at Hemis in Ladakh, and in Marpha, Thame, and Tengboche in Nepal.

To reach Sikkim, you must first travel to Siliguri in the Indian state of West Bengal. Siliguri can be reached by train from Calcutta, but fly to Siliguri's Baghdogra Airport from Calcutta if at all possible; the train ride, which includes a boat trip across the Ganges, is only for hard-core travelers. From Siliguri, the best way to get to Darjeeling is by shared taxi or rented four-wheel-drive vehicle. A narrow-gauge train goes from Siliguri to Darjeeling, but soot from the coal-burning engine makes it a gritty ride. Once you have your permit to enter Sikkim (see next paragraph), you can travel by Jeep from Darjeeling to Gangtok. Your permit will be inspected at Rongphu on the border before you are allowed to enter Sikkim.

Permission to enter (let alone trek in) Sikkim has been difficult to obtain, and because of this, those who can afford to usually go with an organized group. Since 1980, a few groups with at least four trekkers and accompanied by a liaison officer have been permitted to trek from Yuksam village up the Rathong and Prek tributaries of the upper Ranjit Valley to Dzongri ("High Fortress") in southwestern Sikkim. The country is superb. You walk in a narrow north-to-south valley toward Khangchendzonga (28,168 ft.), the world's third highest peak, through Lepcha and Bhotia villages. Less than 2 mi. north of Dzongri is Kaburlam Tso, a high lake. Some people have reached the Goechi La at the valley's head, which commands an unparalleled close-up view of the Khangchendzonga massif.

To initiate the trekking-permit procedure, write to the Indian Embassy or the nearest Indian diplomatic mission and request an application form for entry into Sikkim. When you return this form, it and your photographs will be forwarded by the Indian Embassy to the Home Ministry (Section S-1) in New Delhi. Your application should be submitted at least three months in advance of your expected entry into Sikkim. When the application has been processed, you will receive a letter; if your application has been approved, you can present the letter to the deputy commissioner in Darjeeling, who will issue you the permit for entry to Sikkim (and a trekking permit, if requested). The procedure is lengthy and subject to change, and the application must go through the Home Ministry in New Delhi; don't expect to receive a permit if you should arrive in Darjeeling without the advance paperwork. Areas other than the route to Dzongri may also open up to trekkers; inquire when you are requesting the permit application.

As of the end of 1981, permits for Sikkim also can be obtained on short notice in Siliguri.

Bhutan

Druk Yul, also called the "Land of the Thunder Dragon," is known by those of us outside its borders as Bhutan. This oval kingdom, 100 mi. by 200 mi. at its greatest dimensions, is located directly east of Sikkim and north of the Indian states of West Bengal and Assam. Bhutan's southern border is almost contiguous with the base of the Himalaya Range's jungle-clad foothills that rise from the Assamese rice lands. For the most part, Bhutan's northern boundary follows the ridge line of the eastern Himalaya. Before the northern border with Tibet was closed, three passes in west Bhutan and one in the east were used regularly for north to south trade.

John Kenneth Galbraith, America's ambassador to India in the early 1960s, visited Bhutan and began his tour on the back of an elephant. The building of roads in Bhutan had been forbidden until 1959. After a royal decree in 1960 by King Jigme Dorje Wangchuck, the creation of national roads was undertaken. By 1964 the first all-weather road was completed—from the border to Paro Dzong (*dzong* means fortress) and then on to the new capital of Thimphu. The border town from which the road leads in-country is Phuntsholing, a 3-hour drive from Siliguri's Baghdogra Airport, which can be reached by plane from Calcutta. From muggy Phuntsholing, the road enters lush rain forest, passing waterfalls and rising through conifers and orchards. About six hours of driving are required to negotiate the winding, 112-mi. road through to Thimphu (7,600 ft.). This end of the road is expected to have flights direct from Calcutta—to Paro Dzong, west of Thimphu.

Aside from the Dolpo District in Nepal, Bhutan may well be the most traditional Buddhist region in all of the Himalaya. Despite the ongoing electrification of its larger towns and the road-building program that has already revolutionized access to villages across the land, Bhutan's population is primarily involved in agriculture and pastoralism. A quarter to a third of the populace is of Nepalese extraction and lives in the south, but most Bhutanese are Bhotias of Mongolian origin, called Drukpa, who are Kagyupa Buddhists. Both men and women have closely cropped hair and each sex wears its own version of the national dress. Men don a kimono-like robe that extends to the knees called a *kho* or *gho*. It is held by a narrow belt that creates a loose fold above the waist where money, food, wooden bowls, and all manner of other essentials can be carried. Women dress in a long-sleeved blouse with a lengthy dress closed at the waist by a woven-patterned sash, often one they have made themselves. The food of preference in the south is rice—white, red, or glutinous—while tsampa is eaten in the mountainous northern regions. The Bhutanese, who flavor most foods with chilis, also eat potatoes, eggs, noodles, *choogo* (hard yak cheese), and meat soup called thupa. Like all Bhotias, they favor chang and bouillon-like tea with salt and butter. Bhutanese homes, like the larger dzongs, are made of wood and whitewashed stucco with exposed ceiling beams that are often decorated. Traditional Bhutanese architecture has no nails; all joints are dovetailed. Some large homes and important dzongs built these days have corrugated tin roofs instead of the conventional wooden slats held in place by rocks. Despite such changes, however, many buildings are still protected by thread spirit catchers.

Bhutan has been highly restrictive with visitors from the outside world. Since first admitting tour groups in 1974 and trekking groups two years later, the country's policy has been to allow only a limited number of pricy tours. Every group, whether tour or trek, is escorted by a trained guide of the Bhutan Travel Agency. Only a 50-mi.-wide corridor in the western part of the country has been opened to visitation or trekking as of 1981. The longest and most interesting of the guided treks offered is between Paro Dzong and Thimphu by way of the base of Mt. Chomolhari (23,997 ft.), on the border with Tibet. This 12-day trek ascends the Paro Valley from Drugyel Dzong, crossing two passes en route to the base of Chomolhari. In the high valleys and meadows near the border, musk deer, snow leopard, and bharal are known to live, but trekkers are most likely to see only domesticated yaks and sheep herded by nomadic families. The trek's highest pass, the Nachu La (16,180 ft.), is crossed on the return. The valley you descend is called the Mo Chu, the "Mother River"; to the east is Pho Chu, "Father River."

Most of Bhutan's central regions and nearly all its northern areas have rarely been visited by outsiders. A more complete overview of this country's cultural and physical geography can be written only in the future, when this shy kingdom opens its doors wider, if it will.

In the upper Pho Valley north of Punakha is the remote region called Lunana. Here yak pastures extend up to moraines alongside glaciers that sweep directly from fluted peaks on the border with Tibet. Not only here but across the breadth of the Himalaya in high valleys that are restricted to outsiders, in crisp, upland places with such poetic names as Lunana, Dolpo, Milam, Rupshu, and Shimshal, many of the old traditions survive. Probably it is best that these remote areas remain little touched by the outside world.

14

Himalayan
Natural History

by Rodney Jackson

Introduction

Since the Himalaya's origin less than 25 million years ago, it has moulded the region's fauna and flora by preventing Indian species from moving northward and Tibetan species from moving southward. Because of its youthfulness in geological terms, the Himalaya has not yet evolved plant and animal life uniquely adapted to its terrain; they are instead an amalgam of the forms native to India, Southeast Asia, the Mediterranean, and Europe. Himalayan rivers were in place before the mountains were; consequently, the courses of the rivers have remained unchanged while they have cut ever deeper gorges. These valleys have provided the main avenues of contact between Indian and Eurasian wildlife. Animals adapted to cold climes, such as wolves, brown bears, and rose finches, moved south from Eurasia, while tropical species moved north into the foothills, eventually meeting in the high mountains.

The main Himalaya, stretching for 1,900 mi. and varying in width from 50 mi. to nearly 200, really consists of three parallel ranges. The low hills of the Outer Himalaya, or Siwaliks, adjoin the Indian plain and in few places exceed 3,000 ft. in height or 30 mi. in width. For much of their length the Siwaliks are separated from the main Himalaya by elongated *duns*, or flat valleys, such as the Vale of Kashmir. The Middle Himalaya forms the southern edge of the Inner or Great Himalaya Range, which extends from Kashmir to Bhutan and China. The Middle Himalaya's peaks vary in height from roughly 6,000 ft. to 14,000 ft. This zone supported extensive and magnificent forests of conifers, oaks, maples, laurels, and magnolias until intensive woodcutting in recent years decimated them. The Inner Himalaya is distinguished, of course, by its high peaks, which abut the so-called Trans-Himalaya Range, in reality not a range but a series of ridges, ranges, and plateaux forming the southern edge of Tibet. Examples of individual ranges considered part of the Himalaya include the Zanskar Range, the various Ladakh ranges, the Hindu Kush, and the Karakoram.

The Himalaya is a biological wonderland. Tropical heat and arctic cold are telescoped into a span only 40 mi. wide in the Himalaya of Sikkim and Bhutan, and the region as a whole boasts a richness and variety of plants and wildlife that is perhaps unequalled in the world. On a circuit of the Annapurna massif you will pass from tropical forest to the barren mountain desert of the Tibetan Plateau: two major biogeographical zones. Botanists have estimated that at least 6,500 species of flowering plants grow in Nepal alone. Although the British botanist Joseph Hooker catalogued many Himalayan plants in the mid-nineteenth century, the region's fauna is not well known. A new order of amphibians was discovered in Nepal in the early 1970s, and only recently have the first field studies been conducted on large ungulates (hoofed animals), such as the bharal, or blue sheep.

This trekking guide obviously cannot provide more than a brief glimpse of the area's natural history. The number of plants and animals that can be described here is quite limited, and the descriptions that are included suffer from incompleteness. But if this account stimulates the reader to explore further, it will have served its purpose. In the bibliography you will find references to the most useful natural history books, field guides, and magazine articles. One day the Himalayan trekker will be able to take along a completely portable library, making identification of plants and animals routine. Until then, interest, ingenuity, and perseverance will be the primary tools for exploring life in the Himalaya.

Life Zones

Biologists recognize a number of vertical (or altitudinal) and horizontal (or regional) zones that support distinctive fauna and flora (see the accompanying diagram). The eastern Himalaya is considerably wetter than the western (Kashmir and Kumaon) or northwestern (Hindu Kush and Karakoram) Himalaya, because as the yearly monsoon moves northwestward from the Bay of Bengal, the moisture it carries is rapidly dissipated. And the northern slopes of the Himalaya and the Tibetan Plateau, sequestered in a rain-shadow beyond the monsoon's reach, are dry and practically rainless. As one would expect, then, forests, flowering plants, and wildlife are most diverse and prolific in the east. The eastern Himalaya supports lush tropical montane forests, while at the same elevations in the west are found subtropical thorn or sage scrub. In the north, coniferous or deciduous forests grow on some of the more moist slopes, yet other slopes are entirely unforested. In arid Ladakh, for example, the only trees are those planted near villages and along irrigation ditches. The change from east to west is not abrupt, however. Most biologists recognize the Kali Gandaki River as the eastern boundary and the Sutlej River as the western boundary of a gradient along which plant life changes significantly, with Southeast Asian species to the east and Mediterranean-Eurasian ones to the west.

Vertical zonation results from the changes in temperature and moisture with increasing elevation; temperature decreases while moisture increases to a point and then, at higher levels, decreases. In general, the temperature drops about 11°F (6°C) for every 3,400-ft. rise, and the timberline seems to coincide with elevation levels having a mean temperature of about 50°F (10°C) for the warmest day of the year. Timberline varies from about 12,000–13,500 ft.; it is higher on southern than on northern slopes, and higher in the west than the east.

The permanent snow line is another limit that determines plant and animal populations. Its height varies according to summer temperatures, amount of snowfall, and exposure, fluctuating greatly even within the same range. In the central and western Himalaya the permanent snow line may be 2,000 ft. higher on a north slope than on a south slope and, in the eastern Himalaya, perhaps as much as 3,000 ft. higher on a north slope. Precipitation actually may be less on the higher peaks, and conditions are generally more severe than in temperate

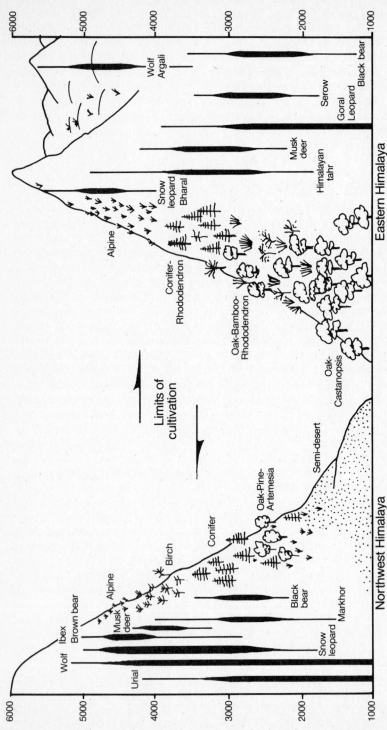

Vertical zonation of vegetation and altitudinal distribution of large mammals in the northwestern and eastern Himalaya. Altitude in meters. (Reproduced courtesy of University of Chicago Press, 1977.)

America or northern Europe, because the steep slopes and strong winds of the Himalaya usually prevent deep accumulations of snow with its moderating effect.

Five major vertical zones have been recognized, and they may be briefly described as follows:

Aeolian (snow line and higher)
Alpine (timberline to snow line)
Subalpine (a narrow transition zone)
Temperate (a broad belt)
Tropical and subtropical (warmer, low-lying belts)

The accompanying table shows how the location of each zone varies in elevation from region to region, and notes the dominant plant life of each zone. (In the table, the Temperate and Tropical/subtropical zones are further subdivided.) The elevations given in the table should serve only as a general guide, for they vary considerably as a result of exposure, soil composition, and such human influences as logging, burning, and grazing. Although the transition from one zone to the next is gradual rather than abrupt, the change may be dramatic: even in the dead of winter you may find grasshoppers active on a south-facing slope, while a north-facing slope a few feet away lies deep in snow.

Aeolian Zone

The permanent snow line is considered the lower limit to this zone. Flowering plants are absent here, and life is limited to bacteria, fungi, insects, and crustaceans that subsist upon airborne food particles blown up from below by the wind. Much ground is exposed, because snow seldom accumulates evenly. Lichens encrust rocks, and spiders, springtails, and glacier fleas are able to survive in protected microclimates among the rocks and in the soil. Jumping spiders have been found at the 22,000-ft. level on Mount Everest, presumably preying upon other insects that live beneath the snow or that are blown there by the wind. Microorganisms have even been found in soil sampled from the very top of Mt. Everest. At the 19,000-ft. level, temporary glacial pools in the eastern Himalaya are known to support large populations of fairy shrimp. And birds and mammals are occasional though transient visitors; the snow leopard, for example, may use high passes to move from one valley to another, and such flocking birds as snow pigeons and cloughs frolic in the thermals. Some birds may rest on high cols as they migrate across the Himalaya, although their flights are usually nonstop.

Alpine Zone

The alpine zone extends from the timberline to the snow line. It is a zone characterized by harsh winters, short summers, shallow soils, strong winds, and a lack of moisture. At the upper limits of vegetation, a few pioneering rock plants grow in sheltered places—beneath rocky ledges and beside protective boulders—where they form small cushions. Typical plants include the stonecrops and rock jasmines, which have basal rosettes of succulent leaves, and the drabas or stoneworts with their densely matted, cushion-like stems. *Stellaria decumbens* has been found at 20,130 ft. and is reputedly the highest plant in the world. Delicate purple or red primroses are often seen flowering immediately

Simplified Vertical Zonations of Vegetation in the Himalaya

Northwest	West	East-Central
Aoelian zone Lower limit unknown Bacteria, fungi, lichens	Aeolian zone 15,000 ft. and higher Bacteria, fungi, lichens	Aeolian zone 15,000 ft. and higher Bacteria, fungi, lichens
Alpine meadows 9,600–? Pioneer plants	Alpine meadows 11,700–15,000 ft. Pioneer plants	Alpine meadows 11,400–15,000 ft. Pioneer plants
Subalpine scrub 9,000–11,400 ft. Birch, juniper, sagebrush	Subalpine scrub 10,200–12,000 ft. Birch, juniper, fir, rhododendron, willow	Subalpine scrub 10,200–12,000 ft. Birch, juniper, rhododendron
Temperate coniferous forest 6,000–10,200 ft. Blue pine, Himalayan edible pine, West Himalayan fir	Temperate coniferous forest 7,500–10,500 ft. Deodar (Himalayan) cedar, East Himalayan fir, Himalayan hemlock, blue pine, cypress	Conifer-rhododendron forest 7,500–10,500 ft. Hemlock, East Himalayan fir, spruce
Forest and sage steppe 6,000–8,400 ft. Oak, chir (long-leafed) pine, sagebrush	Temperate mixed forest 6,000–9,000 ft. Oak, deodar (Himalayan cedar), spruce, West Himalayan fir, blue pine	Temperate evergreen forest 4,500–7,500 ft. Oak, rhododendron, magnolia, maple*
Subtropical semidesert scrub 1,800–6,000 ft. *Capparis, Pistacia,* wild olive	Pine forests 2,700–6,000 ft. Chir (long-leafed) pine	Subtropical montane forest 2,400–4,500 ft. *Chilaune,* chestnut, oak, alder
Subtropical thorn 1,800 ft. Acacia, *Zizyphus*	Subtropical thorn 2,400 ft. Acacia, *Bauhinia, Albizzia*	Tropical evergreen rain forest 150–2,400 ft. Sal, *Bauhinia, Terminilia*

*Chir pine belt dominates in central Himalaya.

adjacent to melting snow. The plants are typically widely scattered and, unless they are in bloom, easily overlooked. The Alpine zone also supports such plants as the eidelweiss or sow's ear, having fuzzy, hairy leaves and a tufted, or clustered, growth pattern (adaptations to the scarcity of water in a form available to plants).

In sedge and grass meadows, wildflowers often form spectacular displays. These profusions of color are greatest where snowmelt collects and where deeper soils have developed over the ages. Some species bloom into late summer, especially at higher elevations and on more exposed sites. Anyone familiar with the mountain flora of North America or Europe will recognize many genera: there are buttercups, anemones, larkspurs, everlasting flowers, asters, dandelions, thistles, saxifrages, cinquefoils, louseworts, geraniums, lilies, and gentians. The diversity is staggering; in Nepal alone more than 67 species of primrose occur, many of them in the alpine zone. Worth looking for are the sky blue *Meconopsis* poppy—the so-called queen of Himalayan flowers— and the delicate purple gentians and poisonous monkshood. Carpets of wildflowers are all the more remarkable in the northwestern Himalaya where soils are absent or thin and water very precious. Small and vulnerable "hanging" alpine meadows relieve the otherwise barren landscape of this region.

Alpine scrub is found along streams and in U-shaped valleys. Typical species include the *Cotoneaster*, a rigid and much-branched shrub that produces an abundance of red berries in the fall; *Caragana*, a member of the pea family that bears thorns and is widespread in central Asia; *Ephedra* or mormon tea; rose; and several species of procumbent (a flattened growth form) rhododendrons and junipers. This community is characteristic of the dry valleys behind the main range, such as Dolpo, Ladakh, and large parts of Tibet.

The high Deosai Plains of Baltistan are vegetated by sagebrush and willow, with moist grassy meadows along the watercourses. In contrast, the alpine zone in Ladakh has very little plant life and virtually no trees, except those people have planted and the odd, stunted juniper that grows in protected places. All plants in this region are adapted to conditions of extreme dryness. Much of the Karakoram consists either of barren scree or arid steppe in which sagebrush is the chief ingredient.

The animals found in the alpine zone tend to be of Eurasian origin, with pre-existing adaptations to the severe conditions of northern latitudes. Typical mammals include the bharal, pikas, marmots, red foxes, weasels, voles, and mice. Lynx, wolves, and brown bears are found near the Tibetan border, and in this zone in the western Himalaya the ibex is a characteristic ungulate. Many species of birds breed in the grassy meadows, and there is the occasional snake or lizard.

Subalpine Zone

The subalpine zone is most accurately considered a transition between the temperate coniferous forest and the alpine belt, in effect delineating the timberline. Stunted, wind-blown birch, juniper, and rhododendron characterize this zone, except in the northwest, which has, instead of rhododendron, sagebrush, poplar, and willow. Fir, pine, or spruce trees are interspersed with these shrubs, and some north-facing slopes support pure birch forests. Birch is easily identified by its pale, peeling bark, which in times past provided the main source of paper.

The birch forest and scrub of the subalpine zone are vital habi-tat for the arboreal birch mouse and the dwindling population of musk deer.

Temperate Zone

Below an elevation of 12,000 ft. is a more or less continuous forest belt. Conifers such as fir, hemlock, pine, cypress, and cedar occupy the higher levels. Undergrowth is sparse in most places, consisting of rho-dodendron, a variety of shrubs, and, in the east, bamboo. In Bhutan, Sikkim, and as far west as central Nepal, a lush, temperate evergreen forest grows between elevations of 3,000 to 5,000 ft. Almost pure stands of evergreen oaks are interspersed with laurels, chestnuts, maples, magnolias, and other trees that rarely exceed 60 ft. in height. In spring the forest is ablaze with white magnolia and white, pink, or red rhodo-dendron blossoms. Mosses and lichens clothe every oak, and numerous orchids and other epiphytes add to the "cloud forest" setting. These forests are frequently shrouded in mist, and they may be remarkably cool even in summer. Some of the steeper slopes support almost pure stands of alder, a tree with deciduous branches that break off easily and lack the moss festoons so characteristic of the oaks in the area. Alders seem to invade areas prone to landsliding and probably play a vital role in stabilizing areas that have slid. Numerous wildflowers, ferns, and orchids occur, especially in moist ravines and near streams. Look for yellow balsams, purple violets, touch-me-nots, begonias, and Solo-mon's seals. The flora and fauna of this temperate-zone belt are truly Himalayan in composition, but they have been little explored, cata-logued, or described.

In west Nepal, Kumaon, and parts of Kashmir, the temperate forests consist mainly of oak, blue pine, and West Himalayan fir with some deodar cedar. Magnolias are absent, rhododendrons sparse, and maples occur primarily near streams or along cool northerly slopes. Farther west yet, the coniferous forests at the same elevation are patchy and steppe-like with such species as oak and sage in the understory.

The northwestern Himalaya is semiarid to arid at this altitudinal zone. Forests, if present, are small and scattered. There are few conifers, and the barren landscape is dominated by shrubs.

The Himalaya is famous for its variety of "rose-trees"—rhododen-drons. The greatest number of species are found in Bhutan and Sikkim. About 29 species are found in Nepal, and most of these are east of Kathmandu. (One, *Rhododendron arboreum*, is the national flower of Nepal.) Rhododendrons range from trees 45 ft. tall to low creeping shrubs and even epiphytic climbers. Flower color is not a reliable means of identification, for a single species can exhibit shades from white and pale pinks to scarlet. The displays are best seen between late March and early May.

Conifers become increasingly abundant as one climbs higher. In the west, the forests are dominated by the five-needled blue pine (*Pinus excelsa*) and the West Himalayan fir (*Abies pindrow*), a species with a smooth silvery bark. Other trees include the famous deodar, a magnificent Himalayan cedar that grows as high as 150 ft. with a girth of 35 ft. Also look for the West Himalayan spruce (*Picea smithiana*), with its flattened leaves (in contrast to the needle-like leaves of firs) and pendulant cones. Spruce branches droop conspicuously. The East Himalayan fir (*Abies spectabilis*) is found from Kashmir to Bhutan but is most abundant in central Nepal and westward. It is differentiated from its western cousin by its rough, fissured bark and lower leaf surfaces that have two dark bands rather than one. Another pine, the Himalayan edible pine (*Pinus gerardiana*) provides food for people in the Hindu Kush and parts of the Karakoram; the seeds, which are protected by thick scales, contain much oil. The leaves occur in clusters of three. Yet another pine that is found in almost pure stands in the central and western Himalaya—the long-leafed or chir pine (*Pinus roxburghii*)—is best distinguished by its long, light-green leaves (in bundles of three) and deeply fissured bark. This relatively fire-tolerant fir is common in west Nepal at elevations of 2,700 to 6,000 ft. On limestone outcrops you may well find dense stands of Himalayan cypress.

Spruce and hemlock are more likely to be found on cool, moist, north-facing slopes, especially in the drier parts of the Himalaya (for example, north of the Annapurna and Dhaulagiri massifs). Larches are found only from central Nepal eastward, while the Himalayan cypress occurs only west of the Kanjiroba Himal of Nepal. Junipers are characteristic of the more arid higher elevations throughout the Himalaya, although they are more common in the alpine or subalpine belts.

The fauna of the temperate zone is diverse and in many respects rather unique. Large mammals include the serow, goral, the takin of Sikkim, Burma, and China, and the Himalayan tahr. At lower elevations macaque monkeys forage on the ground; the langur monkey, which spends much of its time in trees, is found up to around the 12,000-ft. level. Less frequently seen wildlife include Himalayan black bears, forest leopards, yellow-throated martens, red pandas, and a number of small cats. There are numerous small rodents, from wood mice to flying squirrels. And frogs, toads, and snakes, few of which are catalogued, also occur. But the greatest variety is in the avifauna. Most trekkers will attest to mysterious and wonderful calls from birds heard but not seen. The presence of trees, shrubs, and ground vegetation provides many foraging niches for birds that would otherwise compete with one another. Laughing thrushes, babblers, and minias flit about the ground and tangled brush, while nuthatches and tree creepers comb conifer branches for food. Tits and warblers forage among the foliage, and woodpeckers work on dead or dying trees. If you sit quietly on a trailside log, you'll be well rewarded for your patience. Many species will come close enough for you to see without field glasses.

Tropical and Subtropical Zones

Tropical forests occupy the hills bordering the lowlands of the eastern and central Himalaya. The canopy is composed of many deciduous and evergreen hardwoods, including bauhinia and teak, although sal (*Shorea robusta*) is the major species. Its large, rounded leaves, 6 to 10 inches long and a shiny yellowish green, make it an easy species to identify. Although never quite leafless, sal sheds much of its foliage during the dry season. Its flowers are yellow, and it is an important timber and fodder species. Until recently, sal trees formed an almost continuous forest belt along the base of the Himalaya, but in many areas branches have been repeatedly lopped off and the leaves collected for firewood and livestock feed, with the result that the sal's form is typically straight and gaunt. The shrubs, bamboos, palms, and ferns that cover the forest floor decrease in density as you move west so that the sal forest becomes increasingly parklike, until it is replaced by thorn scrub in India and Pakistan. Among the arid scrubs, acacia, *Zizyphus*, and other thorny species dominate.

The tropical forests give way to subtropical montane forests at about the 4,500-ft. elevation in the eastern region. Common trees include the chestnut (*Castanopsis*) with yellow flowers and spiny acorn-like fruits; *Schima*—locally called *chilauni*—which has fragrant white flowers and a nutlike fruit; and in west Nepal, the horse chestnut and walnut. Oaks are also abundant, and alders grow along drainages and on recent landslide scars.

West of Nepal's Karnali River are almost monotypic stands of long-leafed pine, which at higher elevations merges with oak forests. The pines are sometimes 100 ft. tall, and, without an understory of shrubs or vines, the forest has a parklike appearance. Most trees bear witness to past wildfires, to which this pine is specially adapted.

The subtropical fauna is decidedly Indian in composition. For example, this zone, like much of India, has chital deer, tigers, water buffalos, and hog deer, and in times past there were elephants. However, unless you make a special trip to a reserve such as the Chitwan, you are unlikely to see these animals. And because most of these animals are not truly Himalayan, they will not be discussed further.

Himalayan Fauna

Mammals

Langur monkeys, Himalayan orange-bellied squirrels, pikas, and marmots are the mammals most commonly seen on a trek. Many hikers remark on the paucity of large animals, and certainly the water buffalos or yaks you see will be domestic rather than wild ones; except perhaps in the bleak northern desert of Tibet, the wild yak belongs to history. Wild sheep and goats now face a similar demise, as the growing human population in the mountains continues to eliminate these species' habitat and to hunt their remaining members. Because they are on the decline, it is not wise to purchase any wild animal skins or horns—it may in fact be illegal to do so (and impossible to import without a special permit). To see a Himalayan tahr or the urial now, you must go either to a national park or one of the few remaining sparsely populated valleys of the Himalaya.

A few of the larger or more conspicuous mammals you may find on a trek are listed below with brief descriptions. Except where stated otherwise, the species occur throughout the Himalayan chain.

Serow (*Capricornis serow*). Goatlike, standing about 3½ ft. at the shoulder, with a stocky body, thick neck, large head and ears, and short limbs. Horns stout and conical, pointed backwards, and present in both sexes. Color generally black or reddish chestnut with white on limbs. Inhabits forests and wooded gorges, using cliffs for escape. Usually solitary. Found at 6,000–10,000 feet.

Goral (*Nemorhaedus goral*). A common inhabitant of the south-facing slopes of the Himalaya to as high as the 14,000-ft. level in Nepal. Stands about 2 ft. high at the shoulder. Horns short, pointed, and present in both sexes. Color variable, but usually greyish. Solitary, but may be seen in groups of up to five. Usually the goral waits until you are nearly upon it before fleeing—bounding uphill in a zigzag route and disappearing quickly.

Muntjac, or Barking Deer (*Muntiacus muntjak*). Found at lower elevations in montane forest. Recognized by its reddish brown body

Tibetan yak.

with short, dainty legs. The distinctive dog-like bark may be repeated at regular intervals. Partial to rocky, wooded ravines.

Himalayan Tahr (*Hemitragus jemlahicus*). A large, handsome goat that is very partial to the steepest cliffs. Males stand about 3 ft. high at the shoulder and sport large, shaggy shoulder ruffs that are straw colored, contrasting with the black or coppery brown body color. Horns are about 12 inches, close set and curving backward. Females lack the ruff and are much smaller. Tahr are found within a narrow band of land along the southern slopes of the Himalaya from west Kashmir to Sikkim. Readily seen in the cliffs above Langtang village in the Langtang National Park of Nepal.

Bharal (*Pseudois nayaur*). Sheeplike in appearance, the bharal exhibits the behavior of a goat. Males stand about 3 ft. high at the shoulder and are best identified by their slaty blue body color, black flank stripes, and dark chests. Cylindrical horms curve outwards; in older animals, tips are directed backward. Females lack stripes and have thin horns. Bharal are an essentially Tibetan species found north of the main range from Zanskar to Bhutan. Easily seen in India's Nanda Devi Sanctuary, near Shey Gomba in Nepal, and north of Annapurna at the Thorong Pass. Bharal are an important item in the diet of snow leopards.

Urial or Shapu (*Ovis orientalis*). A sheep found in the large river valleys of the Karakoram and the Indus drainage, preferring gently rolling to steeply rolling terrain, up to the 14,000-ft. level (though usually found much lower). A large animal, greyish in color with a long black chest ruff and white bib. Horns massive and strongly corrugated, forming an open half circle that turns inward at the end. Often seen at the lower end of such valleys as the Braldu, Shigar, and Shyok. Now much depleted.

Ibex (*Capra ibex sibirica*). Easily identified by the large scimitar horns and beard so characteristic of the goat genus. Females lack the beard and have smaller horns; males stand about 40 inches at the shoulder. Ibex have a strong predilection for the steepest cliffs. They are excellent climbers, though easily killed by hunters in the winter when deep snows hinder their movements. They spend summers at 16,000 ft. or higher if grassy hanging meadows are available, and their escape is always to cliffs. The most widespread ungulate of the mountains of Pakistan, occurring as far east as the Sutlej River of India.

Markhor (*Capra falconeri*). Another wild goat, with a straight or flaring set of corkscrew horns, a flowing, whitish-grey ruff, and a dark flank stripe. Very localized occurrence in Chitral, Gilgit, Astor, and Indus areas. They live in herds like urial and ibex. Essentially an inhabitant of the low-lying cliffs that receive little moisture and support a dry, shrubby vegetation.

Musk Deer (*Moschus chrysogaster*). The musk deer or kasturi is a primitive deer about as large as a medium-size dog. It has large, rounded ears, no visible tail, and an arched back with long hind limbs. The male sports long upper canines or tusks and has a highly prized musk gland, the contents of which is literally worth its weight in gold. Musk deer are solitary and shy most of the time, and you are more likely to see piles of their droppings than catch a glimpse of an animal. They prefer birch forests and scrub in the upper temperate zone and the alpine zones. Local people hunt them with dogs, snares, and poisoned spears, and for some villagers they provide a major source of income.

Primates. Langurs (*Presbytis entellis*) are long-limbed, long-tailed grey monkeys with distinctive black faces. They live in troops of as many as 50 and are the most commonly seen species in the Himalaya. Like the Rhesus macaque (*Macaca mulata*), this species is sacred to many Himalayan peoples, and even the monkeys that raid agricultural fields are not killed. The rhesus macaque occurs at lower elevations and is brownish red, has a squat form with short limbs, and spends much of its time on the ground. Often seen in towns and villages.

Spotted Cats. If you are exceptionally lucky, you may see a forest leopard (*Panthera pandus*) while hiking through a forest, or even the legendary snow leopard (*P. uncia*) while traversing a high meadow. Either is rarely seen, of course, but to find their sign along the trail is possible—look for the tracks in the snow or mud, and areas scraped bare with droppings nearby. The large cat tracks winding through a village at about 7,000 ft. probably belong to a forest leopard (looking for dogs to eat!). Those seen at the 12,000-ft. level and away from forests probably belong to the snow leopard or the lynx. The forest leopard may weigh as much as 150 pounds and usually inhabits forests lower than 10,000 feet.

Almost nothing is known about the habits of the beautiful snow leopard. This elusive cat can melt away unseen, and invariably spots the human intruder first. Its pelt is smoky grey with a tinge of yellow, its spots forming open rosettes. Best identified by its 3-ft.-long tail and its size—about that of a large dog. Snow leopards rarely descend into the coniferous forest belt and are most frequently glimpsed north of the main Himalaya along the Tibetan border. Ibex and bharal are primary food items in large parts of their range, but with the depletion of native ungulates, snow leopards have turned to livestock for sustenance. This almost guarantees them a short life. Generally solitary, they rarely number more than a half dozen in a particular valley complex.

The lynx (*Lynx lynx*) inhabits the barren uplands of Ladakh, the Karakoram, and Tibet, avoiding forests and deep valleys. Several other species of small cat also dwell in the Himalaya, but you are not likely to encounter them. One of these, the clouded leopard (*Neofelis nebulosa*), is restricted to the lush tropical and semitropical forests from Nepal eastward. It has a marbled appearance and a magnificent coat.

Large Indian Civet (*Viverra zibetha*). May be seen in forests and scrub at low elevations. About 30 inches in length with black and white striped tail and two white throat patches. Short legs, silvery grey fur.

Red Fox (*Vulpes fulva*). Its sign is often seen, because the red fox tends to use the same trails people do. Fairly shy, but not infrequently observed by trekkers. Preys on small rodents, such as pikas and voles. In appearance the same as the European or North American red fox.

Dhole, Jackal, and Wolf (*Canis alpinus, Canis aureus, and Canis lupus*). Jackals and dholes are larger than foxes, with black-tipped tails. The dhole, or Indian wild dog, is the larger of the two and is best identified by its bushy tail and black cheek patch. Both are widely distributed in the Himalaya, but are nonetheless rare. The familiar wolf may be seen in small packs in Zanskar, Hunza, Dolpo, and other border areas. Because wolves kill many domestic animals in some areas, they are often shot or trapped by villagers.

Bears. Three species occur, but you are most likely to see the brown bear (*Ursus arctos*) and the Himalayan black bear (*Selenarctos thibetanus*). The brown bear inhabits alpine or subalpine meadows and scrub in areas bordering Tibet. Its pelage (fur) is sandy or reddish brown and it has a conspicuous hump of longish hair over the shoulder. Uses forefeet for digging out bulbs, grass, and the occasional marmot. The Himalayan black bear is a denizen of temperate forests at elevations of 4,000–12,000 feet. Black in color with a conspicuous cream-colored V on the chest. If you visit the lowlands you may see the sloth bear (*Melursus ursinus*). Give all bears plenty of room—every year locals are severely mauled by bears disturbed intentionally or accidentally.

Martens and Weasels. Species are too numerous for all to be described. The stone marten (*Marves foina*) inhabits the higher mountain steppe, avoiding forests; forests are the primary domain of the Himalayan yellow-throated marten (*M. flavigula*), which, as its name denotes, is yellow throated. Their pelts are greatly prized for making hats. The weasel (*Mustela*) is a small, slender animal with a sinuous body. Frequently bold and inquisitive, a weasel may approach a quietly sitting person. Feeds on voles and other small rodents, and occurs throughout the Himalaya, usually in or near meadows and brush fields.

Red Panda (*Ailurus fulgens*). The red or lesser panda of the eastern Himalaya is easily recognized by its white face, dark eye patches, rich chestnut back, dark limbs, and faintly ringed tail. It's rarely seen but worth keeping an eye out for reclining on a branch.

Pika (*Ochotona*). This delightful relative of the hare is easily found amongst rocks and along mani walls above the tree line. Also known as the mouse-hare, the pika has a short muzzle, rounded ears, and no visible tail. They live in loose colonies, spending summer days collecting grass and forbs, which they store under rocks for the winter. Will allow you to approach closely.

Marmot. Marmots live in large colonies, excavating deep burrows in which they hibernate during the winter. Feed outside burrows during summer. Give loud whistles when sighting an intruder. Most commonly encountered above timberline. The Himalayan marmot (*Marmota bobak*) is about 2 ft. long with a 5-inch tail and occurs along the Tibetan Plateau through the Himalaya. The long-tailed marmot (*M. candata*), whose tail exceeds one-third of its head-body length, has a rich golden-orange pelage. Found in the wetter areas of Pakistan and

Kashmir; common on the Deosai Plains.

Yeti (Abominable Snowman to some). Protected by the government of Nepal, the yeti has yet to be classified by scientists. Since its possible presence was first reported by British Resident Brian Hodgson in 1832, accounts of this ape have been numerous in eastern Nepal and occasionally as far west as the Karakoram (though its existence there is even more open to question). In 1951 mountaineer Eric Shipton took pictures of yeti tracks on the Menlung Glacier, near Everest; these pictures are now considered the "type photos" of the yeti's apelike footprints. Eyewitness accounts generally describe the yeti as a stocky ape 5 ft. or taller with coarse reddish or greyish brown fur, and having a large head with a pointed crown, hairless face, and robust jaw. Its arms reach to the knees, and it moves bipedally with a shuffling gait. If the yeti exists, and some of the available evidence is tantalizing, it probably does so in the dense montane forests of the middle elevations. Presumably it uses high passes to move from one valley to another. But more tangible evidence, in the form of scats, hair, or a conclusive photograph, is needed to decide whether this creature is real or a fancy of the human imagination.

Birds

The Himalaya is an ornithological paradise: Nepal has more than 800 species, and Sikkim and Bhutan many more. Depending upon whose tally one takes, this compares favorably with the 1,200 to 1,800 species found in the entire Indian subcontinent. The abundance of birdlife reflects the diversity of life zones and habitats, as well as the central position of the Himalaya between two major biogeographical zones; the Kali Gandaki River of Nepal is usually considered the dividing line between the eastern and western avifauna. Himalayan birdlife was virtually terra incognita until recently. When Nepal opened to outsiders in the early 1950s, several species new to science were discovered, and the habitat of the spiny babbler, a common bird, was finally determined.

Visitors from Europe and America may recognize a few species from home: the golden eagle and house wren, for example. However, the vast majority of species will be new, sporting such names as crested serpent eagle, large-necklaced laughing thrush, golden-backed three-toed woodpecker, satyr tragopan, hoary barwing, Tibetan twite, white-capped river chat, Hodgson's frogmouth, Mrs. Gould's sunbird, and Guldenstadt's redstart. Birds can be seen even at the highest elevations, and many migrate over the Himalaya. Mountaineers have encountered choughs at 27,000 ft., heard snipes flying over the highest peaks at night, marvelled at geese returning from their Tibetan breeding grounds, and found dead birds on windy cols.

With one of the field guides that have recently been published and a pair of lightweight binoculars, novice and expert alike can look forward to many hours of exquisite bird-watching. If you are interested in numbers, you can expect to enumerate lists at least as long as those back home, even restricting yourself to narrow altitudinal ranges. For the serious ornithologist, summer and spring are the best times to visit the Himalaya because birds are in their breeding plumages and generally much more approachable. You can spend hours watching rose finches, accentors, pipits, and many others amid carpets of alpine wildflowers. However, a word of caution: because of late storms or the monsoon's arrival it may be wet and, at high elevations, cold.

For those trekkers without benefit of binoculars or field guide, opportunities for observing and appreciating are still ample. Most will surely sight a lammergeier—the bearded vulture—as it glides low over Bhotia villages and across knife-edged ridges, or will flush an Impeyan pheasant on its downhill race. A few of the birds you may see are very briefly described below according to their preferred habitat. This introduction obviously cannot mention more than a few, nor can the descriptions provided allow identification of any species with certainty. The emphasis here is on alerting you to birds that are widespread and of prominent size, color, or behavioral features.

Alpine Meadows and Slopes

Impeyan Pheasant (Danphe) (*Lophophorus impejanus*). Nepal's national bird of nine iridescent colors. Invariably glides noisily downhill when disturbed. A heavy bird, the male is easily recognized by its white rump and tan tail. The female is a nondescript brown bird with a white rump. Found on steep grassy or rocky slopes or in winter fir forests.

Snow Cocks. Giant partridges that escape by running uphill. Feed in groups and found as high as 18,000 feet. The Tibetan snow cock (*Tetraogallus tibetanus*) is brownish with white underparts, while the Himalayan snow cock (*T. himalayensis*) is grey with rufous neck streaks and a chestnut chest band. Cannot be mistaken for the snow partridge (*Lerwa lerwa*), which is much smaller and barred grey and white.

Rose Finches (*Carpodacus* spp). Gregarious small birds with thick bills and notched tails that are among the most common breeders in alpine meadows. Many species; most brownish with crimson or reddish breasts in males.

Accentors (*Prunella* spp). Sparrow-like ground-feeding birds with long square tails. They hop about. Many species; most grey or brownish with dark face mask.

Grandala (*Grandala coelicolor*). Unmistakable glistening blue robin of steep rocky slopes well above tree line.

Redstarts (*Phoenicurus* spp). Robinlike birds with dark heads and chests and chestnut brown abdomens and tails.

Pipits and Wagtails. Long-legged birds partial to grassy meadows. Pipits (*Anthus* spp) are heavily streaked, while wagtails (*Motacilla* spp) have whitish or yellow breasts and constantly pump their tails.

Streamside Habitats (Above 8,000 Feet)

Ibisbill (*Ibidorhyncha struthersii*). Large grey bird with prominent, decurved bill that breeds in glaciated valleys. Bobs head and tail.

Forktails. Black and white birds with forked tails. The spotted forktail (*Enicurus maculatus*) has a spotted back and a long tail that it lifts up and down slowly. The little forktail (*E. scouleri*) is a small bird seen moving amongst rocks in rushing streams.

Plumbeous Redstart (*Rhyacornis fuliginosus*). Tame, slaty blue bird that constantly moves its tail up and down. Female with conspicuous rump, male with rufous (reddish) tail.

Dippers. Plump birds that feed by walking underwater. The white-breasted dipper (*Cinculus cinculus*) has a white throat and breast; the brown dipper (*C. pallasii*) is all chocolate brown. Both bob up and down while standing on rocks.

White-Capped River Chat (*Chaimarrornis leucocephalus*). Black and maroon bird with white cap, seen skimming from rock to rock. Also pumps tail.

Oak and Conifer Forests

Blood Pheasant (*Ithaginis cruentus*). Pheasant with coral red legs found east of Dhaulagiri. Quite tame near Tengboche Monastery.

Tragopan Pheasants (*Tragopan* spp). Brilliant crimson pheasants with blue and black faces found in dense forests.

Great Himalayan Barbet (*Megalaima virens*). Green, brown, and dark blue with large yellow bill and red beneath tail. Several may gather at a fruiting tree.

Himalayan Jay (*Garrulus glandarius*). Medium-size gregarious bird that has a white rump obvious in flight. Lacks the dark crest of the blue-throated jay, which occurs in oak forests.

Yellow-Billed Blue Magpie (*Cissa flavirostris*). Yellow bill and long blue tail distinguish this bird from its lowland cousin that has a red bill.

Himalayan Tree Pie (*Dendrocitta formosae*). Noisy bird that feeds in scattered parties. Recognized by its dark grey body and white wing patch. The closely related nutcracker (*Nucifraga caryocatactes*) of pine and fir forests is a large dark bird that continuously flicks its tail, showing white patches.

Minivets (*Pericrocotus* spp). Brightly colored (red, orange, or yellow) long-tailed birds seen feeding amid dense foliage.

Bulbuls. Robin-size crested birds that perch conspicuously on trees and shrubs. The red-vented bulbul (*Pycnonotus cafer*) is found at lower elevations, often in gardens. Note the red patch under its tail. The black bulbul (*Hypsipetes madagasciensis*) has a bright coral red bill and feeds in excited parties that keep up a constant chatter.

Laughing Thrushes. Noisy, myna-size birds; prefer areas of dense vegetation; form large feeding parties. Many species. The white-throated laughing thrush (*Garrulax albogularis*) is olive brown with a large throat patch. The white-crested (*G. leucolophus*) has a "turban" and a brown eye streak. The white-spotted (*G. ocellatus*) is profusely spotted with white. The striated (*G. striatus*) is rich cinnamon with narrow white streaks and is usually found in shady ravines.

Black-Capped Sibia (*Heterophasia capistrata*). Common, light-rufous bird with dark head and crest that is raised upon alarm. Jerks tail up and down, and has a beautiful clear whistle.

Blue-Headed Rock Thrush (*Monticola cinclorhynchus*). Usually found in pine forests and open shady places. The male is an outstanding cobalt blue and orange with a white wing patch evident in flight.

Mountain Thrushes (*Zoothera* spp). Common inhabitant of fir forests and small forest glades. Brown or olive brown with heavily spotted breast and abdomen. Spends much time on the ground.

Whistling Thrush (*Myiophoneus caeruleus*). Blue-black bird with bright yellow bill, often seen near rushing streams and deep cover. Song (consisting of sustained silvery notes at dawn) penetrates above sound of waterfall.

Coal Tits (*Parus* spp). Minute black birds with white cheek patches and dark crests.

Scarlet Finch (*Haematospiza sipahi*). Male a brilliant scarlet with brown wings and tail; seen in heavy forest at low elevations.

Not mentioned are the cuckoos, flycatchers, warblers, leaf warblers, bush robins, nuthatches, woodpeckers, and creepers. Some are extremely numerous and so often sighted; many are difficult to identify without field guide and glasses; and others are simply inconspicuous.

Other Common Species

Soaring birds likely to be seen are the lammergeier or bearded vulture (*Gypaetus barbatus*), with its 9-ft. wingspan and long, wedge-shaped tail; the Himalayan griffin vulture (*Gyps himalayensis*); the golden eagle (*Aquila chrysaetos*), recognizable by the white wing patches and white at the base of the tail that distinguishes it from the steppe eagle; and a variety of buteos or buzzards that have rounded wings and fan-shaped tails. In winter, grey or brown harriers (*Circus* spp) can be seen hovering over open areas.

Fast-flying kestrels and other falcons literally streak by, while snow pigeons (*Columba leuconota*) wheel about in large flocks and feed in open fields like the common rock dove. Snow pigeons have pale necks and abdomens. Near villages you will see ravens or crows, the common myna (*Acridotheres tristis*), house sparrows (*Passer domesticus*), and swifts. The raven (*Corvus corax*) is a large black crow with an unmistakable call: "gorak . . . gorak." Crows (*Corvus* spp) are small and lack the shaggy throat feathers of the raven. Choughs fly about in very large flocks; there are two species, the yellow-billed (*Pyrrhocorax graculus*) and the red-billed (*P. pyrrhocorax*).

Look as well for ducks, geese, and cranes flying over in spring and fall. High mountain lakes provide resting sites for waterfowl, though few species breed there.

Reptiles and Amphibians

Although some 70 species of reptiles and amphibians inhabit Nepal, only 30 of these are typically found in the mountains. Of these, less than a dozen are found above 8,000 or 9,000 ft. Amphibians, like frogs and toads, occur primarily in the tropical zone and the warmer, lower, temperate forest belts, although some live in hot springs at amazingly high altitudes. The number of species also declines as you move westward to the Karakoram. Salamanders are rare, but were recently discovered in the forests of east Nepal. If you are observant, you may find the Himalayan rock lizard, the *Agama* (males have orange heads with bright blue throats), the long-legged *Japalura* lizard of brushy slopes, or the skink species *Leiolopisma ladacense*, which holds the record for being the highest lizard in the world, found at 18,000 ft.

Unless you visit the hot and humid lowlands, or know where to look, you are unlikely to find any snakes in the Himalaya regions. Typical snakes include the rat snakes and racers, which are fast moving with large eyes, slender necks, and broad heads; water snakes, which are, indeed, partial to the aquatic environment; and the mountain pit vipers, which are uniformly dark with triangular heads. Most of the snakes are nonpoisonous. The cobra is occasionally encountered at low elevations. The only other venomous species are pit vipers; fortunately, they too are relatively rare and virtually never seen.

Although they have not been studied in Sikkim and Bhutan, it is likely that numerous species of reptiles and amphibians thrive in the favorable conditions found there.

Appendix A

Map Information

*My experience of mountains is that
the longest way round is the shortest way there.*
Laurens Van Der Post, 1952

The maps in this book are meant primarily for general orientation and as aids for interpreting the descriptions of treks. In nearly all cases, this book's maps, while drawn to scale, lack sufficient detail to be relied on for routefinding.

The best overall series of maps covering the Himalaya outside Tibet is the U.S. Army Map Service (AMS) U502 Series. These maps have a scale of almost 4 mi. to the inch (1:250,000) and a contour interval of 250 or 500 ft., depending on the sheet. The U502 Series was completed prior to 1960, so it does not have current road information, but otherwise the maps are generally accurate in most areas excepting Zanskar and the high mountain regions of northern Nepal. Copies of maps from the U502 Series must be ordered from the Library of Congress, Geography and Map Division, Washington, D.C. 20540 (at a minimum of $7.00 per sheet plus postage). Write first for an index to the series. Better quality reproductions of some, not all, U502 sheets can be ordered from foreign map houses, including Stanford's, Geo Center, and Libreria Alpina (addresses are given at the end of this appendix). Most reproduction copies need to be highlighted: try to emphasize the ridge lines and principal rivers with marking pencils of different colors.

The U502 sheets are the only currently available maps that, taken together, cover the entire Himalaya at such a large scale. Other good maps covering smaller portions of the Himalaya have been made, however. First, let's note the best single map of the Himalaya, a 1:4,000,000 sheet entitled "Indian Subcontinent" that is published by John Bartholomew & Son, Ltd., of England. This map, in Bartholomew's "World Travel Series," is widely distributed and available at most large map stores.

Two atlas-size books published in Japan by Gakushukenkusha, Ltd. (Gakken) contain many large-scale maps of areas covered in this book. The two books are part of a series, "Mountaineering Maps of the World." Edited by Ichiro Yoshizawa, the individual volumes are titled *Himalaya* (1977) and *Karakorum, Hindu-Kush, Pamir and Tien Shan* (1978). Each of these books has a text in Japanese and color photographs. These volumes have, respectively, 23 and 25 two-page shaded relief maps that cover many Himalayan regions. The books can be difficult to locate but when found their maps can be copied for use in the field and are particularly useful for areas with the highest concentrations of peaks.

A series of 18 three-color maps at 1:200,000 scale by various cartographers that depict the Hindu Kush, Karakoram, and parts of the Himalaya (as far east as Garhwal) were published in Japan between 1972 and 1977. These sheets are available from either Geo Center or Libreria Alpina.

Two excellent but very expensive maps of the Garhwal region in India are available with a contour interval of 100 meters and a scale of 1:150,000. These sheets, published in 1978 by Ernst Huber, are named Garhwal-Himalaya-Ost and Garhwal-Himalaya-West. The ost (east) sheet covers the Nanda Devi area, and the west sheet covers from Mussoorie east to Joshimath, including the four sacred pilgrimage places of Yamnotri, Gangotri, Kedarnath, and Badrinath. These two maps can be purchased from German map houses.

An extremely accurate series of maps covering the mountainous areas of both India and Nepal with a contour interval of 100 meters at a scale of one inch to the mile (1:63,360) has been printed by the Survey of India. These excellent maps are highly restricted, and though they are coveted by many they are unlikely ever to become generally available.

One of the best series of maps covering a limited portion of the Himalaya is the set of sheets being edited by the Research Scheme Nepal Himalaya and printed in Vienna, Austria by Kartographische Anstalt Freytag-Berndt und Artaria. These sheets of eastern Nepal are often called the Schneider maps after Erwin Schneider, who supervised the fieldwork and mapmaking. These excellent maps have a scale of 1:50,000 and a contour interval of 40 meters. So far seven sheets have been published and two are in production. The sheets available are: Kathmandu Valley; Lapche Kang (which covers the area from the northern stretch of the road to Lhasa to the western end of the Rolwaling Valley); Rolwaling Himal (covers the Rolwaling Valley); Tamba Kosi–Likhu Khola (covers the middle portion of the trek to Khumbu); Khumbu Himal (covers the entire Khumbu region); Shorong/Hinku (covers the area south of the Khumbu Himal map—the upper Hinku and most of the upper Hongu valleys); and Dudh Kosi (covers the area south of the Shorong/Hinku sheet). Sheets due to be released soon are the Langtang/Jugal Himal sheet and the Khumbakarna Himal sheet that covers the area east of Khumbu (and the Shorong/Hinku sheet) as far as the Arun River.

A map of Sikkim by Pradyumna Karan at the scale of 1:150,000 was published in 1969 by the Association of American Geographers. This map can be ordered for $3.00 by writing to the Program Director of Geography, George Mason University, Fairfax, Virginia, 22030.

Other goods maps of specific areas have been published. The following sources will send lists or catalogues of the maps they sell.

Ordering maps takes time, so begin the process several months in advance to allow time for correspondence.

Stanford International Map Centre
12–14 Long Acre
London WC2E 9LP
England

    Sells some U502 sheets (inexpensive and excellent reproductions) and the Schneider maps of eastern Nepal.

Geo Center GmbH
Honigwiesenstrasse 25
Postfach 80 08 30
D–700 Stuttgart 80
West Germany

    One of the biggest map houses; it also sells some books.

Geo Buch
8000 München 2
Rosental 6
West Germany

    A large map house and book seller.

Libreria Alpina
Via C. Coronedi-Berti, 4
40137 Bologna
Zona 3705 Italy

    Excellently stocked map and book seller.

Appendix B

Staying Healthy

Most people trek for weeks in the Himalaya without experiencing any serious health problems, while a very few hikers barely cross the first ridge without having difficulties. This appendix is designed to help you prevent or treat the most common medical problems you are likely to face while trekking. For complete information on symptoms and treatment of nearly any conceivable malady, consult the bibliography for additional reading, with emphasis on *Medicine for Mountaineering*.

Before You Leave

Read the first section of Chapter 2, on "General Preparation," which stresses the need for vigorous pretrek conditioning and lists the immunizations that you should get before you set off. Being in good physical conditon is vital, because, above all else, trekking is a strenuous activity; and, getting the proper immunizations further ensures your health in Asia. Having physical and dental exams before leaving is also strongly recommended. Take a good medical kit along. The suggested contents of such a kit are listed at the end of this appendix.

On the Trail

Rule Number One is to *walk carefully*. In the "Notes for the Trail" section of Chapter 3 the bent-knee method of walking downhill is suggested. Take short steps when descending, and land with your knee bent to avoid the painful condition called Sahib's Knee. And keep your eye on the trail while you are hiking: walk when you walk and look when you look. Combining the two activities has abruptly halted far too many treks.

The second cardinal rule is to *keep your strength up*. It is essential to eat enough proper food to avoid becoming run down. People on group treks who have Western-style food can tend to forego eating properly, but so can those who are consuming an unaccustomed local diet. If you are eating dalbhat (lentils and rice) or wheatcakes as your staple, keep stuffing them in; these foods have sufficient protein and calories only if you consume enough. Likewise, you need to drink enough liquid (usually tea or iodine-treated water) to keep urine volume greater than a pint a day—particularly at high altitudes, where dehydration can occur quickly. At high elevations you may need to force your liquid intake; in the thin atmosphere, your body can quickly become low in fluid because so much vapor is lost through increased respiration. If you find you are continually fatigued during a long trek, stop and camp earlier in the day.

Food and Drink

Since the most common malady on the trail is either diarrhea or the more serious dysentery, it is important to prevent their occurrence by observing good hygiene and consuming only uncontaminated food and liquids. Small changes in food and water can cause mild "traveler's diarrhea," which soon disappears, but the culprit that activates severe gastrointestinal problems is different. Food and water containing minute amounts of human or animal feces are the primary sources of severe stomach or intestinal trouble: dysentery. The best rule of thumb for avoiding the fecal-oral contamination cycle is: *peel it, boil it, or forget it*.

Let's discuss liquids first. The two sure ways of making certain that water is pure enough to drink safely are to boil it for 10 minutes (longer at high elevations) or to treat it with iodine. Drink only water that you have actually seen boiled for a sufficient period of time. It is not enough to have someone's assurances that water has been boiled.

There are three forms of iodine that can be used to make water safe for consumption. The most convenient is the tablet. In the chemical formulation of tetraglycine hydroperiodide, iodine tablets can be purchased from large outdoor-supply houses. Add one (two if the water is cloudy) to a liter or quart of water and allow the solution to stand for 15 to 20 minutes—longer with very cold water. Keep the bottle of tablets tightly capped or they will rapidly lose potency.

You may also purchase a 2 percent tincture of iodine solution in a dropper bottle. Add eight drops of the tincture to a quart or liter of water and wait 15 to 20 minutes before drinking.

The third method is to use USP-grade resublimed iodine. Resublimed iodine can be difficult to obtain because it is a poison, but it is not harmful in the minute amounts used in solution to disinfect water. Buy four to eight grams of the resublimed iodine crystals and put them in a clear one-ounce glass bottle with a hard plastic screw cap. To use them, fill the bottle with water and shake it to facilitate the saturation process. Then pour half the saturated solution (about 12.5 cc) into a quart (or liter) container of water to be treated, and wait 15 minutes before drinking. The bottle with the iodine crystals can be refilled and used as many as a thousand times.

Before you leave home, try using iodine for water purification to be certain that you are not allergic to it. People with hyperthyroidism should talk with their physician before using any iodine purification method. Alternate methods such as halazone exist; however iodine kills the amoebic cysts that cause dysentery, whereas chlorine and halazone do not.

As to food, remember the "peel it, boil it" stricture. Eat only recently cooked food and avoid all fresh fruits and vegetables that cannot be peeled. Milk will be safe if it is brought to the boiling point before drinking. Sometimes people get sick not from the food they eat but from the container the food or drink is served in. Use your own cup at tea houses where the sanitation may be suspect.

Gastrointestinal Problems

Gut trouble is the big one. Sooner or later on a long trek most people get the runs, despite taking the precautions noted above. Diarrhea is both more common and less severe than dysentery. At the outset, however, it can be difficult to determine which of the two afflictions you are suffering from and what treatment is called for, from benign neglect to a five-day cycle of antibiotics. If you have several loose stools a day that do not contain mucus or blood and you do not have cramps and are not nauseous, then the diarrhea should subside within a few days. In any case, keep drinking plenty of liquids to replace what is being lost, and slow your pace. Mix a few pinches of salt in the water or tea you drink to help with fluid retention (and add sugar for taste, if you wish).

Since in the hills it is impossible to accurately diagnose gastrointestinal difficulties, it can be difficult to determine the most effective but least gut-wrenching remedy. Cramps can often be relieved with Lomotil, paregoric, tincture of opium, or codeine—all relatively benign in small doses. Such drugs as Mexaform, Flagyl, Intero-Vioform and anti-diarrhea tablets containing streptomycin (Renocab and Strepto-magma) are readily available in India and Nepal. All of these nostrums are considered by many authorities to be either ineffective or to have dangerous side effects (or both). Despite being warned about using Mexaform, I have used it with good effect to treat *Giardia Lamblia*, an intestinal parasite that can produce vomiting, stomach gas, "rotten egg" burps, and explosive yellow stools. *Giardia* is not uncommon and, unfortunately, its symptoms are similar to those of dysentery. However, it is probably advisable to try Mexaform before resorting to the more elaborate treatment for dysentery. The dosage for Mexaform is two tablets, then one tablet three times a day until symptoms disappear— usually within one day.

If you believe that you have dysentery with its accompanying fever, weakness, vomiting, and with blood, mucus, or both in your stools, the treatment suggested by many health manuals is a 20-capsule cycle of an antibiotic, such as ampicillin or tetracycline. Begin with 2 capsules (or tablets) and take one every six hours for five days. Flagyl, despite having been shown to be carcinogenic in mice, continues to be recommended by some authorities for acute amoebic dysentery. The adult dosage is three 250-mg tablets three times daily for a minimum of five days. You must avoid alcohol while using Flagyl.

Sunburn

Avoid the sometimes extreme effects of the sun by using an umbrella (the best covering) or wearing a wide-brimmed hat, and by using an effective lotion to block the sun's rays. If you walk on snow, you will need a protective sunscreen with a "sun protection factor" (SPF) of fifteen. Remember, when you walk on snow, to coat all exposed skin surfaces; reflected radiation can burn your lips and even inside your nostrils. Wear high-altitude goggles if you will be on snow for long.

Altitude Sickness

Altitude sickness results from decreased amounts of oxygen in the blood owing to the lower atmospheric pressure at higher elevations. A very few people begin to experience difficulties as low as 8,000 ft., especially if they have flown or driven to that altitude and then begun to exercise. Most people notice at least a mild headache by the time they reach 14,000 feet.

It is difficult to predict who is likely to suffer from altitude sickness. Sex is not a determinant; nor is age between about 25 and 60. Physical condition is important to good altitude adjustment, but often people who are fit ascend too rapidly for their systems to adjust. And sometimes people experience the unpleasant symptoms associated with altitude sickness although they have climbed high in previous years without difficulty.

The main way to prevent altitude sickness is to walk up to higher elevations rather than being conveyed there. And make your ascent gradually; conservative but experienced sources suggest that, above 10,000 ft., you should limit the increase in the elevation at which you sleep to an additional 1,000 ft. to 1,500 ft. daily. Many people will be able to exceed this amount, others will not. You can exceed the recommended limit in the course of taking day hikes—but return to lower elevations to camp, for it is the altitude where you sleep that is most important to acclimatization. The rule is: Walk high; sleep low.

Be particularly careful to drink plenty of liquids while higher than 10,000 ft.; dehydration, which may predispose you to altitude sickness, can occur easily at high elevation. Keep nourishing yourself adequately and try to adhere to a high carbohydrate regimen: eat those taters! Studies have shown that a diet of 70 to 80 percent carbohydrates may reduce symptoms of acute altitude sickness. Also, avoid heavy exertion if you are suffering from the altitude. Rest for a day, or take easy walks. Exhaustion is one of the factors that can help bring on altitude sickness. And, when you are walking at upper elevations, use a rest step.

What are the symptoms of altitude sickness? Rather than one or two, usually a group of symptoms begins to appear as a person gains altitude. These symptoms vary in intensity and in the elevations at which they appear, depending on the individual experiencing them. The predominant characteristic associated with maladaption to altitude is headache. Usually a headache appears in the evening after a long day of ascending. The headache should go away by the following morning. If you have a headache that is not relieved in the morning, consider resting for a day, especially if several other symptoms are manifested in conjunction with the headache. The principal symptoms that accompany the onset of altitude sickness are:

Headache and weakness

Sleeplessness, often accompanied by irregular breathing, particularly at night

Swelling (edema), particularly about the eyes or fingers

Slight loss of coordination (ataxia); it can be mild or severe, depending on the degree of altitude sickness

Dry cough

Mild nausea

Loss of appetite

If you experience a few of these symptoms and they are not severe, you have only a mild case of altitude sickness. Sleep can be difficult at an unfamiliar high altitude; to wake up at night gasping for breath is a sign of irregular breathing and not serious, albeit frightening. I have found that propping up my head at night helps to relieve the "I'm drowning" anxiety. Often facial swelling (edema) that appears in the morning will decrease as the day progresses. Again, note that if the symptoms you or a friend undergo are a mild annoyance, then you should rest until the symptoms subside, before continuing upward slowly. If the symptoms become more severe or do not disappear after a night's sleep, then you should descend until you feel well.

Here are some of the symptoms of severe altitude sickness:

Severe headache

Marked loss of coordination; walking as if intoxicated

Difficulty in breathing even at rest; serious shortness of breath with mild activity

Severe nausea and vomiting

Extreme lassitude (on a trek, this is expressed as a complete loss of desire for food and a disinclination to care for oneself or talk to others)

Abnormal speech and behavior progressing to delirium and coma

Bubbly breath or persistant coughing spasms, particularly coughs that produce watery or colored sputum

Less than a pint of urine secreted in a day (indicating fluid retention)

The basic treatment for severe altitude sickness is immediate descent: altitude sickness can progress rapidly once it becomes serious. When any combination of the symptoms of severity occur, the person afflicted should descend immediately from 1,000 to 3,000 ft., the distance increasing with the extent of the symptoms. The descent may even have to take place at night. An affected person should never return down-valley alone but should be accompanied by someone in good condition. If at all possible, a severely disabled person should be carried down, by a pack animal or a sturdy person. Once severe symptoms of altitude sickness are displayed, time is of the essence; and sometimes a person with altitude sickness will have to be coaxed or ordered to descend. The familiar "I'll be all right, this will go away" attitude does not hold with acute altitude sickness. Even professional athletes and physicians have died in the Himalaya from altitude sickness. Don't assume that *anyone* is immune. Acetazolamide (Diamox) has been used effectively both to prevent and treat altitude sickness. (The adult dosage is one 250-mg tablet twice a day.)

Severe altitude sickness affects few trekkers. Most of us know when to stop and head back down. This brief discussion of altitude sickness is meant to point out the danger signs for those who do experience the severe symptoms, and to note the mild symptoms for the majority of us so that we will not become unduly alarmed.

A Suggested Medical Kit

You will want to take along a small medical kit, although most of its contents will probably remain untouched for the duration of the trek. Minimally, carry iodine tablets, aspirin, an antidiarrheal, and 20 or 40 tablets or capsules (enough for one or two five-day cycles) of a broad-spectrum antibiotic such as tetracycline. I have trekked for weeks using only iodine and antidiarrhea tablets, but you would be wise to be prepared with more than that. Although you might get by with as few items as the four noted above, a more prudent list of what to take would include the items below. If you want to do a physical examination or attempt to diagnose ailments or set fractures, again, the best reference is *Medicine for Mountaineering* (see the bibliography), but note that the book is heavy to tote along.

The asterisked items in the following list have previously been mentioned in the "Compleat List" found in Chapter 2; they are repeated here for emphasis.

Iodine. Use tablets, tincture of iodine solution, or USP-grade resublimed iodine as noted above in "Food and Drink" for purification of water.

Sunscreen. Protect yourself from the strong sun with a lotion having a sun protection factor (SPF) of 12 or higher; 15 or higher if you expect to walk on snow.

Insect repellent. A preparation containing at least 33 percent N, N-diethyl-metatoluamide is best.

Malaria tablets. Chloroquin, if you will be in tropical areas during the monsoon.

Moleskin or elastoplast. As blister protection.

Adhesive tape and gauze. To keep blisters from forming and for cuts.

Elastic bandage. Best for binding strains or sprains.

Aspirin. Or acetaminophen, for aches and colds.

Nasal drops or spray. At high altitudes, your nasal passages often need to be unclogged.

Diazepam (Valium). Good for the flight over or any all-night bus rides. Take one 5-mg or 10-mg tablet to aid the onset of sleep.

Antihistamine. If you have any difficulty with hay fever. A widely used antihistamine found in many over-the-counter drugs is chlorpheniramine. This is also useful for alleviating cold symptoms.

Decongestant. Decongestant tablets may be helpful at elevations above 10,000 to 12,000 ft. if you find, as I do, that your eustachian tubes become blocked.

Cough drops. Medicated cough drops (of a strength for which you would need a prescription in the United States) can be purchased in large towns in Asia. These cough drops help relieve the cough trekkers commonly get at high elevations. Hard candy can help with the dry throat many people get at upper elevations. Codeine (30 mg) is also used to treat stubborn coughs—take one tablet.

Gastrointestinal medicines. See the section earlier in this appendix for comments on some drugs that will treat gastrointestinal problems.

Antibiotics. Tetracycline, penicillin, and ampicillin are the most commonly used broad-spectrum antibiotics. Cephalosporin is a particularly broad-spectrum antibiotic. Once treatment is begun with one of these antibiotics, it should be continued for five days: two tablets (or capsules) to start, then one tablet every six hours.

Ophthalmic ointment. For conjunctivitis caused by smoke in homes or dust-ladened wind. Avoid eye ointments containing steroids, penicillin, or any antibiotic you may take internally. Apply ointment beneath the lower eyelid.

Special medicines. Any you normally need.

Bibliography

The books and articles in this bibliography are only a small fraction of those available about the Himalayan ranges and the people who inhabit or have visited these mountains. Most of the works listed are recently published and, given access to a well-stocked library, should not be difficult to locate. You can find more information about nearly every area mentioned in this guidebook from one or more of the titles below. If your interest continues to grow, you can vastly expand your list of sources from the bibliographies in the books you read.

The Himalaya in General

Braham, Trevor. *Himalayan Odyssey*. London: George Allen & Unwin, Ltd., 1974.
From Chitral to Sikkim, the author has his eyes on the peaks, but he does make some comments on the approaches as well.

Cleare, John. *The World Guide to Mountains and Mountaineering*. London: Mayflower Books, 1979.
Facts about peaks, passes, access, maps, and references, intelligibly presented. Cleare picks up at the snowline where this guidebook leaves off. Fifty pages of the book describe the Himalaya.

Keay, John. *Into India*. London: John Murray, 1973.
Good, anecdotal cross-cultural insights that aid in making some sense of South Asia.

Longstaff, Tom. *This My Voyage*. New York: Charles Scribners, 1950.
Good suggestions on routes in Garhwal, Baltistan, and the Gilgit River Valleys by an early master of the small expedition.

Mason, Kenneth. *Abode of Snow*. New York: E. P. Dutton & Co., 1955.
The basic history of Himalayan exploration and mountaineering.

Mehta, Ved. *Portrait of India*. New York: Farrar, Straus and Giroux, 1970.
Excellent cross-cultural anecdotes; has a substantial section on the Himalaya.

Nicholson, Nigel. *The Himalayas*. Amsterdam: Time-Life International, 1975.
Some interesting sketches of various Himalayan regions.

Shipton, Eric. *That Untravelled World*. London: Hodder and Stoughton, 1969.
Superb writing by a master of the small expedition, about Baltistan, Garhwal, Hunza, and elsewhere.

Singh, Madanjeet. *Himalayan Art*. New York: The Macmillan Company, 1968.
An overview of wall painting and sculpture from Ladakh to Bhutan. Contains many photographs; the text is often quite technical.

Thesiger, Wilfred. *The Last Nomad*. New York: E. P. Dutton, 1980.
Although this book is only about the Himalaya in part, Thesiger does tell how to travel in Asia. He traveled at length and quickly developed a fine attitude about how to approach remote peoples and places. Excellent photographs.

Tichy, Herbert. *Himalaya*. Translated by Richard Rickett and David Streatfeild. Vienna: Anton Schroll & Co., 1970.
Accounts in snatches of voyages by Tichy and others from Chitral to Assam. Tichy has a good feel for the land and people.

The Eastern Hindu Kush and Karakoram

Fairly, Jean. *The Lion River: The Indus*. New York: The John Day Company, 1975.
Factual account of the mighty Indus and the peoples on its shores.

Hurley, James. "The People of Baltistan." *Natural History*, Oct. 1961 (pp. 19–27) and Nov. 1961 (pp. 56–69).
Excellent information on Baltistan and its people in this two-part article.

Keay, John. *The Gilgit Game*. Hamden: Archon Books, 1979.
Interesting narrative of exploration in the Gilgit River Valleys during the latter half of the last century.

Keay, John. *When Men and Mountains Meet*. London: John Murray, 1977.
Well-wrought history of European exploration in the Karakoram Range and Kashmir from 1820 to 1875.

Mariani, Fosco. *Where Four Worlds Meet*. Translated by Peter Green. London: Hamish Hamilton, 1964.
Well-written account of an expedition in Chitral. Tells of an excursion to the Kalash Valleys (long before tourism and the Afghan refugee influx).

Newby, Eric. *A Short Walk in the Hindu Kush*. London: Secker and Warburg, Ltd., 1958; New York: Penguin Books, 1981.
A humorous account of trekking in Nuristan, Afghanistan. Find this one— it's a must.

Rowell, Galen. *In the Throne Room of the Mountain Gods*. San Francisco: Sierra Club Books, 1977.
Photographs of the Baltoro Glacier that make you want to forget everything and see the place. The text about the Baltoro is very informative.

Schomberg, R. C. F. *Between the Oxus and the Indus*. London: Martin Hopkinson, 1935.
Useful background information on early travel in the Gilgit River tributaries.

Shor, Jean Bowie. *After You, Marco Polo*. New York: McGraw Hill, 1955.
An attempt to retrace Marco Polo's route; some facts on Hunza as it used to be.

The Western and Central Himalaya

Barrett, Robert LeMoyne and Katherine Barrett. *The Himalayan Letters of Gypsy Davy and Lady Ba*. Cambridge: W. Heffer and Sons, 1927.
A poetic tale of a year's travels in Ladakh and Baltistan. Hard to find, but very informative about the way things were.

Deacock, Antonia. *No Purdah in Padam*. London: George G. Harrap, 1960.
An insightful narrative of the first women's overland journey from England to Zanskar, in 1958.

Douglas, William O. *Beyond the High Himalayas*. Garden City: Doubleday and Co., 1952.
A discerning account of a 1951 trip from Kulu to Leh. Brief mention of Hunza.

Govinda, Lama Anagarika. *The Way of the White Clouds*. Berkeley: Shambhala, 1971.
A man who was born in the West and eventually became an initiated lama describes his travels in Ladakh and Tibet with many insights into Tibetan Buddhism.

Heim, Arnold and August Gansser. *The Throne of the Gods.* New York: Macmillan, 1939.
The best book on Garhwal and vicinity, with many excellent photographs. They traveled light and really saw the country. Contains accounts of a visit to Mt. Kailas in Tibet and the Tinkar Valley in Nepal.

Murray, W. H. *The Scottish Himalayan Expedition.* London: J. M. Dent & Sons, 1951.
A perceptive book; the Scots enjoyed the locals and describe well the areas traversed. Lots of information about Garhwal.

Pallis, Marco. *Peaks and Lamas.* Third edition. London: The Woburn Press, 1974.
Much anecdotal and well-written information on Tibetan Buddhism with an account of visits to Sikkim and Ladakh in 1936.

Snellgrove, David L. and Tadeusz Skorupski. *The Cultural Heritage of Ladakh, Vol 1.* Boulder: Prajna Press, 1977.
Excellent, authoritative data about the Indus Valley in Ladakh. Many photographs.

Snellgrove, David L. and Tadeusz Skorupski. *The Cultural Heritage of Ladakh, Vol 2.* London: Aris and Phillips, 1981.
Covers the monasteries in Zanskar.

Nepal and the Eastern Himalaya

Bernbaum, Edwin. *The Way to Shambhala.* New York: Anchor Press, 1980.
The inner and outer quest for "hidden valleys" as symbolized in the Buddhist concept of Shambhala.

Bista, Dor Bahadur. *People of Nepal.* Second Edition. Kathmandu: Ratna Pustak Bhandar, 1972.
The best book about the many clans inhabiting Nepal, by Nepal's foremost anthropologist.

Downs, Hugh R. *Rhythms of a Himalayan Village.* New York: Harper and Row, 1980.
A sensitive account in photographs and words of life in a Sherpa village by a person who stayed for two years in the area depicted.

Gurung, Harka. *Vignettes of Nepal.* Kathmandu: Sajha Prakashan, 1980.
Detailed descriptions of many remote areas in Nepal by an extremely knowledgeable native son.

Hagen, Toni. *Nepal.* Third edition. Berne: Kümmerley and Frey, 1971.
A classic book on Nepal. Superb photographs by the author who has still probably seen more of the country than anyone else.

Hagen, Toni, Gunter-Oskar Dyhrenfurth, Christoph von Fürer-Haimendorf, and Erwin Schneider. *Mount Everest: Formation, Population and Exploration of the Everest Region.* Translated by E. Noel Bowman. London: Oxford University Press, 1963.
All the background you want about Khumbu by four eminent scholars.

Jest, Corneille. *Tarap, une vallée dans l'himalaya.* Paris: Seuil, 1974.
Superb documentary photographs of the Tarap Valley in Dolpo. The text is in French.

Kazami, Takehide. *The Himalayas, A Journey to Nepal.* Tokyo: Kodansha Intl., 1968.
Still one of the best inexpensive collections of color photographs on Nepal.

Matthiessen, Peter. *The Snow Leopard.* New York: Bantam Books, 1979.

Along with Schaller's *Stones of Silence* (see "Natural History" section), one of the few recent accounts about a visit to Dolpo.

Olschak, Blanche C. and Ursula and August Gansser. *Bhutan*. New York: Stein and Day, 1971.
Traditional Bhutan; a book with excellent photographs.

Snellgrove, David L. *Himalayan Pilgrimage*. Boulder: Prajna Press, 1981.
Snellgrove's insights make this "scholar's travelbook" of a trip in Dolpo and northern Nepal a very special book. Many trail facts are included.

Tilman, H. W. *Nepal Himalaya*. Cambridge: Cambridge University Press, 1952.
Amusing, well-written account of early trips into the Nyeshang and Langtang regions of Nepal.

Tucci, Giuseppe. *Nepal, the Discovery of the Malla*. New York: E. P. Dutton, 1962.
Account of a trip from Pokhara to Jumla through the Barbung Valley.

Von Fürer-Haimendorf, Christoph. *Himalayan Traders*. New York: St. Martin's Press, 1975.
Dry but very informative account of people in northern border regions of Nepal.

Guidebooks

Armington, Stan. *Trekking in the Himalayas*. South Yarra, Australia: Lonely Planet, 1979.
A misleading title, for the book gives good, detailed descriptions of only a few regions in Nepal. Written basically for people on an organized group trek.

Bezruchka, Stephen. *A Guide to Trekking in Nepal*. Fourth edition. Seattle: The Mountaineers, 1981.
The best trekking guide to Nepal. Packed with detailed, accurate information.

Iozawa, Tomoya. *Trekking in the Himalayas*. Tokyo: Yama-Kei Publishers, 1979.
Good color photographs and maps of some specific areas in India and Nepal. Spotty text.

Kleinert, Christian. *Nepal Trekking*. Munich: Bergverlag Rudolf Rother, 1976.
Informative summaries of various treks in Nepal. Excellent fold-out panoramic photographs.

Raj, Prakash A. *Kathmandu and the Kingdom of Nepal*. South Yarra, Australia: Lonely Planet, 1980.
A fine guide to the Kathmandu Valley in particular.

Rieffel, Robert. *Nepal Namaste*. Kathmandu: Sahayogi Prakashan, 1981.
A good overall guide to Nepal, but hard to locate out-of-country.

Schettler, Margret and Rolf Schettler. *Kashmir, Ladakh and Zanskar*. South Yarra, Australia: Lonely Planet, 1981.
A general guide to Kashmir and Ladakh. Includes some trekking information.

Natural History

Ali, Salim. *Field Guide to the Birds of the Eastern Himalaya*. New Delhi: Oxford University Press, 1977.

Covers Sikkim and Bhutan, describing 535 species and illustrating 366. Detailed natural history information.

Cronin, Edward W., Jr. *The Arun: A Natural History of the World's Deepest Valley.* Boston: Houghton Mifflin, 1979.
Informative account of natural history in the Arun Valley.

Fleming, Robert L., Sr., Robert L. Fleming, Jr., and Lain S. Bangdel. *Birds of Nepal.* Bombay: Vakil and Sons, 1979.
Compact field guide describing about 800 species, including some from Kashmir and Sikkim. Definitely the best available, but has some misleading illustrations.

Hooker, J. D. *Himalayan Journals.* London, 1854 (available in reprint editions).
Account by the first botanist to visit the Himalaya and study it in depth.

Jackson, Rodney. "Aboriginal Hunting in West Nepal with Reference to Musk Deer and Snow Leopard." *Biological Conservation*, Vol. 16, No. 1, pp. 63–72.
Report of the author's field study in the Langu Valley of West Nepal.

Majupuria, Trilok C., editor. *Wild Is Beautiful.* Kathmandu: S. Devi, 1981.
A very useful introduction to the fauna of Nepal, written by Nepalese experts. Also covers conservation and general natural history. Available in Kathmandu bookstores.

Mierow, Dorothy and Tirtha Bahadur Strestha. *Himalayan Flowers and Trees.* Kathmandu: Sahayogi Press, 1978.
Portable guide with many color photographs of trees, shrubs, and wildflowers of Nepal. Well worth taking along.

Mishra, Hemante and Dorothy Mierow. *The Wild Animals of Nepal.* Kathmandu: Ratna Pustak Bhandar, 1976.
Drawings and brief descriptions of Nepal's mammals.

Schaller, George B. *Mountain Monarchs: Wild Sheep and Goats of the Himalaya.* Chicago: University of Chicago Press, 1977.
Detailed facts about Himalayan sheep and goats. Technical but readable.

Schaller, George B. *Stones of Silence: Journeys in the Himalaya.* New York: Viking Press, 1980.
Well-written, factual information on the author's fieldwork in Chitral, Hunza, Dolpo, and the Bhote Kosi Valley.

Medical Information

Hackett, Peter. *Mountain Sickness—Prevention, Recognition and Treatment.* New York: The American Alpine Club, 1980.
The last word on altitude sickness.

Medicine for Mountaineering. Edited by James A. Wilkerson, M.D. Second edition. Seattle: The Mountaineers, 1975.
The most complete how-to medical book; covers nearly everything. Too heavy to carry in toto, however.

Staying Healthy in Asia. Edited by Anne Huckins. Stanford: Volunteers in Asia, 1979. Order from: VIA, Box 4543, Stanford, CA 94305.
Written specifically for Southeast Asia. Has much helpful information on first aid and disease diagnosis, but for treatment often says "see a doctor" (impossible in the hills). Light in weight and easy to carry.

Khowar Glossary

by John H. Mock and Hugh Swift

Khowar, the language of the Kho, is the chief language throughout the district of Chitral, though most side valleys have their own dialects and educated Chitralis also speak Urdu and Persian. Khowar is generally understood in the Kalash valleys and the Lutkoh Tehsil. Pushtu has penetrated the southern valleys. The Chitralis of Turikho are considered to speak the purest Khowar, and it is the first tongue for many in the Ghizar and Yasin valleys, which are in the Gilgit district. Khowar is an Indo-European variant that shows significant Iranian influence, and it is included in the language group known as Dardic.

To briefly sketch the grammar, Khowar has no gender. A plural is formed by adding -an to the singular. Adjectives precede nouns and show no change in gender or number. Khowar has postpositions (prepositions placed after their objects). Its verbs are mostly regular. Infinitive forms end in -ik or -ek. The present-tense endings to regular verbs are as follows. First person singular, -iman; plural, -isian. Second person singular, -isan; plural, -imian. Third person singular, -iran; plural, -inian.

The diacritical marks in the following word list indicate long vowels.

Pronouns

I awa
you tu
it, she, he (near) hess
it, she, he (far) hassa
we ispa
you (plural) pissa
they (near) hamit
they (far) hattet
me, my ma
your ta
his here
our ispa
their hattetan

Colors

black sha
blue otch
green sauz
red krūī
white ishperū
yellow zech

Relations

father tat
mother nan
brother brar
sister īspusār
husband mosh
wife bok
boy daq
girl kumoru
woman kimeri
man mosh

The Body

head sor
ear kar
eye ghech
nose niskār
blood leh
hand host

Time

morning chūchī
noon pishin
afternoon chaghnass
day anūss
midnight chūī barābar
today hanūn
yesterday dush

tomorrow   chūī
day after tomorrow   pinga
day before yesterday   otiri

Numbers

one   ī
two   jū
three   troī
four   chor
five   ponj
six   choī
seven   sat
eight   asht
nine   nyuf
ten   jush
eleven   jush ī
twelve   jush jū
twenty   bishīr
twenty-one   bishīr ī
thirty   bishīr jush
forty   jū bishīr
fifty   jū bishīr jush
sixty   troī bishīr
one hundred   ī shor

Food

apple   palogh
apricot   zhūlī
dried apricot   chambor
apricot nut   zhor
grape   dratch
mulberry   mratch
dried mulberry   kituri
pear   tang
walnut   birmogh
rice   grīnj
whole-wheat flour   peshīrū
bread   shāpik
milk   shīr
buttermilk   shatu
butter   māskah
cream   kambakh
yoghurt   machir
white cheese   shapināk
salt   trupp
egg   aiyukūn
meat   pashūr

Other Nouns

clothes   chellai
bed   zhen
blanket   zhīl
hat   khoī
Chitrali-style hat   pakol
house   dūr
fire   angār
ice   yoz
moon   mas
sun   yor
river   galogh
valley   gol
pass   ān
mountain   zom
water   ūgh
herd   rom
hemp   bong
hawk   yurj
horse   istor
cow   leshū
ibex (male)   ushūng
ibex (female)   mūrū
plain   lasht
polo field   jinali
polo   ghol
ball   plīnj
mallet   ghal o tsun
side   walti

Adjectives

all   chīk
bad   dish
beautiful   chust
big   lut
cold   ushak
good   jam
high   zhang
hot   petch
left-side   kholi
little   phūk
long   drung
right-side   hosk
sweet   shirin
many, very   bo

Verbs

be   assik

be able bīk
bring angīk
come gīk
do korīk
drink pīk
eat zhibīk
give dīk
go bīk
know, understand   hushkorīk
look lolīk
read rek
sit nishīk
sleep oreil
speak lūdīk
take ganīk

Adverbs

how kicha
when kia wat
where kura
who ka
why ko

after āchār
ahead prushti
certainly kha ma kha
now hanisen
probably albātt
slowly lash

Conjunctions

and oche
because koki

Phrases

How are you?   tu kīcha asus?
How are you?   jam taza kosi
 hau-a?
Fine, thanks.   bo jam, mehrbani.
Fine, brother, and how are you?
 jam brar-a, tu taza asūs-a?
Where are you coming from?
 kurār gītī asūs?
I don't know.   ma te malum niki.

Burushaski Glossary

by John H. Mock and Hugh Swift

Burushaski, unrelated to any other Asian language, is spoken in
Hunza and Nagir. Pronunciation varies from the Hunza side of the
valley to the Nagir side. In parts of the Yasin Valley, the closely
analogous Werchikwar is spoken, but in Gilgit and Ishkuman, Shina, a
Dardic language, is spoken.

Burushaski has four genders: male and female (human), and ani-
mate and inanimate (nonhuman). Correct sentence order places the
subject first and the verb last. Long vowels are indicated.

Pronouns

I je
you ūng
he īne
she inagus
we mī
they ne

Colors

black matum
blue shiqam
red bardum
white burūm

Relations

name īk
father ūy
mother mī
woman gūs
man hīr
boy hīles
girl dasīn
infant gīyās
shaman bī ṭan

The Body

head ya ṭis
hand rīng
heart as
ear ltumal
eye lchīn
blood multan

Time

today khūlto
tomorrow jīmale
yesterday sā ati
day after tomorrow hī pulto
day before yesterday yā bulto

Numbers

one hin
two ālto
three usko
four wālto
five tshundo
six shindo
seven talo
eight altar
nine huncho
ten torum
eleven turmahan
twelve turmalto
twenty yalta
twenty-one yaltahan
thirty altar han
forty altu walta
fifty altu walta torum
sixty ski altar
seventy ski altar torum
eighty walti altar
ninety walti altar torum

one hundred tah

Food

apple balt
*apricot ju
dried apricot bater
apricot nut hanī
large, bitter nut balanimidur
mulberry bīranch
pear phesho
walnut balring
pea garken
rice bras
barley harī
buckwheat barū
whole-wheat flour dīram
bread shapīk
inch-thick bread phiti
wide wheat cake giyāl
thick wheat bread duldunī
bread cooked in coals kemishdon
wheat cake fried in ghee
  chamūriki
milk mamū
buttermilk dīltar
butter maltash
cream iran
white cheese burūs
hard cheese rakpin
dry cheese gurūt
salt bayū
egg tīngan
meat chāp
soup dao dho
water tshil

Other Nouns

ice gamū
snow ge
valley bar
pass haguts
mountain chhīsh

*Types of apricots:
whitish, best quality, *brumdru;*
yellow, sweet, *habidru;*
very sweet, *alisakakas;*
white, *kabuli.*

river daria
lake pfarī
tree tom
stone dān
wind tish
cloud kuronch
day gunts
night thap
sun sā
moon halants
star asī
fire pfū
rope gashk
animal haiwāri
bird chīn
hawk bāz
herd dun
he-goat haldin
she-goat tshar
horse khaur
path, way gan
hat pfartsīn
house halle
tent gut

Adjectives

all yon
bad gunīkish
beautiful daltas
big ūyūm
cold chhagūrum
far mathan
good shūā
high thānum
right-side doyum
left-side gāyum
long gusanum
near asīr
new thosh
old (thing) dīganum
small jut
true tshan

very, many būt

Verbs

bathe tam delas
climb dūsas
come jūyas
do etas
drink mīnas
eat shīas
give uyas
go niyas
sit hurutas
sleep guchaiyas
speak yanas
understand henas
walk gutsharas

Adverbs

after īljī
again dā
ahead yar
here khole
how be
now mū
on foot gatal
side pachīmo
slowly thalā
there ele
therefore ītetsum
when ke
where am
why bes
who āmīn

Conjunctions and Prepositions

and ke
because beseke
but thī
with ka

Phrases

How are you? besan hal billa?

Balti Glossary

by John H. Mock and Hugh Swift

Balti is the language spoken throughout Baltistan, whose administrative center is Skardu. It is a form of Tibetan, having a classical resemblance to that language similar to Chaucer's ("whan that April with his showres soote") to today's spoken English.

On pronunciation: *ng* is nasal, pronounced like the *ng* in si*ng*ing, the letters always pronounced together, never individually. *kh, khs, ts,* and *dz* are also pronounced as one letter. Long vowels are indicated on the word list.

Balti indicates only sexual gender: the suffix *-po* indicates male, and *-mo* marks female.

Pronouns

this dyu
these dyung
that do
those dong
what chī
which go
who su

Numbers

one chīk
two ngīs
three khsūm
four bjī
five gā
six truk
seven bdun
eight bgyad
nine rgu
ten phchū
eleven chūschik
twelve chongas
thirteen chuksum
fourteen chubjī
fifteen chogā
sixteen churuk
seventeen chubdun
eighteen chubgyad
nineteen churgu
twenty ngī-shu
thirty khsum-chu
forty ngī shu ngis
fifty ngī shu ngis na phchu
sixty ngīshu khsum
seventy ngīshu khsum na phchu
eighty ngīshu bjī
ninety ngīshu bji na na phchu
one hundred bya

Time

sunday adid
monday tsandār
tuesday angāru
wednesday batu
thursday brespot
friday shukuru
saturday shingsher
dawn sharka
morning zantus
midday tro fed
early afternoon pishin
late afternoon phiro
sunset ngima nub
evening gonghin
moonrise lzod sher
night tshan
today diring
tomorrow bela
yesterday gonde
day after tomorrow snang la
day before yesterday kharchaq la

Colors

black nākpo
green sngonpo
red mārpo
white kārpo

The Body

eye mik
hand laqpa

Relations

father ata
mother ama
woman bostring
man mī
boy butsa
girl bong o
headman trang pa

Food

food zachas
rice bras
egg bjabjun
meat shā
salt payū
whole-wheat flour baq phe
barley flour nas phe
bread khurba
pea paqshan
apricot chuli
dried apricot pading
grapes rgūn
pear nguri
walnut stargah
milk oma
butter mār
whey cheese darbā

Other Nouns

snow kha
ice gang
valley lungma
mountain rī
river rgyamtsho
sun ngīma
moon lzod
rain charpha
water chhu
spring chhumik
path, way lam

clothes gonchas
shoe khafsha
hat nathing

Adjectives

beautiful rgasha
big chhogo
cold grakhmo
good lyakhmo
left khen
hot tronmo
little tshuntse
long ringmo
new sarpha
old sningma
right trang

Verbs

be yodpa
drink thungma
eat za
go shakspa
sit dukpa
speak zerba

Adverbs

here dyuwa
how chi-byase
near ngimore
when nām
where gār

Phrases

Where are you from? khyang gār
pai īn?
Who are you? khyang su īn?
Who did it? su-si byas?
At what are you looking? chī la
hlted?
What is this? dyu chī in?
Oh! what have you done? Le! chī
byas?
How is the road? lam-po chīna
yod?
How are you? chi har ba?

Ladakhi Glossary

by Helena Norberg-Hodge

Ladakhi is classified as a dialect of Tibetan, but though the two are very closely related, they are sufficiently different that Ladakhis and Tibetans often speak Hindi-Urdu with one another. The written language found in traditional (mainly religious) texts is classical Tibetan. Only in the last few years has colloquial Ladakhi been written down.

Ladakhi will seem quite difficult to start with (and it *is*), but it doesn't require much effort to learn a few words, and any effort will be rewarded ten times over. If nothing else, be sure to greet everyone with a "ju-le," and you'll see faces light up with a broad smile as they answer "ju-le" back.

Pronunciation

It would be much too complicated to give a precise phonetic rendering of the words in the glossary, so the following is nothing more than a rough sketch. (Aspirated sounds, for example, are not distinguished from non-aspirated ones. It should nonetheless be sufficient for making oneself understood.

zh is the equivalent of French 'j' as in jour

Long vowels are marked with a horizontal superscript (lō)

Accented syllables are marked with an acute accent (e.g., ku-le'-a)

Word order

Word order is as in Tibetan: subject, object, verb. Adjectives (other than demonstratives) follow the nouns they modify, and adverbs precede the verbs.

nga	specha	galla	chik	daksa	sillat.
I	book	good	one	now	am reading.

I am now reading a good book.

Verbs

The verbs can be very tricky indeed. However, by dropping the infinitive ending *-ches* and adding the following endings to the root, you should be able to get by:

-at (present and future, first person)
yong-ches   yong-at   nga yongat: I am coming.

-duk (present and future, second and third person)
yong-ches   yong-duk   khong yongduk: he is coming.

-(s)pin (past, usually first person)
yong-ches   yong-(s)pin   nga yongspin: I came

-s (past, second and third person)
yong-ches   yong-s   khong yongs: he came

Pronouns

I nga
you nye rang
he, she khong
it ibo
we (including you) ngatang
you (plural) nyerang-gun
they khong-gun
my nge
your nye-rang'-i
his, hers knong'-i
our ngazhe
their khong'-gun-i

Colors

black nak po
white kar po
red mar po
yellow serr po
blue ngon po
green ljang ku

Relations

mother a mma
father a bba
older brother a cho
older sister a che
younger brother no
younger sister nō mō
brother ming bo
sister shing mo
grandfather mē mē
grandmother a bbī

Time

day zhak
week dun' zhak
month da' wa
year lō
time (o'clock) chu-tsot'
morning nga mo, nga tok'
evening pi ttok'
day before yesterday kar tsan'-
zhak
yesterday dhang
today dring
tomorrow tō-re
day after tomorrow nangs' la

sun, daylight nyi ma
night tsan īsan

Numbers

one chik
two nyiss
three sum
four zhī
five shnga
six tuk
seven rdun
eight rgyatt
nine rgu
ten stchu
eleven chuk-shik'
twelve chuk-nyiss'
thirteen chuk-sum'
fourteen chub-zhī'
fifteen cho nga'
sixteen chu ruk'
seventeen chub dun'
eighteen chub gyatt'
nineteen chur gu'
twenty ni shu'
thirty sum-chu'
forty zhip-chu'
fifty ngap-chu'
sixty tuk-chu'
seventy rdun-chu'
eighty gyatt-chu'
ninety rgup-chu'
one hundred gya
one thousand stong chik
two thousand stong nyiss

Food

bread ta gī'
butter mar
buttermilk ta' ra
cheese (dry) chur pe'
drinking water tung chu'
food zachess, kar djī'
kerosene sa mar'
meat sha
milk ō' ma
rice dass
soup tuk' pa
sugar, sweets ka'-ra

vegetables tsod'-ma
wheat flour pak-pe'
yoghurt zhō
roasted barley flour tsam pa, ngam pe'

Other Nouns

assembly hall (in temple) du khang'
buddha sang'-gyas
buddhist nang' pa
cup ko' re
goat ra' ma
horse sta
house khang' pa
hotel don khang'
illness nat, zur'-mo
kettle ti bril
masked dances cham
medicine sman
monk ta' ba
paper shu gu'
table chog' tse
prayer mon lam'
prayer recitation yangs
prayer wall men dong'
room nang
school lop' ta
sheep luk
shoes pa' bu
spoon turr mangs'
student lop tuk'
teacher lo pon'
temple lha khang'
trail, road lam
water chu
wind lungs po'
wood shing

Adjectives

bad tsok-po
good gyall-a
beautiful rde-mo
big chen mo
small chung-un'
little nyung-un'
many mang po
cold tang mo
warm ton mo
hot tsan'-te

light yang mo
heavy ichin te
light sal po
dark mun dik'
high tonn po
low ma mo
near nye mo
far tak ring'
thin ta-mo
thick, fat rom-po
slow ku-le'-a
fast gyogs' pa
happy that po, skitt po
sad tser' ka, duk po
strong shan te, shet-chan'
breakable thol mo
easy la mo
difficult kaks po

Verbs

arrive lep' ches
buy nyo' ches
come yong' ches
cook skol' ches
do cho ches'
eat, drink don ches' (polite)
eat za' ches
drink tung' ches
leave, go cha-ches
pay skyak ches'
say zer'-ches
see thong' ches
sew tsem' ches
get sick zur' mo yong'-ches
stay, sit duk-ches, zhuk ches
   (polite)
talk spe' ra tang' ches, moll' ches
   (polite)
take nam' ches (polite)
steal shkun'-ma, shku'-ches
teach, learn lap' ches
understand ha go' ches
walk, dul' ches
watch ltat'-ches

Adverbs

early, before sngan la
later sting ne
now dak-sa

Phrases

Yes affirmative of whatever verb
is being used, e.g. ĭ′ nok

No negative of whatever verb is
being used, e.g. mā′ nok

Hello, goodby, thank you,
please ju′ le!

O.K. dig-ches ī-nok

Where are you going? nye rang′
ka′ ru skyo′ dat?

I'm going to (Leh). nga (Le)′-a
chat

How many (kilometers) to Leh?
ine′ le′-a (kilometer) tsam ī′ nok?

Hi, come in. skyo′ dang

What's your name? nye rang′ i
tsan′ la chī zhu chen?

My name is _____. nge minga′
_____ zer chen

How old are you? nye rang′ lo
tsam īn?

I'm (forty). nga lo (zhip-chu)′ īn

Where do you live? nye rang′ kā′
ru zhuk′ sat?

I live in (Leh). nga (Leh) a dū′ gat

Where do you come from? nyer
ang′ kā′ ne īn?

I'm from (America). Nga (America) ne īn

How much does a kilo of (apricots)
cost? (patting′) ki′-lo-a tsam ī′
nok?

Where can I buy _____?

_____ nyo′ sa kā′ ne yot?

Do you have any _____?
_____ zhib mo yo′ da?

How much does that cost? pene
tsam song?

That's expensive. ma rin chan′ rak

Where is the water? chu ka′ ne
yot?

Is this drinking water? ĭ′ bo tung
chu′ ī na?

The food is very good. kar ji′ ma
zhim′ po rak

Where is the path to the gomba?
gon′ pa cha′ se lam ka′ bo in?

Does this path go to (Zanskar)? i
lam′ ne (Zangskar) a lep che′ na? /
I′bo (Zanskari) lam ī′ na?

How long does it take? nyi′ ma
tsam go′ rin?

It takes (nine) days. Nyi′ ma (rgu)
go′ rin

(Two) passes must be crossed. la
(nyiss) gyab-go shen′

Do you have horses? sta yo′-da?

Yes, I have horses. sta yott

Each horse costs (forty) rupees a
day. sta re a, nyi′ me khir′ mo
(zhip chu′) cho chen′

I want a guide. nga lam gyus′ pa
chik gō′ sat

He is a very good man. mi ma
gyall′ a yot

Hindi-Urdu Glossary

by John H. Mock

　　Hindi/Urdu is the lingua franca of the subcontinent. In Pakistan
it's written in modified Arabic script and in India in Devanagari script.
　　Hindi/Urdu pronunciation includes all the sounds of English and
then some. At first the English speaker can't differentiate these sounds.
Careful listening to Hindi/Urdu speakers will clarify the spoken language. This will most likely occur only after you reach Asia. Listening

to tapes before you go can help, and of course the written script makes it totally clear.

Vowels

Hindi/Urdu has three long and short vowel pairs. Two other vowels are only long, and two are diphthongs (in which two vowels are pronounced individually yet as a unit—rolled into one, so to speak).

The pronunciation of vowels is roughly indicated by the following examples. The superscript line indicates a long vowel. *a* as in above; *ā* as in father: *i* as in sit; *ī* as in feet: *u* as in put; *ū* as in too: *o* as in ocean; *au* as in brown; *e* as in weigh; *ai* as in die.

As in French, some vowels are nasalized. The *ṅ* (with the superscript dot) indicates that the preceding vowel is nasalized.

Consonants

Listen to spoken Hindi-Urdu. That "trippingly on the tongue" quality is produced by starting the consonants *t, d,* and *r* with the tip of the tongue on the roof of the mouth. This is called a retroflex consonant and is shown with a subscript dot: *ṭ.* Otherwise, consonants are pronounced as in English.

Listen some more. That breathy feature is called aspiration. Consonants coupled with *h* (such as *ch, chh, bh, gh,* and others) are pronounced with a puff of air. Conversely, unaspirated consonants are given hardly any breath. To overstate the point: "daī hai," "dhaī hain", and dahī hai" mean, respectively, "it's the maid," "it's 2½," and "it's yoghurt."

Grammar

The verbs in the glossary are infinitives, formed by adding *nā* to the verb roots. To use these verbs, drop *nā* and add *tā hai* for the present tense or *egā* for future tense.

For example: "jānā (to go) becomes "wo jātā hai" (he goes) and "wo jāegā" (he will go).

"Hai" is an auxilliary meaning "is." It comes from "honā," the verb "to be," and its form varies according to the subject. For example: "maiṅ jātā hūṅ" (I go) could be converted to "ham, āp, wē jātē hain" (we, you, they go).

For plural subjects in the future, use -*enge*. For example: "ham, āp, wē, jāenge" (we, you, they will go).

Nouns have cases, special endings, and an oblique form. These grammatical constructions are best learned from books and in school. Suffice it here to say that verbs and adjectives agree with subject nouns. Nouns ending with a vowel end with either *ā, ī,* or *e*: adjective and verb then also end in the same vowel. For example: A woman says: "main jātī hūn" (I go). Concerning a woman, one says: "wō jāegī" (she will go). Again, about a woman: "wō lumbī hai" (she is tall), whereas about a man: "wō lumbā hai" (he is tall). Nouns are also either masculine or feminine.

In Hindi/Urdu sentence structure, the verb comes at the end. The subject is at the beginning, and adjectives precede nouns.

Colors

black   kālā
blue   nīlā
green   harā
red   lāl
white   safed

Relations

father   pitā
mother   mātā
brother   bhāi
sister   bahan
husband   pati
wife   patnī
boy   laṛkā
boy child betā
girl   laṛkī
girl child betī
woman   aurat
man   ādmī

The Body

ear   kān
eye   āṅkh
head   sir
nose   nāk
tooth   dāṅt
hand   hāth
stomach   peṭ
knee   ghūṭnā
blood   khūn

Time

o'clock, time   baje
today   āj
tomorrow kal
yesterday kal
day after tomorrow   parasoṅ
day before yesterday parasoṅ

Numbers

one   ek
1½   ḍerh
two   do
2½   ḍhāī

three tīn
four   chār
five   pāṅch
six   chhah
seven sāt
eight āṭh
nine   nau
ten   das
eleven gyārah
twelve bārah

Food

fruit   phāl
apple   seb
banana   kelā
mango   ām
orange   santarā
dried fruit mewā
date   khajūr
almond   bādām
peanut   mūṅgaphalī
vegetable sabzī
cauliflower gobhī
carrot   gājar
eggplant baiṅgan
pea   maṭar
potato   ālū
turnip   mūlī
spinach   pālak
squash   laukī
rice   chāwal
pulse   dāl
chickpea chanā
whole-wheat flour ātā
white flour maidā
bread   roṭī
milk   dūdh
butter   makkhan
cream   malāī
yoghurt   dahī
salt   namak
pepper   mirch
spice   masālā

Other Nouns

thing   chīz

bowl katorī
cup pyālā
glass gilās
metal plate thālī
saucer, china plate plet
spoon chammach
knife chākū
needle suī
thread tāgā
rope rassī
clothes kāprā
hat topī
sandal chappal
shoe jūtā
luggage samān
lock tālā
key chabī
room kamerā
bed chārpoi
blanket kambal
chair kursī
table mez
soap sābun
oil tel
kerosene mittī kā tal
candle mombattī
matches māchīs
path, way rāsta
street sarak
water pānī
mountain parbat
wind hawā
sun suraj
moon chand

Adjectives

a little thorā
ahead angalā
alive zindā
all har
angry nārāz
bad burā
bad, no good kharāb
beautiful sundar
beginning shurū
below nīchā
big barā
cheap sastā

closed band
cold thandā
dirty gandā
dry sūkhā
easy āsān
empty khālī
enough kāfī
equal barābar
excellent barhiyā
false jhūth
famous mashahūr
fat motā
finished khatam
forbidden manā
fresh tāzā
full, complete pūrā
genuine asalī
not genuine nakalī
good acchhā
happy khush
heavy bhārī
helpless mazabūr
high ūnchā
hot garam
how kaisā
hungry bhūkhā
ill bīmār
important khās
inside andar
left-side bāyān
less kam
light halkā
little chhotā
long lambā
mistaken galat
more zyādā
necessary zarūrī
new nāyā
old purānā
old person būdhā
o.k. thīk
open kholtā
ordinary māmūlī
ready taiyār
right-side dāhinā
several kaī
separate alag
straight sīdhā

strong   mazabūt
sweet   mīṭhā
true   sach
useless   bekār
very, many   bahut
weak   kamzor
well made   pakkā
not well made   kacchā
wet   gīlā
wide   chauṛā

Verbs

ask (a question)   pūchhanā
ask (for something)   māṅganā
bathe   nahānā
to be   honā
be able (can)   sakanā
bring   lānā
burn   jalanā
buy   kharīdanā
climb   charhanā
come   ānā
cut   kaṭanā
do   karanā
drink   pīnā
eat   khānā
fall   giranā
give   denā
go   jānā
hear   sunnā
know   jānanā
learn   sīkhanā
look   dekhanā
meet, be available   milanā
move   chalanā
read   parhanā
remain   rahanā
search   ḍūṅdanā
sit   baiṭhanā
sleep   sonā
speak   bolanā
take   lenā
think   sochanā
understand   samajhanā
want   chāhanā
wash   dhonā
write   likhanā

Adverbs

after   bād
after this   is ke bād
again   phir
ahead   āge
always   aksar
approximately   kharīb
behind   pīche
besides   alāvā
besides this   is ke alāvā
enough   bas
front   sāmane
in front of this   is ke sāmane
here (place)   yahāṅ
right here   yahīṅ
here (direction)   idhar
how   kaise
last   ākhir
like that, though   waise
maybe   shāyad
middle   bīch
in the middle of this   is ke bīch meṅ
near (close)   nazadīk
near (with)   pās
no   nahīṅ
now   āb
right now   abhī
on foot   paidal
outside   bāhar
side   taraf
slowly   dhīre
sometimes   kabhī
suddenly   achānak
then   tab
there   wahāṅ
right there   wahīṅ
therefore   is lie
totally   bilkul
until   tak
when   kab

Interrogatives

how   kaisā
what   kyā
when   kab
where   kahāṅ
which   kaunsā

who   kaun
why   kyoṅ

Conjunctions and Prepositions

about (concerning)   bāre
about this   is ke bāre meṅ
and   aaur
because   kyonki
but   lekin, magar
if   agar
or   yā
with   sath

Phrases

Greetings; hello or goodbye
namaste, namaskār
How are you?   kyā hāl chāl hai?
(Literally, what is your "hāl
chāl?")
And is everything o.k.?   aur sab
ṭhīk hai?
Who is he?   wo kaun hai?
He is my friend.   wo merā dost hai.
What is your name?   āp kā nām kyā
hai?
My name is John.   merā nām jān
hai.
Please tell me your name.   āp kā
nām sunaīye.
I am very pleased to meet you.   āp
se milkār bahut khūshī huī.
I am a foreigner.   maiṅ videshī
hūṅ.
I am from America.   maiṅ amerīkā
se hūṅ.
Where are you from?   āp kahāṅ se
haiṅ?
What is your work?   āp kyā kām
karte haiṅ?
They are my companions.   we
mere sātī haiṅ.
They are from America too.   we
bhī amerīkā se haiṅ.
His age is twenty.   us kī ūmar bīs
sāl kī hai.
My age is thirty.   merī ūmar tīs sāl
kī hai.

What is this?   ye kyā hai?

What is that?   wo kyā hai?
What is the name of this?   is kā
nām kyā hai?
What is the name of that?   us kā
nām kyā hai?
What is the name of this spice?   is
masālā kā nām kyā hai?
What is the name of that vegetable?   us sabzī kā nām kyā
hai?
Is there roti?   kyā, roṭī hai?
Is there hot milk?   kyā, garam
dūdh hai?
Is the milk hot?   kyā, dūdh garam
hai?
Are there bananas available?   kyā,
kele milte haiṅ?
Is there sugar available?   kyā, chinī
miltī hai?
Is tea going to be available?   kyā,
chay milegā?
Is a room going to be available?
kyā, kamerā milegā?

Where is he?   wo kahāṅ hai?
Where is he from?   wo kahāṅ se
hai?
Where is he coming from?   wo
kahāṅ se ātā hai?
Where is he going?   wo kahāṅ jātā
hai?
Where is sugar available?   chinī
kahāṅ miltī hai?
Where is tea going to be avail-
able?   chay kahāṅ milegā?
Where will he go?   wo kahāṅ
jāegā?
Which direction will he go?   wo
kidhar jāegā?
Where will we go?   ham kahāṅ
jāenge?
Which direction will we go?   ham
kidhar jāenge?
Where will the bus go?   wo bus
kahāṅ jāegā?
Will the bus go to 'Pindi?   kyā, wo
bus pindī jāegā?
Will he go?   kyā, wo jāegā?

Will you go? kyā, āp jāeṅge?

From where will the 'Pindi bus go?
pindī wālā bus kahāṅ se jāegā?

Where is the 'Pindi bus available?
pindī wālā bus kahāṅ milegā?

Where is this bus coming from? ye
bus kahāṅ se ātā hai?

When will it be? kab hogā?

When will it go? kab jāegā?

When will it be available? kab
milegā?

When is tea going to be available? chay kab milegā?

When will he go? wo kab jāegā?

When will it be finished? kab
khatam hogā?

When will you go? āp kab jāeṅge?

When will we go? ham kab
jāeṅge?

When will the Gilgit bus go? gilgit
wālā bus kab jāegā?

I am ready to go. maiṅ jāne wālā
hūṅ.

Are you ready to go? kyā, āp jāne
wāle haiṅ?

That train is just about to go. wo
gaṛī jānī wālī hai.

When will tea be ready? chay kab
taiyār hogā?

Until when will you stay? āp kab
tak raheṅge?

How long will he stay? wo kab tak
rahegā?

What time is it? kyā ṭaim hai?

What is the time now? kyā ṭaim
ho rahā hai?

By his watch what time is it? us kī
gharī par kyā ṭaim huā hai?

What does it strike? kitane baje
haiṅ?

It is one o'clock. ek bajā hai.

It's two o'clock. do baje haiṅ.

How are you? āp kaise haiṅ?

How are the bananas (more commonly, how much are the ba-

nanas?) kele kaise haiṅ?

How is this (how can this possibly
be) sugar? ye chinī kaisī hai?

What kind of a boy is he? wo kaisā
laṛkā hai?

How is that boy? wo laṛka kaisā
hai?

How does he do that? wo kaisā
kartā hai?

How will they do it? wo kaise
kareṅge?

How will we do it? ham kaise
kareṅge?

How will we go? ham kaise
jāeṅge?

Why not? kyoṅ nahīṅ?

Why will he not go? wo kyoṅ
nahīṅ jāegā?

Why won't we go? ham kyoṅ
nahīṅ jāeṅge?

How much? kitanā?

How much money? kitanā paisā?

How much was it? kitanā huā?

How much will you take? kitane
leṅge?

What is the cost of this? is kā dām
kyā hai?

What is the cost of that? is kā ki-
mat kyā hai?

What is the price of a kilo? ek kilo
[ke gī] kā dām kyā hai?

Please make it a little less. kuch
kam kījiye.

From here to there, how far is
it? yahāṅ se wahāṅ tak kitanā
dūr hai?

Go! Move! chalo!

Please go! Please move! chaliye!

Don't! mat!

Go! jāo!

Please go! jāiye!

Come! āo!

Please come! āiye!

Go, sir! chalo jī!

Listen! suno!

Please listen! suniye!

Give!   de do!
Please give!   de dījiye!
Take!   le lo!
Please take!   le lījiye!
Please give tea!   chay dījiye!
Please take money!   paisā lījiye!
Oh brother, listen!   o bhaiyo, suno!

Do like this!   aisā karo!
Don't do like that!   waisā mat karo!
Is finished; finished   khatam ho gayā
Tea is finished.   chay khatam ho gayā.

An Introduction to Spoken Nepali

by Charles Gay

As recently as 10 years ago, a village Nepali assumed that any Westerner encountered alone on the trail spoke the Nepali language. Today, on the more heavily traveled "tourist routes," this assumption is no longer made and the Nepali expects from the trekker no more than the greeting "Namaste" and the Hindi word for tea, *chai*. Indeed, the villagers and innkeepers who have had contact with trekkers now know enough "trekking English" to overcome the traveler's lack of Nepali, but they would still rather speak Nepali, so even on well-traveled routes the Westerner who makes the effort to learn any amount of the language is richly rewarded. And in the farther reaches, where a trekker still can spend days on the trail without hearing a word of English, speaking a few words is all the more beneficial in easing your way.

Since the Devanagiri script appears imposing, it is fortunate that, because signs are unknown in rural Nepal, a knowledge of the script is entirely unnecessary for the trekker. In fact the spoken language is both fun and easy to learn.

The intent here is to provide information sufficient for anyone except the serious student to acquire as much facility as he or she desires, from speaking a few words for food and shelter to forming simple sentences and understanding considerably more. Traveling with a porter or guide is an excellent way to practice Nepali, although if he speaks any English he will probably want to use that with you, instead. But your Nepali may shortly exceed his English in depth and scope anyway since, after all, you are studying the language.

Pronunciation

Nepali is an Indo-European language. Its being written in the Devanagiri or Sanskritic script means it is based on an alphabet and is not a tonal language. As in Hindi-Urdu, Nepali has consonants that are difficult for the English speaker to master; a good ear is as important as in-depth study here, and in fact, you will likely not be able to discern the difference between some aspirated and nonaspirated consonants and between some dental and retroflex consonants—not to mention be able to actually use them in speech. Nonetheless, in the fairly standard roman transliteration of this glossary, some differentiation of these sounds is made. For the trekker, more important than to be academically rigorous is to plunge right in and win friends, and then to imitate their speech. Realize, however, that most Nepali you will hear on the trail will be spoken by villagers (Tamang, Rai, Gurung, Sherpa, Magar, Newar) for whom it is a second language. The native Nepali speakers (Brahmin, Chhetri) will naturally understand you anyway.

The Vowels

Pronunciation of the romanized vowels is as follows:

a	as in "about"
aa	as in "father"
i	as in "pit" (the long *i* has a similar sound)
u	close to "input" (the long sound as in "too")
e	as in "pay"
ai	a dipthong; *a* as in "about," *i* as in "be"
o	as in "toe"
au	a dipthong; *a* as in "about," *u* as in "put"
~	denotes nasalization of a vowel sound

The Consonants

The Nepali alphabet groups the consonants into five categories according to where in the mouth they are produced. We need only be concerned with two of these distinctions, the dental and the retroflex consonants. Like several of the other consonants, these are either aspirated or unaspirated; in our transliteration, they will be followed by an *h* when aspirated. Aspiration is both hard to master and difficult to detect in native speech; make an effort to differentiate it, but not to the point of distraction. Hold your hand in front of your mouth: when you pronounce an aspirated consonant, you should feel a puff of air. The vowel sound that follows is the same whether aspirated or not.

Dental and Retroflex Consonants

The pronunciation of the romanized dental and retroflex consonants is as follows:

t	dental, unvoiced, as in tight
th	dental, unvoiced, aspirated but still hard, not like *th* in "the" (Nepali has no English-style *th* sound)
T	retroflex (tongue arched back and in contact with the roof of the mouth), as in "baaTo" (trail)
Th	retroflex, unvoiced, aspirated, as in "kaaThmaanDu"
d	dental, voiced, as in "dot"
dh	dental, voiced, aspirated, as in "dharma"

D   retroflex (with tongue as in *T*, above), voiced, as in "kaaTh-maanDu"

Dh   retroflex, voiced, aspirated, as in "Dhokaa" (door)

Listen closely to native speakers as they say the Nepali words used above. You should be able to distinguish between dental and retroflex, aspirated and nonaspirated sounds.

Other consonants that appear unaspirated and aspirated are:

k   unvoiced, as in "kite"

kh   unvoiced, aspirated, as in "khaanu" (to eat)

g   voiced, as in "gaai" (cow)

gh   voiced, aspirated, as in "ghar" (house)

ch   similar to *ch* in "church," not aspirated; this is the only exception to the *h* denoting aspiration.

chh aspirated, as in "chha" (is); no equivalent in English

j   voiced, not quite like the English *j* as in "judge"; contains an element of *z*, as in "bajaar" (bazaar).

jh   voiced, aspirated, as in "jholaa" (handbag)

p   unvoiced, as in "paani" (water)

ph   aspirated, somewhere between *p* as in "pop" and *ph* as in "photo." (Nepali has no *f*.) Used in "phohor" (dirty), for example

b   voiced, as in "baaTo" (trail)

bh   voiced, aspirated, as in "bhitra" (inside)

Other Consonants

These consonants are never aspirated:

m, l, s, h   as in English

y   almost a vowel sound, as in "yes"

r   not an *r* sound as in English—more like the rolled Spanish *r*. Used for example in "raamro" (good) and "saari" (dress)

Emphasis is normally on the first syllable of a word unless the first syllable has a short sound and the second a long vowel. For example: "raam' ro (good); but "tarkaa' ri" (vegetables).

Grammar

Not only is Nepali fun to learn, because everybody will want to help you and it often has a humorous ring, Nepali is fairly simple to learn—largely because of its spareness. No plural is necessary, typically there is no gender, and very little future tense is in common usage. Also, if you are disinclined to study the conjugations, one verb ending will get you by. The neutral, present-tense ending *-ne* is widely heard and used and is really the only verb ending needed for simple communication in Nepal. It can be used with any personal pronoun. A typical exchange might be as follows. Villager: "tapaaī kahāā jaanuhunchha?" (proper ending), meaning, "You where are going?" Trekker: "(ma) pokharaa/ maa jaane" (neutral ending), meaning, "(I) Pokhara/to am going." Therefore, you should at least be familiar with the proper verb endings that will be frequently heard.

Conjugation of simple present of *jaanu*—to go:

Pronoun	Affirmative	Negative
I ma	jaanchhu	jaanna
we haami	jaanchhaū	jaandainaū
he, she u	jaanchha	jaandaina
they uniharu	jaanchhan	jaandainan
you (familiar) timi	jaanchhau	jaandainau
you (polite) tapaaī	jaanuhunchha	jaanuhunna
he, she (polite) wahāā	jaanuhunchha	jaanuhunna

Nepalis denote a person's rank, station, or closeness by the second- and third-person pronouns and their verb endings. "Timi" is for a close friend, relative, or person of lower stature, such as a porter. "Tapaaī" is polite and connotes respect, greater age, or high caste. The same applies to "u" and "wahāā." Trekkers tend to call everyone "tapaaī," of course. And they try to verbalize "thank you" out of politeness. Nepali does not have an equivalent to our "thank you," and although "dhanyabaad" is common enough in its misuse for this purpose by Westerners, it is not natural for Nepalis. A nod of the head will suffice as thanks, and be correct.

Sentence Structure

The basic sentence is arranged subject-object-verb:

haami   bhaat   khaanchaū.
we   rice   eat.

In questions, the sentence structure remains the same. Generally raise your voice at the end of the sentence, or emphasize the appropriate word:

Jumla   jaane   baaTo   kun   ho?   (the stress is on *kun*)
Jumla   going   trail   which   is?

To answer questions, repeat the question's verb in the response:

Yo   ke   ho?   Yo   putali   ho.
This   what   is?   This   butterfly   is.

BaaTo   raamro   chha?   chha   or   chhaina
Trail   good   is?   is (yes)   or   isn't (no)

The Imperative

There is also no "please," as such, in Nepali. The polite imperative form of the verb is used, such as: "aaunos" (come), "basnos" (sit down), or "chiyaa dinos" (give tea "me" is implied). The suffix -*na* on the imperative is very polite and is close to "please," as in "aaunosna" (please come).

Ho and Chha

The verb "to be" (hunu) has two forms. They are not interchangeable. Ho (the negative is "hoina") is used for defining something or somebody.

Yo	ilaam	jaane	baaTo	ho.
This	Ilam	going to	trail	is.

Chha (the negative is chhaina) is used to locate things and people, or to state their quality.

BaaTo	raamro	chhaina,	or	BaaTo	naraamro	chha.
Trail	good	is not,	or	Trail	not good	is.

Possessives

Forming the possessive is accomplished with the suffix -*ko* added to the noun or pronoun, demarcated by a slash (/):

Yo	gaaũ/ko	naam	ke	ho?
This	village's	name	what	is?

Tapaaĩ/ko	naam	ke	ho?
Your	name	what	is?

A few important exceptions are:

mero (my), haamro (our)
timro (your, familiar)
usko (his, hers)

Prepositions

Prepositions are actually postpositions in Nepali, and also are demarcated as romanized here with a slash (/) after the noun:

maa (in, on, or to)

Bholi	ma	ghar/maa	baschhu (basne).
Tomorrow	I	house/in	will stay.

The suffix- *laai* must be attached to the subject when the verb is impersonal (see "Some Additional Grammar") and also to indicate the preposition "to":

Ma/laai	bhaat	dinos.
Me/to	rice	give.

Conversational Situations on the Trail

Life on the trail settles into a routine that encourages the repetition and mastery of several basic exchanges. With the above fundamentals in mind, and when you have heard how the language sounds, the following phrases and vocabulary for a typical day on the trail should enable you to travel from the lowest valley to the highest settlement on your own. The acceptable simpler *-ne* verb form is in parentheses.

Food and Lodging

No Nepali traveler camps when houses are nearby.

tapaaĩ/ko	ghar/maa			
Your	house/in			
yahãã		basna	paainchha?	
Here		staying	is available?	
kahãã				
Where				

Khaana	tyahãã	paainchha?
Food	there	is available?

Utaa	paainchha.
Over there	is available.

Maasu		pakaaunos.
Meat	(for me)	cook.

Ali ali	maatra	dinos.
A little bit	only	give.

Kursaani	nahaalnos.
Chili pepper	do not put in.

It is customary to pay for food, wood used, and lodging just prior to departure:

Hisaab	garnos.	[in a house or inn]
Bill	make.	

Bil	dinos.
Bill	give.

Jamaai	kati	rupiyãã?
All together	how many	rupees?

La,	jaaũ	e?	namaste
So	let's go,	eh?	farewell

Porterage

ma/laai	(eutaa, duitaa, tintaa)	kulli	chaainchha.
To me	(one, two, three)	porters	are needed.

Kata	jaane,	saab?
Where	going,	sahib?

Annapurna	sanctuari/maa	jaane.
Annapurna	sanctuary/to	going.

Hiũ/maa	jaanuparchha	(jaane).
Snow/in	must go	(going).

Timro	nyaano	lugaa	chha	ki	chhaina?
Your	warm	clothes	yes	or	no?

Chha,	saab.
Yes,	sahib.

La,   dekauu.
Well,   show them [to me].

Chhaaina,   saab,   kinnuparchha (kine).
 No,   sahib,   must buy   (buy).

 Din/ko   kati   rupiyãã?
A day/for   how many   rupees?

Khaana   khaaera   ki   na khaaera?
 Food   eating (and. . .) or not eating (and . . .)?
[With or without food supplied?)

Khaana   khaaera   pandhara   rupiyãã   pugchha
 Food   eating (and. . .)   fifteen   rupees   is enough.

Mero   doko   chhaaina,   saab.
 My   basket   isn't,   sahib,
[I don't have a basket.]

 Bis   rupiyãã   pugdaaina.
Twenty rupees   isn't enough.

 Ke   garne?
What   to do?

Ma eklai   jaanchhu   (jaane).
 I alone   will go   (go).

Pharkana/ko laagi   din/ko   kati   rupiyãã chhaaincha?
 For returning   a day/for how many rupees (do you) need?

Route-finding and Resting

Remember there are no signs but many trails in Nepal. For directions, hail the nearest farmer:

e daaju   (man older than you, older brother)
   daai

e bhai   (man younger than you, younger brother, boy)

e didi   (woman older than you, older sister)

e bahini   (girl younger than you, younger sister)

e baabu   (old man, father)

e aamaa   (old woman, mother)

Manang   jaane   baaTo   kun   ho?
Manang going to   trail   which is?

Yetaa baaTa jaane
Here   from   go
[This way.]

 Utaa   baaTa jaane.
There   from   go.
[That way.]

Namche   kati   taaDa   chha?
Namche   how   far   is?

Dui   kos.
Two   kos.

[One kos is something more than two miles. This is a common response; it means, "not too far."]

Kati   ghantaa   laagchha?
How many   hours   (does it) take?

[Nepalis will tell you how long it would take them to cover the distance. It will take you longer.]

BaaTo   dherai   ukaalo   chha?
Trail   very   uphill   is?

Ukaalo   oraalo   chha?
Uphill   downhill   it is?

Hoina,   samaai   chha.
No,   level   it is.

Kata?
Where   (are you going)?

Kata
Kahãã } baaTa?
Where } from   (are you coming)?

Kata   pugera   aaunubhayo?
Where (did you) arrive and come (from)?

BaaTo/maa   beding   samma   jaanasakchha?
Trail/on   Beding   as far as   (one is) able to go?

Sakdaaina.
Not able.

Haat bajaar   kahile   hunchha?
Weekly market   when   is?

Bistaari   jaaũ.
Slowly   go.

[also said upon someone's departure: "Take it easy"]

Chitto   jaaũ
Fast   let's go.

Sital/maa   basaũ.
Shade, cool/in   let's sit.

(Ma/laai)   araam garnuparchha (garne).
(I)   must rest.

(Haami/laai)   bholi   ekdam   bihaana/maa jaanuparchha (jaane).
(We)   tomorrow extremely morning/in   must go.
                      (early)

(Ma/laai)   pisaab garnuparccha (garne).
(I)   have to urinate.

Raato   maato,   chhipalo   baaTo.
Red   dirt,   slippery   trail.
[trail proverb]

Nepali Time

If you have a visible watch, you will be asked the time. If you inquire about time, you will get widely disparate answers; every watch in village Nepal shows different time. You can usually generate a lively discussion by asking what day of the week it is:

Aaja   ke   baar   (ho)?
Today   what   day   (is)?

Aaja   aitabaar   (ho).
Today   Sunday   is.

[or]   sombaar Monday
       mangalbaar Tuesday
       budhabaar Wednesday
       bihibaar Thursday
       sukrabaar Friday
       shanibaar Saturday

Kati   bajyo
What time is it?
[literally, how many struck?]

Chaar   bajyo.
4 o'clock.

Pāāch baje   tiraa   basnuparchha (basne).
5 o'clock   around   must or should stop (sit).

Chha baje utnuparchha   (utne).
6 o'clock   should arise.

Kahile   jaane?
when   are (you) going?

Bholi-parsi.
Tomorrow or the next day.
[the Nepali equivalent of "mañana"]

   Kati   din   basnuhunchha (basne)?
How many   days   are you staying?

   Tin   din   baschhu   (basne).
Three   days   I will stay.

Medical Problems and Evacuation

It is still possible to find yourself several days' walk from a wireless and even farther from a landing strip (hawai-jahaaj giraund). If you must get out, walking or being carried is the only possibility, short of helicopter rescue.

Ma/laai   kulli   chaainchha.
Me/to   porter   is needed.

Jomosom   samma   ma/laai   boknos (bokne).
Jomosom   as far as   me   carry.

Mero   saathi   biraami   bhayo   (or chha).
My   friend   sick   is.

Ma   biraami   chhu.
I   sick   am.

Mero   peT   dukhchha (dukhne).
My   stomach   hurts.

KaaThmaanDu/maa   samaachaar   pathaaunos (pathaaune).
Kathmandu/to   message   send.

Bargaining

For a Westerner to bargain in Kathmandu is not as easy as it once was. However, the same ancient rules still apply in the village and at the haat bajaar in the mountains.

Suntalaa   kati   parchha?
Tangerines   how much   cost?

Rupiyãã/ko   duitaa.
For a rupee   two.

Rupiyãã/ko   tintaa   dinos.
For a rupee   three   give (me).

Hunchha.
Allright.

Yasko   kati   rupiyãã?
For this   how many   rupees?

Das   rupiyãã.
Ten   rupees.

Mahango   bhayo (or   chha),   ma   aaTh   dinchhu (dine).
Expensive   it was (or   it is),   I   eight   will give.

La,   linos.
Very well,   take (it).

Chatting

The phrase for chatting is "gaph garne."

Aamaa,   baabu   chhan?
Mother,   father (your)   are?
[Are your parents living?]

Bihaa   gareko chha? [or] Tapaaĩ/ko bihaa   bhayo?
Marriage (your) has been.   Your   marriage   was?

Bhaat   khaanubhayo?
Rice   have you eaten?

Kina   nepaal/maa   aaeko?
Why   Nepal/to   have you come?

Ghumna jaana   aaeko.
To sightsee   (I) have come.

Himaal herna   aaeko.
Snow peaks to look at   (I) have come.

Tapaaĩ/ko   desh/maa   gaai/ko   maasu   khaane?
Your   country/in   cow's   meat   (do they) eat?

Tapaaĩ/laai   kasto chha?
You/to   how is?

[How are you?]
Sanchai,   tapaaĩ/laai?
Fine,   (and) you?

Some Additional Grammar

Impersonal Verbs

Some important concepts are expressed in Nepali with impersonal verbs, which are not conjugated, and the subjects of which always take the postposition -laai.

Need: use chhainchha or the negative, chhaindaina.

Ma/laai   maddat   chhainchha.
Me/to   help   is needed.

Tapaaĩ/laai   ke   chhainchha?
You/to   what   is needed?

Haami/laai   phul   chhaindaina.
Us/to   eggs   is not needed.

Necessity: "parchha" or (negative) "pardaina" is affixed to the infinitive form of a verb to express "should" or "have to."

Haami/laai   jaanuparchha.
We   have to go.

Timi/laai   yo   boknupardaina.
You   this   don't have to carry.

Like and dislike: use "man parchha" or (negative) "man par-daina."

Ma/laai   chang   dherai   man parchha.
I   Tibetan beer very much   like.

Haami/laai   raksi   man pardaina.
We   local wine   don't like.

Tapaaĩ/laai   haamro   desh   man parchha?
You   our   country like?

Dherai   man parchha.
Very much   (I) like   (it).

Desire or want: "man laagchha" or (negative) "man laagdaina" are affixed to the -na form of a verb to express desire.

Haami/laai   yahãã   basna man laagdaina.
We   here   do not want to stay.

Tapaaĩ/laai   gompa/maa   jaana man laagchha?
You   chapel/into   want to go?

Ma/laai   chiyaa   khaana man laagchaa
I   tea   want to eat (drink).

Feelings: use "laagyo" to make a phrase.

Ma/laai   I am   bhok laagyo   hungry
Tapaaĩ/laai   you are   thakaai laagyo   fatigued

Haami/laai   we are   tirkhaa laagyo   thirsty
                          nidraa laagyo   sleepy
                          raksi laagyo   drunk
                          jaaDo laagyo   cold
                          garmi laagyo   hot
                          Dar laagyo   scared
                          haawaa laagyo   wind-blown

Simple Negative

Add "na" to any verb or adjective to negate the concept:

na raamro   not good
na jaane   not going

Simple Past

Transitive verbs: Add *-le* to the subject noun or pronoun and *-eko* to the verb root (remove the suffix *-unu* or *-nu*).

Tapaaĩ/le   ke   gareko?
You   what   did do?

Intransitive verbs: *-le* is not used, *-eko* is affixed to the root.

Ma   junbesi/maa   baseko.
I   junbesi/in   stayed.

Irregular verbs: some common verbs are irregular in the simple past as well as in other forms.

Ma   Jumla/maa   gaeko.   [from *jaanu*]
I   Jumla/to   went.

Vocabulary

Food

fruits and vegetables   phalphul ra
  tarkaari
apple   syaau, nashpati
banana   keraa
chili   khursaani
leafy greens   saag
  (spinach)
lemon, lime   kaagati
mango   ããp
onion   pyaaj
orange, tangerine   suntalla
potato   aalu
pumpkin   parsi
bread (unleavened)   roti, chapaati
corn   makai
flour   pitho
  (roasted barley)   tsampa
                          (Tibetan)

millet   kodo
rice
  in the field   dhaan
  in the store   chaamal
  cooked   bhaat
  pounded   chiuraa
beans   simi
lentils   daal
peanuts   badaam
soybeans   bhaTmaas
butter (clarified)   ghiu
egg   phul
  boiled   umaaleko phul
fish   maachhaa
meat   maasu
  buffalo   raango/ko maasu
  chicken   kukhura/ko maasu
  cow   gaai/ko maasu
  goat   kasi/ko maasu
milk   dudh
yoghurt   dhai

beer
  bottled istar biyar
  Nepali jaãr
  Tibetan chang
local wine raksi
oil tel
tea chiyaa
water
  drinking khaane paani
  boiled umaaleko paani
  hot taato paani
  washing dhune paani
garlic lasun
relish (hot) achaar
salt nun
sugar chini
sweets miThai

Verbs (infinitive form)

ask sodhnu
ask for maagnu
bathe nuhaaunu
boil umaalnu
buy kinnu
carry boknu
chat, gossip gaph garnu
close banda garnu
come aaunu
cook pakaaunu
do garnu
eat, drink khaanu
enough (to be) pugnu (pugyo)
forget birsanu
get up, awaken uThnu
give dinu
go jaanu
hear (listen) sunnu
kill maarnu
laugh haasnu
learn siknu
light (a lamp) baalnu
look hernu
look for khojnu
meet bheTnu
open kholnu
put (down, in) raakhnu
read paDhnu
repeat, say again pheri bhannu

(please repeat pheri bhannos)
return pharkanu
see dekhnu
sell bechnu
send pathaaunu
sing git gaaunu
sit, live basnu
sleep sutnu
speak bolnu
take linu
talk, say bhannu
teach sikaaunu
understand bujnu
urinate pisaab garnu
walk hĩDnu
wash dhunu
work kaam garnu

Nouns and Pronouns

afternoon diũso
baby bachha
bamboo bããs
book kitaab
bottle sisi
boy keTaa
bridge
  large pul
  small saanghu
cat biraalu
children chhoraa-chhori
clothes lugaa
country desh
cow gaai
creek khola
daughter chhori
day din
dog kukur
door Dhokaa
evening beluka
eye ããkhaa
face mukh
field khet
fire aago
firewood daura
floor bhuĩ
fly (house) jhingaa
foot khuTTa
foreigner bideshi

forest ban
friend saathi
girl keTi
government (His Majesty's) shri
  paanch/ko sarkaar
hair kapaal
hand haat
head Taauko
help maddat
hill or ridge lekh, DanDaa
holy man (Hindu) saadhu
ice peak himaal
inn bhaTTi
junk, knickknacks jilli-milli
kerosene maTTitel
king raaja
knife chakku
  (Gurkha-made) khukari
lake taal, pokhari, tso (Tibetan)
lamp (kerosene) batti
launderer dhobi
leech jukaa
luggage, stuff saaman
man, person maanchhe
mat (grass) gundri
match solaai
medicine ausadhi
morning bihaana
mosquito laamkhuTTe
mountain pahaaD
name naam
night raati
outhouse chharpi
pass, saddle bhanjyang
            la (Tibetan)
place Thaaũ
plate Thaal
porter kulli, baariya
queen raani
rain paani (parchha)
religion dharma
resting place (on the trail)
  chautaara
river kosi
road motor jaane baaTo
room (in a house) koThaa
shed goTh
shirt kamij
shoes juthaa

shopkeeper saahuji
sir hajur! (in response to being
  addressed)
snow hiũ
socks mojaa
son chhoraa
spoon chamchha
stone, rock Dhungaa
store pasal
stove (of mud and stone) chulho
sun ghaam
things chij-bij
tiger baagh
trail baaTo
tree rukh
village gaaũ
water buffalo (female) bhaisi
  (male) raango
week haptaa
what ke
  (is this?) yo ke ho?
which kun
who ko
window jhyaal
woman aaimai
work kaam

Adjectives
ago aghi
all sabai
bad (or not good) na raamro
big Thulo
bitter tito
cheap sasTho
clean saphaa
cold chiso
colorful rangi-changi
  (multicolored)
delicious miTho
different pharak
difficult muskil
dirty phohor
downhill oraalo
easy sajilo
good raamro
hot (temperature) taato
hot (spicy) piro
how many (or much) kati
little saano

little
  (a little bit)   ali-ali
long   laamo
many   dherai
new   nayāā
o.k. (it is)   Thik (chha)
old (things)   puraano
  men   buDho
  women   buDhi
only   maatra
short   chhoTo
sick   biraami
sour   amilo
sweet   guliyo
tall   aglo
that   tyo
this   yo
uphill   ukaalo
whose   kasko

Adverbs

after   pachhi
again   pheri
always   sadhaī
down   tala
far   TaaDhaa
fast   chhiTo
here   yahāā
how   kasari
inside   bhitra
near   najik
outside   baahira
secretly, on the sly   luki-luki
there   tyaahāā
today   aaja
tomorrow   bholi
up   maathi
very   dherai
where   kahāā
why   kina
yesterday   hijo

Conjunctions

also   pani
because   kina bhane
maybe   holaa

Money

coins   paisaa
1½ rupees   DeDha rupiyāā
1 rupee = 100 paisaa
sukaa = 25 paisaa
mohar = 50 paisaa
rupiyāā = 100 paisaa

Numerals

one-half   aadha
one   ek
two   dui
three   tin
four   chaar
five   pāāch
six   chha
seven   saat
eight   aaTh
nine   nau
ten   das
eleven   eghaara
twelve   baarha
thirteen   terha
fourteen   chaudha
fifteen   pandhara
sixteen   sorha
seventeen   satra
eighteen   aThaara
nineteen   unnais
twenty   bis
twenty-five   pachhis
thirty   tis
thirty-five   paītis
forty   chaalis
forty-five   paītaalis
fifty   pachaas
fifty-five   pachpanna
sixty   saaThi
sixty-five   paīsaThi
seventy   sattari
seventy-five   pachhattar
eighty   asi
eighty-five   pachassi
ninety   nabbe
ninety-five   panchaanabbe
one hundred   sae
two hundred   dui sae
one thousand   ek hajaar

Tibetan Glossary

by Milan M. Melvin

The following list of Tibetan words and phrases is all too brief but sufficient for you to acquire the basic necessities and, depending on your inclination, to get out of or into trouble. Tibetans are wonderful, fun-loving people and even this small snatch of their language can launch you into some unforgettable relationships. You will undoubtedly encounter Tibetans in the upper hills of India and Nepal.

Pronunciation

The vowel "a" must be pronounced like the "a" in "father"—soft and long, unless it appears as *-ay*, in which case it is pronounced as in "say" or "day." A slash through a letter indicates the neutral vowel sound *uh*.

Word Order

Simple Tibetan sentences are constructed as follows:

Noun (or pronoun)	Object	Verb
I	mountains	going
Nga	kang ree la	dro ge ray

The verb is always last.

Verb Tenses

Tibetan verbs are composed of two parts: the *root*, which carries the meaning of the verb, and the *ending*, which indicates the tense (past, present, or future). The simplest and most common verb form, consisting of the root plus the ending *-ge ray*, can be used for the present and future tenses. The root is strongly accented in speech. In order to form the past tense, substitute the ending *-song*.

"nyo ge ray" means, loosely, "buying, going to buy"
"Nyo song" means "bought"

Only the verb roots are given in this glossary; remember to add the appropriate endings.

Pronouns

I Nga
you (singular) kirang
he, she, it korang, ko
we nga-tso
you (plural) kirang-tso
they korong-tso
this dee la
my, mine nge, ngay, narang kee
your, yours (singular) kirang kee
his, hers, its korang kee
our, ours narang-tso yee
your, yours (plural) kirang-tso yee
their, theirs korong-tso yee

Relations

name ming la
child poo goo
boy poo
girl po mo
man, husband cho ga
woman, wife kyee men
brother poon dya
sister poon kya, ah jee la

father   pa ba, pa la
mother   ah ma

Time

minute   ka ma
hour   tchø zø
day   nyee ma, shak ma
week   døn ta
month   da wa
year   lo
day before yesterday   ke nyee ma
yesterday   ke sang
last night   dang gong
today   ta ring
tomorrow   sang nyee, sang
day after tomorrow   nang nyee
now   tanda, ta ta
always   tak par
morning   sho kay
afternoon   nyeen goon
night   tsen la, tsem mo

Numbers

one   cheek
two   nee
three   soom
four   shee
five   nga
six   trook
seven   døn
eight   gye, kay
nine   koo, goo
ten   tchoo
eleven   tchoop cheek
twelve   tchoog nee
thirteen   tchook soom
fourteen   tchoop shee
fifteen   tchoo nga
sixteen   tchoo trook
seventeen   tchoop don
eighteen   tchup kyay
nineteen   tchur koo
twenty   nee shoo tamba
twenty-one   nee shoo sak cheek
twenty-two   nee shoo sak nee
twenty-three   nee shoo sak soom
twenty-four   nee shoo sup shee
twenty-five   nee shoo say nga

twenty-six   nee shoo sar trook
twenty-seven   nee shoo sub døn
twenty-eight   nee shoo sap kay
twenty-nine   nee sar koo
thirty   soom tchoo tamba
forty   sheep joo tamba
fifty   ngup tchoo tamba
sixty   trook tchoo tamba
seventy   døn tchoo tamba
eighty   kyah joo tamba
ninety   koop tchoo tamba
one hundred   gyah tamba
two hundred   nee gyah
three hundred   soom gyah

Food

barley   droo, nay
roasted barley flour   tsampa
beef   lang sha
breakfast   sho kay ka lak
butter   mar
cheese   choo ra
chicken meat   cha sha
chili peppers   mar tsa
cigarette   ta mak
corn   droo
egg   go nga
flour   to sheep, pak pay
food   ka lak
fruit   shing dong
lunch   nyeen goong ka lak
dinner   kong dak ka lak
meat   sha
milk   o ma
millet   ko do
onion   tsong
potato   sho ko
rice   dray
sugar   chee ma ka ra
tea   cha
vegetables   ngup tsay, tsay
wheat   tro, dro
delicious   shimbo

Other Nouns

bag   gye mo, gye wa
blanket   nya tee, gam lo, nye zen
book (common)   teb

book (religious) pay zya
boots som ba, lam
bridge sam ba
cave trak poo, poo goo
dog kee, kyee
donkey poon goo
fire may
house kang ba
hill ree
kerosene sa noom
kettle tib lee
knife tee, tree
lake tso
matches moo see, tsak ta
medicine men
  pill ree poo
moon da wa
mountain kang ree
mountain pass la
cooking pot hai yoom, rak sang
rain char pa
river tsang po, tchoo, chu
rock do
room kang mee
snow kang, ka
spoon tur ma, too ma
star kar ma
stomach tro ko
sun nyee ma
thread koo ba
Tibet Pø la
Tibetan people Pø pa
Tibetan language Pø kay
trail lam ga
umbrella nyee doo
water tchoo, chu
Westerner in gee, pee ling
wind loong bo chem bo
wood shing
candle yang la
cup mok, cha gar

Verbs

arrive lep
bring kay sho
buy nyo
carry kay
feel cold cha

come yong
cook ka lak so
drink toong
eat shay sa
forget jay, chay
get up lang
give tay, nang
be hungry tro ko tok
learn lap
look meek tang
make, fix so
see ton
sell tsong
be sick na
sit, stay day, shook
teach lap
go dro, do
wait goo
work le ka chee

Adjectives

lost lak song
thirsty ka kam
good yak po
bad yak po min doo
big chem bo
small choon choon
weak shook choon choon
strong shyook chem bo
empty tong ba
full kang
beautiful dzay bo
expensive gong chem bo
cold trang mo
hot tsa bo
different kye per, cheek be ma ray
same nang shing
few tet see tet see
much, many mang bo
light yang bo, yang
heavy jee po, jee ba tsa po

Adverbs

up ya la
down ma la
near nye bo
far ta ring bo, gyang bo
here deh roo

there   pa roo, pa ge
left   yom ba
right   yay ba
slow   ka lee
quickly   dyok po, dyok po
really, very   she ta, she tai

Miscellaneous

and   tang, ta
another   yang ya
how much, how many   ka tzø
maybe   cheek chay na
sometimes   tsam tsam
other   shem ba, shen da, yem ba
what   ka ray
where from   ka ne
where to   ka ba, ka par, ka roo
who   soo
why   ka ray chay nay

Phrases

hello!, greetings!   tashi delay
enough!, stop!   deek song
finished   tsar song, deek song
I do not understand   ha ko ma song
I understand, I know   ha ko gee

doo, ha ko song
right!, really!, yes   ray, la ray
very important   kay chembo, ne ka
    chem bo
what is this called?   dee ming la
    ka ray see ge ray? dee ka ra ray?
how much is (this)?   (dee la) gong
    ka tzø ray?
it doesn't matter   kay kay chee ge
    ma ray, kay kay so ge ma ray
be careful, slowly   ka lee ka lee
I am hungry   nge tro ko to kee doo
are/is there any (onions)   (tsong)
    doo-ay, (tsong) doog-ay?
please bring (onions)   (tsong) kay
    sho ah
o.k., thanks   la so
goodnight   sim jam, sim jam nang
    ro
how far is (Lhasa)?   (Lhasa la)
    gyan lø yø ray?
how are you?   kirang sook po day
    bo yeen bay?, kirang ko sook day
    be yeen bay?
I am fine   sook po day bo yeen, day
    bo doo

Index